MANAGEMENT EDUCATION AND DEVELOPMENT

DRIFT OR THRUST INTO THE 21st CENTURY?

MANAGEMENT EDUCATION AND DEVELOPMENT:

DRIFT OR THRUST INTO THE 21st CENTURY?

Lyman W. Porter

Graduate School of Management
University of California, Irvine

Lawrence E. McKibbin

College of Business Administration
University of Oklahoma

McGRAW-HILL BOOK COMPANY

New York St. Louis San Francisco Auckland Bogotá Caracas Colorado Springs
Hamburg Lisbon London Madrid Mexico Milan Montreal New Delhi Oklahoma City
Panama Paris San Juan São Paulo Singapore Sydney Tokyo Toronto

MANAGEMENT EDUCATION AND DEVELOPMENT:
Drift or Thrust into the 21st Century?

2 3 4 5 6 7 8 9 0   DOCDOC   8 9 3 2 1 0 9 8   ⌐

ISBN   0-07-050521-7

This book was set in Times Roman by the College Composition Unit
in cooperation with Monotype Composition Company.
The editors were Kathleen L. Loy and Peggy C. Rehberger;
the production supervisor was Denise Puryear;
the cover was designed by Carla Bauer.
R. R. Donnelley & Sons Company was printer and binder.

LIBRARY OF CONGRESS
Library of Congress Cataloging-in-Publication Data

Porter, Lyman W.
    Management education and development: drift or thrust into the
21st century? / Lyman W. Porter, Lawrence E. McKibbin.
        p.   cm.
    Bibliography: p.
    Includes index.
    "Outcome of a three-year study commissioned by the American
Assembly of Collegiate Schools of Business"—Introd.
    ISBN 0-07-050521-7
    1. Management—Study and teaching—United States.   I. McKibbin,
Lawrence E.   II. American Assembly of Collegiate Schools of
Business.   III. Title.
HD30.42.U5P67 1988   88-650
658'.007'1173—dc19   CIP

CONTENTS

INTRODUCTION

This book is the outcome of a three-year study commissioned by the American Assembly of Collegiate Schools of Business (AACSB) on the future of management education and development. Earlier projects between AACSB and its overseas counterpart, the European Foundation for Management Development (EFMD), served as precursors.

The study is unique in that it not only looks at management education as traditionally delivered through colleges and universities, but also focuses on other educational delivery systems, such as corporations and third-party providers, which the earlier conference reports predicted would play an increasingly significant role in the years ahead. As knowledge bases continue to grow and demands to enlarge the business school curriculum increase, the relationships among these three providers and decisions about who should teach what become more important than ever before.

While the conclusions, interpretations and recommendations in the report are entirely those of the authors and are not necessarily endorsed by the AACSB Board of Directors, this project's findings are significant and come at a crucial point in the development of management education. Business schools, in attempts to respond to the growth and diversity of their constituencies, will find the book helpful in envisioning what changes will be necessary in teaching, research, and service functions in order to prepare graduates for the challenges and opportunities of the 21st century. The book also will be useful in identifying alternatives to the changes that schools, corporations and third-party providers may want to make.

The report documents the first systematic study of its type in over 25 years and exemplifies an internally generated evaluation of management education, as compared to the externally driven Ford and Carnegie reports of the late 1950s. As such, changes that come about likely will be internally driven rather than stimulated by external forces.

The following contributors provided generous support for the project over the years:

AT&T Foundation
Atlantic Richfield Foundation
American Academy of Arts and
  Sciences
Arthur Andersen & Co. Foundation
The Arthur Young Foundation
BankAmerica Foundation
The Bristol-Myers Fund, Inc.
Caterpillar Foundation

Citicorp/Citibank
Emerson Electric Co.
Ernst & Whinney Foundation
Exxon Education Foundation
Ford Motor Company Fund
Gannett Foundation
General Electric Foundation
International Business Machines
  Corporation

John Wiley & Sons, Inc.
The Mead Corporation Foundation
Mobil Foundation, Inc.
Nestle Enterprises, Inc.
The Peat, Marwick, Mitchell
  Foundation
Pfizer Inc.
The Pfizer Foundation, Inc.

Phillips Petroleum Foundation, Inc.
Price Waterhouse Foundation
The Procter & Gamble Fund
Tenneco Inc.
3M Foundation
Time Inc.
The Touche Ross Foundation
Whirlpool Corporation

As the professional organization and sole accrediting agency for collegiate schools of business and management in the United States, AACSB is pleased to have had an opportunity to play a role in making this study possible and in bringing the results and conclusions to the attention of those concerned with the quality of management education in this country. One of the conclusions points to a widespread lack of concern on the part of business schools toward making needed changes in the way management education is taught. Clearly, schools must decide whether they will forcefully address, both collectively and individually, the exciting new era of the 21st century, or whether they will be satisfied to merely drift into the next century. AACSB's agenda, in turn, will continue to be one of leadership and service, a facilitator for future changes.

Thomas A. Bausch

1987–88 AACSB President
Dean, College of Business Administration, Marquette University

Robert K. Jaedicke

1988–89 AACSB President
Dean, Graduate School of Business, Stanford University

FOREWORD

Almost 30 years have passed since the last comprehensive review of American management education. That is a long time, considering the size, diversity and importance of the field. Those years have seen large, even momentous, changes in business schools themselves, in business institutions and practices, and in the broader environment within which management education must serve, adapt and, hopefully, prosper. Those of us who care about the health and viability of education for business owe a debt to Lyman Porter and Larry McKibbin for their bold and successful effort to describe its current state and to prescribe how it must change in the next decade or two. Our gratitude should also be extended to the project's sponsors and to others who participated in it. As one who was involved in a similar study, I especially appreciate the effort and contribution that Porter and McKibbin have made.

Porter and McKibbin draw on their predecessors (see Chapter 1) where useful: a special feature at the beginning of each section is a brief description of the state of management education at the time of the Gordon-Howell and Pierson "Foundation" reports juxtaposed with the relevant developments in the 30 years since then. The reader is thus efficiently prepared to consider the authors' own data, analysis, conclusions and recommendations. Happily, Porter and McKibbin do not hesitate to strike in new directions when necessary. Both newcomers to the subject and long-time observers will appreciate this approach.

Another important feature is the authors' comprehensive surveying of opinions on each major topic. This is particularly important since many of the popular criticisms of contemporary management education involve sharp differences of *perception* by the several parties. Is the field too analytical or quantitative? Are social and ethical issues ignored? Are faculties too research-oriented? Is doctoral training too narrow? Are "people skills" underemphasized? Readers will gain a new perspective on the parochial premises behind the criticisms implied by such questions.

All institutions must adapt to changing conditions if they are to merit legitimacy and support, and higher education is no exception. But continuous self-evaluation and concomitant actions are particularly necessary for business schools as they struggle with changes in a variety of dimensions—student abilities and aspirations, faculty strengths and weaknesses, shifting and sometimes volatile social and political institutions, global interdependencies, explosions in science and technology and, not least, evolving management problems and practices. Porter and McKibbin have done an admirable job of capturing the flavor of this maelstrom, and their conclusions and recommendations demonstrate a wisdom that those in management education and development ignore at their peril. The report, despite its sponsorship, also looks critically but fairly at AACSB. One hopes the Assembly, too, will give urgent attention to its recommendations.

James E. Howell

Theodore J. Kreps Professor of Economics
Graduate School of Business
Stanford University
Coauthor of *Higher Education for Business* (1959)

FOREWORD

Two decades ago, Peter Drucker observed that the corporation was the first social institution to learn how to bring together a diversity of knowledge in a common effort to pursue a coordinated series of goals. In doing so, it developed what he called "an almost insatiable appetite for all kinds of knowledge and conceptual skill."

Now, as we approach the final decade of the 20th century, that appetite has grown more voracious than ever. Businesses of all types require more and more managers who have both the depth of business expertise to operate the complex mechanisms of finance and industry, and the breadth of knowledge to do so wisely and ethically, in accordance with the demands of the wider society.

This makes the education and development of the nation's business managers a subject of critical importance, not for just the companies themselves, but for the entire country. This book provides valuable insights into that education and development. As such, it is the culmination of efforts by AACSB to look ahead to the skills and knowledge that will be required of managers and executives in the 21st century, and to determine how management education can respond to those needs.

Its authors, Professors Lyman W. Porter and Lawrence E. McKibbin, base their conclusions on a landmark study of management education today. The study provides valuable information on how business schools and their students and faculties, on the one hand, and companies and their managements, on the other, are dealing with the need for management education.

As a corporate manager, business school graduate and participant in the Porter-McKibbin study, I urge my fellow business leaders to consider carefully the conclusions and recommendations in this book, so as to better understand what is happening in business schools before students graduate, and how that can be changed for the better. America's corporations, and the country itself, have an important stake in determining how we best use our national resources—and that includes our brightest students.

In publishing this book, AACSB has performed an important service, continuing its performance as a significant force in business education, especially during the past 25 years, and reaffirming its role in the future.

I trust you will find this enlightening and enjoyable reading.

Philip L. Smith

Chairman
General Foods Corporation

PREFACE

This report represents the culmination of a multi-year effort by many people and organizations, especially the American Assembly of Collegiate Schools of Business (AACSB). As detailed in Chapter 1, it was the AACSB as an organization that made the decision to undertake a major new study of the current status and future directions of management education and development in this country. In particular, it was the 1983 Futures Committee ("Committee on the Future of Management Education and Development") of AACSB that formulated the specific idea for this Project. The members of that committee, who were most generous to us in offering their sagacious advice and counsel, included Max B. E. Clarkson, Thomas R. Horton, E. F. Krieg, Claude W. Rodgers, Robert F. Vizza, and Boris Yavitz. Robert H. B. Wade, then Director of International and Governmental Programs for AACSB, was staff member to the committee, and he worked diligently to prepare a proposal for presentation to the Board of Directors for approval to initiate this Project and to begin the fund-raising that would be necessary to finance it. Bob subsequently worked with the Project's co-directors on its early phases, and we are most grateful to him for his help and encouragement. Throughout the Project, we have received the unstinting assistance of a number of members of the AACSB staff, including Sharon L. Barber, Milton R. Blood, Charles W. Hickman, Eunice K. Lange, Richard T. Wines, and, especially, Executive Vice President William K. Laidlaw, Jr. It is no exaggeration to state that this report would never have become a reality without Bill Laidlaw's prodigious efforts and talents. We salute him, and thank him, for his innumerable contributions.

We also wish to express our appreciation to the individual business/ management schools around the country for their cooperation in various phases of this study. In particular, we thank the deans of the sixty-one schools listed in Appendix B for their help and efforts in arranging for the several hundred university-based interviews. In addition, we appreciate the assistance of the deans of over 400 of the AACSB member schools in completing their own questionnaires and in distributing the other sets of questionnaires to the several different categories of university respondents. Likewise, we thank all those university-affiliated individuals who contributed time for our interviews or who filled out our survey instruments.

This Project also could not have been completed successfully without a high degree of cooperation from a large number of companies and firms. We specifically want to acknowledge with gratitude the generous financial support for the Project provided by the thirty-one organizations and their respective foundations listed in the Introduction. Not once during the entire study did any of these organizations ever attempt to influence in any manner the issues we investigated, the methods by which we obtained our data, or the contents of this report. That is support of the finest type. Many other companies and firms contributed in other ways by assisting us in setting up interviews (see the list of these companies in Appendix B) and by distributing our corporate questionnaires to relevant categories of respondents. As was the case with universities, we express our great appreciation to those corporate-affiliated managers and executives who consented to be interviewed or who completed our questionnaires.

The final version of this report benefited greatly from the comments of a number of distinguished scholars and practitioners who reviewed various sections of the draft document. These individuals were: Paul A. Albrecht, Francis N. Bonsignore, Earl Cheit, James E. Howell, Thomas R. Horton, Nancy L. Jacob, Clark Kerr, Edgar H. Schein, and Noel M. Tichy. Their comments were universally incisive and constructive, and while we were not always able to incorporate all of their suggestions we did consider them carefully and in fact made a number of changes in the draft document that reflected their recommendations.

A project of this magnitude and scope could not be carried out by only two people. Throughout the entire conduct of the study, we had the very able assistance of two outstanding doctoral students: Douglas Kiel and William Cowie. These two ''supermen'' contributed not only brawn—by performing a large number of mundane but crucially important tasks—but, also, especially, brains. They constantly bombarded us with ideas and suggestions about how our procedures could be improved and our thinking sharpened. Their skills and abilities, not to mention hours and hours of sheer hard work, made this a far more productive Project than it ever would have been otherwise.

Others who contributed major efforts in the conduct of the research investigation and the preparation of this report included Hal Gregersen, Umesh Shroff, Michael Renfro, Alice Watkins, and, especially, Emily Glasgow. As the Project's primary secretary, Emily was a source of perpetual cheerfulness and expert support, often under trying (and rushed!) circumstances.

A person who played a special role throughout the course of the Project was Professor G. William England. Bill was our principal technical advisor in the area of research methodology, but we also used him in many other ways, not the least of which was to ask him to read and comment on the first drafts of almost all the chapters of the report. His vast store of knowledge about both methodology and content was of immense help to us at all stages of the investigation and the subsequent writing of the report. He holds no responsibility, of course, for any errors or omissions, but this final report document has been enhanced by his contributions in many (not always visible) ways. We can sum up the role he played in this Project in a phrase: he was very influential!

We also are indebted to our own two schools—the Graduate School of Management at the University of California, Irvine, and the College of Business

Administration at the University of Oklahoma—for their institutional support throughout the entire Project.

Our final acknowledgments go to the two most important people in the world to us—our respective wives, Meredith and Hilda—for not only their continuous encouragement but also for their apparently inexhaustible supply of patience during what must have seemed to them like a never-ending quest. Since we spent a great deal of time away from home collecting data for this report, we unintentionally put to the test the old adage: absence makes the heart grow fonder. Fortunately for us, we passed the test.

A report of this nature inevitably reflects, to some degree, the frames of reference and the experience of the authors, and this is certainly the case in this instance. We came to this Project from different backgrounds of academic preparation—one of us majored in a liberal arts discipline and the other in business—but we both have "lived" in business/management schools for the past several decades. Despite these sources of obvious bias, we nevertheless have attempted to approach the Project and the data we collected with as even-handed a stance as possible. We did not see our task as one of either defending business/management schools and corporations, or attacking them. Instead, we sought to learn as much as possible about our subject matter, to report our findings as accurately as possible, and then to draw our conclusions with as much wisdom and insight as we could muster. No study of this type is ever the last word, particularly with respect to activities as dynamic as management education and development, but our aspiration for this report is that it might provide a basis for stimulating thoughtful consideration by a number of relevant parties concerning how these significant endeavors can be improved and strengthened in the years ahead. In conclusion, we want to stress that this has been a truly *collaborative* effort throughout. We have enjoyed doing the Project together, and we ourselves have learned a considerable amount in the process. We only hope we have been able to transmit at least some of this learning to our readers.

Lyman W. Porter

Lawrence E. McKibbin

MANAGEMENT EDUCATION AND DEVELOPMENT:

DRIFT OR THRUST INTO THE 21st CENTURY?

PART ONE

INTRODUCTION

CHAPTER 1

INTRODUCTION TO THE PROJECT

The focal subjects of this report—management education and management development—are of major concern to a wide range of institutions, organizations, and individuals: universities, business/management schools within universities, corporations and firms, government agencies, students, parents, and managers, among others. Each group has its own parochial interest: budgets, supply of and demand for managerial personnel, admission policies, job prospects of graduates, accreditation standards, and the like. Also, however, there are fundamental concerns that transcend the narrow interests of particular groups: How, as a nation, can we best educate and develop those individuals who now have—and will have in the future—responsibility for managing, leading, and directing our organizations, particularly those organizations engaged in business-type activities? How, in short, can we make the best use of available—and clearly limited—educational and developmental resources to enhance the quality of management? That, in essence, is the overriding question of the Project being reported here.

The aims and goals of the Project, and the issues to be addressed by it, are, of course, more complex. Their elaboration will be presented shortly. First, though, it is important to gain some understanding of the origins of the Project—how and why it came into existence.

BACKGROUND OF THE PROJECT

The Project ("Future of Management Education and Development" or Futures Project for short) that forms the focus for this entire report has had a somewhat lengthy gestation period, due in part to the circumstances by which it came about. The chief raison d'etre of the Project is that it represents the culmination of efforts by the American Assembly of Collegiate Schools of Business (AACSB) to look ahead to what management would be like in the early part of the 21st century and how management education could best meet those future needs. Other motivating conditions were present also, however, including the fact that the two most recent comprehensive studies of business school education (the so-called Foundation studies) were now a quarter-century old, the fact that a number of criticisms had recently been leveled at collegiate business education, and the appearance of growing interest in postdegree management development activities and the corresponding concept of lifelong learning for management. We review each of these background factors in turn.

Joint Efforts by AACSB and EFMD

As early as 1975 (Walton, 1982), representatives from AACSB and its closest European equivalent, the European Foundation for Management Development (EFMD), met informally to discuss how their respective associations and members might begin to address the "needs of managers" and face effectively the educational challenges that would develop by the turn of the century. These informal meetings subsequently led to a series of collaborative conferences sponsored by the two organizations.

Windsor Castle and Arden House Colloquia   Plans emerged from the initial and subsequent discussions between the AACSB and the EFMD to launch a three-phase *joint* project to be carried out over the course of several years. That project (hereafter referred to as the EFMD/AACSB Joint Project) was organized to analyze the following fundamental issue: "Management and Management Education in a World of Changing Expectations." The Joint Project was to focus on the 30-year period 1980–2010. This time frame was selected on the premise that "those who will be senior executives of major corporations and organizations in the year 2000 have already graduated from our institutions; [and thus] if the project was to influence the future executive, it had to look beyond the year 2000" (Paris Conference Report, 1981, p. 3). Each phase of the Joint Project was designed to explore a broad dimension or aspect of the overall problem, and for each phase a corresponding conference would be held to consider that dimension in detail. The three phases were designed to deal with the following basic topic areas:

1 The changing expectations of society in the next 30 years
2 The implications for management
3 The implications for management education/development

The first two areas were to be examined by means of small invitational conferences (or colloquia, as they were termed by their sponsors). The first such conference was held in Great Britain at Windsor Castle in February 1979.

The forty attendees represented both business and academic organizations in Europe and the United States, including some scholars and commentators not directly associated with business schools or the business world. The topics discussed there included the following (Arden House Report, 1979, p. 10):

- Changing values in postindustrial society
- Availability of resources
- Relations between various parts of the world
- Institutions in society
- Groups: women, youth, senior citizens, minorities
- Shift from products to services
- Vulnerability of advanced societies to disruption
- Need for global approach, one that takes into account both east-west and north-south (i.e., "developed" and "less-developed" countries) issues

The Windsor Castle Colloquium was designed to raise issues and questions rather than provide answers or concrete recommendations for changes in direction. Consequently, a large number of subtopics were discussed and explored, all of which carried with them potential implications for management and management education in the future. Illustrative examples (provided by one of the participants, Boris Yavitz, then dean of the Graduate School of Business at Columbia University, and contained in the subsequent report of the Arden House Colloquium), among many, included the following:

- What are the effects of "growing public skepticism toward traditional institutions"?
- What are the implications for the "role of the manager as an agent of growth or contraction, stability or change"?
- How will managerial authority be affected by "a series of dynamic shifts in balance of power between individuals, organizations, national governments, and international institutions"?
- Is "the traditional work ethic fading? What values are replacing it?"

The Windsor Castle Colloquium was followed 9 months later by a similar invitational colloquium at Columbia University's Arden House conference center in November 1979. Again, the participants included educators and business executives from both Europe and the United States. The group at Arden House focused on the implications of societal changes and expectations for management. More concretely, this second conference addressed three major subissues:

1 The legitimacy and authority of management and the governance of organizations
2 The functions of managers
3 The motivation, satisfaction, and morale of managers

These three themes were examined in the context of several crucial questions posed to the participants: "What are the likely major constraints on managers in the future? What are managers actually doing today to meet those demands and pressures? And, what *should* managers be doing over the next 30 years to deal effectively with problems of function, legitimacy, and morale?" (Arden House Report, 1979, p. 23). While the previous Windsor Castle Colloquium focused primarily on question-raising, those at Arden House attempted as much as possible to provide answers to these and more specific questions. (The report of that colloquium, drafted by Clarence Walton, provides details of the positions taken by the conferees on these challenging queries.)

The Paris Conference   The Windsor Castle and Arden House Colloquia were designed, as it were, as warm-ups for the final phase of the EFMD/AACSB Joint Project, a major international conference that was held in Paris in June 1980. This meeting, which subsequently came to be labeled "The Paris Conference," focused on the topic of ultimate interest to the two associations and their members: the education and development of managers for the 21st century. Specifically, attention was directed to two major issues:

1 "The manager's future educational and developmental needs"
2 Action steps to meet those needs

As the report of the Paris Conference emphasizes (p. 4), "this meeting was different from all previous efforts to explore the meaning and needs of management education and development because..."

• "It was the first large-scale international meeting of management school [educators] as well as leaders from corporations and other organizations."
• "Momentum for the meeting came from *within* [emphasis added by the present authors] the field of management and management education."
• It involved a large number of individuals—more than 600—and thus "differed sharply from past reform efforts in which single individuals took the initiative to blueprint future needs in management education."
• It "involved people who came not simply from a few nations or a single geographic region but from all continents throughout the globe."
• It "was genuinely participative in that everyone had opportunity for input."
• It "signaled the emergence of European management schools as equal partners with U.S. schools."

It is not possible here to do adequate justice to the breadth of specific issues dealt with in the Paris Conference nor to the kinds of general conclusions reached by the participants as a result of their extensive discussions. [The interested reader is referred to the report of the conference, *Management for the XXI Century,* published jointly by AACSB and EFMD in 1982, especially to some individual observations and reflections prepared by Maurice Saias and Clarence Walton. Also, an excellent summary of the conference and its results can be found in an article by William Dymsza, prepared for the *Journal of International Business Studies* (Winter, 1982).] Suffice it to say, however, that this conference, as will be explained later, served as a major impetus for the initiation of the Futures Project, which is the subject of this report. The conference provided both stimulating ideas and considerable momentum for embarking on the present large-scale Project, primarily because it had forced those present—especially the management educators (and in particular the American contingent of deans)—to face up to the troubling question, given that the future seems certain to bring about major and fundamental changes affecting society, organizations, and managers, what do *we* as management educators *do* about it?

Subsequent Initiatives by AACSB

One more conference that helped lead to the current Futures Project followed Paris, this one being initiated solely by AACSB rather than jointly in conjunction with the European organization. This later meeting was held at the Wingspread (Wisconsin) conference center of the Johnson Foundation and also came to be known by its location. The central topic at the Wingspread Conference, held in March 1982, was "Lifelong Learning for Managers." As the author of the subsequent report stated: "Of the practical problems identified [at Paris], none received greater attention than the manager's need for lifelong learning and the necessity to determine what should go into that learning package." Conference participants—from both academia and the business community—proceeded to address two major subissues related to the focus on lifelong learning: (1) "ways for improving cooperation and interaction between business schools and corporate management development programs, and (2) [relevant] changes that may be necessary in the curriculum, organization and resources of business schools [to carry out such tasks]." The deliberations at this conference resulted in a number of suggestions and challenges for both corporations and business, individually and collectively, for dealing with the problems and opportunities relating to lifelong learning. Those at the Conference concluded that, indeed, lifelong learning issues were crucial for management education and likely to become more so in the future. However, the conference also ended with the perennial question, particularly for AACSB as an organization, where do we go from here?

To answer this question, the Board of Directors of AACSB proceeded later in 1982 to appoint a new committee, the Future of Management Education and Development Committee (informally referred to as the Futures Committee). This committee was charged with making recommendations to the Board regarding specific follow-up steps that the organization should take to implement the general conclusions from the preceding series of conferences (especially the last two, Paris and Wingspread). After considering this assignment for several meetings, the Futures Committee concluded that they could not make the requested recommendations in the absence of concrete data on (1) the current system and structure of management education and development, and (2) the views of those involved in both the university and corporate settings regarding the types of changes that would be needed in the future. In short, the committee felt that it would not be wise to proceed in the absence of a valid data base. Therefore, since, in their opinion, such an up-to-date data base did *not* exist, the committee recommended to the Board of Directors that such a study be conducted, that the committee be authorized to select a person or persons to direct the study, and that AACSB develop plans to raise external funding to carry out such a study. These recommendations were approved by the Board in 1983, with the anticipation that the project would begin in mid-1984. Thus the "Future of Management Education and Development Project" was born.

It is important to note several things from this brief history of the origins of this Project:

1 The decision to undertake it followed logically from a series of prior initiatives by the organization (AACSB) that were strongly future-oriented and which had the potential for requiring changes by both the association and its members.

2 The particular conclusions from the conferences themselves indicated that it would be highly desirable to obtain as comprehensive a set of data as possible regarding how the current system was working and where it seemed to be heading if changes were not made.

3 The impetus for the Project did *not* come from some outside agency or organization. In effect, the decision to authorize the Project (and, particularly, the extensive efforts that would be needed to raise the funds for it) stemmed more from a *pro*active than a *re*active decision. In this respect, the Project differed from its antecedents, the Foundation projects of the late 1950s, which represented a more-or-less direct response to widespread disaffection and concern.

While the history outlined above traces the specific lineage of the actions that led up to this Project, it should be acknowledged that several other factors had a synergistic impact on reinforcing the decision to proceed with such a major study. Three of these conditions are noted briefly below:

1 *The Foundation studies were 25 years old* The Futures Committee was well aware that 1984 would mark exactly a quarter-century since the publication of the two most recent landmark studies of higher education for business: the so-called Foundation studies of Gordon and Howell and of Pierson. These were so labeled because the former study was sponsored by the Ford Foundation and the latter by the Carnegie Corporation. As anyone who has had any association with university business schools in the last 25 years is well aware, these studies, particularly that of Gordon and Howell, had profound impacts on this sector of the university. The Futures Committee of AACSB believed that sufficient time had elapsed since those reports were published in 1959 that it was necessary to monitor what changes had taken place since then and how current conditions differed from those prevailing 25 years earlier. Thus, this view lent additional support to the idea of initiating a new study. It is important to stress, however, that although the current Project is in many ways a direct lineal descendant of Gordon and Howell and of Pierson, it is not intended to be identical in design, scope, coverage, or content. It is a near relative—perhaps a niece or nephew—but not a son or daughter. (Some of the ways it differs, especially in focus, will be indicated later in this chapter.)

2 *Recent criticisms of business education* As mentioned previously, AACSB's Futures Committee was aware of the spate of articles critical of business education that had appeared and were appearing in the early 1980s. While they, and the Board of Directors of AACSB, did not believe that the criticisms required direct response—in contrast to the 1950s, member school deans were not clamoring for reform—it is probably safe to say that such criticisms provided additional incentives to find out as much as possible about what was "really happening out there" and especially how a broad spectrum of individuals in different types of positions within universities and within the business world viewed modern-day education provided by business schools. If certain basic criticisms were indeed valid, then they would need to be identified and subsequently dealt with by means of major changes. If other criticisms lacked substance and support when evaluated in the light of empirical data, then they should not be given the attention they sometimes were receiving. Thus, it is probably accurate to state that one of the expectations of the committee that commissioned this Project was that the study might shed light on the relative validity of various criticisms as a way of providing guidelines for changes that are needed versus those that are not or that even might be counterproductive.

3 *Increasing interest in management development and lifelong learning* One other development played a key role in both affecting the decision to launch this type of project and shaping the scope and nature of the Project. That development, which had been gathering momentum for the past couple of decades, was the ever-increasing interest on the part of both individual managers and companies in continued enhancement of managerial skills and knowledge beyond what could be obtained from formal degree programs. Of course, this was the subject of the Wingspread Conference and had been prominently discussed in the prior Paris Conference. However, these events only served to reinforce a growing sense of urgency that university-based schools of business needed to examine more intensively than they ever had before how they—and corporations as well—should respond to apparently rapidly expanding needs and demands for management development over and above what could be provided in the long-traditional undergraduate and master's degree programs in business. Again, the issue is not that university business schools had not already been responding to such needs for at least several decades—in fact, the reports by Gordon and Howell and Pierson back

in 1959 had each devoted a chapter to this area. Rather, the issue was one of degree
and centrality of attention and focus. The Futures Committee, rightly in our opinion,
wanted to make this area one of the *primary* concerns of the new Project, whereas
it had been of only relatively peripheral interest in the earlier studies.

OBJECTIVES OF THE PROJECT

The overall purpose and intent of this Project can be summarized by listing three
broad objectives, as proposed originally by the sponsoring group (the AACSB's
Futures Committee): (1) to evaluate the *current* (mid-1980s) status and condition
of management education and development (MED), (2) to analyze the likely future
directions of MED *if* no major changes were to be made, and (3) to provide a
set of recommendations concerning where MED *should be* heading in the future.
We discuss each of these objectives briefly at this point.

Evaluation of Current Status and Condition of MED

As noted earlier, the Project's sponsors determined that first and foremost a
detailed assessment needed to be made concerning the current status and
condition of management education and development in the United States.
How well is it functioning in relation to the needs of both the providers and
consumers (including, in the latter category, the country at large)? What are the
positive accomplishments, what are the problems, what are the apparent unmet
needs? In other words, if one took a snapshot of the current scene, so to speak,
what would it look like? To meet this objective, it would be incumbent on the
Project and its directors to develop a sufficient data base about how management education is presently being carried out. Such information not only would
permit an evaluation of the changes that have taken place in the past 25 years
(i.e., since the publication of the Foundation reports), but also would provide
a foundation for future recommendations.

Analysis of Future MED Directions in the Absence
of Major Changes

This second objective of the Project emphasized the intended forward-looking
nature of the Project. That is, the committee that commissioned the Project
very deliberately put the word *future* in both its formal and informal titles.
Therefore, the data to be collected were to be analyzed with special attention
to their implications for likely future trends and developments. As much as
possible, the principal investigators were charged with looking past immediate
conditions and circumstances to how the "system" (using that term broadly) is
changing and where it will be heading in the near-term future in the absence of
deliberate actions to change it on the part of business schools, associations,
corporations, or other organizations.

Recommendations for Future Action

The third major objective proposed for the Project by the Futures Committee was to produce a set of recommendations for future action based on the data and the analyses. In effect, this goal was to focus directly on the issue of "where *should* the system be going?" Clearly, then, this third objective had a distinctively normative cast to it and was intended to take the study beyond merely researching the status quo. One logical question that might be asked in this connection, however, is, to *whom* would any explicit or implied recommendations be made? This issue was discussed at some length by both the Futures Committee and AACSB's Board of Directors prior to authorization of the Project. Obviously, recommendations to AACSB (i.e., its Board of Directors) and its collective members regarding actions that should be taken would be appropriate and could be expected to have some potential for direct influence. Recommendations involving other organizations and associations could only be regarded as suggestive and would carry no influence other than moral suasion, so to speak.

To fulfill this third major goal of the Project, we have provided (in the chapters in Parts 2 and 3) our own comments and thoughts about the findings we obtained in a number of different areas and (in Chapter 15) our conclusions regarding the total set of results from the study. It is our considered opinion that a list of explicit recommendations could easily end up as superficial and trivial generalizations that not only would be ineffective, but also largely or totally ignored. That, in fact, was our impression concerning many of the recent articles that have contained critiques of management education and offered what we regard as overly simplistic prescriptions for change. Given the wide variety of types of institutions and schools involved in management education and development and the great differences in the circumstances within which they operate, almost any set of highly specific recommendations would be either severely limited in their applicability to particular situations or so broad and general as to be nearly meaningless. Consequently, we instead have chosen to highlight what we believe to be the most critical issues that must be confronted if American management education and development are to be improved in the future, and have suggested some productive approaches to constructive change. In sum, we have endeavored to supply relevant data and supportable rationales that will assist individual schools and companies in charting their own strategic courses of action.

ISSUES ADDRESSED BY THE PROJECT

Given the background and history of the origins of this Project, as described earlier in this chapter, it would have been presumptuous of the principal investigators to develop *de novo* a list of issues and problems to be studied and analyzed. That, in effect, was a principal outcome of the several colloquia and conferences held in the 5 years preceding the start of this Project in 1984. Those meetings were intended to bring together a large number of knowledgeable people from a wide variety of institutional and organizational settings to identify, as it were, the most important problems and challenges confronting management education and development as these activities faced a future of major societal and organizational changes. Thus, the work of "agenda setting" for the current Project was largely finished before the Project was formally initiated.

However, one further small invitational conference took place prior to the actual start of Project data-collection activities in mid-1984. This conference—which was held at the St. Charles (Illinois) conference center of Arthur Andersen and Company in March 1984—was organized by the Futures Committee of the AACSB explicitly for the purpose of providing suggestions and guidance to the principal investigators regarding the types of issues that would be important to try to address in a large-scale study such as that which was being planned. It was recognized by the twenty or so who attended (from universities, corporations, and training organizations) that no single study, no matter how well (or poorly) designed, could adequately delve into all the dozen or so complex issues that were proposed for investigation. Nevertheless, it is probably instructive to mention a few of the provocative questions (issues) that were posed at the St. Charles Conference. They included, for example, the following:

- What are the comparative advantages of different providers of management education and development?
- What are the constraints and opportunities for business/management schools, considering that they must typically operate within *a larger university context?*
- What is the impact of AACSB accreditation?
- What is the role, process and purpose of *research* in business/management education?
- What should be taught? To whom? At what stages in their careers?
- What criticisms, if any, of current management education appear to have validity?
- What is the appropriate balance between breadth and depth in formal management education?

As those who read this report will see, some of these questions will be addressed more directly by data and observations gained from the Project than will others. This is so because some issues and questions are more amenable to this type of investigation than are other equally important but exceedingly difficult (complex, sticky) ones. Thus the directors of this Project see the overall objective of this study as an attempt to shed useful light on some of these central and critical issues but not to provide definitive answers to *all* major relevant questions.

Since, in an investigation of this magnitude and intended scope, some taxonomy of the content of the study is essential, the authors have attempted to group issues around a limited set of major topic headings. These correspond, basically, to the order of chapters in the middle two parts of the report:

- Curriculum (degree programs)
- Students/graduates
- Faculty
- Teaching/instruction
- Research/scholarship
- Business school relations (within and outside the university)
- Accreditation
- Executive education/management development (i.e., lifelong learning)

We well recognize that any such grouping, and certainly any particular ordering, of issues is purely arbitrary. However, these categories seem to us to include and embrace most of the more specific issues that were generated at the various conferences that preceded the start of the present investigation. Also, we should emphasize that we were extremely cognizant of the fact that a number of important issues and concerns cut across these categories and cannot easily be pigeonholed. Therefore, we attempted to be especially alert to those issues which span particular categories. This will dictate that some specific topics will be discussed at more than one place in the report because they are pertinent to more than a single area.

DESIGN OF THE PROJECT

The array of issues that had been identified and developed prior to the initiation of the Project formed the basis for considerations of how to design it. Since we consider the rationale for the design of the Project and its data collection efforts to be crucial to understanding and interpreting our report, we will present a brief summary of it here in Chapter 1 rather than leaving all the design features to an appendix, as is customarily done in a research study report of this type. We have followed convention to some extent, however, by putting certain additional details of the design and its execution in an appendix (Appendix A, in this case) for those interested in more information concerning exactly how the study was carried out.

Early on, it was decided that three major types of data would form the heart of the data base:

1 Factual "on the shelf" statistics from a variety of relevant sources

2 Data from interviews conducted by the principal investigators and their assistants

3 Questionnaire data obtained from survey instruments designed specifically for this study

In addition to the collection of these three basic sets of data, our design called for an examination of two particular sets of literature: books and articles focusing on forecasts (and forecasting) of the future, and published criticisms of business/management education and the schools providing that education. Our procedures for obtaining and organizing each of these five types of data and information will be summarized in turn, starting with the latter two first.

Analysis of the "Futures" Literature

Our attempt here was not to invent our own scenarios of the future, but to examine what those with expertise in futures forecasting (if that is not an oxymoron) were saying about the salient features of the future most likely to affect universities, management, and management education and development. Consequently, our purpose in this part of the study, as will be seen in Chapter 2, has been to bring to bear what "relevant others" have forecast that might have an impact on the basic subject matter that is the focus of the Project. A project entitled The Future of Management Education and Development (FMED) would seem to call for some look at the F per se as well as at the MED.

Analysis of the "Criticisms" Literature

As noted earlier in this chapter, the existence of recently published criticisms of university-based business/management education was a factor that helped to reinforce the decision to undertake this Project. Because of this, and because we felt that an analysis of the criticisms would help to sharpen issues for focus in this study, we collected, summarized, and categorized these criticisms. They will be grouped by topic area and noted at appropriate places in the respective chapters of Part 2.

Collection of "Factual" Statistical Data

To build a sound data base, it was first necessary to update some of the most important factual information that appeared in the 1959 Ford Foundation (Gordon and Howell) report. Also, however, we wanted to include other types of factual data that had become available or more salient since 1959. To meet both these objectives, we canvassed a number of sources, including AACSB, the Graduate Management Admissions Council (GMAC), the U.S. Department of Education, the American Society of Training Directors (ASTD), and others.

Interview Data

As did Gordon and Howell in their study in the late 1950s, we too decided to invest considerable effort (not to mention dollars) in conducting in-person interviews with key individuals in universities, corporations and firms, and several other organizations engaged specifically in providing management development services. Essentially, we faced three major decisions in planning our interview data-collection activities: (1) how to select a sample of universities and business firms in which to conduct the interviews, (2) how to select different categories of respondents in each of these organizations, and (3) how to structure the interviews themselves. Briefly, these decisions were approached as follows:

Sampling of Organizations   For the university sample we set a target of visiting approximately 10% of the some 620 (at the time of the beginning of the study in 1984) member institutions of AACSB. To select the target group of 60 schools, we used a cluster sampling technique by designating six different geographic areas (e.g., Boston and vicinity, the entire state of Kansas) that each contained approximately 10-or-so AACSB member schools. This type of sampling, while clearly not a pure random sample, was designed to give us a wide variety of types of schools (e.g., urban and rural, large and small, accredited and nonaccredited) that would be roughly representative of the total AACSB membership. This sampling method also had the great advantage of cutting down considerably on the costs that would be incurred in visiting all sections and areas of the country to secure a pure random sample. We should point out that we did limit our "universe" (and hence our sample) of universities to those whose schools of business and management are members of AACSB. This meant that several types of institutions were excluded: small liberal arts colleges that provide some type of business education (e.g., a few introductory courses) but which have not chosen to become AACSB members, junior colleges, and vocational-technical schools. Even though each of these institutions has a connection—at least partially—with business education, we felt that given the general thrust of the Project (as well as the ever-present limitations on resources), we should concentrate on the primary providers of collegiate business/management education in the United States: the 4-year college and university members of AACSB, who supply roughly 85% of the degrees granted in this country.

The sample of corporations and firms was selected on a somewhat different basis. We arbitrarily set a target number of approximately 50 companies at which to interview. Almost all the organizations we selected met at least *one* of two criteria: (1) they had been nominated by a panel of human resources experts as leaders in management development activities, (2) they were significant employers of business school graduates. Also, several other firms were selected for one or a variety of special considerations, including, for example, a regional as opposed to a national orientation. Our final sample of over 50 firms consisted, therefore, of mostly larger or at least medium-sized organizations in their field. To sample opinions of managers and executives in smaller firms, we relied on our questionnaire survey data. (See Appendix B for a complete list of all universities and business firms at which interviews were conducted.)

Categories of Interviewees within Organizations   The second decision regarding interviews was to designate specific categories of individuals to interview in each organization. Our primary objective in choosing these categories was to obtain views and observations from a variety of relevant sources in relation to the kinds of issues and content areas on which the Project was focusing. Thus, for example, to obtain multiple perspectives on business schools within the university setting, we wanted to talk to others in addition to just the dean and several faculty members. For universities, then, six categories of respondents were tapped: the academic vice president or provost, the dean of the business/ management school, faculty members, the director of executive education (EE) for the business/management school (if the school had this type of activity), the director of placement for the business/management school, and a member of the school's Business Advisory Council (BAC) from the business community (again, if a school had such a council or similar advisory body whose members were drawn from the business world).

In the case of corporations and firms, we aimed for the following five categories of respondents, to give us a similarly diverse perspective on business school graduates, business education, and management development: the CEO or nearest equivalent top-level officer, the vice president for human resources (who typically was responsible for both college recruiting and management development), the director of college recruiting, the director of management development, and lower-level operating managers who could be expected to have had supervisory contact with recent business school graduates (and who also, frequently, would have experience attending various types of management development activities).

Content of Interviews   The third issue to be resolved with respect to the planning for interviews was their content. The basic overall philosophy that dictated how we decided on content areas for each category of respondent was to attempt to cover those issues previously identified in the pre-Project meetings that were most relevant to the particular respondent group (e.g., academic vice presidents, BAC members, operating line managers, directors of management development, etc.). (Appendix C provides a complete listing of the major content categories for each set of respondents in universities and corporations.) This meant that some interviews covered a much narrower range of subject matter than did others. For example, directors of college recruiting in firms were asked mostly about recruiting matters; and directors of executive education in business schools were asked mostly about that particular content area. Somebody with a broader set of responsibilities, such as a CEO or provost, would be asked about a fairly wide range of different topics and issues.

In addition to interviews carried out in universities and business firms, a small set of other interviews was conducted with the leaders of several professional training and development firms or associations. The focus of these interviews was consistent with the Project's strong emphasis on the topic of lifelong learning for executives, and the interview results helped round out the picture of the major "players" in management development: universities, corporations, and professional training organizations.

Questionnaire Survey Data

Questionnaire surveys formed a major part of the data collection efforts of this Project. We believed that with all their many well-known limitations (and the potential irritation produced in those individuals asked to fill them out), structured questionnaires represented the best means of producing data that would significantly supplement our interview findings. In particular, they would provide the most feasible method of broadening our sample of respondents by greatly increasing the number and types of universities and firms that would be contacted to participate in the study. Also, there was one other compelling reason for including questionnaire surveys as part of the overall research design: The data from these surveys would have the potential for providing a basis for future longitudinal studies of this type. Later researchers would have the benefit of mid-1980s responses to specific questions for comparative purposes, should they so desire.

The same basic research design questions faced us in deciding how to carry out this part of the study: how to select the sample of organizations to be contacted, how to select the categories of respondents within organizations, and how to decide on the content (and structure) of the questionnaires. Some of these design issues were relatively easy to resolve; others were not. On the first issue—selecting the sample of organizations to be contacted—the decision was straightforward for universities: All 620 member schools of AACSB were requested to take part. In effect, the sample of schools and the total population of schools were identical. On the corporate side, no such easy sampling decision could be made because the total population—and, therefore, its parameters—is difficult to define. Our final decision was to sample across a broad spectrum of leading large, medium, and small companies, although the bias was toward larger, more visible firms (see Appendix A for details).

Respondent categories for both universities and corporations were essentially the same as for the interview portion of the study. [An additional category was included for the corporate survey sample, however; namely, senior corporate executives (SCEs), who constituted a group of line executives at the vice-presidential level.] The content of the questionnaires, likewise, paralleled the content categories of the semistructured interviews, but of course more exact questions could be asked, since the surveys were designed for relatively rapid completion by the respondents through extensive use of closed-end questions. (The methods of distribution and return of the questionnaires are described in Appendix A.)

By means of questionnaires, we also were able to sample several other important groups that could not be easily covered in interviews for various logistical reasons: graduating undergraduate and MBA business students, alumni (both bachelor's degree and MBA) from business schools, and managers/owners of extremely small firms.

There was still one other feature of the questionnaire methodology that we utilized in our data analysis. By means of "fact sheet" questions at the end of the questionnaire forms, we had the potential to group respondents by type of organization. This was carried out for the data collected from universities, where for certain comparisons we divided business schools into three "Categories" based on four (arbitrarily selected) criteria: AACSB accreditation status (accredited/nonaccredited), existence of a Ph.D. program (yes/no), type of master's degree program (primarily full-time students/primarily part-time students), and self-rating of school (top quartile or above/below top quartile of all business/management schools). (The self-ratings turned out to be quite candid, in our opinion.) Those schools which met all four criteria were designated as Category I, those which met at least the first criterion (AACSB accredited) but not all four were placed into Category II, and those schools not accredited by AACSB were put into Category III. There were, from the factual data we collected from each respondent, other ways that schools could have been categorized for analysis purposes, but the criteria selected were believed to represent a reasonable basis on which to make a rough classification of schools.

To conclude this section of the discussion of the Project's design, we can note that while interviews gave us *intensive* data on opinions and attitudes from the more than 500 individuals interviewed, questionnaires permitted us to obtain an *extensive* sampling of views from more than 10,000 individuals who have some type of relationship with management education and management development. Thus, most of the relevant categories of persons directly affected by management education and development activities, as well as the institutions and organizations (in this country) that carry them out, have been given an opportunity to express their opinions in the course of this study.

Limits to the Scope of the Project

We have noted previously several practical limits in the design of the Project (e.g., the sample of universities for both interviews and questionnaires). Here, we want to highlight three major limits regarding the overall scope of the Project. These are as follows: First, the data collected for the study, and indeed the Project itself, focus on management education and development in only one country: the United States. No data were collected from any other country, and no analyses were made of how management education activities are carried out in other countries. Second, only one arena of management education was studied: that pertaining to the management of business enterprises. No analyses or generalizations were made with regard to public administration education, health administration education, etc. Third, doctoral-level education for business was not studied, although we did collect indirect information relevant to this academic degree level. All these topics—management education outside the United States, management education relating to organizations other than business firms, and doctoral-level education for business—are quite important, and each deserves major, comprehensive investigation in its own right. The reason that each of them was omitted from the present Project is straightforward: finite resources in terms of both time and money. Thus, decisions had to be made by the principal investigators concerning what could and could not be accomplished within certain parameters. On the positive side, those topic areas omitted provide a stimulus for interesting studies to be carried out by other teams of researchers in the future.

STRUCTURE OF THE REPORT

The remainder of this report is organized in the following manner: The next chapter, entitled Views of the Future, completes the introductory section. Part 2 contains an examination of the basic issues facing university degree programs (undergraduate and master's) in business and management, as listed earlier in this chapter. Part 3 focuses specifically on postdegree executive education and management development activities as those are conducted in the several major settings: universities, corporations, and professional training organizations. In this part, particular attention is paid to the comparative advantages (and disadvantages) of these various providers. The final part of the report, Part 4, contains an overview of the findings and the principal investigators' major conclusions.

CHAPTER 2

VIEWS OF THE FUTURE *

An imaginary German prophet was asked in 1928 to forecast the future. He said that by 1933 Germany would have suffered 5 million unemployed and be in social disarray. His listeners concluded that this spelled disaster for Germany. No, said the prophet, by 1943 the German flag would fly over most of Europe. Ah, said his audience, a Renaissance. No, said the prophet, by 1948 Germany would be in ruins and its production would have fallen to 10% of the 1928 level. From this his audience inferred that anyone born in 1948 would have a tough time indeed. Not so, said the prophet. By 1968 Germans would have real income four times that of 1928 and own boxes that would soon show live pictures of a man landing on the moon.

The prophet was locked up as a madman.

Clifton C. Garvin, Jr.
Former chairman of Exxon, quoting Zbignew Brzezinski,
Advances in Strategic Management, vol. 3, 1985, p. 299.

In order to evaluate the management education and development system and its ability to prepare the leaders of tomorrow for the world of tomorrow, it would seem appropriate to take a look into the future for which they are to be prepared. However, as the preceding passage illustrates, this is much easier said than done. In this chapter we will review what others have predicted for the future as it pertains to a world that includes management. As pointed out in the previous chapter, our goal is not to provide the definitive view on the future, nor is it to formulate our own views of the future, since that would be a major

*The initial draft of this chapter was prepared by William Cowie.

exercise in itself. A more appropriate approach—the approach followed in this chapter—would be to extract from the vast amount of "futures" literature only that which we deem relevant to our area of interest, namely, the future as it pertains to management and management education.

Three groups of variables meet our criterion of relevance to the field of management. These are economic, demographic, and societal variables. In considering these sets of variables, those having implications for either the external environment within which management has to operate or the internal organizational environment with which it has to cope were included. In the consideration of each of these categories of variables, their impacts on the external and/or internal environment facing management were assessed. In other words, one could view the discussion from a matrix framework:

	External (Environment)	Internal (Organization)
Economic variables		
Demographic variables		
Societal variables		

Another point to consider when reviewing the literature dealing with the future is the time horizon that is used. The period focused on in the project is 10 to 20 years into the future, that is, into the first decade of the next century. In order to get a workable sense of this time horizon, it is helpful to think back 20 years or so to, say, the mid-1960s and to think about what has changed since then (and what hasn't), how quickly (or how slowly) things have changed, and finally, what the impact (or lack of impact) has been on business, management, and management education. An example of this would be to consider the state of air travel. Jet aircraft had only relatively recently (late 1950s) begun to appear, and since then, the technology has been refined but not changed radically. However, no new technology was required to spur the growth of the car-rental market which burgeoned alongside the growth in hotels and air travel itself, changes that did indeed alter the way business is conducted—distant travel today is taken much more for granted as a way of conducting business compared to earlier use of train travel or even air travel. Several observers predicted that this would happen, but most of them did not fully realize the length of time it would take for the change to have its full effect. Because the United States is a large and complex country, it takes longer than some expect for many systemic changes to become part of "the landscape." When reading about expected future changes, therefore, caution is needed concerning predictions about the *speed* at which at least some of them will have a major effect. Looking *back* two decades on almost any issue mentioned in this chapter will provide a useful perspective for the pages that follow (as well as for the entire project), a perspective that is often lost when one is focusing only on change and the future. (Incidentally, we have chosen to follow this mode—that of looking back first—in the consideration of major topic areas covered throughout this report.)

In this chapter, each of the three sets of variables will be reviewed. The emphasis will be somewhat heavier on the first category, economic variables, since management education and development, by their very nature, tend to be concerned more with economic factors. In the final section some summarizing comments will be made to set the stage for the rest of the study.

GENERAL OVERVIEW OF THE LITERATURE

There is no shortage of predictions about the future. Rather, an observer's first impression of the "futures" literature is likely to be centered on the overwhelming amount of speculating and forecasting that goes on. This ranges from astrological predictions to such large studies as the famous Limits to Growth Study by the Club of Rome and the Global 2000 Study commissioned by President Carter. Likewise, one finds a wide range of assumptions about the future held by various authors, resulting in a pronounced variation in their views of the future, even though most of them work from the same data base. Such assumptions can be viewed on an optimism/pessimism scale, and Kerr and Rosow (1979) have provided perhaps the best summary of the two extreme views of the future:

    1 The utopian vision, with Herman Kahn as one of its leading proponents, seeing productivity and living standards rising all over the world
    2 The doomsday vision, with resources running out and social systems deteriorating into anarchy, or one of its many variations, such as the gradual smothering of innovation into another Middle Ages, a "last fling" before the "great doom"

The task (and not a trivial one!) facing someone reviewing this literature is to decide which of the many conflicting opinions to pay attention to. As the first step, and probably the most important, one has to acknowledge the fact that the future remains unpredictable, at least with any precision. (This is probably the only thing upon which there is universal agreement among futurists!) Therefore, because of this, there is no science of the future, with an established paradigm, leading scholars, reputable journals, and the like.

    It is possible, however, to view most predictions along a conceptual continuum, with at one end predictions with no basis in fact (e.g., the world will end tomorrow) and at the other end predictions based in history that can be regarded as somewhat more probable. Since human beings have not yet found a surefire way to predict the future of people, organizations, and societal institutions, it probably would be wrong to assume that any particular approach is better than another. Having said that, however, it is possible (and we believe necessary) to take a statistical view of the performance of forecasts, and it is reasonably safe to say that a higher percentage of history/trend-based predictions are bound to be accurate, as opposed to those with less basis in history and/or existing trends. Therefore, despite the much-quoted statement that one should not look into a rearview mirror to move ahead, the truth of the matter is that there probably is no alternative with a systematically higher probability of yielding a better forecast than doing just that. (Unlike the situation facing the driver of a motorcar, however, there is no visible road ahead to look at!)

ECONOMICS

In this section we will look at the following variables which are expected to influence the future environment within which business leaders will have to be prepared to operate:

- The change of the American economy from one based on industry to one based on service and information
- The impact of technological changes
- The increasingly international nature of the world economy
- The growth in entrepreneurism
- Changes in the nature of work

The Service/Information Economy

Of all the variables affecting the future within which American business leaders will have to operate, this is perhaps the most pervasive and significant one, what Toffler calls "an eco-spasm," the move away from an industrial society to what has been termed the postindustrial society, with its emphasis on services. Cetron (1985), Jones (1982), Bell (1973), and Naisbitt (1982) explain the meaning of this: In the previous century, most of the population was employed in the agricultural sector of the economy. This could be described as the first stage of economic development. With mechanization and industrialization, machines increasingly did the work formerly done by humans in agriculture, and output was increased while the number of people working in agriculture declined, both in absolute terms and as a percentage of the labor force. This led to the second stage of economic development, where people became employees of large industrial organizations, up to the point in the first half of this century when more people were employed in manufacturing than in any other sector of the economy. There are not one, but two key elements of this "second wave": (1) the fact that the country became a nation of employees, as opposed to being self-employed, and (2) the fact that the workers became employees of large industrial organizations.

Presently, according to these and other authors, we are in the third stage of development of the American economy, as typified by the major type of employment. The change presently under way is to what Bell (1973) called the postindustrial phase, where the manufacturing output is not necessarily decreasing, but the number of people employed in manufacturing is. More people are now employed in the service sector of the economy than in any other, and the share of total wealth produced by the service sector is increasing relative to manufacturing and agriculture (which is not to denigrate the importance of these two areas). This is the shift that Naisbitt (1982) calls the shift from an industrial society to an information society, summarizing it with the phrase "farmer, laborer, clerk" to typify the changing occupation of the majority of Americans. (He also cites the example that New York City's leading export isn't apparel anymore, but legal services.) This shift moves society's emphasis away from pitting physical person against nature (farming) or physical person against machine (manufacturing), to pitting mental person against mental person.

This transition from one type of economy to another is a profound one. One of the best ways to understand just how profound it is, as well as to obtain a perspective on how deeply it could affect the developments of the next decade or so, is to take a closer look at the transition from the agrarian economy to the industrial economy as it actually happened. One such review is offered by Muller (1970), in which he points out the extent to which institutions we accept as "given" today were products of the industrial revolution. Some examples are the workday with fixed times (instead of working with the sun), not living at work (on the farm or above the store) and the concomitant commuting, urbanization and suburbanization, large corporations into which capital could be pooled to afford expensive machinery, large bureaucracies required to manage these behemoths of industry, and the mass employment and trade unionism they created, to mention only a few. None of these existed before the shift to industrialism. Equally significant, but more subtle, were such concepts as working to a pace set by others; the "capital perspective," where returns are not measured per person (as before), but rather per dollar invested; the philosophy of capitalism itself; the view of human labor as merely another resource, interchangeable with machines (the very product of the industrial revolution); and also, of course, the increase in living standards and economic freedom brought about after the initial poverty and disruption.

The unspoken implication (of this history) is that as we move out of the industrial phase, some of these now taken-for-granted integral aspects of our lives could themselves be greatly altered in the future. Each of these concepts is accepted today as given, and yet when one looks at their roots as being in the industrial revolution, one realizes that they could be susceptible to change with such a global shift in the nature of the economy. Indeed, a few changes are already evident, such as the decline of trade union membership and influence.

Impact of Technological Change

In the 1980s technological changes will undoubtedly affect working environments massively, powerfully, often unpredictably, often perniciously. (Skinner, 1979, p. 204.)

Wickham Skinner's quote is a succinct summary of most of what has been said about the impact of technology on the working environment. If ever one subject relating to the future has suffered from a case of overexposure, the impact of technology probably is it. But not without good reason. Looking back into history, it is easy to see how technology has changed not only the way business operates, but also the whole way we live. Automobiles gave "micro" mobility, air travel gave "macro" mobility, radio and television gave exposure, telephones gave instant communications, and combinations of these gave rise to whole new markets; e.g., as we noted earlier, car rental is the outflow of air travel and automobiles. Computers have already made a major impact on the way business is done, and they are an obvious source of more future changes— especially those connected with the ultimate effects of developments in artificial intelligence (AI).

According to most observers, there appear to be two areas of impact of technological change, namely, industrial automation (also referred to sometimes as "robotics"), which is expected to influence the blue-collar aspects of work, and computerization, which is expected to affect the way in which white-collar work is done. With regard to blue-collar implications, Hunt and Hunt (1983) studied the human-resource implications of robotics. They attempted to separate fact from hyperbole and forecast the robot population in the United States by 1990, taking into consideration forecasts made by others (including General Motors), to be between 50,000 and 100,000 robots, of which 25% to 30% would be in automobile manufacturing. In terms of displacement of workers, they expect this to be insignificant overall (100,000 to 200,000 jobs, or less than 1% of all jobs will be affected), but significant in particular job categories, e.g., welding and painting. Furthermore, they view displacement as different from retrenchment, arguing that a displaced worker need not necessarily be terminated. On the other hand, they expect to see between 30,000 and 60,000 new jobs created by the new technology. An important observation here is their statement that it is the nature of these job changes that is important, not merely the numbers, since the jobs to be eliminated are low-skill jobs, while the new jobs are high-skill jobs requiring significant technical background. This "upscaling" of work, in their view, is the important consequence. Therefore, they view robotics as yet one more step in the evolutionary path of technological innovation in manufacturing technology and thus not worthy of any more or less attention than any other technological innovation on the shop floor. They identify three factors working against the quick introduction of robots, namely, the shortage of skilled personnel to design, install, and operate them; the financial resources required to acquire them and make them operational; and the organizational commitment required to make them work. (Recent media reports about some companies' failures to introduce robots at the pace they had planned to tends to support this assessment.)

The second area of significant technological change is in the white-collar arena, where the primary technological change seems to be computerization in its many forms (including, as previously noted, future developments related to artificial intelligence). Computers have a critical impact on the way information gets processed and, consequently, on the way white-collar workers work (and where they work). Regarding this, Miles and Snow (1986) have postulated that improved information-processing technology is giving impetus to a new form of organization, which they call "dynamic networks." In essence, dynamic networking could be viewed as the opposite of vertical integration, because businesses use outside vendors to perform such functions as design, manufacturing, and distribution, functions which historically have tended to be performed in-house. Although Miles and Snow offer no empirical evidence, it would appear that this phenomenon has close links to the predictions on entrepreneurism and globalism discussed earlier. It is also closely linked with the network approach discussed in the "International Perspective" section.

Cetron (1985) makes a distinction between mechanization (which typified the industrial revolution) and automation (powering the information revolution). Mechanization substituted machines for muscle, while automation substitutes machines for people's minds. Consequently, while mechanization extended purchasing power by providing almost everyone with a secure factory job producing low-cost goods, automation is shrinking purchasing power (in spite of raising productivity) by eliminating workers and raising skills levels needed to gain employment. Thus Cetron foresees a gradual decline of the middle class, citing the view of Lester Thurow that new technologies are turning the United States into a two-tier economy (a leisure class and a worker class and nothing in between) as support for this prediction.

While some reports in the popular media tend to create the impression that this is happening, especially with regard to young blacks, single parents, and ghetto inhabitants "caught" in a position and seeing no way out, Cetron cites no evidence to support his contention that the middle class (itself a product of the industrial revolution) will disappear. Using Muller's approach of looking into the rearview mirror, one could equally well cite the initial disruption, poverty, and other less desirable faces of the early industrial revolution, notice the parallels with the infant stages of the current revolution, and predict that just as the industrial revolution eventually sorted itself out and led to increased prosperity, the information revolution will eventually overcome its birth pains as society adjusts itself to the new technology. Further, just as manufacturing jobs were deskilled to a level where plentiful labor was available, one could likewise expect information jobs to become sufficiently deskilled to allow the majority of workers to find employment in the information economy. This does not constitute endorsement of such a view, but merely represents a counterpoint to demonstrate alternative ways in which the future may develop in terms of the growth or shrinkage of the middle class.

Regarding management as a particular form of white-collar work, it is appropriate to consider the impact of technological change on the work of managers. On the one hand, one can look back over the 20th century and all the innovations that have revolutionized many aspects of our daily lives and conclude that the basic relationships, responsibilities, and activities of managers have not changed much. Managers still have to get work done through others, still use secretaries, and still talk to subordinates, peers, and superiors. Yet one has also to acknowledge that with technological advances have come advances in the sophistication of management, along with increased complexity of the job. Most of the popular literature seems to focus on what computers can do to enhance the efficiency of managers, whereas it appears that a case could rather be made that technology (from the telephone, automobile, and airplane to computers) has its primary impact not on the efficiency of management, but on its effectiveness—enabling managers to *do more*. Examples could include the enhanced ability of managers to understand increasingly intricate mergers and acquisitions, organization forms, and other areas of increased complexity. The popularity of personal computers using spreadsheet programs appears to offer some support for this point of view, since personal computers do not necessarily allow managers to do more with less (efficiency) as much as they allow them to do more than they were able to do previously.

Then, of course, there is the impact of technology on markets. This is probably the subject of most "Who would have thought..." types of conversations, where whole new markets are created by new inventions and some markets disappear (e.g., slide rules). Fascinating and vital to managers as this aspect of technological development no doubt is, it is arguably one of the most treacherous minefields for futurists, littered with the skeletons of technological predictions (such as, for example, personal flying cars) that have not become reality. The important point for this study is to realize and accept that new markets will be created by new technological developments, which will need to be managed, but it is virtually impossible to make accurate predictions in this area.

International Perspective

The international perspective is a subject that needs no introduction following the highly visible debates about trade deficits and protectionist sentiments. The international issue has been talked about for many years, with the focus of the discussion in the sixties and seventies centered around the role, morality, and legitimacy of multinational organization. Of late, the dialogue in this country seems to have moved to a concentration of attention on the growth of the so-called Pacific Rim countries and the degree to which that is globalizing the world's economies, especially that of the United States. As Kahn (1979) put it, by 1990 the United States will no longer be the overwhelmingly dominant economy it was a decade or two ago, but will simply be the largest of many large economies. He uses the concept of gross world product (GWP) to give his ideas concrete expression, and he sees America's relative share of the GWP declining, even though its own domestic economy may be growing, primarily because other countries, especially the Pacific Rim countries, are growing faster and boosting their share of the GWP.

More important than its relative size, though, is the role of the United States in the whole world economy. From being predominantly an industrial exporter since World War II, America now may be faced with greater equality among countries, such as Japan and various developing nations with vigorous economies, in the arena of industrial goods. Naisbitt links this phenomenon back to the postindustrialism discussed earlier by noting that the United States is unlikely to ever regain its industrial supremacy because it no longer has an industrial economy. Industry will be increasingly dominated by the third world, with their more numerous, and lesser-paid, work forces. In this he is supported by many others, who seem to agree that the United States should focus on the new information economy. Using history as a model, Cetron predicts that the countries emerging as the leaders in the new (information/service) economy will also be the leaders in most aspects of global affairs. What observers see happening is American firms dealing more and more with the information and service aspects (such as, say, management and distribution) while forging links with others taking care of the industrial (mining and manufacturing) aspects. Examples of this would include such arrangements as having a product assembled in a third world country from components bought from several other countries (including the United States) for an American firm, to be sold worldwide. This trend will be driven to an increasing extent by disparities in wages, as other barriers are reduced by advancing technology. Thus Kahn sees the percentage of GWP coming from world trade increasing; i.e., a greater proportion of the world's wealth will come from trading among nations. This is, of course, based on the assumption that free trade will be allowed to grow, rather than decline through trade-restriction policies, which tend to be spurred by trade imbalances.

There is ample evidence of the growth in international cooperation in the design, production, and distribution of an increasing number of products. Cetron characterizes this by posing the rhetorical question, which is the American car, the Ford made in Mexico in a plant jointly owned by Mazda and Ford from parts made in Japan or a Volkswagen made in Pennsylvania from parts imported from Germany as well as bought locally? Likewise, AT&T personal computers (PCs) are made in Italy by Olivetti, and the ubiquitous IBM PC began with less than 30% of its value made in America. In such an environment it is only natural to expect the role of international, multinational, or transnational corporations to increase rather than to decline.

The growth in the economic power of Japan has been commented on exhaustively in recent years. An aspect of this growth that has not been emphasized as much is the fact that Japan's economy has a much higher international component, due to its small size and population, relative to the United States, whose domestic economy has been large enough to afford growth without necessarily looking abroad to obtain it. What the futurists seem to be saying is that if the United States wants to keep its position of preeminence, it will have to develop a similarly high international trading component. To put it simply, in Kahn's terms, an increasing part of the GWP will be international trade. Any country wanting a prominent position in the future world economy cannot afford to neglect this arena. What is interesting, though, is that few of the futurists feel confident to venture their guess as to whether or not the United States will in fact respond to this challenge, and therefore, it is difficult as an observer to predict whether in the future the role of the United States in the global economy will be smaller or greater or remain about the same.

Another topic which figured prominently in earlier debates is the role of the third world. What has emerged since the seventies is a two-tier division of the third world. The first half are those countries which have made economic progress over the past decade, such as South Korea and Taiwan. The second half are mainly countries in Latin America, the Caribbean, and sub-Saharan Africa, which have shown more promise than progress. The distinction appears to be based on the predominant nature of the exports of third world countries. Countries that have made progress are those which have industrialized and for whom industrial exports form the major category, while the others are characterized by the fact that their economies are to a large degree based on the export of a few commodities. An extreme example is Madagascar, whose whole economy received a major setback when Coca-Cola made the (as it turned out, short-lived) switch to the "new Coke," which did not require vanilla beans (an ingredient in the old formula, and Madagascar's staple export), as was the case before.

Entrepreneurism

Concurrent with the changeover in the U.S. economy, and an integral part of this shift, is the increase in what has become known as entrepreneurism—the growth of small business. Naisbitt argues that this is to be expected, that every previous changeover of this magnitude was accompanied by a rise in the number of new small ventures and entrepreneurs who brought new technology to the marketplace. However, his view is that this is a temporary phenomenon; as this economic order matures, he says, the current wave of entrepreneurism will wane accordingly. Williamson (1975) supports this with his summary of studies done on several industries, showing that major new inventions tend to come from outside established, large organizations. This implies that the surge in entrepreneurism is not a fundamental characteristic of the information economy, but merely a characteristic of the beginning stages of any new economic order, and therefore, that the current wave of entrepreneurism will subside in the next decade or two. As Williamson describes it, this is the transformation from the major breakthroughs to the more minor improvements, which tend to come from the more established, and larger, firms. However, this time around, it is not clear that the concentration which followed the industrial revolution will be reproduced automatically in the service economy. It has to be noted that concentration is not inevitable—agriculture never was as concentrated as manufacturing became—and therefore, it should not be accepted without question that the service/information economy will become as concentrated as the industrial economy became.

There are several arguments to support this view. For example, the nature of manufacturing lends itself to physical concentration more than does agriculture or the provision of services and/or information. As Drucker pointed out, the large business enterprise arrived with the industrial revolution, and very few large companies are based in agriculture. Although many large firms are based on the provision of services and/or information, the reconcentration implied by Naisbitt and Williamson may not necessarily be inevitable. This is so because several entropic forces in evidence at present (which are discussed below) were not as strong during the manufacturing economy.

The pace of change in the information/service sector is intrinsically greater than it was during the industrial era, because service innovations typically require fewer resources and less time to bring to market. For example, for a restaurant to add an item to its menu or for a bank to add a new service takes less time and capital investment in physical plant tooling and preparation than, say, the production of a new automobile model. The lower "front-end" investment in new services normally leads to a shorter product life cycle, since new offerings are more easily introduced and existing products/services have less investment to amortize before they too can be changed. Stability, therefore, carries less of a premium as compared with manufacturing organizations, and adaptability becomes more important. Under circumstances such as these, largeness tends to be a vice rather than a virtue, since large organizations often cannot move as quickly as small ones; also, there are fewer natural barriers to entry to protect large organizations from competition by newer, smaller competitors.

Further, as will be discussed in more detail in the "Societal Variables" section, there has been a change in values among the "new breed" (Yankelovich's expression), putting a premium on individuality, and entrepreneurism is the economic face of this expression. According to Cetron (1985), this is likely to be supported by a change in individualistic values stressed in the educational system. The stereotype for this change is the individual who no longer is satisfied with taking orders from someone he or she does not consider to be his or her superior and who strikes out on his or her own, often competing with the former employer with the know-how obtained during that employment. Dissatisfied employees are no new phenomenon, but the barriers that have limited their mobility (such as high capital investment required for production tooling) in the industrial era have now disappeared to a greater degree, since it requires less up-front investment to get a service/information business going. Indeed, such businesses are often started by employees who are moonlighting, which enables them to build their own businesses to a viable point before leaving their original job.

Finally, as Robert Noyce of Intel put it, the new industry has become a brain-intensive industry—not a capital-intensive one—which no longer requires concentration in order to obtain the critical resource. This, combined with romanticized visions of the entrepreneurial successes of such people as Steven Jobs of Apple and Bill Gates of Microsoft, makes it more difficult for a large organization to retain its "brains," which increasingly are becoming its critical resource. This does not mean that there will be no concentration or large organizations in the service/information economy. Banks, restaurant chains, information companies, media organizations, and many other examples abound where there are obvious benefits to concentration. But the forces mentioned above may reduce the extent of concentration compared to what it was in the manufacturing economy. Also, and more important, it may be a different type of concentration—looser linkages and more dispersed (even if within one organizational shell).

Another aspect which has received ambivalent treatment is the question of whether staff services will tend to be moved in-house or subcontracted. While some research tentatively indicates that increased use of computer technology may increase the ability and desire of businesses to move staff services (previously contracted out) in-house, Cetron argues that the increased drive to entrepreneurism will lead to the opposite state of affairs, namely, that more and more staff services will be performed on a contract basis, often by former employees.

Therefore, although it would appear that the transition to a new type of economy has introduced a new wave of entrepreneurism, there are forces (e.g., the maturing of new technologies) pushing toward increased concentration and the consequent reduction of entrepreneurism. However, other forces (e.g., volatility of technology, low capital requirement) seem to push in the opposite direction toward deconcentration. While it may be impossible to predict which of these forces will win out in the end, it seems reasonable to conclude that even if the level of entrepreneurism declines with the maturation of the service/information economy, it is likely to stabilize at a higher plateau than in the industrial economy because of the forces endemic to the service economy (e.g., lower capital investment).

Nature of Work

If there is one arena where current changes are put into sharp focus, it is in the workplace. Not since the beginning of this century have so many forces, from so many angles, been pressing simultaneously for change in the way Americans work. Not only is the nature of the work we do (what gets done) in the midst of a major structural change (farmer, laborer, clerk), but the composition of the work force (who is doing the work) is also changing. On the one hand, there is a clear demographic trend toward aging as the baby-boom population bulge ages. On the other, there is a change in social values leading to a dramatic increase in the number of women in the work force. Further, the technology employed in the workplace has had an impact on how the work is done, differential patterns of economic growth have had an impact on where the jobs are located, and the educational level of the work force, among other things, has had an impact on how the labor force is organized. These topics are covered elsewhere, and therefore, only issues pertaining to the nature of work in the future that are not treated in other sections in this chapter will be discussed here.

One of these aspects is the phenomenon of corporate bureaucracy, which is a by-product of the large organizations created around the turn of the century. Observers pointed out some time ago that the computer is likely to replace mid-

dle managers—e.g., Muller predicted that in 1970. Yet, as pointed out in a special issue of *Business Week* dealing with this trend (September 1984), there is
little systematic evidence of it having happened on a major scale in the intervening 14 years. Since our time horizon for the future is not much longer than
that, it is at this point still difficult to say whether this trend will strengthen or
prove to be merely a temporary phenomenon. The forces pushing for a reduction of middle management appear to be related to computerization, while those
pushing for increasing the need for middle management are related to the increasing complexity of the internal and external work environment.

Several authors (e.g., Best, Cetron, and O'Toole) expect the computer revolution to contribute to such trends as increased working at home and deur-
banization, as commuting is replaced by computer communication links. As
yet, there is no strong evidence of such trends gaining strength, but likewise,
nobody at the turn of the century foresaw that a new technology (the automobile) would radically alter the way people relate home to work either. With the
change from an agricultural society to an industrial society, there came a fundamental change in the nature of work. Workers no longer lived where they
worked (above the grocery store or on the farm). Instead, urbanization and
commuting were essentially outcomes of industrialization. With the change to
a service/information society, it is not impossible that such a fundamental shift
may occur again. Cetron (1985) links the growth in entrepreneurism (mentioned
earlier) with the emergence of new technology that enables people to sever physical ties not only with the workplace (e.g., through "telecommuting") but also
with their employing organizations, reverting to the status of independent outside contractors for services rather than employees. As the story of the German prophet at the beginning of this chapter illustrates, it is impossible to say
which direction this phenomenon may take in the near future.

Organized labor came to prominence with the industrial revolution, and just
as the postindustrial revolution is chipping away at employment in blue-collar
occupations, membership in labor unions has shown a steady decline for the
past few decades. Bluestone (1979) acknowledges this from a union perspective but sees the problem as only one of a negative public perspective and one
which not only could, but will, be overcome. However, as yet, the statistics do
not bear out such proclamations. One could speculate on the likelihood of unions
gaining a foothold in the so-called hi-tech manufacturing environment, since
they mostly use assembly-line personnel in almost the same way as the older
manufacturing industries. On the one hand, there are arguments supporting a
revival due to the low wages that get paid, the lack of job-tenure agreements,
and other aspects of hi-tech employment that increasingly resemble employment in the older industries which tend to be unionized. On the other hand,
there are arguments that a broader section of the work force (e.g., women) are
involved, the work is less demanding physically, the surroundings of the job
are more pleasant, etc., all of which make unionizing efforts more difficult. However, it is too early to present definitive evidence for either point of view, and

therefore, there are few observers capable of making a persuasive case one way or the other.

DEMOGRAPHICS

Of the three categories of variables affecting this study, demographics is probably the easiest to forecast, since everyone needing management education and development in the next two decades has already been born! In this section we will focus on three specific demographic variables:

- The baby-boom population bulge
- Aging and retirement
- The role of women

The Baby-Boom Population Bulge

The first variable to be considered is the so-called baby boomers, those 70 million people born between 1946 and 1964, about whom so much has been written lately. By the year 2000, this bulge will be reflected in the 40 to 55 age category, the age when most of those who have the potential to be managers would already be in management. The second issue relates to the first in a delayed sense, namely, retirement. Will managers (and/or other categories of employees) retire earlier or later, and what effects will that have on the need for management education and development?

   Regarding the population bulge phenomenon, there is very little that can be said that is not already well known. One of the more visible changes this demographic phenomenon has wreaked already is on the higher-education system, with many smaller liberal arts and junior colleges striving to avoid severe enrollment declines as the "bulge" moved beyond the traditional college attendance age. The growing interest in lifelong learning is no accident as the baby-boom cohort accelerates overall demand for ongoing education merely by their numbers. The fact that these people find themselves in an era of rapid change and increasing sophistication simply reinforces this demand, of course.

Aging and Retirement

Turning to the second issue, aging and retirement, it is expected that the over-65 age group is going to grow substantially in the next two decades for two main reasons. First, the trend of continued longevity shows no sign of abating, meaning that, on average, people live longer once they have reached retirement age. Since the turn of the century, the average American life expectancy at birth has increased by more than 25 years (from 48.2 to 73.2 years by 1978) (Butler, 1981).

The second reason is the aging of the baby-boom generation. Glickman (1982) highlights Census Bureau projections, which show that by 2015 the first wave of baby boomers will be in the traditional retirement age. He points out that at present there is one General Motors pensioner for each 3.3 current employees, but by 1999 it is expected that there will only be 2 employees per pensioner and this trend could be expected to continue beyond that.

Copperman and Keast (1983) provide one of the best analyses of the retirement issue, focusing as they do on the underlying factors affecting retirement. On the premise that older employees base their employment and retirement decisions on the incentives and disincentives established by public and private policies, the authors examined such policies and noted that, currently, less than 20% of individuals aged 65 or older are delaying their retirement. Most workers are continuing to retire between the ages of 62 and 65 years. The authors contend that this is due to values and policies which have traditionally emphasized the "making place" by older workers for younger workers. This point is also supported by Honig and Hanoch (1981). Specific factors mentioned include the following:

• Current Social Security rules encourage retirement with full benefits at age 65 (and age 62 with reduced benefits). These rules are a major factor in the retirement decision.

• Full-time work past retirement age is discouraged by taxation policies, which increase the opportunity cost of working (in terms of foregone leisure).

• Benefits lost by not retiring at age 65 are not recouped at a later retirement age, but are lost. This also provides a disincentive to delay the retirement decision.

• Employers are not required to continue pension benefit accruals past the normal retirement age—usually 65.

• Most private pensions suspend benefits if retirees return to work for their old employer. Because of several factors, these retirees are reluctant to attempt employment at a new employer and therefore withdraw from the labor market completely.

• Traditional personnel policies generally require full-time work. Suitable part-time positions are not yet widely available.

The baby-boom generation will begin to approach retirement in the next two decades. Social security is but one aspect of a potential intergenerational conflict that could be triggered, according to these (and other) authors. While acknowledging that no one knows exactly what will happen, because no one knows how these various policies will be modified over time, these authors point out that employers could make a major difference by adopting policies that make it more attractive for themselves as well as for the potential retirees to continue employment. The point is that these corporate decisions, made individually, will collectively influence the outcome, and at present it is too difficult to discern which way (earlier or later retirement) the outcome will lean. Similarly, the direction of government policy changes is unknown, but based on the history of the equal-opportunity issue, it would not be unrealistic to expect legislation to involve employers in some way or another if this issue begins to cause increased friction. Sheppard (1982) points out that this issue, which he calls "ageism," has many similarities with those of sexism or racism and, therefore, has the same potential for ending up in the public policy arena, with similar consequences for employers (i.e., more regulation).

Apart from the possible impact the issue of aging/retirement could have on managers through the avenue of governmental regulation, it is a relevant issue because of the vast amount of knowledge contained in the minds of increasingly healthier and longer-living senior employees. The intergenerational conflict theory advanced above holds basically that the current retirement system "pushes" older people out of the labor market to make place for the (promotion of) "youngsters." Yet, if this were true (for the sake of argument), and further, if it were true that one of the main demographic reasons for this conflict could be the (more numerous) baby boomers "pushing" their predecessors out, then it could be expected that as the baby boomers start retiring, this "push" will subside because there is no longer a more numerous cohort behind them competing for their positions. Then the "push" may be replaced by a "pull" from the workplace, which would be losing workers faster than it could replace them. If this line of reasoning holds true, then one would expect employers in the 1990s to start changing their thinking about retirement and other related policies and begin aiming at keeping employees active longer. This would increase the long-term importance of ongoing training, in all its forms, even more.

The Role of Women

According to Maret (1983), about 43% of the total labor force consisted of women in 1980, up from 33% in 1960 (about the time the Foundation reports were published). Several studies point out that the participation level of women has not yet reached its equilibrium point, meaning that in the next two decades an even greater percentage of women is likely to be active in the work force and, in concert, a greater percentage of almost all occupations (including management) will be held by women. Maret adds that the more education a woman has, the greater is the likelihood that she will seek paid employment. Among women with 4 or more years of college, about two out of three were in the labor force in 1979. This is also reflected in the fact that the average female worker is as well educated as the average male worker, both having completed a median of about 12.6 years of schooling. The segment of women accounting for the fastest rise in employment has been married women. Between 1950 and 1980, labor force participation for this category of women increased from 12% to 45%.

The two major differences between male and female workers at present are the degree of continuity of employment and the status of occupations. The degree of continuity of employment for women, while still lower than that of men, has increased significantly in the past two decades. The highest tendency to part-time work is among married mothers, while unmarried women are more likely to be full-time employees. In addition, Maret shows that the highest proportion of full-time female workers comes from divorced or never-married single women. Maret lists seven factors linked to high labor force participation rates:

1 Having had a mother employed outside the home
2 Having had a good education
3 Living in highly urbanized areas
4 Being unmarried or having a liberal spouse
5 Having small families
6 Having a taste for market work
7 Having jobs which are economically rewarding

If one projects each one of these factors to the end of the century, it appears that this trend will continue. Other authors, e.g., Smith (1979), identify the same or similar factors, e.g., the ratio between male and female compensation. Smith also sees a continuation of the trend toward later marriages. For example, he expects the percentage of women who have never married in the age group 20 to 24 to increase from about 40% to about 50% within the 15 years between 1975 and 1990, while the overall percentage decreases. This means that more women will marry, but they will marry later, with obvious implications for participation in the labor market. Cetron (1985) adds another factor, namely, the decline in blue-collar work, which tended to be physically and emotionally undesirable for women, and the increase in white-collar employment (and one could add hi-tech production employment), which will lead to an increase in the number of employment opportunities realistically open to women.

Regarding earnings and status, the data unquestionably show that full-time women employees earn significantly less than their male counterparts with equivalent education. However, the gap is smaller at younger ages, which could signify some correction "working through" the age groups. To debate the reasons falls beyond the scope of this study, other than to note that it is an issue that is likely to increase in its intensity, given the increase in proportion of female workers. Moreover, it may be safe to predict that if management as a whole does not address this issue to the satisfaction of women, the issue could result in yet another increase in government regulations affecting business.

The increase in female participation in the labor force is a major change in the face of the American labor force and is probably the biggest single change that will affect it in the two decades to come. Regardless of any immediate relevance this trend could (or could not) have for management education and development, it is definitely a major change in the workplace that managers will be facing in the next 20 years.

SOCIETAL VARIABLES

In this section the less tangible, yet nevertheless important, aspects of the environment within which managers and providers of management education and development will have to operate will be addressed. In particular, the following issues will receive attention: (1) societal values, (2) technology and society, and (3) political structures.

Societal Values

Kerr (1979) postulates that the U.S. labor force is presently undergoing its fourth period of great evolutionary change in its composition, character, and the rules for its conduct. The first three periods were

1 The enormous influx of immigrants and the rise of heavy industry, beginning in the 1880s
2 The great internal migration and depopulation of the countryside, beginning around World War I
3 Introduction of social controls over the use and conduct of the labor force, accelerated by the New Deal and again by events in the sixties and seventies

Kerr sees the fourth evolution as a great cultural transformation in attitudes and expectations within the labor force. Some examples of this would be that more people want jobs and more people want "good" jobs, with the emphasis on self-fulfillment. The work ethic, according to Kerr, has not disappeared, but the aesthetics of work has taken on a great new significance, and this constitutes the central theme of the new evolution. He believes that there is a long-term trend toward greater job satisfaction, rising incomes, more leisure, and improved working conditions. This will be accompanied by an increased demand for flexibility in terms of jobs held by employees; e.g., many women want part-time work, and flexible hours are sought by more workers.

This scenario is supported to some degree by Yankelovich (1979), who describes what he terms "a new breed of Americans" embracing a new and different set of values compared with those of their predecessors. As a departure point, he identifies the social symbols of success (such as automobiles, houses, and appliances) and the subordination of individual desires to a complex network of obligations (family, employer, etc.) as predominant values that existed in the fifties and sixties, accompanied by relative social stability. This value set he posits as leading in the past to the success of employment practices which relied on motivating people with money and status, as well as relying on their unquestioning loyalty. These values, as viewed by Yankelovich, are being superseded by newer sets of values, as success acquires new and somewhat ambiguous meanings, such as "keeping on growing" and "fulfilling potential." Another, related, trend is the increasing ethic of duty to oneself and of less obligation of loyalty to others. These value changes are (according to Yankelovich) at least partly responsible for such other trends as increased "job hopping," women seeking paid employment (because being "just a housewife" is regarded as a poor means of maintaining self-esteem), and the increased insistence by workers on having control (others call it "voice") over their jobs. As a consequence, Yankelovich sees the responsibility for providing meaningful incentives to this new breed of employees as being on management's shoulders. For example, he sees the need for more diversity and less uniformity in compensation systems, less emphasis on economic incentives, and more knowledge of and provision of such things as recognition and responsibility earlier in careers, accompanied by education and training activities aimed at developing these employees.

Another interesting perspective on value change is offered by Gordon (1969), who argues that changes in technology have a profound impact on values, but that values do not have such a great impact on technological development. Therefore, to come to grips with the direction of value changes that will occur in the future, it would be important to understand the impact of technology on values. This would allow one to make more informed assessments of the future consequences of technological change. These effects, according to Gordon, occur along four paths of influence:

1 *Enhanced attainment* The attainment of desires or values is enhanced by a particular technology. An example of this would be the value enhancement of time efficiency behind the technology of instant coffee, frozen food, etc. With such technology being available, these products will be used more and their increased use will inspire a value change.

2 *Novelty* Continuous new technology changes create expectations of change and an increase in the value of change, with slow or no change regarded as boring and undesirable.

3 *Redistribution* Technological advancements allow new value standards to be rapidly spread around. An example would be television and now satellite communication, carrying images, along with embedded values of what is wrong and what is right, across the world. This leads to cultural cross-pollination and increased value homogeneity.

4 *Restandardization* New understanding of technology changes concepts and values. An example offered by the author is privacy, which used to mean 100 acres between neighbors, while today it means an untapped telephone.

Looking at these four paths, it is possible to gain an understanding of how technology influences values. The next section deals with technological change in more detail.

Technology and Society

The impact of technology on societal values was dealt with in the previous section, and the impact on work-related issues was dealt with earlier. In this section, attention is focused on one more issue related to technology, namely, the broad effects of technological change on society in general. There can be no question that technological development has a strong impact on society. Examples of inventions that have dramatically changed the way we live are electricity, automobiles, telephones, radio and television, and many more. Much has been written about these changes, e.g., the suburbanization brought about by the automobile. Often the impact comes in stages, most of which are difficult to foresee. For example, turning again to the automobile, the first stage of impact could be viewed as the increased mobility, which led to more discretionary travel. Other stages of impact followed, one of which (many years later) was a society increasingly dependent on oil, which turned out to have a complete set of ramifications in its own right. It is also important to bear in mind, however, that some things have not undergone any significant change or have changed relatively slowly, such as newspapers. Some changes, e.g., jet engines, have altered the cost/benefit ratios and in so doing have increased the use of the technology (in this case, air travel) without making any deep and sudden changes in society. Nevertheless, it is becoming increasingly clear that technological change is having an impact not only on business and its immediate environment, but also on society at large in ways that sometimes are easy to predict and sometimes are less so.

Political Structures

Since politics could be regarded as social aspirations and movement put into an organizational framework, it needs to be looked at, however cursorily, in the context of this study. An aspect of the change to an information/service society that is mentioned by many commentators and futurists is the growth of government. The reason is that as the demand for services and information grows, it would appear natural that the largest provider of services and information—government, in all its various forms—would grow, which would have obvious implications for the environment within which business operates.

This leads to a related consideration, namely, the blurring of the distinction between government and business. Lindblom (1977) observed that if one defines government as the provision of services, then one has to take the view that some services are provided by politically appointed providers and others by market-appointed providers. Several commentators in the public policy arena have observed that it is becoming increasingly difficult to distinguish between the public and private sectors. An often quoted example is the military-industrial complex, where private contractors have adapted to their public-sector customers to the point where their internal operational procedures bear close resemblance to those in the public sector itself. Another example is the increasing willingness of government to consider the "privatization" of certain government services. Yet another is education, where the intrinsic product of the private sector may be indistinguishable from its public counterpart.

A related issue of politics and government is that of regulation. While it is impossible to formulate a "regulation index," there seems common consensus that in recent years there has been more deregulation than expansion of regulation, examples being airlines and banking. Again, there are commentators who predict that deregulation will continue further, while others maintain that the current wave of deregulation has run its course and in the future it could be expected that some new administration could reinstitute regulation. This is an issue that directly affects business and hence deserves attention. Notwithstanding the obvious importance of this area, however, developments are virtually impossible to forecast accurately, and therefore, it would be inappropriate to do so other than to emphasize that this is one more area of uncertainty and change.

On a more global level, it is interesting again to use Muller's perspective, namely, looking at the changes in world political power wrought by the previous change in the predominant economic system, the change from an agrarian to an industrial society. The industrial revolution wrought a massive change in the geopolitical power balance. By 1920 it was clear that the countries which embraced the new economic structure were the new world leaders. The new system produced more wealth and technology, which translated into more resources with which to acquire more effective weapons (e.g., tanks), without which no opponent could any longer compete. At this point there is no clear sense of the direction in which the transformation to a service/information economy will affect the global political order, but it seems a fairly safe assumption that the latter will be altered in some important ways.

COMMENTARY

In this concluding section we want to comment on three issues relating to the future: the approaches used by futurists in making their forecasts, change as a permanent feature of the future, and responses to anticipation of the future.

Approaches Used by Futurists

As pointed out at the beginning of this chapter, there are basically two types of approaches to viewing the future. The first is used by those who are commonly referred to as the doomsday prophets, who tend to predict cataclysmic events—events based on obscure information that is not widely regarded as having a significant influence on the predictions. A variation on this would be those who also base their views of the future on something not typically regarded as being a significant causal variable, e.g., patterns in tea leaves. These predictions may or may not be true, but others not initiated in the intricacies of these methods have difficulty in relating the causal variables to the outcomes predicted. Much more often, however, futurists tend to provide views of the future based on existing trends, the data of which are commonly available for others to inspect and test. The causal relationships tend to be spelled out by the futurists, and critics are free to agree or disagree with the conclusions and inferences drawn from the data. Since the data, assumptions, and conclusions are easy for most people to follow, this approach tends to have a larger following among those interested in the future.

Inherently, however, there are limitations to this latter approach which ought to be kept in mind when one evaluates the resulting predictions, because each forecast, projection, or prediction has a significant risk of being wrong. This has less to do with the quality of the information used, or even the quality of the forecaster himself or herself, than it does with the essential uncertainty of the subject matter. As someone once said, there are no experts on the future, only experts on the past. Therefore, before making decisions based on a certain set of views about the future, it is necessary to take a closer look at the factors that characterize this approach to forecasting.

Influence of the Times   Most predictions tend to be unduly influenced by whatever is happening at the time they are made. An example, mentioned earlier, is the predictions made in the seventies, when inflation was rampant and commodity prices were rising, of a future with high inflation and commodity scarcity as permanent features of the scenario ("limits to growth" being one of them). These predictions were widely regarded as accurate, since nobody knew what could or would happen to change the then current circumstances. Today, with hindsight, one can see the flaw in those views of the future, because inflation has been proven to be not necessarily a permanent phenomenon and, at least for the time being (which may or may not last for more than a short period), commodity prices are in a worldwide slump. Likewise, with the current decline in inflation and commodity prices, it would not be surprising in the next decade to see visions of a future that included worldwide gluts (e.g., in farm produce) and problems of overproduction. The missed predictions of the 1970s were not due to any deficiency in the methodology used by futurists, or even to their acuity. Rather, they were due to the simple fact that the world we live in is very complex, with so many factors across the globe interacting with one another and often conflicting with one another that our knowledge of these factors and their interaction is still limited. Therefore, it frequently happens that a variable, overlooked before, becomes critical in a certain situation and causes unpredicted results.

A variation of this qualification on the capacity of futurists to predict the future is the influence of the economic cycle on forecasts at any particular point in time: During a recession forecasts tend to be gloomy, while during boom times they tend to be rosy. The fact is that both slumps and expansions happen, but it is almost impossible to predict *when*. Therefore, on the optimism/pessimism scale, the best approach seems to be to assume a swinging of the economic pendulum and not to assume a long-term gloomy outlook or a long-term rosy outlook.

Continuation of Existing Trends   The second problem inherent in using trend-based forecasting is the tendency such approaches have to assume the continuation of the trends they are based on. Sometimes this is what occurs, but it often happens that an unforeseen event changes everything and renders plans based on the continuation of those trends largely useless. For example, in the literature dealing with the increasingly global nature of the world's economies, Japan is often cited as the prime example, followed by Korea, Taiwan, and Singapore, while China (until quite recently) has been relatively ignored. The reason is that until several years ago it was not evident that China had ambitions to become a world player in this arena. Now, however, it is clear that, with the recent initiatives to "liberalize" their internal economy, China indeed has the potential of becoming a major player in the international trade arena. Predictions made in the next few years about the global economic order will almost certainly have to include China, based on their economic development. However, should there be a significant internal cultural backlash within China against this economic development, it is quite possible that this advance could just as easily be reversed, making the "new, updated" forecasts out of date once again.

Pace of Change   Most forecasts deal with things that are expected to change, especially those things which are highly visible and are expected to change quickly. It is necessary to counterbalance this expectancy of high growth with an awareness that there are also many things that are not changing and with the perspective that sometimes the more things change, the more they stay the same. For example, road systems went through a period of change when a new technology, i.e., freeways, was introduced, but over the past few decades road systems have not changed in any major respect, except for the addition of new highways.

Furthermore, many things change at a slower pace than predicted, at a pace of decades rather than years. An example is the automobile, which admittedly changed the travel habits of America profoundly, but took a period of 50 to 60 years to do so. The large number of personal computers has prompted some predictions in the popular press that home shopping via linked computers will replace traditional retailing. While it is possible that this will indeed happen, it has to be considered that social changes such as these seldom happen overnight, and in the light of the pace of change, 20 to 25 years, as opposed to 5 years, is a possible length of time for a change of that type to become salient. Even the "rapid" institutionalization of supermarkets took several decades. Therefore, it is important to consider the relative "slowness" with which change *sometimes* is assimilated.

When reviewing futurists' predictions, therefore, it is necessary to remember that the variables mentioned in this chapter are subject to unforeseen change and, furthermore, that some changes could take longer (or shorter) than predicted before they become reality. This is no idle disclaimer—events such as the unanticipated oil price hikes and later an unforeseen oil price drop do happen, and when they do, they often ripple out to produce many other second-order events, such as high inflation, which in turn cause still other changes.

Furthermore, it would appear that the frequency with which unexpected events do in fact disrupt the carefully laid plans of futurists and the ordinary person is growing, owing to the increasingly interlinked world in which we live.

Change as a Permanent Feature

Whatever else may be said about the future, and no matter how hedged are the predictions of the futurists, the inescapable conclusion seems to be that *change* has indeed become (perversely) a steady fixture on the landscape of 20th-century life. This report is itself an attempt to come to grips with changes anticipated in the area of business, management, and the education of those who will have the responsibility to lead the organizations of the future. In later chapters, changes that have taken place in business education will be dealt with in more detail, and it will be seen that in some areas fairly substantial changes have occurred. Some of these changes had their origin from within the field (e.g., the reports by Gordon and Howell and by Pierson), while others had their origins in external factors (e.g., the growth in the college attendance age group). It seems unlikely that change will go away—rather, it appears to be as certain as death and taxes!

When we started doing background preparation for this chapter, we were headed in the direction of attempting to picture a likely scenario within which managers and management educators would have to function for the next 20 years or so. Once we started reviewing others' comments and predictions about the future, however, we were reminded of Zebulon Pike, who reputedly predicted, after scaling (what later came to be called) Pike's Peak, that very few people would ever be able to climb it. Today, of course, one can easily drive to the summit in an automobile (and thousands do so) in less than an hour, showing not only the fallacy, but the extremeness of the fallacy of many predictions, even those made by acknowledged "experts." As we progressed in our review, it became increasingly clear that it was unlikely that we would arrive at such a scenario, owing to many things that were pointed out earlier in this chapter. Instead, as we were forced to qualify arguments and positions, it became obvious that to attempt to arrive at one scenario was not the correct approach because of the suddenness with which major unanticipated events and changes can happen and the correspondingly strong impacts of such phenomena. A more appropriate approach—to us, at least—to dealing with the future appears to be one that not only notes the probable direction in which some major variables appear to be heading, but more importantly, acknowledges the *inevitability of change* and the related *inability* to predict the future with a high degree of accuracy.

An explanation often advanced for the inevitability of change is that the world we live in seems to have become more and more complex, and indeed, there is no shortage of evidence to support such a view. However, one might argue that this is somewhat of a misstatement of the problem, since the real problem seems to be more that—as our capacity to handle complexity expands (through accumulating research, as well as through new technological aids to understanding)—we seem to discover more ingredients of complexity we feel compelled to try to manage. Whichever way one looks at it, the change and complexity we can expect in the future raise major challenges to those charged with preparing managers to function at the limit of their potential, heading off the threats and utilizing the unique opportunities offered by such an environment.

Response to the Future

All the preceding raises the persistent question of how we ought to prepare prospective managers for the future, and that is at the heart of this Project. While it would be premature to relate our conclusions at this point, it is necessary to reiterate one of the basic themes running through the remainder of this report: namely, it is fallacious to seek to identify a particular scenario as a future context for any specific recommendations. Rather, it seems more appropriate to advocate an acceptance of change as a way of life in the future. Instead of recommending changes in the system to cope with some specifically identified changes in the environment, *we believe that the system itself should be made as responsive as possible to major changes which may occur*. This would require attention to sensing changes as they occur and flexibility with which to address them. In other words, we recommend *institutionalized flexibility* to cope with what has become institutionalized change.

Advocating institutionalized flexibility does not necessarily mean the abandonment of systems and structures that have been built up painstakingly through the years. Nor does it mean only intraorganizational flexibility (as opposed to system-wide flexibility). Instead, as will become clear from the remainder of this report, there are some identifiable areas where changes seem to be called for, but the focus of those changes will not be to cope with a particular set of future circumstances. Rather, the intent will be to prepare individuals more effectively for an environment where change has become a permanent feature.

UNIVERSITY-BASED MANAGEMENT EDUCATION: DEGREE PROGRAMS

CHAPTER 3

CURRICULUM

As others have noted (e.g., Pierson, 1959), the curriculum serves as a useful and logical starting point to examine academic degree programs. What universities do with—and to—students is in large measure a function of the curriculum. The curriculum specifies what is taught to students and in what order or sequence. Thus the curriculum provides the *structure* for the educational delivery system of an institution. If the faculty can be thought of as the "senders" and the students as the "receivers," then the curriculum, along with teaching, can be considered as an essential part (the structure) of the "transmission" process. The nature of the curriculum content and design, along with, of course, the abilities and qualifications of the faculty, therefore has a significant impact on the quality of education that students receive.

The curriculum of a degree program also serves another very useful purpose. For observers, it provides excellent *diagnostic* indicators of several key features of the academic program, particularly the kinds of educational objectives that a given set of faculty thinks should be pursued. This point has been well stated elsewhere:

> A college curriculum is significant chiefly for two things: it reveals the educated community's conception of what knowledge is most worth transmitting to the cream of its youth, and it reveals what kind of mind and character an education is expected to produce. The curriculum is a barometer by which we may measure the cultural pressures that operate upon the school. (Hofstadter and Hardy, 1952, p. 11; cited in Gordon and Howell, 1959, p. 147.)

Given the importance of the curriculum in any overall assessment of current degree programs in business/management and their possible modifications in the future, we focused considerable attention on this topic in our interview and survey data-collection efforts. Our aim was to concentrate primarily on *major* curriculum issues rather than on more micro details of specific curriculum components. Thus, in this sense, our treatment of the curriculum area will differ somewhat from the way in which the topic was handled in the two Foundation reports 25 years ago. Because of the circumstances existing in business education at that time (see the next section of this chapter), both those reports not only covered the larger curriculum issues, but also went into a fair amount of detail regarding the specifics of curriculum composition (e.g., going so far as to suggest the number of semester hours that should be devoted to particular courses). As a result of the various changes that have taken place since that time—including, as will be noted subsequently, many that were strongly influenced by those reports—and the somewhat different objectives of the current Project, the reader will not find that level of detail in this chapter.

The first sections of this chapter will review the situation 25 years ago as analyzed in the Carnegie and Ford Foundation reports and then will summarize the developments that have taken place between then and now and the criticisms that have been directed toward current features of curricula in business/management schools in the 1980s. The data portions of the chapter will be organized around our findings separately for the undergraduate and master's degree programs. The chapter concludes with a discussion of what we think is the import of the results we obtained, as well as a presentation of certain of our own views about particular curriculum issues.

THE SITUATION 25 YEARS AGO

In this section we will first consider the situation for undergraduate programs (where we use the initials BBA to designate the most common undergraduate business degree, the Bachelor of Business Administration) at the end of the 1950s, followed by a separate look at the condition of master's degree curricula of that era. Throughout this section we will rely heavily on the Ford and Carnegie reports. Not only did these reports describe what undergraduate and graduate business curricula were like at that time, but they also made major recommendations for curricular change that were extremely influential over the course of the next couple of decades. It would be impossible to understand the *current* state of business school curricula without extensive reference to those reports. Also, citations to their major conclusions in this area supply an essential context for placing the curriculum findings from the present Project, and our associated commentary, in perspective. Thus, the reader should not be surprised to find a liberal use of direct quotations from those earlier studies in this section. This is done deliberately.

Undergraduate (BBA) Programs

Since undergraduate business degree programs have had, for many years, two major components—general education (liberal arts) and professional (courses directly related to business/management topics) requirements—we examine the state of each as they existed at the time of the Foundation reports in 1959.

General Education Requirements The authors of both the Carnegie and Ford reports had serious concerns about the general education portion of the undergraduate business curriculum in the 1950s. They anchored their analyses in strongly held views that this set of requirements constitutes a vitally important component of the 4-year undergraduate business degree program. Their mutually consistent positions on the critical role of these general education (liberal arts) requirements can be summed up in the following brief statements:

> Undergraduate preparation for business necessarily rests on a number of subjects in the liberal arts area. The work in these subjects should be pursued beyond the first-year introductory level. The student should be given every opportunity to transfer general knowledge to applications in the business area. (Pierson, 1959, p. 163.)

> Undergraduate schools of business clearly have a responsibility for general (or "liberal") as well as for professional education. The school of business cannot avoid this responsibility by confining its jurisdiction to the last two years, leaving the first two years for whatever the student wishes to study or for whatever the liberal arts college chooses to require. (Gordon and Howell, 1959, p. 148.)

What the two studies found, basically, was that (in the views of their authors) insufficient attention was being given to this area of requirements by most undergraduate business schools. In the words of Pierson (1959, p. 164):

> Typically [based on "interviews conducted...at approximately seventy undergraduate schools in all parts of the country"], the work which students do in liberal arts subjects appears to have little relation to their studies in business and economics and not infrequently consists of a certain number of courses to be gotten out of the way as quickly and painlessly as possible.

Even more important was the discrepancy between the then-existing AACSB Standard regarding general education requirements and the reality of what schools—members as well as nonmembers—were actually requiring. The applicable AACSB Standard stated:

> *At least 40%* [italics added] of the total hours required for the bachelor's degree must be taken in subjects other than business and economics....

Data obtained from surveys and curriculum analyses carried out in the two studies showed that "in more than seven out of ten cases the schools require less than 40 per cent of the work to be taken in these [liberal arts] subjects" (Pierson, 1959, p. 174). Even more telling, "it appears that a little under one-half of the 4-year [AACSB] member schools did not meet the association standard" (Pierson, 1959, p. 174). This state of affairs regarding AACSB member schools' relative noncompliance with this part of the curriculum standard of their own organization was bluntly summarized by Gordon and Howell (1959, p. 152):

We visited every one of the [thirty-seven] institutions included in our sample of Association schools, and there is no doubt that many member deans are aware that member schools often violate with apparent immunity both the letter and the spirit of the Association's Curriculum Standards.

To rectify the situation they found with respect to the general education portion of the curriculum, both Foundation reports made highly specific, but basically similar, recommendations for changes. These recommendations were directed at two main elements of the requirements: (1) the amount of time that should be devoted to the liberal arts part of the 4-year program, and (2) the content of this part of the total curriculum. With respect to the former, both reports recommended an increase in the minimum percentage of time to be spent by students in taking general education courses: from the 40% figure contained in the AACSB Standard to 50 to 55%. With respect to the content of this set of courses, both reports urged schools to specify in more detail which types of courses (in designated subject matter areas) students should be required to take rather than leaving it to their discretion. The spirit of these recommendations, especially the latter, is captured in the following summary statement by Gordon and Howell (1959, pp. 174–175):

> It cannot be emphasized too strongly that our recommendations are intended to imply something about the *kind* or *content* of the courses to be offered. . . . The business school that permits its students to graduate with even less than 40% of their work in nonbusiness courses, with little or no college-level work in science and mathematics, and with their preparation in English confined to business letter-writing, is not experimenting in an attempt to implement better the desirable educational goals. It is simply offering a poor grade of education which inadequately prepares the student either for life or for a responsible business career.

The Professional (Business) Curriculum   The so-called professional part—i.e., courses in business and business-related aspects of economics—of the BBA degree curriculum was no less a target of the Foundation reports than was the general education section. The basic stance taken by both reports was summarized by Pierson (1959, p. 196):

> There is considerable evidence that the business curriculum has expanded beyond justifiable limits at most undergraduate business schools. There is need for a general tightening of standards in terms of the scope of the core studies, the variety of majors, the number of courses that can be taken in a major, and the kind of electives students can choose.

The applicable AACSB Standards at that time gave considerable latitude to schools in designing this part of the curriculum. They specified that "at least 40% of the total hours required for the bachelor's degree must be taken in business and economics subjects..." and that "...in general, candidates for the undergraduate degree shall receive basic instruction" in the fields of "economics, accounting, statistics, business law, finance, marketing, and management." Also, "opportunities beyond the basic course shall be available in at least three of the above fields." The curriculum standard also added the following admonition: "However, a proliferation of courses which might serve to diminish the effectiveness of the staff in meeting its obligations toward fundamental areas of training is not to be encouraged."

The Foundation reports were not as concerned about the thrust of these standards as much as they were about how the standards were being implemented in many schools. They focused mainly on two general issues: (1) the composition of the required "core" in business; and (2) "specialization" in particular areas beyond the core. With regard to the core, the Ford report, for example, made specific recommendations about which types of courses should be *excluded* as well as about which ones should be included. The exclusion suggestions received the most attention after the report was published and were of three types. First, there were "courses which are excluded because something else has been put in their place; for example, no money and banking or public finance and no business law of the conventional sort...[and also] the conventional kind of production management." Second, subject areas for which "we feel there is little or no justification for their inclusion. Conventional business mathematics, business English, and letter writing fall under this heading....In addition, we have excluded the sort of freshman survey course usually entitled Introduction to Business." And third, "courses (for example, transportation or insurance) which may have a legitimate claim to be in the catalogue, but which we do not think need to be included in the core" (Gordon and Howell, 1959, pp. 210–212). Pierson's views about the then-existing sets of core courses in various schools were generally similar, and he was especially concerned about the total number of core courses many programs required: "It is difficult to believe that some reduction in the number would cost much in terms of essential educational preparation" (Pierson, 1959, p. 201).

The issue of specialization beyond the core, i.e., the role of majors within the business curriculum, was given particular attention in both Foundation reports, and again the two sets of authors were in virtual agreement in their assessments of the existing situation. Gordon and Howell, for example, stated (1959, p. 217):

> It seems to us that the time has come to face up to the fact that "specialization has been running riot" in American business schools. Dozens of minor fields of specialization have been permitted to develop that never should have been introduced at all. Many of these involve specialization in the problems of some industry, and...there is little evidence that business itself needs this kind of specialized training at the undergraduate level.[1]

---

[1]Gordon and Howell point out that the concern about specialization was not new in the 1950s and that as far back as 1931 Bossard and Dewhurst in their published study on university business education expressed the same concern: "One wonders whether much of the purported specialization in the collegiate business schools, most of it perhaps, is not mere window dressing designed to impress students and businessmen...For the most part, the real reasons for the development of any extensive specialization have to do with matters other than that of the educational interests of the students" (Bossard and Dewhurst, 1931, p. 313).

The arguments that Gordon and Howell advanced against excessive special-ization were "both positive and negative." "On the positive side...the primary need is for a broad business and general education....[On the negative side] there is the...argument that any considerable investment of time in special-ized training in the undergraduate years reduces below the minimum accept-able level the time available for general education and the basic business sub-jects [i.e., the core]" (1959, p. 212). Gordon and Howell did acknowledge that accounting represented somewhat of a "difficult problem" with regard to the issue of specialization, and they (somewhat reluctantly, apparently) recom-mended that accounting students be able to take 12 semester hours "in that one field." Pierson advocated limiting majors to six or seven areas at the most and limiting the number of courses permitted within a major to four or five. He, along with the authors of the Ford Foundation report, was particularly con-cerned about the danger of vocationalism, and he cited some (then) current examples of "absurd major offerings," such as the following:

> ...an eight-course major at a large Southern university in baking science and man-agement which includes courses in Principles of Baking: Bread and Rolls; Principles of Baking: Cakes and Variety Products; Bread and Roll Production—Practical Shop Operation; and finally Cake and Sweet Baked Products—Practical Shop Operation. (Pierson, 1959, pp. 219–220.)

(He wryly added in a footnote that this school's catalog "states that its pro-gram will help students 'secure the broad vision of economic affairs and the understanding of fundamental economic courses which are today essential for successful business leadership.'")

On a positive note, the authors of both reports argued for continued exper-imentation by schools in both the general education and professional segments of the undergraduate curriculum. In the words of Gordon and Howell (1959, p. 222), "Continued improvement implies the willingness to experiment, and [throughout] we have urged the need for experimentation—and for publicizing the results of experiments that seem promising." Pierson expressed similar views and noted (1959, p. 195) that "the important consideration [in making changes in such areas as the general education requirements] is the broad purpose and direction of the recommendations."

Master's Degree Programs

Any assessment of the condition of curricula in master's degree programs in the late 1950s should take into account the size and number of those programs compared with the current scene in the 1980s. The Ford Foundation report pointed out that in 1957–58 only "about a fifth of the approximately 600 col-leges and universities with degree programs in business administration offered the master's degree in business." The authors also went on to note that

> While approximately 125 institutions confer master's degrees in business, graduate training is heavily concentrated in a small number of the larger business schools.

Nine schools accounted for more than half of all the master's degrees awarded in 1955–56. About 25 per cent of the total was awarded by two institutions, Harvard and New York University. (Gordon and Howell, 1959, p. 247.)

The number of master's degrees awarded in business in 1955–1956 was approximately 4500, compared to well in excess of 60,000 thirty years later.

A number of curriculum issues relevant to master's programs were identified in both reports. For Gordon and Howell, the issues were

1 The relative effort that business schools should put into master's level versus undergraduate education

2 The relative degree to which master's programs should stress breadth (preparation of students for general management careers) versus specialization (preparation for staff roles in particular areas)

3 Whether the degree should be a "professional" or a "graduate" degree

4 What the best kind of undergraduate preparation is (i.e., type of undergraduate major) for a master's degree program in business

For Pierson, the issues facing master's education in business were largely variants of the same issues facing undergraduate programs. Chief among these issues, stated in question form, were

1 "Where should the balance be struck between breadth and depth?"

2 "How much of the...program should be required [in the core]?"

3 "How much of the required work should be in traditional tool and functional business areas?"

Pierson also identified two major and sticky issues ("difficulties") specific to graduate business programs:

1 "There is no clear distinction between the undergraduate and graduate [business] studies."

2 "There is no clear direction which schools can follow in putting business studies on a genuine graduate level even if they are determined to do so."

In Pierson's view both these issues stemmed from the same fundamental problem:

Business administration is a vague, shifting, rather formless subject in which neither the foundations at the undergraduate level nor the super-structure at the graduate level can be sharply defined. (1959, p. 233.)

Prior to 1958, the AACSB, as the accrediting agency for business programs, had never developed standards for master's degree programs. In that year, a set of such standards was adopted, and they included the following Standards pertaining to the curriculum:

- As a minimum, the school shall offer one full year of course work or equivalent (open only to graduate students in their final year) in at least three of the following areas: accounting, finance, marketing, statistics, economics, and management....
- It is assumed that the minimum requirement for a Master's degree shall be the equivalent of one academic year of full-time work for the holder of a baccalaureate in business. Up to one additional year may be required for holders of other baccalaureate degrees....

The Ford report's authors were not impressed with this first ("cautious") step by the AACSB at the graduate level. They commented that

> The minimal character of these recommendations [pertaining to the curriculum and other aspects of the graduate program] will be all too obvious to the reader.... Its minimum of graduate offerings... are no more than a small start toward the bare essentials of a satisfactory master's program. The question of a minimum core is not touched, nor is the problem of prerequisites. And in general these standards would require little change even in the more unsatisfactory master's programs.... It is significant also that failure to live up to these standards would not jeopardize a school's membership in the Association. (Gordon and Howell, 1959, p. 290.)

The data analysis and recommendations of the two Foundation reports regarding master's programs revolved around three basic issues:

1 *Type of program* The Ford report identified three types of master's programs in existence by the 1950s: First, there were "integrated 2-year programs which assume no previous preparation in business subjects and require a substantial core of graduate level courses oriented toward managerial problem-solving.... [Such] schools are found chiefly in exclusively graduate schools..." (of which, according to Pierson, there were twelve at that time). Second, there were "'hybrid' programs that require from 1 to 2 years of work, depending on the student's background" (i.e., whether or not the student majored in business as an undergraduate). And third, there were "strictly 1-year programs built on a set of undergraduate [business] prerequisites." Both reports strongly favored the integrated 2-year program requiring a substantial core and displaying a strongly managerial orientation.

2 *Graduate core* The Ford study found that most of the exclusively graduate business schools required a set of core courses amounting to at least a year or more of academic work. However, it also found that "a different situation prevails among the schools offering both the bachelor's and master's degree. In these cases, there is apt to be little in the way of a graduate core beyond the undergraduate prerequisites" (Gordon and Howell, 1959 p. 257). As noted above, both reports recommended that a required set of core courses

constitute a "substantial" portion of the master's program. The Ford report proposed that the core should cover "essentially the same professional areas" as were recommended for the undergraduate program, but with "more rigorous analysis," "more emphasis on managerial problem-solving," and "more of a systematic attempt to develop the other basic skills that are important." That report also stated that "the need for an integrating, case course in business policy in the master's program is too obvious to call for much comment." The report went on to note that "of the thirty-three 'mixed' schools [i.e., those with both graduate and undergraduate programs in business] in our sample which are members of the Association, only nine required a course in business policy." Gordon and Howell's view of this situation (1959, p. 269) was that "here is an excellent illustration of the failure of most business schools to adapt their master's programs to the new emphasis on managerial problem-solving and on training for administrative careers in business."

3 *Specialization* The Carnegie study found that "among 64 schools offering MBA degrees in 1955–56 (out of 66 institutions known to have such programs), 12 offered no majors as such...; of the 52 other schools, 28 offered 7 majors or more, and 15 offered 10 or more" (Pierson, 1959 p. 258). In commenting on this, the Carnegie report stated that "it seems likely that unless counteracting steps are taken the number of graduate majors available at these [MBA granting] schools will increase still more over the next five or ten years" (Pierson, 1959, pp. 258–259). Not surprisingly, both reports indicated concern with this state of affairs and advocated that only a moderate degree of specialization be permitted for the MBA degree.

DEVELOPMENTS DURING THE PAST 25 YEARS

In our opinion, in addition to variable and shifting market influences there were three principal driving forces behind the curriculum changes that have taken place in business schools in the quarter century between 1960 and the mid-1980s: (1) the recommendations contained in the Foundation reports, (2) the work of the Ford Foundation in the 1960s to provide financial and other support to facilitate the implementation of the reports' recommendations, and (3) the revisions made in the AACSB curriculum standards. These three forces were not unrelated. The changes that at least some business school deans and faculty members already thought should occur were supported by the reports' recommendations and by various implementation activities financed by the Ford Foundation. Likewise, some of the changes advocated in the reports and propelled by Ford Foundation grants to various schools were translated into the reality of revised "accreditation law," with its associated sanctions, by successive sets of AACSB Standards Committee members. These members (deans and representatives from the business community) undoubtedly were influenced in part by the two reports and by the new initiatives that certain schools were beginning to take to modify their curriculum structures. In the paragraphs that follow, each of the three interrelated forces is examined briefly.

Impact of the Foundation Reports

Those deans, faculty members, and others who were affiliated with university business schools in the 1960s and 1970s will have their own views about the amount of impact that the reports by Pierson and by Gordon and Howell had in the curriculum area during this era. Our assessment, and that of many other knowledgeable observers, is that the overall effect of the reports was substantial and *especially so* on curricula—both in undergraduate and graduate programs. There are probably several reasons why the reports' curriculum recommendations were so influential, but chief among them were the following:

1 The curriculum analyses were based on empirical data, which provided solid support, not easily challenged, for the arguments advanced by the reports' authors. The data for this part of the two studies consisted primarily of analyses of official catalog descriptions of curriculum requirements, answers to questions on surveys sent to business school officials, and interviews at selected schools.

2 The recommendations contained in the reports (which, as previously noted, were generally quite similar) were consistent with what some prominent leaders of business education were already advocating and, in a few schools, beginning to put into practice. Thus the curriculum reforms urged by Pierson and by Gordon and Howell were quite in line with the developing "winds of change" as they related to business schools. The foundation reports' authors didn't necessarily start the curriculum revolution,[2] which probably would have occurred eventually with or without the two studies, but they certainly abetted, accelerated, and spotlighted changes that many knowledgeable people felt were necessary and long overdue.

3 The Ford Foundation provided financial support explicitly for implementation of the recommendations (see the following section).

The general nature of the foundation reports' recommendations regarding the curriculum in business schools was described in the previous section and can be summarized briefly here:

1 Increase the percentage of the curriculum devoted to general education to at least 50%.

2 Do not leave to student choice what types of subjects and courses are taken to satisfy the general education requirement; specify the areas of subject matter to be taken (e.g., mathematics, social sciences, etc.), and make sure that the courses listed to satisfy those requirements are solid, college-level courses and not remedial in nature.

3 Require a comprehensive core of basic business courses that all students must take, and ensure that this core includes rigorous analytical, quantitative, and behavioral components.

---

[2]In the words of Howell himself: "We didn't cause that revolution, Gordon and I; we were part of it, and we were catalysts, but it was going on before our report" (*Schmotter*, 1984 (Spring), p. 9).

4 Except for the accounting area, greatly reduce in number and length (or even eliminate entirely) any majors permitted within the business curriculum; do not permit students to overspecialize in any one area of business.

5 Eliminate from the curriculum highly specialized and narrowly vocational elective courses, particularly those which are industry-specific (e.g., transportation, insurance, etc.).

The Influence of the Ford Foundation

It would be a mistake to conclude that the Gordon and Howell study was the initial stimulus that persuaded the Ford Foundation to embark on a set of actions to reform higher education for business. Rather, their project and its eventual report were part of a series of steps that key Ford Foundation officials and their academic consultants had begun earlier to improve American business education. In the mid-1950s these individuals not only perceived significant problems with the way business education was being conducted by universities, but they also believed that a comprehensive study would serve to document these issues and bring them to wider attention. Thus, the Ford Foundation report was commissioned.

Furthermore, these Ford Foundation officials knew that change could be accelerated if certain influential schools were to lead the way by example. Therefore, once the Gordon and Howell project was completed, the Foundation over the next 10 years or so proceeded to back up the recommendations contained in its report with more than $30 million of financial support to institutions and individuals. Grants were made to a number of schools to initiate the kinds of changes that would be consistent with the report's recommendations (the thrust of which had been largely anticipated by Foundation officials). Grants also were made to sets of faculty members at the forefront of different disciplines to provide (during summer workshops) instruction to their colleagues from around the country on how to update their courses to incorporate the most rigorous and advanced analytical techniques and approaches. These faculty members, in turn, were expected to return to their schools and help persuade their local colleagues to revise the curriculum and course contents in these new directions. In summary, it seems safe to conclude that curriculum changes—ones that some schools were starting, some schools were only thinking about, and still other schools had not even contemplated—were greatly hastened by the infusion of Ford Foundation funding.

Changes in AACSB Curriculum Standards

The undergraduate and graduate curriculum sections of the AACSB Standards changed rather markedly between 1960 and 1985. This can be seen in an overall sense in Table 3.1, which presents the complete statement of those sections of the Standards pertaining to the curriculum for undergraduate and graduate degrees in 1960 and in 1985. The major specific changes that occurred along the way during this 25-year span are enumerated below separately for (1) the undergraduate general education requirements, (2) the business courses section of the curriculum (for both undergraduate and master's degrees, and (3) curriculum matters specific to the master's degree.

TABLE 3.1
AACSB CURRICULUM STANDARDS: 1960 AND 1985

1960

UNDERGRADUATE

Standards for Membership

(3) The curricula shall approximate, quantitatively and qualitatively, the standards in effect in recognized collegiate schools of business, due allowance being made for the meeting of regional or other special objectives. A portion of the four years of college work for the undergraduate degree may be taken in some other college, such as liberal arts or engineering college of approved standards. At least forty per cent of the total hours required for the bachelor's degree must be taken in business and economic subjects; the major portion of the courses in this group shall be in business administration. At least forty per cent of the total hours required for the bachelor's degree must be taken in subjects other than business and economics provided that economic principles and economic history may be counted in either the business or nonbusiness groups. With respect to the latter, breadth not specialization is the objective.

(4) As the foundation for training in business administration, instruction shall be offered in the fields of economics, accounting, statistics, business law, finance, marketing, and management. (Management is here used to denote Industrial or Production Management, or an integrating course in organization and management or a business policy course. Finance is used as a generic term to describe courses in Money and Banking, Business Finance and Investments.) In general, candidates for the undergraduate degree shall receive basic instruction in each of these fields. Opportunities beyond the basic course shall be available in at least three of the above fields. However, a proliferation of courses which might serve to diminish the effectiveness of the staff in meeting its obligations toward fundamental areas of training is not to be encouraged.

GRADUATE

Standards for Membership

II. *Graduate Offerings.* As a minimum, the school shall regularly offer one full year of course work or equivalent (open only to graduate students in their final year) in at least three of the following areas: accounting, finance, marketing, statistics, economics, and management. For purposes of comparison, "a full year of course work" shall correspond to 6 semester hours in a conventional university program. A thesis course shall not be considered as meeting the area requirement.

III. *Curriculum Requirements.* It is assumed that the minimum requirement for a Master's degree shall be the equivalent of one academic year of full-time work for the holder of a baccalaureate in business. Up to one additional year may be required for holders of other baccalaureate degrees. At least half of the student's work in his final year shall be in courses open only to graduate students.

TABLE 3.1 *(Continued)*

1985

IV. Curriculum

The purpose of the curriculum shall be to provide for a broad education preparing the student for imaginative and responsible citizenship and leadership roles in business and society—domestic and worldwide. The curriculum shall be responsive to social, economic, and technological developments and shall reflect the application of evolving knowledge in economics and the behavioral and quantitative sciences. To facilitate the foregoing, the Accreditation Council encourages continuing development and appraisal of both new and existing curricula.

> There is no intention that any single approach is required to satisfy the worldwide dimension of the Curriculum Standard, but every student should be exposed to the international dimension through one or more elements of the curriculum.

An undergraduate school of business should concentrate its professional courses in the last two years of a four-year program, and should offer only a limited amount of work below the junior year. The objective of this is to provide a foundation of work in those academic areas necessary for an appropriate combination of descriptive and analytical approaches to the study of business administration. Such foundation work would normally include courses in communications, mathematics, social sciences, humanities, and the natural sciences.

> Examples of courses which might be offered at the lower division level are: principles of accounting, principles of economics, business law, statistics, and introduction to business. Examples of courses which should be offered only at the upper division level are: principles of finance, principles of management, and principles of marketing.

Normally, 40 to 60 percent of the course work in the baccalaureate program shall be devoted to studies in business administration and economics. Normally 40 to 60 percent of the course work shall be devoted to studies other than business administration and economics.

> The major portion of the courses in the first group shall be in business administration. Credit for remedial courses of subcollegiate level shall not be considered toward meeting the Standards of the Accreditation Council. Up to nine semester hours of lower division economics may be counted in either of the curriculum segments.

To provide students with the common body of knowledge in business administration, programs shall include in their course of instruction the equivalent of at least one year of work comprising the following areas:

(a) a background of the concepts, processes and institutions in the production and marketing of goods and/or services and the financing of the business enterprise or other forms of organization;

(b) a background of the economic and legal environment as it pertains to profit and/or non-profit organizations along with ethical considerations and social and political influences as they affect such organizations;

(c) a basic understanding of the concepts and applications of accounting, of quantitative methods, and management information systems including computer applications;

(d) a study of organization theory, behavior, and interpersonal communications;

(e) a study of administrative processes under conditions of uncertainty including integrating analysis and policy determination at the overall management level.

TABLE 3.1 *(Continued)*

1985

There is no intention that the work for each of the five areas should be taught in either separate or one-year courses. Nor is it intended that the five areas described should take the same fraction of the total of at least one year's work, and reasonable variation in proportions is acceptable. By "the equivalent of at least one year of work" is meant 25 percent or more of a normal four-year baccalaureate program.

Schools may choose to meet this Standard in a variety of ways. Some may prescribe individual courses in each area; others may organize learning in different ways. Further, some coverage of the common body of knowledge may be in courses outside the school. There is no intention that two concentrations within a school necessarily should meet the common body of knowledge in the same way, nor that two students in the same concentration should meet the common body of knowledge in the same way.

In the spirit of the accreditation philosophy, a school may develop curricula somewhat at variance with the common body of knowledge when it demonstrates that overall high quality is maintained.

Opportunities for advanced work in some of the subject areas should be provided consistent with the school's objectives and capabilities.

Masters degree programs in business administration must require students to have completed, either at the undergraduate or graduate level, the equivalent of the common body of knowledge in business administration as set forth above.

The common body of knowledge may be satisfied by undergraduate or graduate work. The requirements of less than 30 semester hours of undergraduate courses or 20 semester hours of work in courses reserved exclusively for graduate students to satisfy the common body of knowledge is presumed to be insufficient. This presumption may be overcome by evidence to the contrary. Average weekly contact hours and credit hours should normally bear an approximate relationship of one-to-one for most courses offered in the business unit.

For the MBA degree, it is expected that the program in addition to the courses identified as satisfying the common body of knowledge shall be broad in nature and aimed at general competence for overall management.

"Breadth" means that the student must earn at least 15 semester credit hours or equivalent of work in addition to that in the common body of knowledge outside the field of specialization.

For other masters degrees, the limitation on specialization will not apply.

For the MBA degree, it is expected that the programs will require for most students a minimum of two semesters of academic work in addition to the common body of knowledge and the baccalaureate degree in classes reserved exclusively for graduate students.

The word "most" means 90 percent or above. The phrase "two semesters" means 24 semester credit hours (36 quarter hours).

For other masters degrees, it is expected that programs will require for most students a minimum of two semesters of academic work in addition to the common body of knowledge and the baccalaureate degree of which at least two-thirds of two semesters of academic work will be in classes reserved exclusively for graduate students.

The phrase "two-thirds of two semesters" means 16 semester hours (24 quarter hours).

Undergraduate General Education Requirements
1961
- *Credit for remedial courses* Added: A statement that such credit "shall not be considered toward meeting the standards of the Association." (Note: This statement was subsequently put in the "Interpretations" of the Standards in 1969.)

1969
- *Timing of general education requirements* Added: A statement that "Professional courses" (i.e., business courses) should be "concentrated" in the last 2 years of a 4-year program and therefore "only a limited amount" of [professional] work (e.g., principles of accounting, statistics) should be offered at the lower division so that the student could use this time to "acquire a foundation of work in the basic arts and sciences."
- *Content of general education requirements* Added: A statement that specified what the arts and sciences (general education) foundation of the student should normally include: "work in mathematics, social sciences, humanities, and the natural sciences."
- *Percentage of time devoted to general education requirements* Changed: The statement "At least 40% of the total hours" was changed to "normally, 40 to 60% of the course work in the undergraduate program...shall be devoted to studies other than business...."

1980
- *Additional specification of content of general education requirements* Added: "communications" to the four areas previously specified (mathematics, social sciences, humanities, and the natural sciences). No further major changes were made to the general education requirements after 1980.

Business Courses Section of Curriculum
1969
- *Use of phrase "common body of knowledge" (CBK)* Changed: Previous phrasing "foundation for training in business administration" to phrase "common body of knowledge in business and administration."
- *Amount of work in core (CBK) areas* Changed: Previous statements that "instruction shall be offered in..." and "candidates for the undergraduate degree shall receive basic instruction in..." were changed to "programs shall include in their course of instruction the equivalent of at least one year of work " in the collective areas comprising the CBK.
- *Content of core (CBK)* Changed: Core was significantly restructured: previous seven "fields" (economics, accounting, statistics, business law, finance, marketing, and management) were regrouped into five "areas" by combining the fields into three areas and adding an area on organizational theory and behavior and an area dealing with business policy.
- *Advanced courses beyond the core (CBK)* Changed: Wording of "opportunities for advanced work" to "opportunities for advanced work in some of the subject areas should be provided consistent with the school's objectives and capabilities."

1974

• *International dimension of curriculum* Added: As part of the stated purpose of the (entire) curriculum, the phrase "domestic and worldwide."

• *Means for satisfying CBK requirements* Added: An "interpretative" paragraph stating that there is "no intention that two schools meet the CBK in the same way."

1980

• *International dimension of the curriculum* Added: An "interpretation" (to the "domestic and worldwide" phrase in the stated purpose of the curriculum): "...every student should be exposed to the international dimension through one or more elements of the curriculum."

• *Content of CBK* Changed: Part of the third CBK area dealing with "information systems" was redefined to "management information systems including computer applications."

1982

• *Means of satisfying CBK requirements* Changed: The "guideline" (formerly "interpretation") concerning "no intention that two schools must meet CBK in the same way" was modified to "Schools may choose to meet this Standard [CBK] in a variety of ways."

• *Means of satisfying CBK requirements* Added: An interpretative guideline regarding the necessity to provide "justification" by those schools that "wish to develop uniquely focused curricula somewhat at variance with the CBK."

1983

• *Means of satisfying CBK requirements* Changed: The preceding guideline (regarding experimental curricula) was modified to put it in a more positive way: "In the spirit of the accreditation philosophy, a school may develop curricula somewhat at variance with the CBK when it demonstrates that overall high quality is maintained." No further changes were made in the business courses section of the Curriculum Standard after 1983.

Curriculum Matters Specific to Master's Degree Programs   Note that no mention of the master's degree was made in the Standards until 1958.

1961

• *Separate section of Standards* Changed: From "Graduate Programs" to "Master's Program Accreditation."

• *Content of graduate standard relating to the curriculum* Changed: Entire section was rewritten to emphasize: (1) the equivalent of the undergraduate core must be taken at the graduate level or have been taken at the undergraduate level; (2) for the "MBA degree" (the first time this term was used in the Standards), "it is expected that the program beyond the core shall be broad in nature and aimed at general competence for overall management"; (3) "for other master's degrees the limitation on specialization beyond the core will not apply"; and (4) the expectation that "for most students a minimum of two semesters...of work beyond the core and the baccalaureate degree in classes reserved exclusively for graduate students" will be required.

1969
- *Separate section of Standards* Changed: Section deleted and replaced by specific statements pertaining to master's degrees in the Curriculum Standard section.

1975
- *Interpretation regarding completion of CBK* Added: An "interpretation" stating that a "requirement of less than 20 semester hours" of course work "reserved exclusively for graduate students" was "insufficient" to satisfy the CBK requirement.

1977
- *Interpretation regarding completion of CBK* Added: Preceding interpretation was modified to include the additional phrase of "less than 30 hours of undergraduate courses." No substantive changes were made after 1977 to statements pertaining specifically to the curriculum for master's degrees.

The major changes listed above that were made in the AACSB Standards can be compared to the summary of the Foundation reports' curriculum recommendations presented previously:

1 The minimum percentage of the curriculum that was required to be devoted to general education (liberal arts) requirements was left at 40% instead of being increased to 50%. However, those schools that wanted to do so were explicitly permitted by the revised Standards to allow students to take as much as 60% of their course work in these areas.

2 The recommendation that students' choices of liberal arts courses to be taken to satisfy the general education requirements should be concentrated in certain areas and in certain types of courses was partially incorporated in the Standards when (in 1969) the statement was added that such course work should "normally include work in mathematics, social science, humanities, and the natural sciences." The types (nature) of specific courses that should be taken in these areas have so far never been specified in the Standards.

3 A comprehensive core has been specified by area in the common body of knowledge (CBK) part of the current Curriculum Standard. Quantitative and behavioral components have been identified in the CBK requirement.

4 The current Standards do not speak to the number and length of majors permitted within the business curriculum.

5 The Curriculum Standard is silent with respect to the issue of highly specialized and narrowly vocational elective courses.

As can be seen, the first three of the five major types of curriculum recommendations contained in the Foundation reports have been incorporated to a large degree in the current Standards. The other two recommendations concerning majors and vocational-type elective courses have not been addressed in the Standards. In toto, the reports appear to have had a major—but not totally comprehensive—influence on the the AACSB Standards that today guide the curriculum decisions of a large number of business schools.

CURRENT CRITICISMS OF BUSINESS SCHOOL CURRICULA

The curriculum of business schools that has evolved over the past two decades or so has recently come in for sharp criticism from a number of sources, both in the academic community and in the world of business. Space does not permit an exhaustive listing and discussion of these critiques, but we will attempt to characterize them in general and to group them into what seem to be five or six major categories.

Nature of Current Criticisms

Collectively, the current criticisms of business school curricula at both the undergraduate and master's degree levels represent a wide array, something of a "laundry list" as it were. That is, particular critics focus on particular deficiencies of commission or omission in the curriculum, but there is not always a high degree of agreement from one observer to another. What may seem like a vital weakness to one critic is sometimes given only minor consideration or is even omitted by another. This is not to say that there is no consensus at all across often perceptive commentators, because that would clearly be incorrect, but only that the criticisms as a group are not concentrated in just one or two areas but instead constitute a fairly diverse and broad list.

The total set of criticisms includes concerns about both what subject matter is overemphasized in today's business schools as well as, especially, what is underemphasized. Thus, an examination of a large sample of critical articles and comments would seem to point to more concern with what is left out of the curriculum or not given sufficient attention as compared with what is given too much emphasis. However, some of the critics who point to various "sins" of omission do not then go on to give much consideration to how adding topics and subjects will affect the total length of the curriculum. The critical issue of how to fit an ever-expanding list of seemingly important subject matter areas into a curriculum program of finite length seldom gets addressed head on. A few suggestions (as noted below) have been made in this regard, but generally, the task of finding what to cut from the curriculum often seems to be left to business school deans and faculty—the very individuals usually held responsible by the critics for creating the problems in the first place.

Major Types of Criticisms

General Criticisms   There appear to be two general types of criticisms of business school curricula:

1 *Insufficient emphasis on generating "vision" in students*   This criticism typically takes the form of stating that current business school courses focus more on problem solving than on problem finding, more on analyzing solutions than on creating novel approaches, and more on locating safe or acceptable courses of action than on taking prudent or moderate risks. Obviously, considered most broadly, this criticism goes beyond a concern only with curriculum matters to include, also, problems with instructional methods, faculty and student attitudes, and the like. Nevertheless, the curriculum, in terms of the types of courses offered, is viewed as one of the chief culprits responsible for this state of affairs.

2 *Insufficient emphasis on integration across functional areas* The Foundation reports strongly came out in favor of a "capstone" type of course in business policy/strategy that would be designed to show how knowledge from the various functional areas could be combined in addressing real-world business problems. The need for such an integrative approach (but not the necessity of confining it to a single course) was subsequently put into the AACSB Standards as one of the five required CBK areas. The issue, from the perspective of some critics, is, does the typical business school curriculum—particularly at the undergraduate level—provide sufficient attention to both the need to and the means to use specialized functional knowledge in an integrated approach to the increasingly complex, fast-changing, and multidimensional problems of contemporary business?

Criticisms Addressed to Specific Topic Areas

1 *Too much emphasis on quantitative analytical techniques* If there is one area that many critics seem to agree receives *too much* attention and emphasis in the modern business school, it is quantitatively based analytical techniques. The focus of such criticism is that while it may be useful for students to learn many of these sophisticated techniques, the amount of time spent on them is too much relative to what could be spent on other, more useful areas, and also that too much attention to these techniques reinforces undesirable tendencies in students to believe that all business problems are amenable to quantitative-solutions. Frequently, this supposed curriculum imbalance is linked by critics to the previously mentioned issue of students' lack of vision.

2 *Insufficient attention to managing people* This is not a new concern. In fact, the point that some critics make is exactly this: Business schools, for all their changes in the last 25 years, have not made much progress in developing students' leadership and interpersonal skills. The curriculum, coupled with other elements in the total degree program, is seen as a major avenue for doing so if business schools and their faculty were inclined to use it in this way. The problem, say at least some critics, is that they (the faculty) by and large are not oriented in this direction and hence tend to ignore this problem or at best give it only passing attention in the curriculum.

3 *Insufficient attention to communication skills* Here again, this is a long-standing criticism of business schools and was mentioned as a common complaint by respondents in the Gordon and Howell and Pierson studies. This type of criticism usually contains the observation that many business executives and managers complain that the students they hire out of business schools are not good communicators, either orally or in writing. If this is accepted as fact, then the presumption is usually made that the business-school curriculum did not provide sufficient opportunities for students to develop their skills in this area.

4 *Insufficient attention to the external (legal, social, political) environment* This criticism voices the concern that business schools have been overly concentrated on the internal operations and management of business—the traditional functional areas such as accounting, finance, production, etc.—and have generally tended (except in the area of marketing) to neglect the necessity for coping effectively with the external environment. It is mismanaged relationships with various aspects of the social, political, and legal environment, say the critics, that have caused some of the most serious problems for American business firms in the last decade. Business schools, so the reasoning goes, have contributed to these problems by not modifying their curricula to keep up with important developments in the external context in which modern-day business organizations must operate.

5 *Insufficient attention to the international dimension of business* As is glaringly obvious to any observer (especially American observers) of today's business world, the international aspects of business have grown increasingly crucial in recent years. The need to pay attention to the international as well as domestic aspects of business was recognized officially by AACSB in 1974 when the first paragraph of its Curriculum Standard was modified by adding the phrase "domestic and worldwide" to the statement about the purpose of the curriculum. This element of the Curriculum Standard was further emphasized by the addition of an "interpretation" in 1980 that stated that "every student should be exposed to the international dimension through one or more elements of the curriculum." Thus, in recent years (and before that in certain business schools), the international component of the curriculum has received emphasis both from the organization of business schools (i.e., AACSB) and from individual schools. The issue, for some of the critics, again, is: is there enough emphasis being put on the international area? Does actual curriculum practice strongly (not weakly) support the stated intention of the above-cited Standard interpretation?

6 *Insufficient attention to entrepreneurism* This criticism, briefly stated, is that business schools traditionally have been far too much oriented toward preparing students for working within large, already established organizations rather than also encouraging and teaching students how organizations can be started and how small organizations operate.

7 *Insufficient attention to ethics* Unethical behavior in all walks of life has, unfortunately, always been with us. However, in the eyes of some critics, examples of such inappropriate conduct in business have been on the rise in recent years, and business schools are given some of the blame for this. The charge is that in the typical business curriculum ethics is seldom given direct, explicit attention in either separate courses or as designated parts of other courses. The net result, say critics, is that business schools, while certainly not solely to blame for any increase in unethical business behavior, have not sensitized their students sufficiently to the ethical components of business problems and issues.

THE UNDERGRADUATE (BBA) CURRICULUM

In this section we review the findings from our interviews and questionnaire surveys in both the university and corporate communities regarding a number of facets of the undergraduate degree (BBA) curriculum: the general education part of the degree program, breadth/specialization within the business portion of the curriculum, quantitative/behavioral emphases, the need for change in the required (CBK) core curriculum, specific content areas, emphases on skills and personal characteristics, emphases on preparation for coping with change, and the future of the undergraduate business degree. In each case, differences across groups of respondents will be highlighted as well as the general trends of their viewpoints.

General Education (Liberal Arts) Components
of the BBA Degree Program

Deans and faculty were asked whether they believed that the nonbusiness (liberal arts) component of the undergraduate degree program in their respective schools ought to be increased, decreased, or remain about the same. The results showed that while the majority favored the current situation, almost a third (29 and 32%, respectively) of the deans and faculty members in the survey think that this component should be *increased* and only about 10% (6 and 13%, respectively) think that it should be decreased. These percentages, however, varied significantly (statistically) by type of school: The percentage of deans in Category I schools who believe that this component ought to be increased (56%) is almost double that of Category II school deans (31%) and more than double that of Category III deans (23%). The faculty responses showed a similar pattern by type of school.

Breadth/Specialization within the Business Curriculum

The issue of whether there should be more or less breadth in the undergraduate business curriculum was investigated with four of the university-based groups of respondents in the survey: deans, faculty members, graduating BBA students, and BBA alumni. (Although the word *business* was not specifically included as a modifier of the term *curriculum* in the particular questionnaire items, the context of the surrounding questions clearly implied that they referred to the business school portion of the total undergraduate curriculum.) Views across these four groups differed. Some 27% of deans think that the curriculum needs to be "significantly broadened," while only 8% think that the curriculum should "emphasize specialization to a significantly greater extent." The comparable figures for faculty members, however, are 23 and 21%. Thus, for those deans who think that there should be a change from the status quo, considerably more want increased breadth rather than specialization; faculty members wanting change, on the other hand, are about equally split between these two alternatives. (There was some tendency for Category I deans and faculty to be more strongly in favor of increased breadth compared to those from the other two categories of schools, but the differences were not statistically significant.) Of course, it should be emphasized that a clear majority— about 60 to 65%—of both groups, deans and faculty, prefer the present balance of breadth versus specialization.

The majority of undergraduate students and alumni also feel that the present breadth/depth balance is about right. However, of those who do not in both groups, more believe that there is "too much breadth" (31% of undergraduates and 34% of alumni) compared to those who believe there is "too much depth in a particular specialized area" (7 and 13%, respectively). These findings would appear to show that student and alumni opinions on this matter differ rather decisively from those of deans and somewhat from those of their faculty mentors. (Additional findings relating to the issue of breadth versus specialization will be found in Chapter 4.)

Quantitative and Behavioral Emphases in the Curriculum

As indicated earlier, one set of major issues that has emerged in recent years is the degree of emphasis that business schools currently give to two broad dimensions of the curriculum: quantitative methods and behaviorally oriented subject matter. Certain critics have been especially concerned about what they regard as an overemphasis on the former. The less frequently expressed concerns about the behavioral side, if raised at all, have been addressed more to the issue of whether there is enough such emphasis in the curriculum. Each of these themes—the quantitative and behavioral—appear in curricula in at least two ways: as separate courses in their own right and as important elements of other courses (e.g., quantitative aspects of finance and behavioral aspects of marketing).

Our survey questions on these issues did not pit the two emphases against each other in an either/or choice, since we do not regard them as in any way antithetical to each other. A particular business school curriculum can be relatively strong in both, in neither, or in one and not the other. Also, the current AACSB Curriculum Standard virtually ensures that accredited schools will give more than minimal attention to each. Both academic and corporate respondents were asked whether they believe that the current emphasis on quantitatively (behaviorally) oriented subject matter is "too much," "about right," or "too little." (The particular questions in our surveys on this matter did not ask separately about master's degree and undergraduate curricula. They used the phrasing "...the emphasis in the current curricula in your school"; "...in business schools" in the corporate survey forms.)

Quantitatively Oriented Subject Matter   Table 3.2 presents the results for the question concerning quantitatively oriented subject matter for both sets of respondents (academic and corporate). As can be seen, deans and the two sets of alumni generally regard the current emphasis as about right, with the remain-

TABLE 3.2
VIEWS CONCERNING THE AMOUNT OF QUANTITATIVE EMPHASIS IN THE BUSINESS
SCHOOL CURRICULUM

	Deans	Faculty	BBA Alumni	MBA Alumni	CEOs	SCEs	VPHRs
Too much	16%	14%	14%	14%	35%	33%	42%
About right	70	59	68	73	57	57	54
Too little	15	27	17	13	8	9	4

Note: All columns total 100%, with rounding.

TABLE 3.3
VIEWS CONCERNING THE AMOUNT OF BEHAVIORAL EMPHASIS IN THE BUSINESS
SCHOOL CURRICULUM

	Deans	Faculty	BBA Alumni	MBA Alumni	CEOs	SCEs	VPHRs
Too much	11%	17%	6%	8%	9%	4%	7%
About right	68	60	48	62	24	30	21
Too little	21	23	46	30	67	66	72

Note: All columns total 100%, with rounding.

der splitting fairly evenly between too much and too little. The majority of faculty agree that the current amount of emphasis on quantitative material is about right, but about twice as many of the remainder think the emphasis is too little instead of too much. (It is also worth noting, however, that the views of both deans and faculty members differ significantly by category of school: Thirty percent of all Category I deans and 25% of Category I faculty think the emphasis is too much, while only 10% of Category III deans and faculty hold that same view. The percentages of Category II deans and faculty are intermediate at 19 and 12%, respectively.)

The views of corporate respondents on this issue are markedly different from those of the faculty and most of the deans (especially deans from Category II and III schools) and business school alumni. Just over half of chief executive officers (CEOs), senior corporate executives (SCEs), and vice presidents for human resources (VPHRs) in our sample (57, 57, and 54%, respectively) believe that the current level of quantitative emphasis in the curriculum is about right, but of the remainder, about 80% (that is, 35% of the total sample) believe that such emphasis is too much. As will be seen next, these figures are decisively reversed when the question concerns the amount of *behavioral* emphasis in present-day business schools.

Behaviorally Oriented Subject Matter The distribution of responses regarding the degree of emphasis on behaviorally oriented subject matter in current business school curricula is presented in Table 3.3. As can be seen, again the majority of deans and faculty believe that the current curricula in their schools give this type of subject matter about the right degree of emphasis. Those who have any qualms about this tend slightly more (faculty) or somewhat more (deans) to say that the current emphasis should be increased. On the other hand, as Table 3.3 clearly demonstrates, all three sets of high-level corporate respondents do *not* believe that the amount of current emphasis is correct and by sizable margins indicate that this area receives too little rather than too much attention. The contrast between the percentages of CEOs and SCEs (67 and 66%, respectively) who believe that this area is given too little emphasis and the percentages of these two groups (9 and 4%) who think that it gets too much emphasis represents one of the most dramatic trends in the findings obtained in this entire study. Even the similar contrast between the two percentages for undergraduate alumni (46 and 6%) and MBA alumni (30 and 8%) of business school programs is quite pronounced.

Perceived Need For Change in the Required (Business) Curriculum

The question of whether deans and faculty see a need for a change in their school's required undergraduate business curriculum was addressed by two parallel survey items as well as by interview queries. The survey items asked about whether new topic areas "need to be introduced into the required curriculum" and whether "major topic areas need to be deleted or greatly deemphasized." Based on both the survey findings and our interview results, we would conclude that there was *not* a strong mandate for major systemic changes in the basic core curriculum on the part of either deans or faculty, although there was some sentiment in favor of specific changes. About half the deans and faculty (46 and 50%, respectively) did answer "yes" to the survey question about whether new topic areas should be introduced into the required curriculum, but the other half preferred the status quo. (There were no significant differences in these percentages by category of school, either for deans or faculty members). Members of both groups made varied suggestions about which particular areas they thought should receive more emphasis (see next section), and some deans and a few faculty members in interviews expressed concern about the need for more integration in the curriculum across functional areas. When the question turned to whether or not (any) particular topic areas should be dropped from the required core, about seven of ten individuals in both groups said "no" (with this percentage being significantly greater for Category III deans).

Specific Content Areas of the Curriculum

For those deans and faculty members who believe that some changes are needed in the required undergraduate curriculum, survey and interview questions explored which specific topics or areas should be emphasized *more* and which should be emphasized *less*. (The survey questions presented some fourteen listed options of topic areas, plus the opportunity for checking "no area" or to write in the names of areas not listed.) Deans and faculty showed strong agreement about which particular areas they think should receive increased emphasis: The top four for both groups are business communications (first for both groups), entrepreneurship (second for deans and fourth for faculty), international business/management (third for both), and management information systems (fourth for deans and second for faculty). (Our interview findings, incidentally, strongly reinforced the survey findings regarding these four topic areas.) BBA alumni, on the other hand, showed no consensus on which areas they think should receive more emphasis in the curriculum. Their survey responses were widely dispersed across the dozen or more listed alternatives. However, they did show more consensus in response to a question that asked them to indicate the areas that had been of most use in their careers to date. The three areas ranked highest were (1) accounting, (2) general management, and (3) marketing.

The survey question regarding which areas should receive less attention in the required undergraduate curriculum showed the strongest plurality (50% of the deans and 48% of the faculty) by far for "no topic should be emphasized less." Of those deans who thought at least one or more topics should be de-emphasized, the highest percentages went to quantitative analysis (15%), general management (11%), and economics (10%). The areas receiving the largest faculty votes were general management (17%), organizational behavior (11%), and quantitative analysis, economics, and accounting (all tied at 10%).

Emphases on Skills and Personal Characteristics (SAPCs)

An issue that received special attention in our study, in part, at least, because of a recent extended project by AACSB that focused heavily on this general domain, was the extent to which the curriculum should emphasize the development of various skills and personal characteristics (SAPCs). Both deans and faculty were asked how much each of nine particular SAPCs were currently emphasized in the curriculum and how much each should be emphasized. The results are presented in Tables 3.4 (for deans) and 3.5 (for faculty). The first of these tables shows that deans perceive wide gaps between the current situation in the curricula of their own schools and what they think should be the situation. As can be seen, analytical skills and planning/organizing are the only SAPCs where there is even a semblance of comparable percentages (and these are not closer than 25%) checking that the skill/characteristic both should be emphasized very much and is in fact being emphasized to this degree in the curriculum. All the other seven SAPCs showed considerable discrepancies between perceptions of current reality and beliefs about what ought to be taking place. Interestingly, for two of the SAPCs (analytical skills and computer skills) a statistically significant higher percentage of strong current emphasis was reported by deans of higher category schools, and in two other SAPC areas (initiative and oral communication) a significantly higher percentage of Category III deans reported that the areas receive strong emphasis. For the remaining SAPCs, there were no significant differences by categories of schools. Overall, then, neither the reported amount of attention currently being given to these

TABLE 3.4
DEANS' VIEWS OF THE EMPHASIS THAT IS CURRENTLY
GIVEN AND SHOULD BE GIVEN TO THE DEVELOPMENT OF
VARIOUS SKILLS AND PERSONAL CHARACTERISTICS
(SAPCs) IN BBA PROGRAMS IN THEIR OWN SCHOOLS
(Percent Checking "Emphasized Very Much")

	Current	Should Be
Analytical	50%	76%
Computer	32	65
Decision making	33	71
Initiative	14	53
Leadership/interpersonal skills	18	68
Oral communication	16	75
Planning/organizing	20	47
Risk taking	3	30
Written communication	24	84

nine skills and personal characteristics nor the amount that deans think should be given to them seemed to vary systematically by type of school. Put another way, the large gap perceived by deans between what is and what "should" be the amount of emphasis given to the development of SAPCs is relatively consistent across schools with quite different types of missions, programs, and circumstances.

Faculty views about how much emphasis is and should be given to these same SAPCs are shown in Table 3.5. As with the deans, the differences in percentages checking that a particular SAPC is currently emphasized very much and checking that it should be emphasized to this extent in the curriculum are quite large. Also, again, differences across categories of schools are not consistent for perceptions of the current situation, although there is a tendency for

TABLE 3.5
FACULTY VIEWS OF THE EMPHASIS THAT IS CURRENTLY
GIVEN AND SHOULD BE GIVEN TO THE DEVELOPMENT OF
VARIOUS SKILLS AND PERSONAL CHARACTERISTICS
(SAPCs) IN BBA PROGRAMS IN THEIR OWN SCHOOLS
(Percent Checking "Emphasized Very Much")

	Current	Should Be
Analytical	28%	78%
Computer	18	52
Decision making	20	68
Initiative	7	48
Leadership/interpersonal skills	11	52
Oral communication	8	71
Planning/organizing	12	42
Risk taking	3	27
Written communication	12	81

Category I faculty to have somewhat smaller percentages checking that the various SAPCs should be emphasized strongly in the curricula in their own schools. (While the percentages checking "should be emphasized very much" are statistically significant across categories of schools for most of the SAPCs because of the large number—about 2000—of faculty respondents involved, the practical differences tend to be mostly moderate or small; for example, for initiative, the relevant figures for the three categories of schools are 36, 50, and 51%, and for oral communication, they are 66, 71, and 76%.)

One other group of respondents in our sample that provided their views on the extent to which the typical BBA program is emphasizing the development of these skills and personal characteristics was comprised of undergraduate business students themselves. Specifically, they were asked "to what degree" each of the SAPCs was "currently emphasized in your school's...program." Table 3.6 shows the percentages of BBA undergraduates checking "currently emphasized very much" (out of three alternatives that also included "very little" and "somewhat"). Somewhat surprisingly, perhaps, these percentages are higher than are those of deans (Table 3.4) or faculty (Table 3.5) for seven of the nine SAPCs. Only on analytical skills and computer skills were the BBA students' percentages about equal to or lower than those of the deans. Apparently, undergraduate students are not as critical as deans and, especially, faculty concerning the amount of emphasis placed on these skills and personal attributes in the contemporary business school curriculum. Of course, as will become evident in the following chapter, skeptics may argue that BBA students do not have a very realistic baseline—because of a general lack of work experience—for gauging whether the emphasis they perceive represents in fact a lot or a little. Nevertheless, the divergence of their views from those of their mentors is noticeable.

Corporate views on the extent to which SAPCs *should* be emphasized in business school undergraduate programs were obtained only from human resource executives (VPHRs) and the small sample of managers of small busi-

TABLE 3.6
BBA STUDENTS' VIEWS OF THE EMPHASIS THAT IS
CURRENTLY GIVEN TO THE DEVELOPMENT OF VARIOUS
SKILLS AND PERSONAL CHARACTERISTICS (SAPCs) IN
THEIR OWN SCHOOLS
(Percent Checking "Emphasized Very Much")

Analytical	51%
Computer	18
Decision making	55
Initiative	28
Leadership/interpersonal skills	35
Oral communication	38
Planning/organizing	46
Risk taking	11
Written communication	44

nesses (MSBs). (SAPC items were not included in the survey forms for other sets of corporate respondents only because of the paramount necessity to keep the survey instruments as short as possible.) The percentages checking "very much" for both groups are shown in Table 3.7, where it can be seen that there is strong agreement between these two samples. Except for computer skills and risk taking, high percentages of both the VPHRs and small business executives endorsed the idea that the undergraduate business program should strongly emphasize the development of these skills and characteristics.

Emphases on Preparation for Coping with Change

Three groups of respondents, deans and faculty members on the university side and VPHRs from the corporate side, were asked to rate, on a ten-point scale, how well business/management schools prepare graduates to cope with change. (Note: This question was not specific either to undergraduate or to MBA programs.) The results showed that deans were definitely more positive than either faculty or human resource executives on this issue. The former gave a mean rating of 7.3, while the mean ratings of both the latter two groups were below the scale midpoint (5.5) at 5.1. It would appear that important constituent groups in both the academic and corporate sectors are not convinced about the effectiveness of business school programs in this seemingly important aspect of preparation for a management career.

Future of the Undergraduate Business (BBA) Degree

One other aspect of the undergraduate business program was explored through a question about the perceived future of the BBA degree. Although such a question has a broader focus than just the curriculum, we have included the data from this question in this chapter because the curriculum is such a critical component of any degree program. Respondents were given five alternative re-

TABLE 3.7
VIEWS OF VPHRs AND MSBs REGARDING THE EMPHASIS THAT SHOULD BE GIVEN TO THE DEVELOPMENT OF VARIOUS SKILLS AND PERSONAL CHARACTERISTICS (SAPCs) IN BBA PROGRAMS
(Percent Checking "Emphasized Very Much")

	VPHRs	MSBs
Analytical	73%	59%
Computer	38	47
Decision making	61	65
Initiative	67	71
Leadership/interpersonal skills	78	76
Oral communication	76	76
Planning/organizing	56	59
Risk taking	29	18
Written communication	76	71

sponses, ranging from "[the degree] is important to the business world now and will become even more important in the future," to "[the degree] is unimportant...now and will not become more important in the future." The results for seven sets of respondents—two from the university perspective and five (including BBA alumni) from the corporate perspective—are shown in Table 3.8. Generally speaking, the seven categories of respondents were in remarkable agreement in believing that the BBA degree is important to the business world now and will either remain so or become even more important in the future. Only about 15 to 20% of the various respondent groups felt that the degree was either likely to decrease in importance or was already unimportant.

MASTER'S (MBA) CURRICULUM

In this section we examine several of the same issues explored with regard to the undergraduate curriculum but with the focus on the master's degree level of education. Although business/management schools sometimes offer several different master's degrees, by far the most prevalent one is the Master's of Business Administration (MBA), and thus our survey and interview questions were addressed to curriculum matters related to that degree. These include the breadth/specialization issue, the perceived need to change (or not to change) the required part of the MBA curriculum, specific content areas, emphases on SAPCs in MBA programs, and the future of the MBA degree.

Breadth/Specialization within the MBA Curriculum

Only relatively small percentages (14 and 17%, respectively) of deans and faculty believe that the present MBA curriculum needs to be broadened, but somewhat larger percentages (21 and 32%, respectively) believe that it needs to emphasize specialization to a significantly greater extent. These latter feelings were more pronounced (significantly so among faculty) in Category II and III schools.

TABLE 3.8
OPINIONS ABOUT THE FUTURE OF THE UNDERGRADUATE BUSINESS (BBA) DEGREE: SEVEN RESPONDENT GROUPS
(Percent Checking One of Five Alternative Responses)

	Deans	Faculty	BBA Alumni	CEOs	SCEs	VPHRs	MSBs
Important now/more in future	22%	23%	25%	17%	15%	17%	18%
Important now/same in future	64	57	63	60	62	65	71
Important now/less in future	12	15	10	8	13	9	12
Unimportant now/but more important in future	0	1	1	2	2	1	0
Unimportant now/same in future	2	5	1	13	8	7	0

Note: All columns total 100%, within rounding.

The majority (63 and 65%, respectively) of both MBA students and MBA alumni believe that the balance between breadth and specialization that they are experiencing (students) or have experienced within the past 10 years (alumni) is appropriate. However, of the approximately one-third who believe that the balance is not appropriate, most (by a factor of 5:1) think there is too much breadth (in business areas) and not enough depth (in a specialized area of business) in their MBA programs. (Again, the following chapter will present additional data on the breadth/specialization issue as it pertains to MBA students.)

Perceived Need for Change in the Required (Core) MBA Curriculum

Deans and faculty were each split about 50-50 on whether they thought that new topic areas need to be introduced into the required (core) MBA curriculum. (There were no differences in these 50-50 splits by category of school.) However, as with undergraduate degree programs, only about one-fifth of each of these respondent groups said that major topic areas needed to be deleted from the required curriculum.

Specific Content Areas of the Curriculum

For MBA programs, deans believe that the two areas that are in greatest need of additional emphasis in the curriculum are international business/management and management information systems (MIS). About 40 to 45% of all deans think that each of these areas deserves more attention. Interestingly, however, there were some statistically significant differences in responses by categories of schools. It is Category I deans who have the highest percentage of respondents (55% versus 41 and 26% for the other two categories, respectively) who indicate that the international area needs more emphasis. However, the highest percentage of deans advocating more emphasis on MIS comes neither from Category I schools (28%) nor from Category III schools (also 28%), but from Category II schools (47%). Faculty are generally in accord with deans in indicating that the two areas needing greater additional attention are MIS and international business. About 30% of the faculty think that these areas should receive increased curriculum emphasis. In addition, almost 30% believe that the area of business communications needs greater emphasis in the MBA curriculum.

MBA alumni, in response to a question about which curriculum areas had been most useful to them in their careers to date, voted most often for accounting (23% rank it first), finance (15% rank it first), and general management (11% rank it first). A follow-up question regarding which areas they would have liked to have had emphasized more in their programs drew scattered responses, although clearly MIS was the area most consistently ranked first.

Emphases on Skills and Personal Characteristics (SAPCs)

As was done in the case of undergraduate programs, deans and faculty were queried with respect to the extent to which the development of various skills and personal characteristics (SAPCs) is emphasized in the MBA programs in their schools. The percentages of deans checking that a particular SAPC is emphasized very much in their MBA programs are shown in Table 3.9. Similar to the situation for BBA programs, response percentages are quite different with regard to what is happening currently versus what deans think should be happening with regard to the development of most SAPCs. Only in the case of analytical skills is a gap virtually nonexistent. A comparison of the first columns in Tables 3.9 and 3.4 will show that only slightly higher percentages of deans believe that SAPCs are being emphasized to a strong degree in their MBA programs vis-à-vis their undergraduate programs. For computer skills, even this small differential is reversed. While 32% of the deans think that this skill is receiving great emphasis in undergraduate programs, only 20% feel this way about their MBA programs. (Of course, the same deans are not involved in the two comparisons, since some deans head schools with no undergraduate programs and others are at schools with no MBA programs; however, since a large number of schools have both degree programs, the comparisons can be considered meaningful to an extent.)

The responses for faculty regarding SAPCs emphases in their MBA programs are shown in Table 3.10. The "current" versus "should be" gaps are consistently large, as they were in the case of deans' opinions. Also, as with deans, a comparison of Table 3.10 with Table 3.5 regarding undergraduate programs shows that faculty think the various SAPCs are only slightly more emphasized at the graduate level. The fact that 11% of faculty members believe that leadership and interpersonal skills are strongly emphasized in their undergraduate programs, for example, and only 14% think that this is the case with their MBA programs would seem to suggest that the typical MBA program is not providing much beyond what an undergraduate program does in this area. At least, this is how business school faculty view this situation.

MBA students, as is the case with undergraduate business students, are more positive (that is, a higher percentage are more positive) than faculty members

TABLE 3.9
DEANS' VIEWS OF THE EMPHASIS THAT IS CURRENTLY GIVEN AND SHOULD BE GIVEN
TO THE DEVELOPMENT OF VARIOUS SKILLS AND PERSONAL CHARACTERISTICS
(SAPCs) IN MBA PROGRAMS IN THEIR OWN SCHOOLS
(Percent Checking "Emphasized Very Much")

	Current	Should Be
Analytical	64%	76%
Computer	20	58
Decision making	50	81
Initiative	16	59
Leadership/interpersonal skills	25	76
Oral communication	21	78
Planning/organizing	30	57
Risk taking	6	38
Written communication	23	85

TABLE 3.10
FACULTY VIEWS OF THE EMPHASIS THAT IS CURRENTLY GIVEN AND SHOULD BE
GIVEN TO THE DEVELOPMENT OF VARIOUS SKILLS AND PERSONAL CHARACTERISTICS
(SAPCs) IN MBA PROGRAMS IN THEIR OWN SCHOOLS
(Percent Checking "Emphasized Very Much")

	Current	Should Be
Analytical	38%	80%
Computer	15	49
Decision making	32	76
Initiative	11	52
Leadership/interpersonal skills	14	61
Oral communication	14	73
Planning/organizing	18	51
Risk taking	5	34
Written communication	15	81

about the emphasis provided by their programs on SAPCs. Their views—shown
in Table 3.11—generally are similar to deans' perceptions, except with regard
to planning/organizing and written communication. Also, and rather interestingly, the percentages of MBAs indicating that a given SAPC receives strong
emphasis in their programs are generally *no higher* than the percentages of undergraduates describing their programs.

The views of corporate personnel executives (VPHRs) and the managers of
small business firms (MSBs) regarding whether various SAPCs should be emphasized very much in MBA programs are quite similar (though the percentages are slightly higher) to their views about undergraduate programs that were
presented previously in Table 3.7. Thus these percentages are not presented
here in tabular form.

Future of the MBA Degree

The opinions of seven groups of respondents were solicited with respect to the
future of the MBA degree, as had been done also for the BBA degree (see Ta-

TABLE 3.11
MBA STUDENTS' VIEWS OF THE EMPHASIS THAT IS CURRENTLY
GIVEN TO THE DEVELOPMENT OF VARIOUS SKILLS AND PERSONAL
CHARACTERISTICS (SAPCs) IN THEIR OWN SCHOOLS
(Percent Checking "Emphasized Very Much")

Analytical	62%
Computer	14
Decision making	51
Initiative	21
Leadership/interpersonal skills	26
Oral communication	28
Planning/organizing	51
Risk taking	8
Written communication	42

ble 3.8). The results are shown in Table 3.12 and indicate that not only are deans and faculty quite positive about the future of the MBA degree, but so also are all the corporate groups, with the exception of the small sample of managers of small business firms. CEOs and SCEs are, if anything, even more positive, as Table 3.12 illustrates, about the future of the MBA degree than are deans and faculty members. Only about 14 or 15% of the two top executive groups believe that the degree will become less important in the future or that it is not important now.

COMMENTARY

For both BBA and MBA degree programs, the typical business school curriculum in the United States in the 1980s, at least the curriculum of those schools already accredited by the AACSB or striving to qualify for accreditation, is substantially different from what it was in the 1950s. It is anchored firmly on a base of at least 40% of total credit hours in liberal arts subjects at the undergraduate level, it has explicit quantitative and behavioral components, it requires all students to take a set of core courses in basic subject matter areas pertaining to business, it provides at least a (bare) minimum exposure to international aspects of business, it incorporates at least one course designed to provide integration across functional areas, and it has eliminated many overly superficial and unduly specialized vocational courses. In short, it has become far more academically solid and thus considerably more academically respectable. Viewed from almost any angle, it provides a better foundation for students entering the business world in the 1980s than did the curriculum 30 years ago for those starting their careers in business at that time. The key question, however, especially in light of the objectives of this Project, is whether the current curriculum is as appropriate for the future—the 1990s and beyond—as it ought to be. Unfortunately, that is not an easy question to answer. The question is a simple one to ask, but the answer is complex.

The structure and content of any curriculum that hopes to be relevant to future needs must take into account one inescapable fact that we emphasized

TABLE 3.12

OPINIONS ABOUT THE FUTURE OF THE MBA DEGREE: SEVEN RESPONDENT GROUPS (Percent Checking One of Five Alternative Responses)

	Deans	Faculty	MBA Alumni	CEOs	SCEs	VPHRs	MSBs
Important now/more in future	23%	26%	29%	22%	22%	23%	6%
Important now/same in future	56	51	54	62	64	60	38
Important now/less in future	20	21	13	11	9	15	38
Unimportant now/but more important in future	1	1	1	1	1	2	12
Unimportant now/same in future	0	1	2	3	3	1	6

Note: All columns total 100%, within rounding.

in the preceding chapter: this is a *changing,* not static, world. Although it is difficult, if not impossible, for anyone to predict specific future events and trends with a great degree of accuracy, the designers of curricula must nevertheless be highly tuned to the need to sense relevant current basic changes in the environment (broadly speaking) and those major changes in the near future that can be anticipated with reasonable confidence. This also implies that over time a curriculum needs to have enough flexibility built in such that innovations and adaptability to changing conditions can be nourished and encouraged rather than stifled and discouraged. The challenge to those responsible for the curriculum, of course, is to be able to discern—and then have the curriculum adapt to—those changes which are important and fundamental rather than superficial and trivial.

The previous chapter outlined some of the basic changes to which a business school curriculum aiming at preparing graduates for the next decade and the beginning of the next century must be responsive. Most crucial, perhaps, for this country at least, is the continuing change from an industrial to a service- and information-oriented society. No matter how one views the magnitude of this change, it is a virtual certainty that graduates of the future will, in toto, be working in a different configuration of companies/firms/organizations than has been the prevailing pattern for the past 50 years—organizations that are likely to be different in form and structure and the way in which they are operated compared to the typical examples of firms of the 1960s, 1970s and 1980s. The employees of these organizations will, collectively, enter the work force with more diverse backgrounds and with changing patterns of needs and expectations. The age distribution within the work force will be different by the year 2000. The trend toward increasing globalization of the world's economy is hardly likely to subside. The United States, with its former secure position as the world's dominant national economy in jeopardy, will almost certainly face continuing intense competition from other countries. The role of business in relation to that of government in this as well as other countries is likely to continue to evolve through the years. The recent sensitivity to the ethics of business behavior is not likely to go away. Overlaying these changes, of course, are the inevitable technological advances in the physical and life sciences. Given all this flux of change, some of it relatively slower and more evolutionary and some of it rapid and near-revolutionary, how well and how fast are business school curricula adapting? What did we find "out there"?

Satisfaction with the Status Quo

In marked contrast to the situation reported in the 1950s, we found *no forceful push for systemic curriculum change emanating from business schools themselves.* This is a strong statement that undoubtedly will be disputed by some deans and faculty members, particularly those who believe that they are doing exactly this—pushing for major changes in their own particular schools. However, we can say in response, first, that our survey data from a broad and representative sample of institutions and individual deans and faculty members lead us to no other conclusion. Furthermore—and this will not be obvious from the (mainly) survey findings reported in the previous section—during the course of our some 300 interviews in more than sixty schools of widely diverse types we were particularly struck with what we regarded as a general level of *complacency* about the basic thrust and nature of the present curriculum. In our view, this stemmed not so much from an unwillingness to consider possible changes and modifications as it did from a pervasive satisfaction with the status quo; there were few expressions of a felt *need* to make major, fundamental *systemic* changes. The majority of deans and faculty with whom we talked may be correct that such changes are not needed, but we seriously question whether this is not a dangerous stance to be taking—an academic version, as it were, of generals (and troops) planning to fight the last war!

Some facts from the survey findings seem clear: The majority of deans and faculty members do not believe that the liberal arts (general education) proportion of the undergraduate curriculum should be altered up or down, about half do not believe that there need to be any specific additions to the required curriculum and nearly 70% do not believe that there need to be any deletions, most believe that the current curriculum in their school has the right balance between breadth and depth, and clear majorities believe that the present emphases on both the quantitative and the behavioral components of the curriculum are about right.

Maybe all these majority opinions are correct. Maybe there need to be very few or even no fundamental changes. Maybe changes occurring within specific individual courses add up to enough total change. However, from our interviews we did not detect many strong desires to test these assumptions; nor did we encounter any very great willingness to experiment in imaginative ways with the basic curriculum. Whether these attitudes arise from a reluctance to deviate from what are interpreted to be clear-cut AACSB Standards or from a fear that employers will not be attracted to graduates from schools with unconventional curricula, or for other reasons, is not clear. This general play-it-safe approach, however, occurs even though the Standards state that "schools may choose to meet [the Curriculum] Standard in a variety of ways" and "innovation [in the curriculum or other aspects of a school's program] that furthers the school's objectives and substantially advances the overall high quality of programs is encouraged." Also, the inertia persists even though the business community registers serious reservations about some aspects of the current curriculum.

It would be misleading and incorrect to convey the impression that business school deans and faculty have entrenched opposition to any change at all. The facts clearly argue otherwise. Although those tending to favor the curriculum status quo appear to be the majority, figures (percentages) cited earlier in this chapter suggest that there is a not insignificant minority who want at least limited changes. As the survey findings illustrated, however, there was not a great deal of consensus on what these changes should be. Certain areas—such as MIS, international business/management, entrepreneurism, and business communications—were singled out for additional curriculum emphasis by some deans and faculty more often than were other topic areas, but our interviews indicated that the mention of these areas tended to represent scattered individual preferences rather than elements of more comprehensive plans for change. Also, we need to stress what was stated earlier: a number of suggestions were made for additional emphasis on particular subject matter areas, but in very few instances did we encounter careful consideration of what might be deleted from the curriculum to make a place for those additions. Thus, potential additions almost never were weighed against the total structure of the curriculum: either what would have to be deleted *or* how the total length would have to be adjusted (i.e., increased). In short, there was little overall evidence of thinking that might lead to bold, new initiatives.

Curriculum Content Issues

There are a number of particular curriculum issues that deserve discussion, most of them dealing with curriculum content and most of them revolving around the various criticisms that have been leveled by observers in both the corporate and academic communities. These were summarized and outlined previously, and the commentary that follows will be organized around that set of general and specific criticisms. We will provide our appraisals of them in light of the data collected for this project and reported in the earlier results sections of this chapter.

Vision   In our view, this criticism—that there is an insufficient emphasis on generating vision in graduates of business school programs—has as much or more to do with the way various courses are conducted and taught as it does with the content of the curriculum. While curriculum content is not irrelevant, it is only one factor affecting how much problem-finding/creative-solution-generating vision students emerge with when they complete a BBA or MBA program. In any event, we were not able to obtain very much reliable data on this important issue in relation to the curriculum and its content. Our impression, subjective as it is, is that there is some validity to this concern and that it is not often enough discussed in relation to curriculum objectives in business school settings. One thing is certain: we did not find it spontaneously raised as an issue in those parts of our campus interviews which pertained to the curriculum. (Additional data relating at least peripherally to this issue will be found in Chapter 4.)

Integration Across Functional Areas   Unfortunately, for today's business school graduates, let alone those who will be graduating in coming years, the modern world of business is not very accommodating; it does not present problems and decisions neatly packaged and exclusively within a marketing, finance, accounting, or some other single functional box. The implication is clear: The manager of the future must understand more than a narrow discipline or functional area. Yet, our interview data indicated that many schools, perhaps most, are relying on the single "capstone" business policy course to cope with this all too obvious fact of business life by having it carry the major integrative load across functional areas. This raises several subissues: Is this enough, is this the only way to provide integration, and should such integration occur only at the very end of a (BBA and MBA) degree program? Our own answer to each of these questions would be "no," but we do not have quick solutions to suggest. Again, as with the vision issue, we believe that our interview soundings strongly support the assertion that cross-functional integration is not receiving the attention it deserves from business schools. To put this somewhat differently, we encountered a large degree of casual acceptance of the single business policy course placed at the finale of the program as sufficient, and this attitude seemed to be coupled with the view that any alternative approaches were either not feasible or not worth the bother of trying to implement them. Should and can more effective integration be provided within the limits of the total time available in BBA and MBA programs? This is a question worth attempting to answer.

The issue of integration across functional areas also is not unrelated to the issue of the balance between breadth and specialization in the curriculum. Most (not all) deans, faculty, and business school alumni are satisfied with the current balance. However, our findings, especially at the MBA level, suggest that those who want any change at all prefer the balance tipped toward more specialization. If this were to become a stronger trend of opinion—at the present time it is difficult to predict whether it will be, but there are signs that it may be somewhat likely—one can ask how this would affect the need for increased integration across functional specializations. On the surface, at least, it would appear that the two ideas are in conflict. Our own preference is for more of the one (integration) than there is now and no more of the other (specialization) than there is now, because we think that this is the type of curriculum that will best prepare students for the uncertain future. Our *prediction*, however, is that both issues—how much integration to build into the curriculum and how much specialization to allow students to take within the curriculum—will be continuing major battlegrounds and never definitively settled within business schools in the foreseeable future. (See, also, further comments on these issues in the following chapter.)

Quantitative Emphasis in the Curriculum Has the Foundation reports– inspired revolution that urged the insertion of much toughened and more rigorous quantitative requirements into the curriculum gone too far? As documented in the survey findings presented earlier, most academic and corporate respondents do not think so. There was a preponderance of opinion among all parties—deans, faculty members, BBA and MBA alumni, and senior corporate executives—that the present amount of emphasis on quantitative-oriented subject matter throughout the business school curriculum is about right. However, there were enough corporate executives who disagreed to warrant further examination of the issue. Most (by a factor of about 4:1) of those in the corporate sector who think the amount of present emphasis is not appropriate want it decreased. Our interview findings, however, seemed to corroborate the majority opinion among corporate survey respondents, namely, that the present degree of emphasis is approximately correct. While we almost never found anyone in the corporate world in our interviews who wanted the quantitative aspects of the curriculum increased, most, when pressed on this issue, also thought it should not be decreased. In other words, whatever else they thought about the curriculum and what might be emphasized more, there was virtually no call for less quantitative emphasis. To the contrary, we found a general level of admiration and appreciation of the level of quantitative skills that business school graduates possessed as part of their overall strong mastery of analytical skills (see Chapter 4). In short, based on our total set of data, both survey and interviews, we find little or no basis for recommending any major change—up or down—in how much quantitative analysis should be emphasized in the curriculum. This is, however, decidedly not the case with the next curriculum area.

Behavioral Emphasis in the Curriculum   The Foundation reports were also insistent in recommending that business schools give far more attention to the behavioral science aspects of their curriculum than they ever had before. This, as noted earlier, was accomplished beginning in the 1960s by most schools requiring students to take courses in areas such as organizational behavior and organizational theory and by the inclusion of a relevant element in the CBK part of the revised AACSB Curriculum Standard adopted in 1969. As reported previously in this chapter, our survey findings point to a relatively high degree of concern in the corporate sector that behaviorally oriented subject matter is *not* being emphasized enough in the curriculum. This view represented two-thirds of all senior corporate respondents and significant percentages of BBA and MBA alumni and, furthermore, was strongly reinforced in our corporate interviews (which included members of middle and lower management as well as upper-level executives).[3] Deans and faculty, on the other hand, on both the surveys and in interviews were mostly of the opinion that the present degree of emphasis was about right. Clearly, there are substantial differences of opinion between academia and the corporate world on this score (as will be further elaborated in the following chapter) which need to be explored and analyzed in greater depth than has been true to date.

All our data relating to SAPCs presented in this and the next chapter highlight a perceived gap in the corporate world between (1) the extent to which behavioral skills are seen as being emphasized currently in the curriculum and demonstrated by business school graduates, and (2) the extent to which the curriculum and other elements of the total program *should* emphasize such skills. Either the expectations of the business community in this area are too high and unrealistic, or business schools are not placing enough attention on this area. We suspect there is truth to both these assertions, but as with most important educational matters, there are no simple, quick solutions that go much beyond the level of rhetoric or gimmicks. We will have more to say about this critical issue, however, in our concluding chapter.

---

[3]Since one of the codirectors of this project is himself from the behavioral area, we were acutely conscious in interviews about the possibility of leading the interviewee into making statements about this area that he or she did not intend or would not have made otherwise. Although we would have a hard time proving that we did not do this, we made every effort to try to guard against this possibility. In point of fact, both of us were struck by how often respondents offered spontaneous comments about the behavioral area even when we were discussing other topics.

Communication   This has been an area of criticism aimed at business schools for many years. Our survey findings strongly indicate that most deans and faculty think that communication is still not sufficiently emphasized in the curriculum. Corporate views relating to this issue will be found mostly in Chapter 4, where we present data on perceptions of the degree of skills possessed by business school graduates in this and other areas. Further comments will be reserved for that chapter.

The External Environment   The external legal/social/political environment, as an area of the curriculum, did not elicit especially strong concern in our interviews of either academic or corporate officials, although there was a moderate level of sentiment in both sets of respondents in the surveys in favor of placing more emphasis on this area. We believe that because of the increasingly complex environment in which business operates, business schools must give more consideration to whether they have the appropriate balance between an internal and an external focus. (This is also related to the previously discussed issue of the need for integration across functional areas.) We were somewhat surprised that this did not seem to be as salient an issue as we thought it should be. Part of the reason may be that it is more of a subtle and diffuse issue than some other curriculum issues, but that does not mean it is any less important. In our opinion, failure to address it in a more head-on fashion now will likely generate more pressure to do so in the not too distant future. However, that pressure does not appear to have developed very much to date.

International   This is an area of the curriculum where we found a considerable amount of, at worst, lip service, and, at best, serious concern on the part of deans and faculty (but, we should point out, *not* on the part of most corporate-sector respondents). It was, as we reported earlier in the chapter, one of the four specific areas most often mentioned in both interviews and on the surveys as needing more emphasis in the curriculum. The problem, as most acknowledged, is how to implement this—whether to do it through adding more specific courses on international business, international finance, international marketing, and the like or by putting more emphasis on international issues in courses already in the curriculum. This whole area has been the object of much discussion within the business school community, and we probably cannot shed much additional light on the curriculum aspects of the matter except to say this: Although there seems to be an increasing awareness among business school deans and faculty that more ought to be done to emphasize this area, this awareness or sensitivity so far does not appear to us to have been translated into a great deal of action. More is being done now than 10 years ago, and this seems clearly demonstrable by an examination of curricula and in interviews with knowledgeable observers, but much more needs to be done.

Entrepreneurism   This area, as did the international area, received a relatively high degree of endorsement as a topic needing more attention in the curriculum. Clearly, some schools have in recent years added specific programs in this area and have given it considerable attention already. Others have not addressed this subject to any great extent at all. Since we seem to be in an era of the downsizing of large corporations and a corresponding increase in emphasis on "intrapreneuring" within them and on starting new firms and related entrepreneurial activities, this would appear to be an area that will be given more attention in the typical business school curriculum in the future than it has in the past. More than likely, however, there will be a wide variance in how much attention it will receive from school to school. To allocate it more emphasis in the curriculum will, as with other such expanding areas, require consideration of what will be given less attention. Furthermore, as with the international area, schools will have to decide whether to spread the topic throughout the curriculum or give it separate, discrete treatment.

Ethics   This is an area somewhat like the international area insofar as the curriculum is concerned, because the issue is whether to treat this as a specific topic (like marketing, finance, etc.) or as an important consideration in any course. Because our own view is that ethics should receive attention throughout the total business school program (including the entire curriculum), we did not list it as a specific item in our survey question dealing with topic areas needing more (or less) emphasis. It was, however, viewed as such by some (not a large number of) deans and faculty respondents. It was listed more frequently than any other area as an open-ended response to "other areas needing more emphasis." Our interviews uncovered some general concern about how to achieve a stronger emphasis on ethics in the curriculum, but also an accompanying uncertainty about how best to do this. No reasonable person, in our opinion, could argue that business schools should ignore ethical aspects of business behavior and business decisions or should emphasize this less than currently, but how best to implement an increased emphasis is the challenge. Even more difficult is the question of how to make a concerted focus on ethics in the business curriculum have an impact on graduates' subsequent behavior, to go beyond merely making faculty and students "feel better" because they have discharged their obligations by giving consideration in their courses to moral standards and principles of conduct.

Future of the BBA and MBA Degrees

Although there have been a relatively large number of criticisms directed against business schools in general and aspects of the curriculum in particular in recent years, our survey and interview findings among corporate respondents did not point to any great disenchantment with either the BBA or MBA degrees as preparation for careers in the world of business and management. As we noted in reporting our findings earlier in the chapter, senior corporate executives are at least as positive as (and in the case of the MBA degree, slightly more positive than) deans and faculty members about the future of these degrees—in terms of their importance to the business world. This will no doubt disappoint some critics who are inclined to paint a more gloomy picture about the current condition of business education, but it appears to testify to the positive impacts of the generally strengthened curricula that business schools individually and collectively have put into place during the past two decades. However, to return to a point made earlier: Too much self-satisfaction with this current level of acceptance of business school degrees can—as has perhaps been the case with much of U.S. industry—lead to unpleasant consequences if "eternal vigilance" is not given to the challenge of making continuing changes and improvements. As we have attempted to point out elsewhere in this chapter, there appear to be certain curriculum issues and areas that need more monitoring and concerted attention than they are now receiving. We return to such issues in the final chapter of this report.

CHAPTER 4

STUDENTS/GRADUATES

If university business schools were considered from a *systems* perspective, students could be thought of as a key "input" and graduates as one of the two most important "outputs" (the other being research, which is discussed in Chapter 7). Students entering business schools are the basic raw material, so to speak, and graduates leaving are the product of that input plus the transformation brought about by the faculty (Chapter 5) utilizing the curriculum (Chapter 3) and various teaching methods (Chapter 6). As many people have pointed out, if the student input is of high quality, almost anything the faculty members do (within limits) will fail to prevent quality graduates from exiting. Conversely, if the input is inferior, it will be extremely difficult to transform low-quality students into high-quality graduates. Although most business schools face neither extreme, the challenge for *all* schools and their faculties is to develop further whatever the degree of talent they inherit in entering students.

This chapter focuses on some facts about entering students, including their own self-perceptions, and especially on how the "transformed" students—i.e., the graduates of business schools—are viewed and evaluated by both their academic mentors and their corporate employers. Since business/management education that is aimed at turning out graduates who will enter the "real world" of business involves two basic levels of programs—bachelor's degree and master's degree programs—our analysis will treat each student group separately. We will concentrate particularly on the perceived strengths and weaknesses of each type of graduate, as well as on a key issue relating to the range of their developed talents: their relative breadth versus depth of knowledge for both entering positions in the business world and for later positions of significant leadership. Throughout our analysis and discussion it is essential to keep in mind that graduates of business schools represent some *combination* of their degree of talent and experience at entrance, the natural maturing that would take place during the particular 2 to 4 years that a student is in a business school program regardless of what took place during that period, and—most important for our purposes—the success (or lack thereof) of intellectual and other developmental processes engendered by the school through its faculty, instructional programs, and other resources.

THE PAST 25 YEARS

In this section we begin by reviewing the situation regarding business school students/graduates as the two Foundation reports found it at the beginning of the 1960s. This will be followed by a discussion of developments during the past 25 years and critics' assessments of the graduates that are currently being turned out by business/management schools.

The Situation at the Beginning of the 1960s

The authors of the Ford and Carnegie reports had quite serious concerns about the quality of students entering business schools in the late 1950s and, therefore, also about the quality of the graduates from those schools. The overall views of these two reports with regard to students were summed up well by Pierson (1959, p. 5):

> Hardly any undergraduate business schools…follow selective admissions policies. Judged on intelligence-test scores, undergraduate business students do not compare favorably with other important student groups. These findings are modified, but only in part, at the graduate level. Both undergraduate and graduate business students regard education primarily in career-value terms.

The analyses in the two reports focused on two major problem areas: (1) the intellectual quality ("mental aptitude" as Gordon and Howell termed it) of the students, and (2) their motivation, interests, and other personal characteristics (or "nonmental traits," to use Gordon and Howell's term). It is instructive to look at these two problem areas in more detail in order to place our own findings of the 1980s in broader perspective. Of the two concerns, clearly the one of greatest importance to both Pierson and Gordon and Howell was the first: the intellectual quality of students choosing to major in business and subsequently being selected for admission. The latter authors put this issue in the form of a question: "Do business students have the mental aptitude to handle and benefit from the more rigorous kind of program recommended [in this report]?" (Gordon and Howell, 1959, p. 323). To substantiate the basis for their question, Gordon and Howell cited the data in Table 4.1 (Table 20, p. 324, from their report) and pointed out that "it is clear that business schools and departments enroll a disproportionate share of very weak freshmen" (p. 325) and grad-

TABLE 4.1
INDICATIONS OF STUDENT ABILITY BY FIELD OF STUDY

| Field of Study | Selective Service College Qualification Test, 1951–1953 | | | | College Graduates (ACE Psychological Examination) Median Score (AGCT Scale) |
| | Freshman | | Seniors | | |
	Mean Score	Percent Exceeding Critical Score (70)	Mean Score	Percent Exceeding Critical Score (75)	
All fields	70	53%	74	50%	121
Agriculture	68	40	71	29	119
Biology	71	60	73	46	121
Business	68	38	73	43	119
Education	66	28	69	20	117
Engineering	72	68	76	67	124
Humanities	70	52	74	47	122
Physical sciences	72	66	76	68	127
Social sciences	70	56	74	51	120

Note: A Selective Service College Qualification Test score of 70 corresponds to 120–121 on the AGCT scale.
  Sources: Freshmen and senior scores on the Selective Service College Qualification Test are from Educational Testing Service, *Statistical Studies of Selective Service Testing, 1951–1953* (Report SR-55-30, 1955). Median scores of college graduates (bachelor's level) on the American Council on Education Psychological Examination (converted to the AGCT scale) are from the Commission on Human Resources and Advanced Training, *America's Resources of Specialized Talent* (prepared by D. Wolfle, director, 1954), and are based on test scores of a sample of 10,000 men and women students who graduated in 1950 from forty-one colleges and universities. [Reproduced from Gordon and Howell, 1959, p. 324.]

uate only a small proportion of the best students from a campus. However, they also noted that at the undergraduate level those receiving bachelor's degrees in business more closely approximated the average degree recipient from throughout a campus because business schools typically had high attrition rates among poorer-quality entering students. Pierson believed that a major part of the problem revolved around the fact that "most business schools have had to adapt their programs to the abilities and interests of extremely large and diversified student groups…[and thus] the majority of these schools cannot expect to establish high academic standards comparable to those found in the advanced professions" (Pierson, 1959, p. 55).

The major solution to this problem that was advocated by both reports was to raise the standards both for admissions and for performance once in the school. Pierson's thesis, for example, with respect to the latter objective was that "business schools could raise the content and quality of their programs materially and still meet the needs of the bulk of their students" (p. 55). Gordon and Howell strongly believed that the AACSB could be a major force in promoting higher standards for student admissions and performance. The AACSB should, they said, "give more attention than it has so far done to the admission and performance standards of present member schools as well as of those newly applying for membership" (p. 331). Both reports indicated that this type of attention needed to be addressed to both the graduate (i.e., master's) and the undergraduate programs in business. In other words, their data indicated that the situation for master's (MBA) students was not significantly better than that for bachelor's degree students. Action to raise academic standards was imperative at both levels, they felt. Gordon and Howell, however, went on to point out that if graduate standards were raised and undergraduate specialization in business simultaneously discouraged, "there would be an ample supply of good candidates for the master's degree" (p. 334).

With respect to the second major area of concern—the attitudes, values, and interests of business school students—the reports were somewhat less confident that data existed from which to draw firm conclusions. Gordon and Howell found a distinctly bimodal (actually trimodal) split in the motivation of students to enroll in a business school program. One group of students was majoring in business for indirect rather than direct reasons. These students were not choosing business as an academic area of concentration out of any strong conviction that it was a stimulating and intrinsically interesting area of study. As indicated by the following comment from Gordon and Howell (p. 335), this was probably not an insignificant proportion of students:

> We discussed the question of motivation with groups of students and individual faculty members on several dozen campuses. The impression was widely held that relatively few undergraduates concentrate in business administration because they are intellectually attracted to the subject....Often they major in business because they feel that they will wind up in business and that it is therefore only reasonable to take a business degree.

A second group of (undergraduate) business majors appeared to be exactly the opposite in motivation: They majored in business because they (in the words of Gordon and Howell, 1959, p. 335):

> ...quite positively want and are seeking what they consider to be a career in business....[Such students] often express[ed] a desire for a "practical" education which will...give them higher starting salaries and higher lifetime earnings than any alternative.

The third category of business majors in the 1950s, as identified by Gordon and Howell, were "those who are in the business school by default. [They are] the residual element." These were students who could not find any other major that interested them and/or who anticipated that business courses would be easier than those in other majors. In short, they were the students of that era who "have given the undergraduate business schools a reputation for having weak students." Again, this third set represented more than a tiny minority: "So far as we can determine, they are found in significant numbers in nearly every undergraduate business school" (Gordon and Howell, 1959, p. 336).

Pierson appeared to be most concerned about an exceedingly "practical" orientation on the part of many (if not most) undergraduate business students and especially their tendency to pile up as many business courses—and as few nonbusiness courses—as possible in their programs of study. Aside from the potential negative effects of such a narrow focus for the great majority of business students, Pierson also was doubtful that the better students among them were finding enough intellectual stimulation in most of these business courses.

The challenge thrown down to business schools and to the AACSB by both the Ford and the Carnegie reports with respect to the quality of students being admitted and the kinds of standards those students would be expected to meet in their academic programs was forcefully expressed by Gordon and Howell:

> The kind of educational program recommended...requires a more carefully selected student body than can be found in most business schools today. Clearly the average quality needs to be raised, more by eliminating the students at the lower end of the scale than by increasing the number in the top few percentiles....The program proposed here also implies a student group with a reasonably high level of positive motivation toward careers in business....Many students now in the schools meet this stipulation. But many, as we have seen, do not [p. 338].

Further:

> All of this presents a problem to the AACSB which thus far it has apparently been reluctant to face....We think that the time has come for...[the AACSB] to concern itself...with the quality of students and standards of student performance [p. 340].

Developments during the Past 25 Years

The overwhelming development that occurred during the past 25 years relating to business school students and graduates was the immense increase in their numbers. The other significant development was action by the AACSB to set basic minimum standards for admission of students (particularly master's degree applicants) to accredited and would-be accredited schools. Both these developments had powerful effects on the attempts of business schools to meet the challenge of improving student quality that was put forth in the two Foundation reports. In the remainder of this section of Chapter 4 we will look at each, in turn, and then examine data relating to the current levels of intellectual aptitude of business school students versus those in other areas of the university.

Enrollment Growth in Business Schools   As is well known to anyone who has been connected with university-based business/management schools in the past 25 years, enrollment (as predicted in both Foundation reports) has surged throughout the period from 1959 to the early 1980s. This can be seen clearly in Table 4.2, which shows a steady and strong increase in the number of bachelor's and master's degrees granted. The number of bachelor's degrees doubled during the decade of the sixties and redoubled again in the seventies. The increase in master's degrees granted was even more dramatic, in terms of percentage increase. Master's degrees earned in business quadrupled in the sixties and then almost tripled again in the seventies. The last column in Table 4.2

TABLE 4.2
EARNED DEGREES IN BUSINESS: 1960 TO 1983
(Rounded to Nearest 1000)

Year	BBA Degrees	BBA/Total Bachelor Degrees	Master's (MBA) Degrees	MBA/Total Master's Degrees
1959–1960	52,000	—	5,000	8.2%
1962–1963	54,000	13.1%	6,000	6.3
1967–1968	80,000	12.6	18,000	10.1
1972–1973	128,000	13.8	31,000	11.8
1977–1978	161,000	17.5	48,000	15.6
1982–1983	227,000	23.4	65,000	22.5

Source: National Center for Education Statistics.

shows that the increase in undergraduate business enrollment outstripped that of the rest of the campus, as the percentage of bachelor's degrees awarded in business rose from 13.8% in the 1960–1961 academic year to 22.6% in 1981–1982. Thus, business school enrollments during the 25-year period were increasing both absolutely and relative to total university enrollments.

This growth was accomplished both by additional universities and colleges offering business programs and by enrollment increases in existing programs. However, as Table 4.3 shows, the latter factor appears to be most important in recent years. The number of institutions offering business degrees increased, but not in proportion to the total enrollment growth. This would indicate, not surprisingly, that those colleges that chose to add a business program had smaller numbers of students majoring in this area compared with those institutions already offering such programs. Thus, new entrants came into "the market," but they were less of a factor in total growth of business school enrollments than the "old" players.

TABLE 4.3
NUMBER OF INSTITUTIONS GRANTING DEGREES IN BUSINESS AND MANAGEMENT: 1974 TO 1982

Year	Granting BBA Degrees	Granting Master's Degrees	Total
1973–1974	1057	389	1079
1974–1975	1099	412	1104
1975–1976	1136	428	1156
1976–1977	1156	463	1177
1977–1978	1177	480	1201
1978–1979	1197	511	1224
1979–1980	n/a	n/a	n/a
1980–1981	1233	539	1258
1981–1982	1244	544	1277

Source: National Center for Education Statistics.

These very large increases in the number of students wanting to major in business at both the undergraduate and master's degree levels had at least two major impacts. First, of course, as we discuss in the following chapter, schools had to scramble to obtain qualified faculty and other related resources in order to staff the increased number of courses. Second, and most important for consideration in this chapter, in principle, schools could be more selective in deciding whom to admit from the deluge of applicants. In practice, however, many schools, especially at the undergraduate level, had to keep accepting all university-enrolled students who wanted to major in business because of university-wide policies, and hence their selectivity did not increase. They were, in effect, forced to tread water with regard to improving student quality. However, the more elite private schools offering undergraduate programs and almost all schools offering master's (typically MBA) degree programs had the "luxury" of being more selective *if* they chose to do so. Whether this in fact happened, of course, depended greatly on the individual circumstances of various schools. Some held their enrollments virtually constant and hence automatically became more selective as the number of applicants increased. Other schools simply enlarged their programs more or less in proportion to the applicant increase and thus maintained a fairly steady level of student quality. Still others, if they chose—and some schools undoubtedly did—could (if they were not concerned about the relevant AACSB Accreditation Standard) take advantage of the greater numbers of applicants by admitting a high percentage of those who applied largely irrespective of their quality.

Across the entire range of all schools, therefore, the impact on student quality of the increased number of students desiring to take business curricula at either the undergraduate or graduate level was highly variable. At some schools quality no doubt increased, at many other schools it remained constant, and at others it may have dropped. The question of whether business students in toto, relative to the rest of the campus, were stronger academically than their 1950s counterparts will be addressed after we examine the steps that the AACSB took to strengthen accreditation standards relating to student admission.

Changes in AACSB Standards   Prior to 1961, the AACSB had no accreditation standards relating to admissions at either the graduate or undergraduate level. By 1965, still no mention of admissions standards was made at the baccalaureate level. However, by this time, a rudimentary standard regarding admissions at the graduate level did appear in the published Standards. It stated (in part) that "it is expected...that admission will be granted only to students showing high promise of success in postgraduate business study. Various measures may be used..." to assess this "promise." The "various measures" listed included test scores on the Admission Test for Graduate Study in Business (the ATGSB, which was the forerunner of the current Graduate Management Admission Test, the GMAT), undergraduate grades, and the candidate's rank in "his [sic] collegiate graduating class." However, it is important to note that no quantitative cutoff criteria were specified, only that "ordinarily...the candidate will stand well above average by most of the measures" (AACSB Standards, approved 1961 and updated in 1963 and 1965).

Gradually, more and more specific language was adopted that was intended to have the effect of setting an unambiguous level of minimum quality for entering students, *especially at the graduate level*. By 1969, the relevant undergraduate Standard stated that "admission and retention standards should compare favorably to those of the university or college as a whole." The applicable standard for master's degree students was, by 1974, understandably more specific and has changed little in the past 10 years. The current Standard states that "it is expected...that admission will be granted only to students showing high promise of success in postgraduate business study." Furthermore, and most important, "high promise" was specified in terms of "at least 80% [of newly enrolled students]" meeting specific quantitative cutoff criteria involving a numerical formula of students' undergraduate grade-point averages and their GMAT test scores. To show just how much of a change this was from the situation existing in the late 1950s, one has only to consider that in the Carnegie report Pierson noted that only "some ten or twelve schools apply quite strict entrance requirements, and [only] eighteen institutions now stipulate that all applicants must take the admission test for graduate study in business" (p. 64).

As these progressively changing Standards indicate, the AACSB did respond (although not immediately) over the next two decades to the Foundation reports' recommendations that more emphasis be placed by schools on raising admission standards. Since virtually all undergraduate programs are under the jurisdiction of university-wide admission standards, the AACSB Standards have less direct influence at that level. However, at the graduate level where business schools have much more direct control over their own admissions, the Assembly moved to adopt increasingly tougher and more precisely specified Standards. (The other major concern in the Gordon and Howell and Pierson reports relating to student quality involved the necessity for schools to hold students to higher standards of performance—providing them with more rigorous academic programs—once admitted. Since this issue has more to do with curriculum matters, it was dealt with in Chapter 3.) These higher admission requirements imposed by the changing Standards at the master's level, coupled with the steady increase in applicants, permitted (indeed, required) accredited AACSB member schools to make definite improvements in student quality. At the undergraduate level, for the reasons indicated, the possibilities were much more limited.

The Current Situation   In the past few years, the rate of growth in the flow of applicants to business schools appears to have begun leveling off somewhat. Since the numbers of those desiring a business education could not be expected to increase indefinitely, enrollments may be reaching an asymptote. If so, the question is whether, in a few years, there will then begin to be a substantial drop-off in the number of applicants. The present Project was not designed for the purpose of making short-term predictions, nor for engaging in elaborate analyses of enrollment projections. (The AACSB itself and other agencies, such as the Graduate Management Admission Council, have the appropriate resources for such projections.) However, to the extent that employers' actions in deciding to hire or not hire graduates with certain types of academic backgrounds affect students' choices of majors, we will be able to offer some data (later in this chapter) that may be relevant. These data appear to indicate that, at the present time, most firms do not expect to decrease their emphasis (relative to what it is at present) on hiring business school graduates—either at the undergraduate or the MBA level. Of course, there is nothing to prevent a change at any time in such expectations on the part of employers if other factors change.

Recent data on the intellectual aptitude of undergraduate business students *across all schools* requiring the American College Test (ACT) for admission indicate that there has been no major change in the their ranking when compared to students entering other majors. This is shown in Table 4.4. The average composite score for those indicating a preference for majoring in business has remained constant from 1974 through 1984, and this score places this group below the physical and biological sciences groups, very near the social sciences group, and just above the fine arts and education preference groups. (Relative standings of any of these groups changed very little during this 10-year period.) A somewhat similar conclusion can be drawn from data supplied by the Graduate Management Admission Council concerning GMAT scores by undergraduate degree for years between 1977 and 1982 (see Table 4.5). Applicants (to graduate business programs) with undergraduate business majors did improve their scores substantially during that period, but so did almost all other groups (except those from fine arts and education). Thus, undergraduate business majors retained more or less their same ranking: well below engineer-

TABLE 4.4
ACT COMPOSITE SCORES OF HIGH SCHOOL SENIORS BY INDICATED CONCENTRATION PREFERENCE

	Average Composite Scores		
Concentration Preference	**1974–1975**	**1979–1980**	**1984–1985**
Biological sciences	21	21	22
Education	19	18	18
Engineering	21	22	22
Fine/applied arts	19	18	18
Medicine	23	23	23
Mathematics	25	23	23
Physical sciences (general)	24	24	23
Physics	26	27	26
Social sciences	20	20	20
Business (general)	19	19	19

Source: American College Testing program.

TABLE 4.5
GMAT SCORES BY UNDERGRADUATE DEGREE

Degree	Average Composite Scores					
	1977–1978	1978–1979	1979–1980	1980–1981	1981–1982	1982–1983
Fine arts	472.69	469.94	468.64	499.94	473.97	479.27
Economics	469.29	470.78	472.55	482.13	488.49	499.61
Education	443.17	442.51	441.99	448.48	447.95	447.83
Psychology	463.88	465.38	468.29	473.64	476.80	483.23
Engineering	490.87	497.22	500.48	505.28	509.57	526.36
Mathematics	518.64	528.25	525.27	530.78	532.48	539.94
Physics	523.90	533.99	524.65	540.44	538.95	548.25
Accounting	444.92	446.79	451.20	458.91	463.83	473.59
Finance	449.60	450.95	454.55	464.09	465.62	476.31
Management	418.95	423.21	422.94	430.91	434.94	443.30
Marketing	423.85	427.67	427.14	432.91	435.23	441.72

Source: Graduate Management Admission Council

ing, mathematics, and physical science majors, and also below economics and psychology majors. Those with undergraduate business majors specializing in finance and accounting had (by 1982) pulled even with fine arts and surpassed education majors, but that was not true of those specializing in management and marketing (who were still below fine arts and about even with education majors). Overall, then, it appears that the quality of those graduating from high school who plan to major in business (Table 4.4) has not increased, and both entering and leaving undergraduate business students do not rank substantially different relative to all other undergraduates in 1982 than they did 5 or 10 years earlier.

An important caveat must be noted with respect to these data: They do not differentiate by type of business school. Thus, it is not possible to compare scores for accredited versus nonaccredited schools, nor to track either group across time. If tightening AACSB Standards has had any effect at the under-graduate level, it is not possible to determine this from these data, which come from a complete cross section of schools that fall on both sides of the accred-itation line. What would be more definitive from the standpoint of drawing con-clusions in this area would be data that track graduates across time from AACSB-accredited schools as a separate group. So far as we could determine, such data do not presently exist.

Also, it should be stressed that Tables 4.4 and 4.5 supply data only with respect to undergraduates. No reliable data are available to compare the intel-lectual aptitude of students applying to master's programs in business versus those applying to other similar-level professional programs (master's level en-gineering programs, graduate architecture programs, law schools, education schools, etc.). Again, for such comparisons it would be useful to differentiate those applying to or graduating from AACSB-accredited schools from those attending nonaccredited schools. Such data, if available across time, would per-

mit a direct assessment of the effects of the very specific changes made in recent years in the AACSB Standards for graduate programs.

Current Criticisms of Business School Graduates

In contrast to questions about the quality of students at entry into business
school programs, which were a central concern in the two Foundation reports
25 years ago, today's critics talk more about what students are like as they
leave business programs as graduates. It is obvious, of course, as we noted
earlier, that graduates are the products of their academic programs as well as
the maturing of their own personal characteristics. Hence, criticisms leveled
against graduates are, fundamentally, criticisms also addressed to the types of
programs that helped produce them.

If one reviews the various articles and other published critiques relating to
business school graduates, it becomes clear that most of the comments appear
to be directed more toward MBA graduates than toward bachelor's degree graduates, although frequently a critic will not make this explicit distinction. Furthermore, some of the criticisms of MBA graduates are even more narrowly
focused on those from the so-called top ten schools because they have the highest proportion of the "high-salary" MBAs going into the most prestigious consulting, financial, and other types of firms. This category of MBAs makes a
highly visible and (from some perspectives) appealing "target."

The critics of current business school graduates have singled out four major
areas of concern:

1 *Overly high expectations* This is a criticism that is particularly aimed at
MBAs rather than at business school undergraduates. A typical version of this
complaint was voiced by a personnel director quoted in an article on business
schools in the early 1980s:

> Would I employ an MBA? The short answer is "no." First, we don't like the "crown
> prince" syndrome. Second, we're not really prepared to pay the very high salaries
> they ask for. (*International Management,* August 1981, p. 87.)

The high expectations that are the cause of this concern (once an MBA is hired)
usually refer to the issue of advancement opportunities and the related subissues of salary increases and high-level, "exciting" tasks to perform. The charge
is that MBAs are impatient and expect to begin to carry out functions normally
assigned to upper-level managers very shortly after their arrival in a firm. "They
expect to be CEO in two years," would be a typical, albeit cynical, version of
this complaint.

2 *Lack of organizational loyalty* This criticism is related to the first one. If
MBAs have unrealistically high expectations that cannot be met, and if they
are, as alleged, rather impatient, it would seem to follow that they would not
hesitate to change organizations frequently. And this is the charge that is often
made in the popular press. For example, a top executive who was quoted in

Time magazine in 1981 appeared to sum up the beliefs of a number of critics when he said, "They [MBAs] tend to be more loyal to their personal careers than to any company."

3 *Poor communication and interpersonal skills* This is a criticism that appears to be applied to both graduates of business bachelor's degree programs as well as to those from master's programs, although perhaps in greater intensity to the former than to the latter. Various surveys carried out in the early 1980s indicated that there was a widespread perception in the practicing world of business that business school graduates were deficient in communication skills—both oral and, especially, written. Often such criticisms also included the area of interpersonal skills, even though that capability is at least as much related to leadership as to communication.

4 *Lack of leadership skills* As noted above, one component of leadership relates to interpersonal skills, and this area has been identified by some critics as, at best, not a strength of business school graduates and, at worst, a significant deficiency. Another major element of leadership as typically defined can be summed up in such concepts as "vision" and a "willingness to take calculated risks." Here, again, critics frequently fault business school graduates. One claim is that they are overly focused on the short term at the expense of taking a broader, deeper, and longer-range perspective. Also, they are seen by some observers as too cautious and afraid to take actions that cannot be backed up by detailed, quantitative analyses. (It might be noted, in passing, that on the surface this criticism could be seen as somewhat contradictory to the first criticism cited, namely, that MBAs want to assume the decision-making responsibilities of top-level jobs in the organization too quickly.)

Much of the data on students and graduates that will be presented in the next sections of this chapter will relate to these and other criticisms, although, as we stated in Chapter 1, the Project was not designed to address each and every criticism directly. We begin with a look at undergraduates, followed by a separate discussion of master's students and graduates. Each group will be viewed from both the university and the corporate perspective.

UNDERGRADUATES

In this section (and similarly in the following section on master's students/graduates) we will consider five issues pertaining to undergraduate business students and graduates: (1) their self-described reasons for selecting a business major, (2) their overall quality as seen by university and corporate observers, (3) their specific strengths and weaknesses as evaluated by members of these two observer groups, (4) their perceived breadth versus specialized depth in business-related subject matter, and (5) the recruiting policies of business firms as they relate to this category of business school graduates.

Students' Self-Described Reasons for Choosing a Business Major

Any self-report descriptions of motives for taking actions are always suspect because of a presumed need for individuals to provide socially acceptable reasons for their actions, whether or not those are the "real" reasons (which in any event are impossible to know). With this admonition in mind, one can see from Table 4.6 that about one-fifth of the undergraduate respondents indicated that they chose business as a major for strictly intrinsic reasons; i.e., "this field [business/management] is really interesting." About two-thirds said they were attracted to the field of business/management because of job and career opportunities. With respect to another question about who influenced them the most to choose a major in business/management, about three-quarters of the respondents checked "decided on this major principally by myself," while 16% said that the primary influence was their parents or other family members.

When asked whether they had "serious[ly] consider[ed] another major instead of a business major when... [they] first came to college," half (51%) answered "yes." In a follow-up question concerning why they did not pursue that other major, the most often selected response (out of eleven alternatives offered) was that they thought they would eventually become "bored with that field." The second most frequently checked response was "lack of long-term career opportunities in that field." Interestingly, and indicating a certain degree of candor on the part of the graduating seniors, the third most frequent response was "that major [was] academically too demanding," which was checked by about 10% of the respondents.

Perceived Quality

University Perspective   From the university perspective, undergraduate majors were rated generally on the positive side. On a 10-point scale (with 10 = high), deans rated them ("the typical graduate from your undergraduate program") 7.3, but business school faculty judged them slightly lower at 6.8. (Deans from Category I schools rated their undergraduates significantly higher than did deans from Category III schools.) Provosts, on the other hand, were in

TABLE 4.6
BBA STUDENTS' SELF-DESCRIPTION OF PRIMARY
REASON FOR DECIDING TO MAJOR IN BUSINESS
(Percent Checking One of Six Alternatives)

"Business...really interesting"	21%
"Business...provides...challenging career"	44
"Business...provides...good job upon graduation"	23
"Business...provides...high income"	7
"Business...[provides] high prestige career"	4
"Other"	1

Note: Column totals 100% within rounding.

between, giving them an overall rating of 7.1. Perhaps more revealingly, when provosts were asked to compare business undergraduates with undergraduates from throughout the campus, 43% rated the business students as "somewhat above or well above" those on the rest of the campus, whereas only 9% rated them as "somewhat below or well below" other undergraduates. These questionnaire findings conformed closely to our interview data from provosts. If provosts (virtually none of whom were formerly members of business school faculties) can be assumed to be somewhat objective on such matters, it would seem that the quality of business undergraduates is not a matter of major concern to the campus at large. They seem to be at least representative of, if not slightly above, the quality of undergraduates at large. Of course, there are specific exceptions in particular universities, and occasionally this kind of exception was made clear to us in our campus interviews with provosts.

We also were interested in perceptions of whether the quality of business undergraduates had been increasing, decreasing, or staying about the same during the past 10 years. There was general agreement by all sets of university respondents (deans, faculty members, and provosts) that the quality had increased. Again, to cite provosts' responses, 72% said quality had increased and only 2% said it had decreased.

Corporate Perspective If we turn to the corporate perspective on business undergraduates, we see somewhat the same picture. CEOs and SCEs rate the quality of business school graduates (both undergraduates *and* MBAs, not differentiated) as about 6.9 to 7.0 on a 10-point scale, and members of business advisory councils give business undergraduates an overall rating of 7.3. The latter also believe, by a wide margin, that the quality level has been going up in the last 10 years.

About 90% of vice presidents of human resources (VPHRs), the chief personnel officers of business firms, indicate in response to a questionnaire item that bachelor's degree business graduates have worked out "well" or "very well" in their firms. (This compares with about the same % who responded similarly when asked about "technical," e.g., engineering, graduates and about 80% who believe non-business-school, i.e., liberal arts, graduates have done that well once in the firm.) When these VPHRs were asked to compare business (undergraduate) graduates with liberal arts graduates in terms of "how successful as managers" they have been in their organizations, about half (51%) said that there was no difference in their performance, but 42% said that business school graduates have done better, compared to only 7% who indicated that liberal arts graduates had the advantage. For a variety of reasons, these latter percentages must be regarded with caution, but overall, both the interview and questionnaire data from the corporate sector indicate a general level of satisfaction with the quality of business school undergraduates. There are some definite concerns, however, about certain specific areas, as will be seen in the next section.

Specific Strengths and Weaknesses

University Perspective: Strengths   If we first look at perceived strengths of business school bachelor's degree graduates, then there is one characteristic that deans, faculty members, and placement directors agree on: These students have a high degree of "motivation to work" (see Table 4.7). This was the number one strength (out of thirteen listed characteristics) cited by two of those groups and the second strength mentioned by faculty. The latter regarded "knowledge about a particular content area" as the chief strength of business undergraduates. This item—content area knowledge—was regarded as the second strongest positive characteristic by the other two groups.

A comparison of deans' perceptions of relative strengths by category of school shows that there were five potential strengths for which there were statistically significant differences across schools. These were "motivation," "analytical skills," "content area knowledge," "computer skills," and "appropriate self-confidence". For each characteristic, except for "content area knowledge," the highest percentage of deans giving a rating of "major strength" were Category I deans (with Category III deans using this rating least often for their students). For "content area knowledge", the highest percentage of deans rating it a major strength were the Category II deans.

As one item that will become of interest later on, it should be noted in Table 4.7 that 29% of all deans rated "realistic expectations" as a "major strength," the fourth highest rated strength of undergraduates as seen by deans. This perception can be compared subsequently with corporate perceptions. It should also be noted in Table 4.7 that faculty members were more conservative than deans in applying the label "major strength" to most of the characteristics possessed by undergraduate business students.

TABLE 4.7
PERCEIVED *STRENGTHS* OF *BBA GRADUATES* FROM OWN SCHOOL:
BY FACULTY, DEANS, AND PLACEMENT DIRECTORS
(Percent Checking "Major Strength")

Strength	Faculty	Deans	Placement Directors
High motivation to work	33%	58%	72%
Leadership/interpersonal skills	6	11	29
Analytical skills	16	31	30
Knowledge of a particular content area	40	51	60
Computer skills	9	17	16
Knowledge about how business world really operates	7	11	14
Understanding legal/social/political environment of business	6	11	9
Oral communication	4	10	19
Written communication	4	15	14
Breadth of perspective	10	20	26
Maturity	16	27	33
Realistic expectations	15	29	29
Appropriate self-confidence	15	23	26

Undergraduate business majors (seniors in their final semester) also were asked to rate themselves on the list of positive characteristics. The trait/capability receiving the highest percentage of "major strength" ratings was "maturity", with 72% of undergraduates describing themselves in this manner, versus 27% of deans and 16% of faculty using this rating to describe the maturity of their undergraduates. Another capability where there were substantial differences in how undergraduates saw themselves versus how others saw them was "leadership/interpersonal skills": 47% of undergraduates rated this a major strength, while only 11% of deans and 6% of faculty members believed this to be a "major" undergraduate strength. In fact, on almost all the thirteen listed capabilities, undergraduates rated themselves considerably higher than deans or faculty did, except for one: "content area knowledge" (where they rated themselves similar to how the faculty rated them and slightly lower than the deans rated them).

University Perspective: Weaknesses Clearly, from university-based vantage points, the major weaknesses of baccalaureate graduates from business schools center around communication. Deans and faculty members were agreed that written and oral communication skills ranked as the number 1 and number 2 deficiencies of business undergraduates. Also, this was rather consistently the case across all categories of schools (especially with respect to written communication skills). Although undergraduates agreed that oral communication skills (relatively) ranked near the top of any deficiencies, only 7% saw this as a "serious weakness," compared to 17% of deans and 25% of faculty members viewing it this way. Undergraduates also did not believe that their writing skills constituted an area of serious weakness, with only 6% characterizing this area in this manner, compared to 20% of the deans and 36% of the faculty members. Undergraduates, by a slight margin, rated "lack of understanding about the legal/social/political environment" as their number one (relative) weakness, with 8% seeing it as a "serious" weakness and 47% regarding it as a "moderate" weakness.

Corporate Perspective: Strengths Corporate respondents (specifically, VPHRs and operating managers) agreed with deans and faculty members that the top-ranking positive characteristic of graduates from undergraduate business programs is their "motivation to work". The second-ranking characteristic (in terms of receiving a rating of "major strength") in the corporate perspective is undergraduates' "analytical skills." Also, these corporate respondents accorded a relatively high ranking to "knowledge of a particular content area," but their absolute rating of this capability was much lower than that by deans and faculty members (16% of VPHRs and 18% of operating managers said that this was a "major strength" of business undergraduates as viewed from their experience, compared to 51% of deans and 40% of faculty members). In general, corporate respondents were slightly more restrained in using "major strength" to describe potential strengths of undergraduates, but there were some specific exceptions. For example, VPHRs rated the "analytical skills" and "oral communication skills" of undergraduates higher than did business school faculty (although not higher than did deans). Also, the views of VPHRs differed rather considerably from those of undergraduates of themselves on such traits as "maturity": Only about 5% of VPHRs and operating managers rated this as a "major strength," compared to the previously noted 72% of undergraduates who used this self-rating. On every single one of the thirteen traits/capabilities listed in the questionnaire, the percentages of undergraduates using "major strength" to describe themselves was substantially higher than the percentages of line and staff corporate executives. In this sense, there is a tangible "perceptual gap."

Breadth/Depth of Graduates of Business/Management Programs

University Perspective   Collegiate business schools—ever since the first one was started in this country in 1881 by Joseph Wharton at the University of Pennsylvania—have always faced a nettlesome yet highly important issue: how to set the balance between breadth and depth that a graduate of a program, whether undergraduate or master's, should have. In concrete terms, the issue can be rephrased as follows: To what extent should graduates be prepared for the *first job* after graduation versus a longer-term career in business/management. If the former objective is emphasized, a student may do well when initially out of school but may falter somewhat on the way up the corporate ladder. If the latter is a program's focus, a graduate may have a difficult time in early jobs and possibly never attain (or attain relatively late in his or her career) a job level which emphasizes broader responsibilities and skills. This is an issue with no absolute answers, and schools have struggled in various ways to reach their own position on this matter—often not addressing it directly and letting the issue be decided by default rather than by explicit attention. It is also an issue that is relevant to both undergraduate and master's degree programs. Because it is such an important issue, in our opinion, we devoted several questionnaire items and corresponding interview time to it and thus will discuss it at some length in this chapter. In the paragraphs that follow, we consider it in the undergraduate context, and in a later section we take it up as a graduate-level issue.

In the university setting, four groups—deans, faculty members, placement directors, and undergraduate business majors—were asked to respond to a questionnaire item that asked how well "the typical graduate ["you" in the case of the undergraduates themselves] of your undergraduate program has been prepared *by the program* to assume their *first job* after graduation?" The results are presented in Table 4.8. As can be seen, placement directors were (relatively) the most positive in their answers and undergraduates (graduating seniors) were the least positive. However, all four groups, including the students

TABLE 4.8
RATINGS OF *BBA GRADUATES* FROM OWN SCHOOL IN TERMS OF "HOW WELL
PREPARED [FOR] *FIRST JOB* AFTER GRADUATION":
BY FACULTY, DEANS, PLACEMENT DIRECTORS, AND BBA STUDENTS
(Percent Checking One of Four Alternatives)

	Faculty	Deans	Placements Directors	BBA Students
Very well	27%	40%	48%	34%
Moderately well	63	55	51	59
Moderately under	9	4	1	6
Inadequately	1	0	0	1

Note: Columns total 100% within rounding.

themselves, felt that their respective programs had prepared them at least moderately well for the first job. More than one-fourth of all groups, in fact, felt that the preparation was "very good." There were no significant differences across categories of schools (using responses from deans) in terms of how well the schools were doing in this type of preparation.

Table 4.9 presents the comparable data regarding views about preparation of undergraduate business majors for assuming "eventually a position of significant managerial leadership." Again, all four groups gave generally positive responses. However, for this question faculty were (relatively) the most skeptical; 30% of faculty respondents felt that their own school's undergraduate program had led to moderate *under*preparation or even "inadequate" preparation. In general, if Table 4.9 is compared to Table 4.8, a smaller percentage of respondents answer that undergraduate students have been "very well" prepared for eventual leadership positions compared to first jobs. Also, for the latter question, there was a statistically significant difference across categories of schools with respect to the use of the "very well prepared" alternative: The respective percents from Category I to II to III schools, in terms of deans' responses, were 29, 25, and 14%.

Another questionnaire item asked university-based respondents to describe (*not* evaluate) the "balance" that graduates from the undergraduate program

TABLE 4.9
RATINGS OF *BBA GRADUATES* FROM OWN SCHOOL IN TERMS OF "HOW WELL
PREPARED [FOR] EVENTUALLY A POSITION OF SIGNIFICANT MANAGERIAL
LEADERSHIP":
BY FACULTY, DEANS, PLACEMENT DIRECTORS, AND BBA STUDENTS
(Percent Checking One of Four Alternatives)

	Faculty	Deans	Placement Directors	BBA Students
Very well	12%	19%	40%	20%
Moderately well	58	63	56	67
Moderately under	24	16	4	12
Inadequately	6	1	0	1

Note: Columns total 100% within rounding.

TABLE 4.10
PERCEIVED BALANCE BETWEEN *BREADTH* AND (SPECIALIZED) *DEPTH* WITHIN AREAS
OF BUSINESS/MANAGEMENT FOR *BBA GRADUATES* FROM OWN SCHOOL:
BY FACULTY, DEANS, PLACEMENT DIRECTORS, AND BBA STUDENTS
(Percent Checking One of Three Alternatives)

	Faculty	Deans	Placements Directors	BBA Students
Too much breadth	22%	13%	13%	31%
Appropriate balance	64	73	78	61
Too much depth	13	14	9	7

Note: Columns total 100% within rounding.

have "after going through the entire degree program, between overall breadth
of knowledge in business/management vs. depth of knowledge in a particular
specialized area within business/management." The summary responses are
shown in Table 4.10. A solid majority of all four groups believe that their undergraduate students have an "appropriate" balance. However, in the case of
both faculty and students, those who do not think the balance is appropriate
tend to believe that there is too much emphasis on breadth compared to specialized depth. Also, there are significant differences in deans' perceptions by
type of school. Among those deans (27% of all deans) indicating that there was
not appropriate balance, Category I school deans tended to believe that there
was too much emphasis on specialized depth, whereas Category III deans felt
exactly the reverse. Category II deans, in this respect, were more similar to
those from Category I than III schools.

In a further effort to gain an understanding of how various groups of respondents viewed the breadth/depth issue, several items were placed in most of the
questionnaire forms (both for university and corporate groups) that attempted
to highlight the distinction. This was done by a series of questions that asked
about two hypothetical persons:

Person A

Has a well-developed area of specialized knowledge and is well-prepared to perform
effectively in the *first job* (with a minimum of additional training); however, it is uncertain whether this person's education has prepared him/her for an *eventual* position of significant leadership in an organization.

Person B

Has a broad background and knowledge base that has prepared him/her for an *eventual* position of significant leadership in an organization; however, it is uncertain
whether this person's education has prepared him/her to perform effectively in the
first job without substantial additional training.

The findings relating to this series of questions are summarized in Table 4.11 and are discussed sequentially below.

One questionnaire item asked deans, faculty members, and placement directors to indicate which type of person—Person A or Person B—employers "most like to recruit *currently* as a new-hire graduate from business/management school undergraduate programs." As can be seen in Table 4.11, three-quarters of the deans and two-thirds of the faculty (and 60% of the placement directors) believed that employers prefer Person A graduates (the ones with more specialization). Across categories of schools, Category II deans were most convinced of this employer preference for specialized knowledge.

Another item asked the same question except in terms of the type that corporations *should be* hiring. Thus, this question was aimed at respondents' prescriptive views. The distribution of answers here (obtained from deans and placement directors) was almost exactly the reverse of that for the previous question. About two-thirds of all deans and placement directors (as Table 4.11 shows) felt that corporate employers should be hiring Person B graduates (the ones with a broader background but less suited for the initial job). Deans from Category I schools were virtually unanimous in this view, and deans from Category II and III schools were in favor of recruiting Person B graduates by about a 2:1 margin.

Additional similar questions asked about types of (undergraduate) graduates turned out by business schools in general and by *this* business school. As shown

TABLE 4.11
RESPONSES TO PERSON A/PERSON B QUESTIONS FOR *BBA GRADUATES*:
BY UNIVERSITY-BASED RESPONDENTS
(Percent Checking "Person A" Alternative)

a. Type of BBA graduate employers *"most like* to recruit":

	Faculty	Deans	Placement Directors	BACs
Person A	65%	76%	60%	

b. Type of BBA graduate employers *"should be"* recruiting:

	Faculty	Deans	Placement Directors	BACs
Person A	—	33%	30%	—

c. Type of BBA graduate "being turned out by *business schools in general*":

	Faculty	Deans	Placement Directors	BACs
Person A	—	83%	—	—

d. Type of BBA graduate "being turned out by *your own school*":

	Faculty	Deans	Placement Directors	BACs
Person A	63%	65%	51%	48%

e. Type of BBA graduate *"your school should be turning out"*:

	Faculty	Deans	Placement Directors	BACs
Person A	38%	28%	29%	29%

Note: For all parts of table, A and B answers total 100%.

in Table 4.11, deans (the only group for which this question was asked) believed overwhelmingly—83% versus 17%—that business schools in general are turning out Person A graduates (those with greater specialization), and there were no significant differences in this view in relation to a dean's category of school. When deans were asked which type of person *their* school is producing, the percentage indicating Person A was smaller (65%) but still much greater than the percentage indicating Person B. Interestingly, there were no significant differences by category of school in deans' views of the type of person their own schools were turning out. Faculty members' perceptions were nearly identical to those of deans—63% believed that their own schools were graduating Person A graduates. However, placement directors and business advisory council (BAC) members were much more evenly divided: 51% of the former and 48% of the latter indicated that the school with which they were affiliated is producing Person A graduates.

Perhaps the most crucial question concerned the type of graduate that "*this school should be turning out* 10 to 15 years from now." The results for this question, as shown in the bottom row of Table 4.11, present a rather striking contrast with those for the preceding questions concerning the types currently being turned out. Whereas about two-thirds of deans and faculty members believed that their own schools are currently producing Person A graduates, the reverse was the case when they were asked about the type of person their schools *should be* turning out 10 to 15 years from now. A substantial majority of both groups, as well as placement directors and BAC members, think that their schools ought to be turning out Person B graduates—the ones with greater breadth. Clearly, there appears to be a major difference between what schools are doing now and what those connected with them on the university side (including those members of the business community who have direct involvement with business schools through their BAC membership) advocate they should be doing in terms of the types of bachelor's degree graduates they are producing.

Corporate Perspective   Corporate respondents were much less certain than deans and faculty members that bachelor's degree business graduates are "very well" prepared for the first job. Only about 15% (of VPHRs and operating managers, the two groups asked this question) felt this way, compared with about 40 and 25% of deans and faculty, respectively (see Table 4.8). With respect to how well graduates from undergraduate programs are prepared for "eventual positions of significant managerial leadership," the opinions of the corporate respondents were closer to those of respondents from the university. In fact, the distribution of answers of VPHRs to this question corresponded almost perfectly with that of the faculty, and operating managers also were fairly close to (but slightly more negative than) the faculty response patterns. (As Table 4.9 showed, deans were slightly more positive than faculty members on this question.)

Several sets of corporate respondents were asked about which type of graduate—Person A or Person B—their own organization likes to hire, which type

TABLE 4.12

RESPONSES TO PERSON A/PERSON B QUESTIONS FOR *BBA GRADUATES*:
BY CORPORATE-BASED RESPONDENTS
(Percent Checking "Person A" Alternative)

a. Type of BBA graduate *"this organization prefers to recruit"*:

	CEOs	SCEs	VPHRs	OpMgrs	College Relations	BACs
Person A	33%	33%	35%	46%	35%	45%

b. Type of BBA graduate employers *"should be"* recruiting:

	CEOs	SCEs	VPHRs	OpMgrs	College Relations	BACs*
Person A	—	—	—	32%	—	28%

c. Type of BBA graduate "being turned out by *business schools in general*":

	CEOs	SCEs	VPHRs	OpMgrs	College Relations	BACs*
Person A	57%	58%	62%	—	57%	48%

*BAC members answered for corporate employers in general.
Note: For all parts of table, A and B answers total 100%.

their organization should hire, and which type they say business schools are turning out. With respect to the first of these questions, as can be seen in Table 4.12, corporate respondents were much less likely to say that their organizations prefer the more specialized graduate (Person A) than was the case with university respondents' views of corporate preferences. (Compare the first row of Table 4.12 with the first row of Table 4.11.) The former, by a margin of about 2:1, say that their firms prefer to hire Person B graduates, whereas the view from the university, by a roughly similar margin, is that corporations prefer the narrower Person A graduates. Note, however, that operating managers (OpMgrs), who are lower in the organization than the CEOs, SCEs, and VPHRs, are somewhat closer in their perceptions to university respondents. This is also true of BAC members. The corporate respondents, however, are in general agreement with their university counterparts that the type of undergraduate currently being turned out by business schools is the person (A) with more specialized depth than breadth. Note, again, that BAC members are somewhat less sure of this than other corporate executives or deans and faculty members. (See the bottom row of Table 4.12 compared with the third and fourth rows of Table 4.11.)

Recruitment of Undergraduate Business Majors

University Perspective   Business school placement directors were asked to rank a list of attributes they thought employers value in their recruitment of undergraduate majors. At the top of their list (of what they thought business firms are looking for) was "appropriate knowledge about a particular content area (e.g., marketing, finance)." Tied for second were "highly motivated to work" and "appropriate leadership/interpersonal skills."

Corporate Perspective   Corporate college recruiting managers were asked the same question. The top three checked responses, of the thirteen listed alternatives, for this group were (1) "appropriate leadership/interpersonal skills," (2) "motivation," and (3) "content area knowledge." Thus there was general agreement between those on both sides of the recruiting function—those attempting to place business undergraduates and those responsible for recruiting them—although the corporate recruiters ranked leadership/interpersonal skills slightly higher, giving it the top rank.

Corporate recruiters also were asked, in both interviews and questionnaires, about their own firms' policies in connection with the hiring of business bachelor's degree recipients. Only about 10% said that their firms recruited from *any* college or university, while about half said their firms recruited from a "broadly selected" set of colleges/universities and 41% indicated that their companies recruited only from a "very highly selected set" of institutions. The most important factors affecting the set of schools from which their organizations recruit were, in order, the historic relationship between particular schools and the firm, the particular geographic location of a school, and the general reputation of the school. Ranked last in a list of seven possible factors influencing the choice of schools at which to recruit BBAs was "AACSB accreditation." Only 11 out of some 250 managers of college recruiting ranked this item among the top three (of seven) factors!

Finally, with respect to what they expect to happen in the next 10 years insofar as "this organization's emphasis on hiring BBAs" (for those firms that report they hire BBAs), about 60% of these recruiting managers generally expect their firms to retain about the same degree of emphasis. About one-third expect the emphasis to increase, and less than one in ten expect a decrease.

MASTER'S (MBA AND OTHER DEGREE) STUDENTS/GRADUATES

This section on master's students/graduates will consider the same five issues covered in the preceding section on undergraduate business majors. (For simplicity, in this section we will use the short-hand designation of MBA for all business master's degree students, since 87% of our some 1800 questionnaire respondents in this student group indicated that the title of the degree they were receiving was the MBA. We fully recognize that some schools use other designations for this degree, such as Master of Management, and that there are other more specialized degrees, such as Master of Science in Marketing or Master of Accounting, offered by some schools.)

Students' Self-Described Reasons for Obtaining an MBA Degree

Both full- and part-time MBA students in our sample ranked "high probability of challenging career opportunities" as their number one reason for deciding to obtain this degree. "Intrinsic interest" in business/management was the second-ranking reason given by part-time students and the third-ranking reason for full-time students. The latter indicated that the "high probability of a good job upon graduation" was their second-ranking reason for choosing to enroll in an MBA program.

Almost half (46%) of the current MBA students surveyed reported that they had *not* planned on obtaining an MBA degree at the time of graduation from their baccalaureate program. Thus, a considerable percentage of MBA students seem to have made the decision to seek the degree after they had been out working for 1 or more years following their bachelor's degree rather than having planned to do this while still an undergraduate. Presumably, work experiences of certain types had an influence on whether an advanced degree in business would be worthwhile.

Perceived Quality

University Perspective   As with their evaluations of undergraduate business students, business school deans and faculty members gave moderately high ratings of quality to their MBA students, although faculty (a median rating of 6.9 on a 10-point scale) were not quite as positive as deans (median rating of 7.4). This pattern and level of median ratings were very similar to those for undergraduate majors. (Corresponding to data for undergraduates, there was a statistically significant difference among deans across the three categories of schools, with Category I deans giving their students the highest ratings.) Provosts proved to be slightly more positive than even deans or faculty about their university's MBA students, giving them a 7.5 rating.

Deans were the most emphatic in their belief that the quality of MBA students had been improving the past 10 years, with 81% saying that the quality had increased and only 2% saying that it had decreased. Provosts and faculty members were somewhat more conservative in their views on this question, with their respective percentages being 63 and 2% for the former and 57 and 7% for the latter.

Corporate Perspective   Views of CEOs and SCEs (as explained in the preceding section on undergraduates) regarding the quality of MBAs were not differentiated from those regarding undergraduate business majors. As noted previously, these two groups of top executives rated business school graduates overall at 6.9 to 7.0. Members of BACs gave MBA students in their schools a rating of 7.2 and also were almost unanimous in their belief that the quality of these students had improved over the past decade.

Corporate VPHRs were *not* as positive about their organizations' experiences with MBAs *compared to* business bachelor's degree graduates. Whereas about 90% of the VPHRs had indicated that BBAs had worked out "very well" or "well" in their firms, the percentage dropped to 75% for MBAs. Also, VPHRs were less sure that the first-year performance of MBAs had improved over the past 10 years when compared with the first-year performance of BBAs, although many more of them (44%) thought it had improved rather than deteriorated (4%). When these senior personnel executives were asked about "how successful as managers in their organization" MBAs had been compared to those without this degree, about half (47%) said that there was no difference, 42% said that MBAs had done better than non-MBAs, and only 11% said that MBAs had done worse. The VPHRs did, however, appear to be highly concerned about the rate of turnover of MBAs. Some 41% felt that the turnover rate of this group was "higher than the organization thought it should be," compared with 22 and 17% who thought this about technical graduates and BBAs, respectively.

Corporate college recruiting managers were asked whether their own firms were finding the "attributes they were looking for in the pool of new MBA graduates." About half (47%) answered that their organizations did find these attributes "in a broad sample" of MBA applicants, but at least as many (51%) said that they found the relevant attributes in "only a fairly narrow sample" of MBA graduates. Taken at face value, this latter figure would indicate that many corporations look beyond an applicant's mere possession of an MBA degree and prefer to be highly selective in hiring among this large pool of potential employees. (See the later subsection on MBA recruiting policies.)

Specific Strengths and Weaknesses

University Perspective: Strengths   "High motivation to work," as it had been with business school undergraduates, was seen by deans and faculty members as the greatest strength of MBAs. The second most positive characteristic attributed to MBAs by both these two groups was, however, different than for undergraduates: "maturity." ("Maturity" was not ranked at the bottom for undergraduates, but neither was it at the top.) Deans, especially, and faculty cited "realistic expectations" as the third-ranking "major strength" of their MBA students, which is particularly interesting in light of corporate perceptions to be described shortly. MBA students, in their own self-descriptions, virtually agreed with deans and faculty regarding their relative greatest specific strengths. Sixty-seven percent said that "high motivation" was a "major strength, followed by 64% checking "maturity," 58% checking "analytical skills," and 57% checking "realistic expectations." These percentages are comparable to deans' views but somewhat higher than the percentages of faculty who gave this ("major strength") rating.

University Perspective: Weaknesses   Deans and faculty members both felt that the communication area—both written and oral—was, relatively speaking, the area of greatest weakness in their MBA students. Faculty were (relatively) also concerned about MBA students' computer skills. MBA students themselves regarded their (lack of) computer skills as their primary weakness, relatively speaking, with 20% regarding it as a "serious weakness." Less than 1% of deans and 4% of faculty members believed that "unrealistic expectations" were a "serious weakness" of MBAs. MBA students concurred: Only 1% believed that unrealistic expectations constituted a "serious" weakness, and 77% said that it was "not a weakness".

Corporate Perspective: Strengths   The two groups of corporate respondents asked about specific strengths of recently hired MBAs in their organizations identified their "analytical skills" as their chief (relative) strength. Seventy-five % of VPHRs and 69% of operating managers labeled this skill area as a "major strength" of MBAs. Both groups were in agreement on the next two relative strengths: high motivation (56 and 61% of the two respective groups labeled this a "major strength") and "knowledge about a particular content area" (45 and 38%, respectively, terming it a "major strength"). These "major-strength" rating percentages for analytical skills, motivation, and content area knowledge can be contrasted with the percentages (ascribing "major strength") given by VPHRs and operating managers to the following characteristics (among others): 6 and 6% for "knowledge of how the business world really operates," 5 and 7% for "understanding of the legal/social/political environment in which business operates," 12 and 10% for "leadership/interpersonal skills," and 2 and 3% for "realistic expectations." By contrast, for example, the comparable percentages labeling "realistic expectations" of MBAs a "major strength" by deans, faculty members, and MBA students, respectively, were 53, 29, and 57%! It would appear that there are some major differences of opinion between the university side and the corporate side about the attitudes and expectations of MBAs. We will have more to say about this in the Commentary section.

Breadth/Depth of Preparation for a Career in Business/Management

University Perspective   Table 4.13 presents data for four groups of university respondents—deans, faculty members, placement directors, and MBA students—on how well they thought MBA graduates from their programs are pre-

TABLE 4.13
RATINGS OF *MBA GRADUATES* FROM OWN SCHOOL IN TERMS OF "HOW WELL PREPARED [FOR] *FIRST JOB* AFTER GRADUATION":
BY FACULTY, DEANS, PLACEMENT DIRECTORS, AND MBA STUDENTS
(Percent Checking One of Four Alternatives)

	Faculty	Deans	Placement Directors	MBA Students
Very well	26%	42%	57%	45%
Moderately well	63	53	40	47
Moderately under	10	5	2	7
Inadequately	3	0	0	1

Note: Columns total 100% within rounding.

pared "for the first job." As can be seen, views were very positive. The findings in this table compare rather closely with those in the equivalent table for undergraduates (Table 4.8). The one difference is that a somewhat higher percentage of MBA students and placement directors (compared to the equivalent groups looking at the undergraduate business program) believe that their MBA programs prepare graduates "very well for the first job."

The next table, Table 4.14, presents the equivalent data regarding preparation for "an eventual position of significant managerial leadership." The percentages of three of the four groups checking "very well prepared" are slightly lower than for "first job"; for the fourth group, MBA students themselves, the percentage using this response category to describe their preparation for the longer term is much lower than for "first job" (26 versus 45%). Not too surprisingly, the percentages shown in the first row of Table 4.14 relevant to how well MBA programs prepare graduates for significant managerial leadership positions are modestly higher than the equivalent percentages for undergraduate programs shown previously in Table 4.9. (While Category I deans were more positive than deans of other schools about how well their programs prepared their MBA graduates for long-term career success in management, the difference was not statistically significant.)

University-based observers—as Table 4.15 shows—generally felt that MBA programs have an appropriate breadth/depth balance. However, almost all (by a ratio of about 3 or 4:1) of those who did not believe that the balance is appropriate were of the opinion that there is an overemphasis on breadth. (This was similar to faculty and student views about the undergraduate business program, as previously reported in Table 4.10.) Again, however, as was the case with undergraduate programs, this view differed markedly (with differences being statistically significant) by category of school. For deans who believed that the present balance is not appropriate, those who headed Category I schools were more likely (18 to 8%) to report that their MBA students had too much specialization compared to too much breadth. On the other hand, the reverse was true for Category II and III deans: Only 4 and 3% of them, respectively, said that the balance is too much toward specialization, while 19 and 22%, re-

TABLE 4.14
RATINGS OF *MBA GRADUATES* FROM OWN SCHOOL IN TERMS OF "HOW WELL PREPARED [FOR] AN *EVENTUAL A POSITION OF SIGNIFICANT MANAGERIAL LEADERSHIP"*:
BY FACULTY, DEANS, PLACEMENT DIRECTORS, AND MBA STUDENTS
(Percent Checking One of Four Alternatives)

	Faculty	Deans	Placement Directors	MBA Students
Very well	19%	34%	50%	26%
Moderately well	61	59	48	61
Moderately under	17	7	2	12
Inadequately	3	1	0	1

Note: Columns total 100% within rounding.

TABLE 4.15
PERCEIVED BALANCE BETWEEN *BREADTH* AND (SPECIALIZED) *DEPTH* WITHIN AREAS
OF BUSINESS/MANAGEMENT FOR *MBA GRADUATES* FROM OWN SCHOOL:
BY FACULTY, DEANS, PLACEMENT DIRECTORS, AND MBA STUDENTS
(Percent Checking One of Three Alternatives)

	Faculty	Deans	Placement Directors	MBA Students
Too much breadth	31%	20%	14%	31%
Appropriate balance	61	75	82	63
Too much depth	8	6	4	6

Note: Columns total 100% within rounding.

spectively, said that their graduates have too much breadth and not enough
depth of specialized knowledge (about some area of business). While the majority of deans overall are satisfied with the breadth/specialization balance in
their MBA programs, some are dissatisfied with this balance—and the nature
of that dissatisfaction is distinctly related to the type of school they head.

Questions of the "Person A/Person B type" (well prepared for first job with
specialized knowledge of an area of business versus well prepared for later positions of leadership with broader knowledge base) were used concerning perceptions of MBA programs, as they had been with undergraduate business programs. (See the earlier discussion on p.106 for a fuller description of the format
for this question.) Results are shown in Table 4.16. (Table 4.11 is the comparable table for undergraduate programs.)

TABLE 4.16
RESPONSES TO PERSON A/PERSON B QUESTIONS FOR *MBA GRADUATES*:
BY UNIVERSITY-BASED RESPONDENTS
(Percent Checking "Person A" Alternative)

a. Type of MBA graduate employers *"most like* to recruit":

	Faculty	Deans	Placement Directors	BACs
Person A	47%	50%	42%	—

b. Type of MBA graduate employers *"should be"* recruiting:

	Faculty	Deans	Placement Directors	BACs
Person A	—	16%	18%	—

c. Type of MBA graduate "being turned out by *business schools in general*":

	Faculty	Deans	Placement Directors	BACs
Person A	—	46%	—	—

d. Type of MBA graduate "being turned out by *your own school*":

	Faculty	Deans	Placement Directors	BACs
Person A	37%	29%	29%	39%

e. Type of MBA graduate *"your school should be turning out"*:

	Faculty	Deans	Placement Directors	BACs
Person A	27%	15%	19%	17%

Note: For all parts of table, A and B answers total 100%

The first row of Table 4.16 gives the views of deans, faculty members, and placement directors concerning their perceptions of the type of person they believe employers like to hire. These perceptions (and there were no significant differences among deans by category of school) came out close to 50–50. However, when deans and placement directors were asked (row 2 in Table 4.16) which type of MBA graduate companies *should* hire (again with nonsignificant differences among deans by category of school), there was very strong agreement by a margin of more than 4:1 that it should be Person B graduates (with more breadth). Of the deans sampled, about half (46%) believed that business schools in general are turning out Person A MBAs and the other half (54%) viewed the scene in the opposite way. However, when asked about their own school (row 4 in Table 4.16), only about 30% of the deans (and 40% of the faculty) believed that their own typical MBA graduate is closer to Person A. In other words, there was a tendency for deans to be more likely to view their own schools as closer to producing Person B (with more breadth) compared to business schools in general. When asked about the type of MBA graduate their school *should* be producing, there was fairly broad agreement across deans, faculty, placement directors, and members of BACs that it should be the person with breadth rather than specialized depth.

Corporate Perspective   Corporate executives—VPHRs and operating managers—were fairly close to university groups in viewing MBAs as relatively well prepared for the first job after graduation. (Compare this situation with that for undergraduate business graduates, as discussed previously on p. 108.) In fact, they were even more positive than deans and (especially) faculty. Forty-eight % of the VPHRs and 46% of the operating managers said that MBAs are "very well prepared," compared to (as shown in the first row of Table 4.13) 42% of deans and only 26% of faculty making a similar rating. With respect to preparation for an "eventual position of significant managerial leadership," corporate views were less positive (compared with their own views about preparation for first job) but were at least as positive as faculty and only modestly less so than deans. The percentages of VPHRs and operating managers who believed that MBAs are "very well prepared" for these types of eventual major management positions were 23 and 21%, respectively, compared to 34% of deans and 19% of faculty members.

On the specific comparison of two types of graduates—Person A (depth) and Person B (breadth)—CEOs and other SCEs were inclined to believe, by about a 2:1 margin, that their firms prefer to hire the person with more breadth. This is shown in the first row of Table 4.17. However, lower level operating managers were less sure that this was the case (presumably because they are more likely to come into direct contact with new MBAs in a job situation), with only about half saying that their firm prefers to hire Person B graduates. With regard to the types of MBAs that corporate executives believe business schools are currently turning out, VPHRs were somewhat more inclined than their corporate associates to view MBA graduates as having a specialist orientation.

TABLE 4.17
RESPONSES TO PERSON A/PERSON B QUESTIONS FOR *MBA GRADUATES*:
BY CORPORATE-BASED RESPONDENTS
(Percent Checking "Person A" Alternative)

a. Type of MBA graduate *"this organization prefers to recruit"*:

	CEOs	SCEs	VPHRs	OpMgrs	College Relations	BACs*
Person A	26%	27%	30%	44%	32%	34%

b. Type of MBA graduate employers *"should be"* recruiting:

	CEOs	SCEs	VPHRs	OpMgrs	College Relations	BACs*
Person A	—	—	—	26%	—	18%

c. Type of MBA graduate "being turned out by *business schools in general*":

	CEOs	SCEs	VPHRs	OpMgrs	College Relations	BACs*
Person A	44%	43%	54%	—	46%	39%

*BAC members answered for corporate employers in general.
Note: For all parts of table, A and B answers total 100%.

Recruitment of MBAs

University Perspective   Placement officers of business schools rate the following (in order) as the attributes they think employers look for most when hiring MBAs: knowledge about a particular content area of business, "leadership/interpersonal skills," and "high motivation to work."

Corporate Perspective   By comparison, corporate college recruiters list the same three attributes as the ones their firms are looking for when recruiting MBAs; however, they reverse the order of the first two attributes. By a *wide* margin, they assign the top rank to "leadership/interpersonal skills."

About two-thirds of corporate college recruiting managers report that their firm's recruitment of MBAs is directed toward "a very highly selected set of universities." (This compares with about 40% who reported such recruiting selectivity for undergraduate business majors.) The leading factor affecting this selective recruiting is the "general reputation" of schools, followed by "the historic relationship between particular schools and this organization", and the "geographical location of the school." Again, as was the case with undergraduate recruiting policies, the AACSB accreditation status of schools was ranked last of seven factors potentially determining choice of business schools from which to recruit. About 40% of the firms expect their recruiting of MBAs to *increase* over the next 10 years and less than 10% expect a decrease. The remaining firms (49%) expect their MBA recruiting to stay at about the same level.

COMMENTARY

In this section we will draw on the considerable amount of data that has been presented in the preceding pages to discuss seven major issues: the intellectual aptitude of business students, the degree of commitment of business students to the field of business, the perceived quality of business school graduates, the validity of current criticisms of them, an evaluation of their specific strengths and weaknesses, their breadth/depth balance, and finally, factors influencing their recruitment by employing firms.

Intellectual Aptitude of Business Students

The issue of whether business school *undergraduate* students were sufficiently high on intellectual aptitude was a basic concern in the two Foundation reports 25 years ago. In one sense, there appears to have been little change in the intervening 25 years. Undergraduate majors in business across the country appear to have maintained about their same relative position compared to other sets of undergraduates (physical science majors, humanities majors, etc.). The absolute level of intellectual aptitude of (all) applicants to business administration undergraduate programs, as measured by ACT scores, also appears to have remained relatively constant. Thus, in this sense, the authors (were they all alive today) of the Foundation reports might not have many grounds for believing that progress had occurred. However, what we can report from our interviews is that the issue of the intellectual quality of business school undergraduates does not seem to be one of high salience on campuses in the 1980s. Provosts, who presumably have a reasonably dispassionate overview of campus units, do not seem particularly concerned about business undergraduates and in general find their intellectual attributes at least comparable to the university-wide level of student academic capabilities, if not definitely above on some campuses. The latter phenomenon usually is the case where business schools have been allowed to limit their numbers of majors and hence require higher grade-point averages for admission to the major. Business school deans and faculty, likewise, in most instances seem relatively well satisfied with the quality of their undergraduates, although there are exceptions at particular schools.

The Gordon and Howell and Pierson reports in 1959 were nearly as concerned about the intellectual aptitudes of business master's degree students as they were about business undergraduates. In effect, they did not see quality as being much better at the MBA level. This situation appears to have changed fairly substantially over the past decade or so. The AACSB has specified a Standard (albeit one that is not overly exclusionary) for intellectual capability that 80% of entering MBA students at accredited schools must meet. This has dealt in some measure with the problem of the "weak student" at those schools in a way that did not exist 25 years ago. Furthermore, with mushrooming numbers of applicants to MBA programs in the last two decades, those schools that desired to be selective have been *able* to be more selective. Together, these developments have led to an increasingly higher level of average aptitude of applicants as measured by GMAT scores. Any problem that may have existed in the past concerning whether MBA students, on average, were "smart enough" seems to have evaporated, at least for the near-term future. Almost never in any interviews in either universities or corporations did we encounter a complaint about MBA students/graduates not being bright enough. On the contrary, we often heard just the opposite: how "intelligent" many of them are. In fact, judging from the comments of some (relatively) older middle- and upper-level managers without this degree, the "problem" sometimes appears to center around MBAs being "too bright." The former often feel unduly challenged by the latter.

There is, of course, clearly another side to the MBA coin that ought to be recognized. Many schools turning out MBAs are not accredited by the AACSB and have no particular desire to be accredited. Hence, they are not bound by any specific admissions standards dealing with indices of intellectual capability (e.g., GMAT scores) and are free to admit (within the limits imposed on them by their own institutions) whatever percentage of applicants they wish with whatever academic qualifications such applicants may possess. Thus, they can choose to be very *non*selective and thereby take advantage of the increased interest in the MBA degree that has occurred nationwide over the past couple of decades by merely increasing their own enrollments with little or no attention to quality. (The extreme example of this, of course, is the so-called diploma mill.) A number of executives with whom we talked were well aware that certain business schools with weak programs were accepting almost "all comers" and hence were contributing to what some termed an "MBA glut." They were not impressed with the intellectual qualities of the graduates of such programs. On the other hand, other executives seemed not to be concerned with how many MBAs were being turned out as long as their own companies could continue to be selective in their own recruiting. They were getting the intellectual quality they needed in MBAs, and that was all that really mattered to them.

Commitment of Business Students to the Field of Business

Again, to the extent that commitment to a professional career in business was a problem in the past, it appears to have greatly diminished. This is not to deny the point that there are undoubtedly a certain number of undergraduates who are majoring in business because they do not know what else to do or because it is "easier" than some other majors. (Recall that about 10% our of undergraduate respondents indicated that the latter was the reason they decided to major in business rather than some other subject area they had been thinking about.) However, we seldom, if ever, heard complaints from either faculty or deans about students' lack of interest in the area. Obviously, given the very large numbers of students choosing to major in business, there is a wide range in their degree of intrinsic interest in this field, but our evidence does not indicate that there is a significant percentage of "default" business majors at the present time.

Perceived Quality of Business School Graduates

On the assumption that business school faculty and, particularly, deans naturally would be inclined toward seeing their own students in a relatively positive light, we particularly pressed provosts in our interviews concerning their perceptions of the quality of business undergraduates and MBAs and also noted closely the responses of nearly 300 of them to questionnaire items on this topic. Their views, collectively, were that undergraduate business students were at least comparable to, and at some universities better than, the campus average. (Similar evaluative comparisons for MBA students could not be made easily because of the difficulty in identifying appropriate comparison groups.) This is probably as good evidence as any that business students are viewed in relatively positive (at least not negative) terms on campus. Likewise, corporate executives in both interviews and questionnaire responses indicated that overall they were basically well satisfied with the quality of BBAs and MBAs hired by their firms. Furthermore, they, along with their university counterparts, generally felt that the quality of graduates they were seeing from business schools had been improving over the past decade or so.

All this points to a conclusion that business school graduates are in general highly regarded, but it must always be kept in mind that there are a number of contrary views. In a few companies (as reported by VPHRs), BBAs (according to 1% of the respondents) and MBAs (as reported by 5% of the respondents) have *not* worked out well. As we were reminded repeatedly in our interviews, just because someone possesses an appropriate degree does not in any way guarantee that that person can in fact do a job or a series of jobs well. Furthermore, while most firms that hire business graduates seem *generally* satisfied, they do have some specific criticisms (see following paragraphs). Nevertheless, business school graduates start with the benefit of a relatively positive impression on the part of both those who influenced their education and those who will influence their careers in business.

Criticisms of Business School Graduates

Each of the four major criticisms currently leveled at business school graduates did receive a fair amount of (but far short of unanimous) support in our study:

1 *Overly high expectations* A high percentage of corporate respondents thought realistic expectations were *not* a strength of business graduates (especially MBA graduates, but also BBA graduates). This contrasted sharply with the views of deans, faculty members, and, especially, the students themselves. Of course, these striking differences should not be interpreted to mean that one group is necessarily right and the other group wrong. Business school graduates' expectations may be too high, but on the other hand, they may be appropriate but not regarded as such by those senior to them in the firms they join. What the differences do indicate, however, is that the "producers" and "consumers" of business school graduates are far apart in what they think those expectations ought to be, and this has implications for both how business students are prepared and how business graduates are utilized. A closer meshing of expectations might be advantageous, especially to the graduates themselves. (See our later comments about the recruitment of business graduates.)

2 *Lack of organizational loyalty* This is not seen by the corporate side as a particular problem for BBAs, but it is seen as a fairly major problem with respect to MBAs. That is, a not insignificant percentage (over 40%) of those responsible for the personnel side of firms (the VPHRs) believe that the turnover rate of MBAs is higher than it should be. The key question to be asked, however, is: Whose fault is that? Is it because the MBA graduate is always looking to leave at the first chance to acquire a better or higher-paying job? Or is it, sometimes, because a firm has not utilized the MBA graduates they have hired in such a way that those who really want to stay with the firm believe the firm is making reasonable use of their talents and capabilities? We have no way to resolve this issue on the basis of information gleaned from this study, but again, our later comments on recruiting may be applicable.

The other two criticisms—poor communication and interpersonal skills, and lack of leadership skills—are discussed below.

Specific Strengths and Weaknesses of Business School Graduates

Both sectors agree that a high level of motivation to work is the major specific strength of undergraduates and also a strong point with MBAs. They also tend to agree that analytical skills and knowledge of a particular content area of business are other relatively strong areas for both levels of graduates. The students themselves appear to be able to take a great deal of credit for the former (high motivation), since they presumably enter the undergraduate major or the graduate MBA program already possessing a certain level of work ethic. (It was not too long ago, of course, that social commentators were bemoaning the low level of work ethic in young people, but we saw virtually no such concern about business school graduates in our interviews or questionnaires.) Presumably, the business school program (faculty in combination with the curriculum) can take at least some credit for helping to develop the other two positive strengths typically singled out by corporate managers: analytical skills (particularly of MBA students) and a reasonable level of knowledge of a particular content area of business (e.g., accounting, marketing).

The disagreements between the university and corporate sectors occur with respect to the areas in which business graduates show the *least* strength. The university side (deans and faculty) tends to focus on communication areas, especially written communication. While the corporate side could not fairly be termed as "wildly happy" with the strength of business graduates in this area, they are not as negative as the students' university mentors, and some said that they had seen some definite progress in this area in the last few years. Rather, managers and executives seemed most concerned about two types of attributes of business graduates: their relative lack of knowledge of how the business world operates in practice as well as in theory (especially taking into account that they are *business* graduates, after all) and their relatively low levels of so-called soft, or people, skills—leadership and interpersonal relations. (Judging by students' own self-perceptions, they have a palpable lack of insight into how they are seen by the corporate world in these areas.)

The message for business schools would seem straightforward: The business world regards the student product as relatively well prepared for starting out with a good base of knowledge in a particular business subject matter area and for undertaking analytical tasks. The graduate is not regarded as particularly well prepared for encountering various day-to-day realities of the business world nor for exercising requisite levels of personal skills, including both communications (in the broad sense of being able to get meaning across and to be persuasive) and leadership that is capable of influencing others with whom they work. Even though such shortcomings cannot be totally (or, perhaps, even mostly) laid at the feet of business/management schools, here is a fundamental challenge for these schools in the future. Can they provide "value added" in these areas as well as in those areas in which they already have achieved a fair measure of success?

Graduates' Breadth/Depth Balance

As might be expected, business school educators and corporate executives are generally agreed that business schools do a better job in preparing graduates for the initial job than for long-term career progress and the ability to assume eventual positions of leadership. After all, if business schools have any impact at all, it seems logical to assume that that impact will be felt closer in time to graduation (e.g., in postgraduation year 1) than farther out (e.g., in postgraduation year 20). Therefore, it is easier to attribute the success of a business school graduate in a first job to the quality of his or her formal business education than to be confident that that education will ensure success 20 years later in a more demanding job. Since schools understandably want their graduates to do well after being hired (and often after being heavily recruited), and since first jobs typically involve more narrow duties and responsibilities than later jobs, there is a natural tendency—in the absence of any specific countervailing forces or policies—for most schools to focus on preparing students for the first job. This, in turn, means a tendency to focus on specialization (so that the graduate knows how to "do something"), often at the expense of breadth, which would become of relatively greater importance to the graduate only as time passes. Thus, business schools face the eternal dilemma: how much breadth should be emphasized in relation to specialized depth?

Deans and faculty have, apparently, ambivalent feelings about this issue. On the one hand, most of them believe that the present breadth/depth balance in their own programs is about right. However, if anything is out of balance, more think that there is too much breadth rather than too much depth. On the other hand, at the undergraduate level particularly, deans felt that business schools in general and their own schools in particular were turning out type A graduates (well suited for first job) when they *should be* turning out type B graduates (relatively better suited for later jobs with broader responsibilities compared to the first job). Deans in Category I schools were much more united in their view about the type that business schools should be producing, but even in Category II and III schools a majority felt this way. (At the MBA level, deans' prescriptions were the same, but a higher percentage of them—compared to the percentage thinking this about undergraduate programs—believed that business schools were already doing so at this level.) Corporate respondents generally agreed that their firms *should* want to hire type B graduates, but that business schools (especially at the undergraduate level) were producing type A graduates.

Taken together, the entire pattern of opinions points to a general belief (albeit with many individual exceptions) that business schools should be more oriented than they are now toward emphasizing preparation of the student for a long-term management career—and developing capabilities for assuming later positions of leadership—rather than being too focused on more specialized preparation for the first job. We agree strongly with this viewpoint. Given rapid changes in many of the parameters of relatively specialized jobs and in many aspects of business in general, as well as the increasing complexity of business, it seems to us that both the students themselves and the business world would be better served if graduates have more breadth than they now have. Of course, individual schools face quite different sets of circumstances, as we have repeatedly emphasized in this report, so the amount or degree of this breadth should not be expected to be uniform across all degree programs. The point is that there are "siren song" influences, often including the preferences of corporate recruiters and their immediate superiors, that tend to emphasize the need for immediately applicable job skills in new graduates. In our opinion, such tendencies, if not checked, lead to short-sighted program policies and practices that are, ultimately, not in the best interests of business students and faculty or of corporate employers.

Recruitment of Business School Graduates

This Project was not designed to focus on short-term trends, such as predicted enrollments in business school programs in the next 5 years or employers' hiring plans over that same period. However, we did attempt to gain some information regarding employers' policies concerning whether they believed it was necessary to maintain, decrease, or increase their degree of emphasis on hiring business school graduates. Our questions were not constructed to take into account changes—up or down—in economic conditions that might affect hiring practices, only changes (or lack of changes) in intentions as determined by recruitment policies of the organization. In this context, we did not encounter any trends to decrease BBA or MBA hiring. Most organizations indicated that they were either going to maintain about the same emphasis as currently (about) 30% in the case of BBAs and 40% in the case of MBAs) or that they planned to increase their emphasis on hiring this type of college graduate. The latter figures (obtained from questionnaire responses) must be regarded with caution, but they were generally consistent with the responses to interview questions where we probed extensively. Such recruitment polices can always change on short notice, but for the *foreseeable* future (barring an extended and major economic downturn), it appears that there will be at least as strong a demand for business graduates—at both the undergraduate and graduate levels—as there is at the present time in the latter half of the 1980s.

Both our questionnaire and interview responses indicate that firms do not take into account whether a school is AACSB accredited when they select schools at which to recruit. Those firms recruiting at the "top schools" (as they term them) *assume* such schools have all the credentials that might be applicable and never give any particular credential a second thought. Firms that have a much less selective recruitment policy have particular reasons for recruiting at certain schools—e.g., the historic relationship between that school and the firm or the particular geographical location of that school in relation to the firm— and AACSB accreditation is simply not high on the list of factors involved in those decisions. The import of this for the AACSB is clear: If it believes that companies should give high priority to a school's accreditation status in their recruitment policies, then it (AACSB) will have to provide a much more visible and convincing rationale to potential employers as to what firms would gain by concentrating their recruiting only on those schools. Some firms do this now, but it may be by accident, not design. Other firms are not aware of this type of difference—AACSB-accredited status—among schools.

Finally, with respect to recruitment of business school graduates, there is one clear impression that we gained with our interviews at over fifty firms and companies: Many employers have not considered carefully the match between the types of jobs they have to offer and the types of business graduates (especially MBAs) they are trying to hire. Some firms have consistently attempted to hire only from the "top-ten" or "top-twenty" schools (especially MBA programs), only to find that very few graduates from those schools desire employment in their type of organization. This has led to a considerable amount of frustration and wasted time, effort, and money on the part of those companies and the people they hired. These firms might have been much better off aiming at top-quality graduates from other somewhat less prestigious schools who not only would be more likely to accept offers, but also, perhaps, would work out at least as well or even better for their organizations' particular needs.

A related issue for some other companies who are relatively successful in their initial hiring of MBA graduates from the "tier 1 schools" (to use an employers' term) is that there is a subsequent high (from their perspective) rate of turnover of relatively recent hires. Often (not always), however, this may be due to the lack of sufficient job challenge in comparison to what the graduates not only expect, but are, in fact, capable of meeting. In these instances, such firms should either pay increased attention to how they are structuring the jobs into which they are placing the "tigers" they have hired and which they claim they want, or else they should hire from a broader range of schools where the fit between job requirements and student capabilities is much more synchronized. We were constantly surprised in our interviews at how seemingly unaware otherwise-sophisticated companies were concerning (what we believe to be) a spread of superior student talent across a much wider range of schools (certainly a wider range than only ten or twenty schools) than those schools to which they restricted their hiring. To put the matter as succinctly as possible: Just as some business school graduates do not approach the problem of finding a job in a very intelligent fashion, some firms do not display a great deal of savvy in how they approach the problem of finding graduates to fill the particular (actual, not idealized) jobs they have to offer.

CHAPTER 5

FACULTY

How times have *not* changed in business education:

> The most precious resource which any business school can possess is a highly qualified and highly motivated faculty. (Pierson, 1959, p. 268.)

> The expansion in the student population has already outrun the ability of the business schools to find qualified teachers....One of the most important issues facing the business schools is how, in the face of the pressures created by mounting enrollments, they can not only maintain but improve the quality of their faculties. (Gordon and Howell, 1959, p. 341.)

As these quotations so aptly illustrate, a crucial element—probably *the* crucial element—in university-based management education is the faculty, and the challenge—as in 1959—lies in attempts to secure and develop as high a quality level as possible. In this sense, the times have not changed in the past 25 years. In other respects relating to the faculty component of business schools, considerable change has, in fact, taken place.

In this chapter we will begin by reviewing how business school faculties were evaluated in the late 1950s and the types of developments with respect to faculty resources that have occurred in the intervening decades. This will be followed by a focus on how faculty members in business schools in the mid-1980s are prepared, selected, developed, and promoted. These activities, in turn, provide a basis for relevant observers' current evaluations of overall faculty quality.

THE PAST 25 YEARS

To achieve a comprehensive understanding of issues relating to how, and how well, faculty resources contribute to management education and development in the 1980s, it is necessary to place those issues in historical context. For this reason, in this section we will first provide a brief synopsis of the comments and evaluations made in the two 1959 Foundation studies. This will be followed by an analysis of developments pertaining to business school faculty that have taken place in the intervening decades, and the section will conclude with a brief discussion of current criticisms of the faculty component of business schools.

The Situation at the Beginning of the 1960s

In essence, Pierson and Gordon and Howell in 1959 graded the overall quality of business school faculties around the country at the end of the 1950s, and the grade given (with obvious exceptions at some specific schools) could charitably be described as D and less charitably as a clear F.

Several key problems concerning business school faculties were identified by the two reports:

1 Extensive use of part-time instructors in some schools. [On a national basis, about 40% of all persons teaching in business schools were doing so on a part-time basis (Gordon and Howell, 1959, p. 341).]

2 Heavy teaching loads for business school faculty, leaving little time for research.

3 A "widespread tendency for regular faculty members to take on extra teaching for additional compensation in evening and extension programs" (Gordon and Howell, 1959, p. 342).

4 "Inbreeding" (hiring faculty from a school's own graduates), "a serious problem in some of the large schools that have their own doctoral programs" (Gordon and Howell, 1959, p. 346).

5 A relatively low percentage—"about 40%" (Gordon and Howell, 1959, p. 343)—of full-time faculty members holding an earned doctorate.

6 A general lack of training for, and interest in, research and scholarly activity on the part of faculty in many schools.

Of these several major "problems" regarding business school faculty, probably the most important were the last two: the fact that there was not a high percentage of doctorally qualified full-time instructors and the seeming absence of a strong research orientation on the part of many, if not most, faculty members in a large number of schools. These latter two factors were, of course, related to each other and together contributed to a widely shared belief that business school professors often were not current with respect to the latest developments in their fields. Gordon and Howell summed up their view of the situation by declaring that "significant improvement in the quality of faculty is perhaps the most critical need now facing business education" (p. 354). They went on to state (p. 355) that

> It can be said of only a modest minority of business school teachers that they have a thorough and up-to-date command of their fields....Too many faculty members

view their own areas of interest both too narrowly and too superficially and are too little concerned with what has been called the "intellectual foundations of professional work." This is not merely our own impression. It is confirmed by other informed observers and was further documented by many of the deans and better faculty members to whom we talked during the course of this study....It is fair to say that many business school faculties have been suffering from a creeping intellectual obsolescence.

Not only were business faculties (apart from specific exceptions) judged to be of generally inferior quality on an absolute basis, they also fared poorly on a relative basis. As Gordon and Howell noted, "The intellectual atmosphere in the business school frequently compares unfavorably with that in other schools and colleges on the same campus" (p. 356).

The two Foundation reports went beyond criticism, of course, and offered their own prescriptions for how to improve the situation. These included the more obvious steps of recruiting a higher percentage of research-oriented doctorally qualified faculty, reducing reliance on part-time instructors (especially "businessmen" [sic] with minimal academic qualifications) as much as possible, reducing excessive teaching loads (by lowering student/faculty ratios), and the like. However, both reports also discussed the more subtle and more difficult step of transforming the attitudes and values of existing business school faculty and deans. "In the long run," said Gordon and Howell, "the raising of standards and the improvement in the quality of business school faculties must rest with the schools themselves" (p. 345). Similarly, Pierson stated (p. 286):

> The life force of a school really lies in the ideas of its faculty...There are hardly any undergraduate schools [in the late 1950s], and surprisingly few graduate schools, wholeheartedly committed to developing programs of first-rate academic quality. Here, rather than any marked deficiency in funds, lies the great need in business education today.

Later, in his report, though, Pierson was more optimistic about the future, when he wrote that "On many campuses...the faculties seem ready to move forward if only strong leadership can be provided" (p. 295). Clearly, the task was one for both deans and faculty members together.

Developments during the Past 25 Years

As the result of a number of factors, the overall situation with regard to business school faculty changed considerably in the years since 1960. Three of the most important forces for change were: (1) the Foundation reports; (2) the significant financial support provided to business schools by the Ford Foundation to implement various actions to improve the quality of business education in general and the quality of faculty in particular; and (3) the actions of AACSB, especially with respect to Accreditation Standards. A fourth factor was that which Pierson (and Gordon and Howell also) had hoped would be a significant force: the faculty and deans collectively of various schools. The latter source of influence is harder to document on a tangible basis (since very few, if any, longitudinal studies with relevant data are available), but we believe that it was an important element in the pattern of changes that took place. Many faculty groups and many deans did sense the need for change and did work hard in that direction. This is not to say that there were not footdraggers in a number of schools, but they generally seemed to be a shrinking minority as time went on.

The developments that took place in the past couple of decades or so pertaining to business school faculty can be described in relation to the several specific problems identified by the two Foundation reports and listed earlier in this chapter.

1 *Percentage of classes taught by part-time instructors.* There has been a deliberate attempt by business schools collectively, through the mechanism of AACSB Accreditation Standards—which affect not only accredited schools, but also those schools aspiring to achieve accredited status—to hold in check the amount of classroom instruction offered by non-full-time faculty. The current relevant Accreditation Standard, for example, states that full-time faculty shall be "at least 75 % of the [required] full-time equivalent faculty." (In 1956, the equivalent Standard simply stated that "the majority of members of the teaching staff shall give the greater part of their time to instruction and research." From 1956 through 1968, that Standard read: "It is expected that at least 50% of the teaching credit hours on either the junior-senior level or on an overall basis will be taught by full-time faculty members having terminal degrees.") Of course, there are still a number of nonaccredited schools that do not meet these requirements, and some of these schools, in fact, deliberately use a high percentage of part-time instructors in order to have classes taught by individuals currently working in business or who have extensive consulting practices. What can be said on a factual basis is that the 200-plus accredited schools do limit the use of part-time instructors to less than 25% of total classroom student credit hours, and a large number of other schools also appear to do likewise. This particular faculty "problem" has thus been brought under control by those schools.

2 *Teaching loads.* Again, the applicable AACSB Accreditation Standard determines the maximum limits for many schools. This Standard states that faculty members "should not teach courses in excess of twelve credit hours per week" and also prescribes a "downward adjustment of the teaching load" for other responsibilities, such as "graduate instruction, research direction, and thesis direction." As with other Standards, nonaccredited schools are not bound by these restrictions but often choose to comply with them. Based on our interviews in a number of nonaccredited and accredited schools, it would appear that excessive teaching loads have largely disappeared as a salient issue in most business schools, with many accredited and some nonaccredited schools limiting teaching contact hours well below (to a 6- or 9-hour level) the 12-hour permitted maximum. We heard very few, if any, complaints from faculty members themselves about onerous teaching schedules. The reasons for these changes over the past couple of decades go beyond simply the effect of the applicable Standard and would include the competition among schools for relatively scarce faculty resources (i.e., doctorally qualified full-time instructors). The age-old imperative of supply and demand most likely has helped to hold down any inclinations of universities or colleges to extract very large teaching loads from hard-to-obtain business school faculty.

3 *Additional teaching for additional compensation.* The same Standard as that cited above also has served to control abuses of this particular practice, in which a faculty member would teach a limited number of hours in the regular degree programs of a given school but then also instruct a number of additional hours in that university's extension or nondegree programs or in degree or nondegree programs in other universities. The Standard limits total instruction of any type to 12 hours per week, and this has effectively curbed—for those schools adhering to AACSB Standards—many of these types of excesses. Of course, for schools not attempting to meet AACSB Standards, it is possible to employ individuals who are teaching at several different institutions for well in excess of a total of 12 or even 15 hours. How much this is, in fact, done in the 1980s is difficult to determine, but across all business schools it is probably considerably less than 25 years ago.

4 *Inbreeding.* For years, some universities have had virtually ironclad policies against hiring their own graduates (directly following receipt of their degrees) for faculty positions. This, of course, applied to business schools as well as other units. However, many other universities have not had such stringent policies in this regard, and hence it has been possible for so-called inbreeding to occur. Whether this practice has decreased across business schools in the past 25 years is not easy to verify. As we noted earlier, Gordon and Howell found this to be "a serious problem" in some schools in the 1950s. In fact, they found that at one school they visited "80 per cent of the faculty [had received] their graduate training at that institution." We encountered no such extremes in our visits and would conclude that despite a fairly severe shortage of business doctorates in recent years, the inbreeding problem, to the extent that it exists, is neither severe nor widespread in the 1980s. Not one of the provosts, deans or faculty members we interviewed across a wide range of schools ever mentioned this as an issue.

5 *Percentage of faculty holding an earned doctorate.* As we indicated earlier, both Foundation reports identified the relatively low percentage of full-time faculty holding doctorates as a major problem for business schools. The prominence they gave to this problem, in turn, helped to focus a great deal of attention on it by both the AACSB and individual schools. The result was that a number of schools scrambled to increase their percentage of doctorally qualified faculty. They did this by two means: tightening their hiring standards such that they would only employ new faculty who either had received the doctorate or were in their dissertation phase and would receive it within a specifically limited period of time (typically 2 years), and requiring those full-time members already on their faculty who did not have this terminal degree to take steps to obtain it if they were to remain on the faculty. So-called top schools were

not affected, since almost all their faculty were already doctorally qualified, and likewise, those schools that calculated that they had virtually no chance of ever obtaining accreditation (usually because of the type of institution in which they were located) also made few changes. However, a relatively large number of schools in the middle had both the means and the strong motivation (usually related to AACSB Accreditation status) to do so. Also, considerable pressure in this direction was applied by the AACSB through its Accreditation Standard for faculty teaching at the graduate level, which set 75% (for the percentage of faculty to be doctorally qualified) as the minimum figure required. Since, in the late 1970s, the AACSB required all schools having both undergraduate and master's (MBA and similar degrees) programs to accredit their master's programs, this meant that practically all large state-supported schools had to meet the 75% requirement. As a consequence, definite increases in the percentage of faculty holding doctorates occurred in a significant number of schools. These days, very few schools that want to maintain or increase their academic credibility choose to hire anyone without a doctorate.

6 *Faculty research.* This subject is the focus of an entire chapter in this report—Chapter 7—so it will be discussed only briefly here. The lack of sufficient quality research coming from business school faculty members was perhaps one of the sharpest criticisms leveled by both Foundation reports. As a result, this topic received a great deal of attention and soul searching by schools and their faculty during the 1960s. The result was that most schools, and the AACSB as an accrediting organization, placed considerably more emphasis on research and scholarship than they had before. Its priority level, aided considerably by infusions of Ford Foundation funds, was made paramount for faculty in a number of schools and was sharply increased for those in many other schools. The consequences of this change for faculty as well as for others, such as students and the relevant business community, were many and are still being strongly felt to this day (as documented in Chapter 7).

Current Criticisms Relating to Faculty

Current criticisms of business school faculty fall into two major areas: (1) they are too narrowly educated in a functional specialty, and (2) they frequently lack relevant work experience. Ironically, to the extent that there is some degree of substance in these criticisms, the causes can, in part at least, be attributed directly to some of the changes made in response to the 1959 Foundation reports. The very success of the "revolution," insofar as faculty matters are concerned, has led to an entirely new set of problems in the minds of some observers. It is as if the powerful chemicals used to stimulate the growth of desired new grass in a yard have also unintendedly stimulated some undesired weeds as well. At least, that is how some—both in and out of universities—view the current situation.

The first criticism—the supposed narrowness and overspecialization of faculty members, particularly younger ones—is primarily addressed to the preparation of business school faculty members in their doctoral programs. The charge is that most business school Ph.D. programs concentrate an individual's advanced degree education only in highly specific functional areas (e.g., accounting, organizational behavior, marketing, etc.) or, even worse, in subareas of these functions (e.g., tax accounting, macro organizational behavior, marketing research, and the like). The imputed reason for such specialization, of course, is so that a person can become expert in a clearly defined but limited area and thereby know enough about it to be able to carry out original research. The argument of the critics would be that the pressure for research that has emerged in the modern business school has forced doctoral programs to prepare students in this manner. The outcome, from this perspective, is that many new Ph.D.'s joining business school faculties lack sufficient breadth of understanding of real-world business problems and are not able to see or appreciate how diverse factors and functions interact to influence those problems. In short, whether they have received their doctorates in business or in a related area (such as mathematics or behavioral science), they are not able to provide an integrated managerial approach in their classroom teaching. Even many relatively senior faculty members, according to the critics, are so imbued with the predominant research ethos that abounds in business schools today that they have succumbed to the lure of becoming specialists rather than attempting to retain something of a broader approach to their areas. They, as well as the most junior of faculty members, say the critics, often feel the pressure to publish research articles which lead to a narrowing of focus.

The second major criticism of business school faculty members—that too many of them lack relevant business world experience—is not unrelated to the first. The argument is that most students entering doctoral programs (either in business schools or in departments with subject matter areas closely related to business) have had very little, if any, significant work experience prior to their entrance into those programs. Once graduated with their new doctoral degrees, they ordinarily go straight into business school faculties, knowing a lot about their particular technical specialty but very little about how issues and problems play out in the hurly-burly of the workaday business world. In short, they do not appreciate the complexities and subtleties of business. This, in turn, deprives their (MBA and undergraduate) students of insights and perspectives that will be necessary when they graduate and go out into the practice of management. This line of reasoning is based on the assumption that unless one has directly experienced certain events and situations, one cannot teach effectively about them.

We turn now to findings from our Project that relate to these and other various issues involving business school faculty, including the following: how faculty members are selected, approaches to the development of faculty, the comparative importance of different promotion criteria, and some assessments of faculty quality provided by respondents both in and outside of universities.

PREPARATION AND SELECTION OF FACULTY MEMBERS

With the strong emphasis in recent years on having virtually all business school faculty members doctorally qualified, it is obvious that if there are problems with their educational preparation, then attention must be given to how doc-toral programs are structured and implemented. As pointed out in Chapter 1, this Project did not explicitly examine doctoral education for business because this was judged to be beyond the resources available and outside the bound-aries of the main scope of the Project. However, in the course of the interview part of our study, we did pick up, indirectly, a number of comments and ob-servations that had implications for doctoral preparation. We will have more to say about this topic later in the Commentary section of this chapter. However, for now, we would simply point out that our overall impression gained through-out this investigation is that business schools, collectively, need to give increased scrutiny and attention to the basic rationale and approaches that underlie doc-toral education. This is, in our view, a highly salient issue.

Regardless of the adequacies or inadequacies of doctoral preparation for serv-ing on business school faculties, schools do have a certain latitude in deciding whom to select to serve in those positions. Thus, through both questionnaires and interviews we examined the relative importance attached to various selec-tion criteria, as seen by several different sets of observers.

As might be expected, there is an extremely large variation by category of school with respect to the importance attached to (predicted) competency in teaching versus research when prospective new faculty members (usually those just completing their Ph.D. or DBA programs) are being considered for hiring. This is shown in Table 5.1, where some 75% of Category I school deans say that research is the primary criterion for selection in their schools, whereas only 8% of Category III deans give this answer. Interestingly, schools that have been classified in Category II are more similar, on this issue, to Category III schools than to Category I schools. These figures were virtually reversed for teaching (in degree programs): About 90% of Category III schools rated it as the most important criterion, while only 25% did so in Category I. No other criterion (e.g., potential for contributing to executive education, potential col-legiality, etc.) rated even 1% mention by any category of school.

TABLE 5.1
DEANS' PERCEPTIONS OF THE MAJOR CRITERIA FOR SELECTION OF NEW
TENURE-TRACK FACULTY MEMBERS IN THEIR OWN SCHOOL:
BY CATEGORY OF SCHOOL
(Percent Ranking a Criterion as Primary in Importance)

	Category of School		
	I	II	III
Potential for high-quality teaching (in degree programs)	25%	71%	90%
Potential for high-quality research	75	27	8
Potential for contributing to executive education programs	0	0	0
Potential for building relations with the business community	0	0	0
Potential collegiality	0	0	0
Other	0	1	0

Note: All columns add to 100% within rounding.

When faculty across all schools (and by category of school) were compared with deans from all schools (and by school category) in describing the current state of affairs regarding selection criteria, a considerably higher percentage of faculty thought research was the top criterion. This can be seen in Table 5.2, where 42% of faculty rated research as the key hiring criterion, compared to only 21% of the deans. From these findings it could be inferred that faculty believe that the amount of attention *supposedly* given by schools to the importance of potential for good teaching when hiring new faculty is inflated and that research potential is more important than some deans might admit. Of course, there is no direct way to determine whether faculty, collectively, are more or less accurate than deans in their perceptions. The data only show that there is a distinct difference in views in a particular direction.

When deans, faculty, and provosts were queried on the extent to which an individual's real-world business experience (or lack thereof) should be given consideration vis-à-vis academic credentials in the selection of new business-school faculty members, there was general agreement across the three groups: namely, about 75% of the emphasis should be on academic credentials and about 20 to 25% of the weight should be given to the person's amount and quality of "practical business/management experience." However, these figures were somewhat different for the several hundred BAC members who responded to this question. They put the desired weights at roughly 60% on academic credentials and 40% on prior business experience. These latter figures also were reinforced by some of the interviews with BAC members. We seldom encountered an advisory board member who wanted primary consideration to be given to practical experience instead of credentials, but we encountered more than a few who felt that it should be given more weight than is now the case.

We also explored, in our interviews with different sets of respondents, expectations and desires for future changes in the bases for selection of new faculty members. There seemed to be a rather strong expectation, on the part of both deans and faculty with whom we talked, that research was going to be emphasized even more in the future than it had in the past as the major criterion for selection. (This predicted change is also discussed in greater detail in Chapter 7.) However, some (although a definite minority) seemed concerned

TABLE 5.2
COMPARISON OF DEANS' AND FACULTY PERCEPTIONS OF THE (RELATIVE) IMPORTANCE OF TEACHING POTENTIAL VERSUS RESEARCH POTENTIAL IN THE SELECTION OF NEW TENURE-TRACK FACULTY MEMBERS IN THEIR OWN SCHOOL (Percent Ranking a Criterion as Primary in Importance)

	Deans	Faculty
Potential for high-quality teaching in degree programs	77%	45%
Potential for high-quality research	21	42

Note: Columns would total 100% if other alternatives were included.

that this trend could go too far. For example, one faculty member (at a Category II school) who was representative of those with concerns said, "We're in a self-destructive mode: We're hiring all researchers now (giving them 6-hour teaching loads, etc.)—they do not know much, if anything, about the profession and they're devoting all of their efforts to research and very little to teaching."

One approach to the overall selection issue that was mentioned by about 15% of the deans in our interviews (and by some individual faculty members) as a strong possibility for the future was for a school to move to a so-called dual-track system. In this type of arrangement some portion of the faculty would be hired for a very strong emphasis on research activities as part of their total set of activities, and their evaluations for promotion would be heavily weighted in this area; others would be hired primarily for their teaching skills, and their assignments and promotional criteria would be adjusted accordingly. Under an ideal application of this kind of dual-track system, a school would end up with a defined "portfolio" of skills across the array of faculty members as a group rather than having each faculty member individually expected to be highly competent in each component activity. This approach would make it easy to accommodate, for example, having some limited percentage of the faculty (e.g., 10 to 20%) be hired based almost entirely on the extent and quality of their business experience without the typical expectation or requirement of "research productivity." There are obviously a number of potentially serious drawbacks with such a system (some of which we will discuss later in the Commentary section), were it to be deliberately implemented, but some deans think it should be tried more than it has been to date. Thus, the dual-track system may not be the wave of the future, but it might turn out to be more than a small ripple.

DEVELOPMENT OF FACULTY

Once organizations of any type (business schools, in this case) hire new employees (e.g., faculty), they face the issue of whether further development is required and, if so, how this should be accomplished. We asked, by means of questionnaires, both deans and faculty members what they thought about the effectiveness of their schools' current efforts in this area. Both groups rated their schools as only moderately effective in developing faculty, with deans (as might be expected) being somewhat more positive than faculty themselves. For all deans, the median rating (on a 10-point scale) of effectiveness of what their schools were doing to develop faculty was 5.0. (The rating was higher for Category I schools and slightly lower for Category III schools.) Faculty, for the same question, gave a median rating of 4.1. In terms of the amount of attention that faculty members felt was *currently* given to various areas of development (i.e., faculty skills that could be improved) versus the attention they thought *should be* given to these areas, there was general agreement (as shown in Table 5.3) that considerably more attention was needed, especially with respect

TABLE 5.3
FACULTY VIEWS OF ATTENTION *CURRENTLY* GIVEN AND THAT WHICH *SHOULD BE*
GIVEN BY THEIR SCHOOLS TO DEVELOPING SKILLS IN SPECIFIC AREAS
(Median Ratings on a 10-Point Scale)

	Currently	Should Be
Teaching in Degree Programs	3.4	6.9
Teaching in Executive Education/Management Development (EE/MD) Programs	1.7	4.3
Research	3.4	6.4
Consulting	1.4	3.6

to teaching in degree programs and in developing research capabilities. Furthermore, this finding strongly held for faculty in *all three* categories of schools.

Potential methods of faculty development were discussed in interviews with both deans and faculty. The most common method—according to both groups—was for the school to provide various types of "resources," particularly financial resources, to support research and/or attendance at professional meetings. About 20% of the deans mentioned that there was also some sort of "mentoring" program in their school, although this was reported less frequently by faculty members themselves. Also mentioned by about 15% of the deans (and less often by faculty members) was the existence of a yearly formal appraisal of junior faculty members that was designed to be an explicit aid in their development. About 20% of the deans who responded to the question about faculty development methods currently used in their school admitted that they either were "ad hoc" or did not exist in any form. This compares to a much higher figure of about 50% of faculty interview respondents who gave the same response.

To summarize what we learned about faculty development from our interviews, it seems clear that (1) most schools do not have any systematic program of faculty development beyond simply making available certain types of (primarily financial) resources for individual faculty members to use at *their* (not the school's) initiative, and (2) faculty members on the whole (but certainly not in every school) are much more critical than deans about the amount and quality of faculty development efforts currently provided by their schools. This latter point is reinforced when the two groups were asked whether they expected faculty development efforts to receive more emphasis in the future: About 80% of the deans responding to this question said "yes," compared to only about 55% of the corresponding faculty members. It would seem that faculty are not only more critical about current efforts in this direction but also more skeptical about the prospects for change.

CRITERIA FOR PROMOTION OF FACULTY

After schools hire new faculty and assist them with various kinds of informal and formal development efforts, they eventually face the most crucial personnel decision they will make with regard to any faculty member: whether to promote that person to a tenured position. If this decision is positive, the school and the faculty member will be married for life unless the latter voluntarily chooses to leave. A negative decision, if made incorrectly, could mean that the school loses someone who later on turns out to be a "star" at some other institution. Thus, the tenure decision is vital for both parties, and therefore it becomes a matter of great importance as to what weights are given to different criteria in making that decision.

Our questionnaire results show that, as expected, different types of schools give different weights to the two primary criteria: teaching and research. Category I deans report that about 30% of the weight goes to teaching and 45% to research (with service to school and university, and contributions to the professional community and to executive education accounting for the other 20 to 25% collectively). Category III deans report the weights as about 55% for teaching and only 20% for the research record. It is of interest, also, that although all three categories of deans do not indicate that there *should be* much change in those weights in the future for their respective types of schools, there is a small tendency for Category I deans to indicate that the emphasis on research should be reduced in the future and for Category III deans to say that that emphasis should be slightly increased.

When deans are asked what they *expect* to happen in the future, a somewhat different picture emerges. First, of course, for most of the criteria (except research), a substantial proportion (about 60%) of deans expect no change in their weights. However, for the remainder, there are distinct differences in expectations by Category of school. This is illustrated in Table 5.4. Almost half of Category I deans (who expect any change) expect that there will be more emphasis on *teaching* as a criterion for promotion in the future, whereas no Category I deans expect less such emphasis. Category III deans (of those anticipating any change at all with respect to emphasis on teaching) are about evenly divided between an expected increase versus an expected decrease in

TABLE 5.4
DEANS' *EXPECTATIONS* REGARDING A CHANGE *IN THE NEXT 10 YEARS* IN THE IMPORTANCE OF MAJOR CRITERIA FOR OBTAINING TENURE IN THEIR OWN SCHOOL: BY CATEGORY OF SCHOOL
(Percent Checking "Increase" Versus "Decrease" for Each Criterion):

	Category of School		
	I	II	III
Quality of teaching in degree programs	47%/0%	36%/7%	20%/16%
Quality/quantity of refereed publications	13/25	51/10	68/7
Quality of service to School and University	3/10	11/15	12/15
Quality of contributions to professional community	21/5	30/2	35/9
Quality of contributions to EE/MD	52/0	36/2	32/4

emphasis on teaching. (On this issue, Category II deans are more similar to Category I than Category III deans.) For research, somewhat the reverse occurs: Category I deans are more inclined to expect a decrease rather than an increase in emphasis if there is any change, while Category II and III deans expect an *increase* rather than a decrease by a wide margin. If deans' predictions can be regarded as valid, newly hired junior faculty members can expect that there will be some change in the mix of weights given to various promotion criteria by the time they are ready for tenure evaluation, with the nature of that change in the mix dependent on the type of school in which they are located.

Faculty views on tenure criteria generally parallel those of deans except that they believe that teaching currently counts for less weight relative to other criteria (especially research) compared to the beliefs of deans (across all schools). This is consistent with other faculty/dean comparisons reported earlier in this chapter. In terms of the weights that *should be* given to the several criteria, faculty want slightly more emphasis on teaching than on research, whereas deans' weights go slightly in the opposite direction. Provosts' views are very similar to those of deans in their view of what currently determines tenure and what should determine it in the future. In the case of members of business advisory councils (BACs), however, there is a definite tendency for them to say that less emphasis *should be* given to research in tenure decisions and more to teaching than the comparable weights assigned by deans, faculty members, and provosts. The differences between BAC members and the other groups are not startling, but the direction is clear. (Additional relevant information on this issue is provided in Chapter 7.)

FACULTY INTERACTION WITH THE BUSINESS COMMUNITY

This was a topic that was investigated rather thoroughly in this Project because it relates to an important issue raised by some critics, namely, that business school faculties in general do not have sufficient contact with the practicing business/management community and hence do not know enough about how the business world "really" operates. In our study, the issue was divided into three subquestions: (1) how important is it for faculty to have contact with practitioners, (2) how much such contact does the faculty currently have and how much should it have, and (3) what is the amount of practical experience that business school faculties have in the aggregate?

There was virtually unanimous agreement—with only a few exceptions—among deans, faculty members, and provosts in our sample that it is important for business school faculty to have contact with the practicing business/management community. The only differences were in degrees of importance attached to this activity and not in whether it was a good or bad thing to do. For example, 95% of the faculty members in our interview sample rated it as either "important" or "very important." Only 5% said that it was "not important." Similar interview results were obtained from deans. Even more striking were the answers of university-level administrators to a similar questionnaire item: Not a single provost or academic vice president out of nearly 300 responding answered that it was "not important," and over two-thirds (68%) rated this activity on the part of faculty as "very important."

Deans, faculty members, and members of business advisory councils did not disagree greatly with each other as groups of respondents when asked to rate the current amount of faculty interaction with the business community and the amount that faculty should have. As shown in Table 5.5, BAC members rated faculty slightly higher than faculty did themselves on the current level of their interaction with practitioners. All three groups gave faculty only a very modest rating on how much interaction they currently have (around 4 to 5 on a 10-point scale), and they were in agreement that such contact should be significantly increased in the future.

The only discordant note to this general view that business faculty need to maintain or probably increase their level of interaction with the business/management practitioner world came in interviews with several deans. These deans were concerned that certain of their faculty members had *too much* contact with the professional community and thus were spending too much time in industry. The nature of this problem typically involved an excessive amount of attention devoted to consulting rather than to their primary teaching and research responsibilities.

Estimates of the aggregate amount of practical experience possessed by specific business school faculties were made by deans, faculty members, and BAC members. About two-thirds of the deans and four-fifths of the faculty interviewed indicated that they thought the particular sets of faculty with which they were associated possessed "adequate" or greater amounts of practical business experience. Even in some of those schools where there were doubts about how much actual business world experience was represented on the faculty, there was not a high degree of concern. As one faculty member of a prominent business school said, "The actual experience—time spent in industry—of our faculty is probably low, but our *business-relevant expertise* is high." Of the small number of BAC members asked this question, most (about three-fourths) judged that the faculty of the particular school with which they were affiliated

TABLE 5.5
RATINGS OF *CURRENT* AMOUNT OF FACULTY
INTERACTION WITH THE BUSINESS COMMUNITY AND
THE AMOUNT FACULTY *SHOULD HAVE*:
BY FACULTY, DEANS, AND BAC MEMBERS
(Median Ratings on a 10-Point Scale)

	Current	Should Have
Faculty	4.2	6.9
Deans	4.0	7.1
BAC Members	4.7	7.6

had "adequate" experience. Only about one-fourth of the BAC members rated their faculties as "weak" in this area. Overall, in all our interviews with BAC members and a large number of other corporate managers and executives we did not find a great amount of concern about whether business school faculty knew enough about the business world. There were definite specific exceptions to this generalization, of course, with such concerns being very acute on the part of some executives. On the whole, though, this did not seem to be as much of a burning issue among our corporate respondents as some of the critics of business school education (see our discussion earlier in this chapter) have been suggesting.

QUALITY OF BUSINESS SCHOOL FACULTY

The level of quality of business school faculty members was, as discussed earlier in this chapter, a major issue in both Foundation reports at the end of the 1950s. As we described, however, business schools took a number of steps in the following two decades to upgrade that quality. The results of those actions can be judged partially by assessments made by two knowledgeable groups of observers in our current study: provosts and members of BACs. It is unfortunate that comparable data are not available from the Foundation reports, since this would have permitted a direct comparison across time. Nevertheless, we can infer from those reports that these two groups would have given low, or at best very mediocre, ratings to the quality of faculty members.

By 1985, the situation apparently had changed considerably. On a 10-point scale (1 = low and 10 = high), provosts as a group rated the quality of faculty in their business schools at 7.3. The BAC ratings, again for faculty in the schools on whose advisory committees they were serving, were nearly identical at 7.4. Taken at face value (and one must always approach absolute ratings, as compared with relative ratings, with caution), these two sets of ratings would seem to indicate a general level of satisfaction with the quality of faculty in today's business schools. Also, the view that quality was at least satisfactory or better was widespread and not confined to a small set of high-rated schools. For example, of over 400 BAC members responding to this questionnaire item, only 52 rated their faculty at 5 or below. Likewise, of nearly 300 provosts, a group not known for any particular intrinsic fondness for business schools, only 39 gave a rating of 5 or below. One further piece of evidence in this direction: In interviews and questionnaires, provosts were asked not just about their overall estimate of the quality of the business school's faculty, but also to make direct comparisons with the rest of the campus. The results are shown in Table 5.6. As can be seen, about 55% said that the quality was comparable to that of the faculty throughout the university, about 30% said the business school faculty was better, and only about 15% said the business school faculty was lower in quality. Either raters have gotten easier over the years owing to some sort of creeping rating inflation or else business schools have improved the overall quality of their faculties in a significant fashion. From the total set of data collected for this Project, the latter would seem to be the explanation.

TABLE 5.6
PROVOSTS' RATINGS OF THE QUALITY OF BUSINESS
SCHOOL FACULTY, COMPARED WITH FACULTY "OF
THE REST OF THE UNIVERSITY."
(Percent Checking One of Five Alternatives)

Well above	2%
Somewhat above	28
About the same as	54
Somewhat below	14
Well below	1

COMMENTARY

In this section we discuss the major issues that arise from the findings from our questionnaires and interviews as they relate to business school faculty.

Preparation and Selection of Faculty

The predominant factor in the selection of new faculty members is their academic pedigree. Given the AACSB accreditation requirements that a large number of schools have either met or are striving to meet, this means that faculty members have completed (or are about to complete) a relevant doctoral program. Some also may have spent several or more years in full-time work in business or industry, although this is probably the exception rather than the rule. (We have no direct data on the percentage of new business school faculty members who have had at least 1 year of full-time work experience in business, so we can only assume, based on the hiring patterns with which we are familiar, that for most schools those with that kind of experience would be in the minority. The percentage, however, would vary greatly by school, and the amount and quality of such experience would vary greatly across individuals.)

Because of the fact that most of those being hired for full-time faculty positions in business schools today have an earned doctorate (or are in the final stages of completing a doctoral program), it seems clear that if any changes are going to be made in the preparation of faculty members, such changes will have to come about through changes in doctoral programs. As we indicated earlier in this chapter, a comprehensive study of doctoral education for business was outside the scope of this Project. Nevertheless, through our several hundred interviews with deans, faculty members, and provosts, plus our own direct knowledge of a number of doctoral programs, we believe we are in a position to offer some observations about doctoral training for business.

First, we would have to agree with those critics who claim that most new business school faculty members have, indeed, been educated in a relatively narrow specialty. There are, of course—as with any generalization of this type—exceptions, but by and large, we believe that most new doctorates coming out of business school programs are highly specialized both in their knowledge base and, perhaps even more important, in their orientation toward business/ management issues. We saw very little in all our university interviews to contradict this statement. The reason for such specialization is obvious: This is how one acquires expertise in a given area. This expertise, insofar as university faculty members in general and business school professors in particular are concerned, is what can facilitate not only teaching in a disciplinary area, but also high-quality research. It is rare to encounter a generalist who has made significant research contributions. Thus doctoral students, with the assistance of their faculty mentors, are motivated to narrow their focus so that they can be better prepared to do research, which, in turn, will help them get hired and promoted.

We have no argument, of course, with the necessity for business school doctoral programs to develop defined areas of expertise in their students. We also do not quarrel with the basic approach of most doctoral programs that emphasizes the development of research skills in their students. In fact, we strongly disagree with a recent recommendation that "Ph.D. programs should be redirected to deemphasize research compared with teaching preparation" (Behrman and Levin, 1984, p. 142). We believe that quality doctoral programs should emphasize *both* teaching *and* research preparation. This does not mean that all doctoral graduates necessarily should do research when they join business schools faculties—this depends largely on the type of school and the type of university or college they choose to join—but they at least should be very familiar with the scholarly process and what is required to do first-rate research. In addition, though, we believe that it would be appropriate for doctoral programs to strengthen the preparation of their students for teaching. In fact, we think that most business doctoral programs probably need to begin to exert more quality control on teaching competence at exit analogous to the dissertation requirement for research. However, we are firmly convinced that casting the problem in terms of a research/teaching dichotomy does not address the heart of the issue—the necessity for business doctoral students to see their functional areas of teaching and research specialization in a *broader context*.

The great need, in our view, is for business doctoral students to *add* some breadth to their depth—especially if it is regarded as desirable for their own eventual (BBA and MBA) students to gain greater breadth than they now have (see the preceding two chapters). Doctoral students in accounting, finance, organizational behavior, or any specific area need to acquire a greater appreciation for how major business/management problems cut across different areas and how solutions often depend on an integration of approaches from different functional fields. This would mean more attention to how particular specialized areas relate to such overarching issues as the internationalization of business, the impact of technology, the challenge of improving productivity, and the like. As it is now, the foreground of the student's area of specialization seems to crowd out attention to the background of context, environment, and relations to other areas. We advocate *adding* this type of breadth, not subtracting specialized expertise and research competence.

To sum up our views on current doctoral education for business, we sense a general lack of boldness and innovation in the typical business school doctoral program. Although this is only a hypothesis for which we have little direct tangible data, we think that it is a hypothesis worth testing by means of systematic investigation. We believe that there exists a strong need for the AACSB or some other appropriate organization to initiate a major and comprehensive study of business school doctoral education—both its content and its processes. Such a study, when completed, should culminate in some sort of national conference of business school doctoral providers, so that new approaches to the preparation of future faculty members can be identified and disseminated widely.

The preparation of business school faculty members is closely tied to the issue of how schools go about deciding whom to hire. As we have noted several times, accreditation requirements—as well as many schools' aspirations to increase their academic status and rankings—exert a strong influence in the direction of hiring doctorates, especially those who appear to have a high potential for undertaking research. This has resulted in, among other effects, a rise in the overall quality of business school faculties (as documented earlier in this chapter). No longer, as in the past, are business school faculties considered to be "weak sisters/brothers" on campus. Thus, this type of impact has been quite positive, as seen by both the schools and the universities in which they operate. Our concern, and it was also raised by a few (but only a few) of the deans and faculty members with whom we talked, is whether this has led to faculties too homogeneous with respect to their prior backgrounds. To what extent are new (first time) faculty members alike in significant characteristics: young, lacking in any substantial work experience outside university settings (i.e., naive concerning real-world operations), and highly focused on research in their specialized field as the surest route to promotion? Would an upwardly mobile school hire any other type of first-time faculty member? The issue raised here is whether there is anything to be gained by some of the so-called major schools experimenting with assembling a slightly more diversified faculty. Would a limited dual-track system, as a small number of our interviewees advocated, provide a more stimulating set of faculty in toto for a school? Would students be better served, even—perhaps especially—in highly research-oriented business schools? If 10 to 20% of new hires had a somewhat different education/experience mix than the typical new research-driven Ph.D., would this corrupt the efforts of a school to turn out (on a school-wide basis) quality research and scholarship as well as good teaching? We strongly doubt it, but in any event, we think the matter is worth more consideration than it appears to have received to date.

We believe some modest experimentation in this direction would probably be healthy, even though there are clearly some risks. Just because a person is hired for the reason that he or she has a nontypical background does not automatically make that person a good faculty member. Furthermore, the reward systems in the school (which, in turn, are usually determined by those of the university at large) would have to be structured such that someone who is primarily only a teacher (but with a substantial experiential background) and not a researcher in a research-oriented university could get rewarded for that particular specialized type of activity. The culture—both formal and informal— would have to be supportive for this type of portfolio approach to faculty composition. Also, of course, the benefits to the school would have to outweigh some obvious costs. The objective, in any event, would be to add unique (different) faculty resources to the school, not just to hire a teacher instead of a researcher.

Faculty Development

Our data indicate that most business schools give relatively little systematic attention to the development of faculty members once hired. Most (not all) schools more or less adopt some version of a "survival of the fittest" approach. That is, they rely on the new faculty member's own initiative to obtain whatever advice or assistance he or she needs from fellow colleagues. Also, typically, they make available a set of financial resources (varying considerably by school) to support various professional activities such as attendance at scholarly meetings or seed money to support research activities. Again, it is usually up to the individual faculty member's initiative to take advantage of such resources as are made available. These opportunities are then followed by a periodic appraisal (yearly or every other year, in most cases) of what the individual has accomplished. All of this works quite well, seemingly, for those faculty members who adapt easily to such a laissez-faire approach. However, we would contend that this informal method leaves a great deal to chance and does not ensure that all or even most faculty members develop to their fullest potential. It is one of the great paradoxes of modern-day business/management education that business schools frequently put a large amount of effort into offering various types of planned, systematic management-development programs for managers, yet treat the development of their own faculty in such a casual, often (it would appear from our interviews) cavalier manner.

    If the best-managed corporations believe that it is highly important to devote careful attention and considerable resources to planned development for their managers and executives, one can at least ask why an analogous approach would not be helpful to the development of business school faculty members. The latter ordinarily have two primary functions—teaching in degree programs and research—and several subsidiary functions, including some sort of continuing contact with the practicing profession (often in the form of participation in nondegree executive-development programs). If business schools believe that new faculty members coming out of doctoral programs are fully developed in all these areas, then obviously little time or effort needs be given by a school to their further development. They are "finished products." Common sense as well as informed observation, however, would seem to indicate that this is not the case for most new faculty members and even some (maybe many) senior professors. Our questionnaire data from faculty members themselves suggest that they believe that substantially more development efforts should be provided by their schools than is now the case. While deans (based on our interviews) widely believe that this additional attention to development will take place, faculty members are much more skeptical—probably based on the belief that actions (or the lack thereof) of the past speak louder than good intentions about the future.

We are obviously encouraging schools (deans and faculty collectively) to take a closer look at what they are doing to develop their faculty members and how this could be done in a more comprehensive way in the future. (To carry out such an assessment, they could—in our opinion—often benefit from some reverse consulting: that is, using the advice and counsel of some of the leading management-development managers from industrial and business firms. Such resource individuals not only have a good experience base to judge what will and will not be effective approaches, but also frequently have given more analytical thought to the issues involved in this activity than have deans.) However, we need to stress that a more systematic plan for faculty development does not mean a more *uniform* approach. Some faculty members will need and want certain kinds of assistance in developing their teaching skills for undergraduates and MBAs. Others will consider themselves quite comfortable with this activity but be much less sure how to handle 35- to 45-year-old midcareer managers in executive programs. Still others will (accurately) not see a need for any help with either teaching or research but will want to find ways to have more extensive contact with real-world managerial practices and problems. The best developmental programs will surely emphasize an individualized process, with different developmental activities targeted for different faculty members and with a great deal of direct involvement of faculty members themselves in the planning.

Finally, we want to make clear that we do not think that more extensive approaches to faculty development are some sort of panacea that will always produce the intended effects. There is definitely a danger that schools can move too far and in too rigid a fashion and end up with a minimum of actual development and a maximum of faculty irritation and cynicism. As one of our faculty interview respondents said, "It is a big problem to keep faculty growing and excited about their work [teaching and research], but I am apprehensive about any formal program." We share that apprehension, but we believe that such appropriate concern should not prevent schools from examining what they are or are not doing to develop their faculty. Each school will have to decide for itself what will work best for its particular circumstances, and that may include—in some instances—doing nothing at all beyond what the school is currently doing. At the least, though, this decision should be a conscious one, rather than one made by passive default.

Faculty Interaction with the Business Community

As reported earlier, there was very little disagreement among deans, faculty members, and provosts that it was strongly desirable for faculty to interact directly with the professional management community. In fact, most were agreed that this type of contact needed to be increased in the future (except in cases where certain individual faculty members already were involved to such a great extent that it was interfering with their basic university duties). Thus, such interaction was almost universally viewed as "a good thing." While we would not argue to the contrary, we believe that it is also important for business school administrators and faculty not to lose sight of potential risks—risks which did not always seem to be fully recognized in a number of our interviews. Such concerns were well stated by Pierson in his report (1959, p. 278) of 25 years ago:

> A feel for the feasible and the relevant in a business environment is a highly desirable quality...but it is unlikely that there is any simple means of determining its existence. The opposite danger is probably more serious. Institutions of higher education which prepare for careers in a particular field always court the risk of becoming mere followers of the particular group they serve. In their zeal to please, i.e., to be realistic and practical, they may fail to provide any leadership.... Business school faculties should strive to break new ground for business, playing the role of informed questioners and constructive critics.... Thus, a sense of the practical is desirable only if it does not crowd out the element of originality, the very quality which is the hallmark of first-rate academic work.

In a similar vein, Howell, in a recent interview (Schmotter, 1984, p. 12) states the following viewpoint:

> A business school has to serve the profession, but that doesn't mean that it should always do what the profession wants it to do. Its obligations are to its students and to the profession as it's emerging, not necessarily as it exists today. I think it's important that business schools stay some distance away from the business community.

These admonitions, from Pierson a quarter century ago and Howell only recently, are cogent and to the point, in our opinion. (In fact, Pierson reported that interviews conducted for his study indicated that "the emphasis on the practical appears to have had [the result of crowding out the element of originality] on many campuses.") Nevertheless, such concerns should not deter schools and their faculty members from searching for innovative ways to supply or increase this experience for those faculty members who could benefit from it. We think that such efforts would show a net benefit despite the possibility that some members and indeed even some schools might get so "cozy" with the business world that they would lose some degree of independence of action and judgment. The potential gain in helping faculty members to see how their own particular disciplinary area of knowledge and interest ties in with other areas probably outweighs the potential danger of losing one's capacity to evaluate current practices critically and generate creative suggestions for change.

Increasing the amount of faculty contact with the world of business practice can be thought of as an aspect of faculty development. Here again, as with other elements of development, the need is highly individualized and the approach to meeting this need also should be correspondingly individualized. Not all faculty members need more of it, and a few, in fact, probably need less of it. For some, limited-period internships in business may be appropriate. For others, spending sabbatical time in industry would be useful. For still others, merely having more opportunity to talk with managers would be sufficient. Finding the right approach for each (particularly younger) faculty member who wants (and could utilize effectively) more contact with the professional community will not be easy, however. The issue was well summed up by a senior faculty member in one of our campus interviews: "I would like to see practical experience emphasized more as a young faculty member develops. The problem is: how to encourage this type of contact (and have it happen) but not let it interfere with teaching and research—that is, take precedence over those activities." This is, indeed, a formidable problem, but also one that we would contend could be met more head-on if there is the motivation to do so.

Faculty Quality

Data from our study are consistent across different groups of observers in showing that the quality of the typical business school faculty is at least equal to, and in the view of provosts even slightly better than, the average of the rest of the campus. Business school faculties, with very rare exceptions, are no longer the objects of derision either from the university or from the business community. In this sense, the collective authors of the two Foundation reports of 25 years ago can claim credit for having helped stimulate a major improvement in this element of business/management education. Likewise, recent and current business school deans and faculty members can take a degree of pride in how both the academic and business worlds generally view faculty members' overall level of competence. They have no need to apologize on this score now, compared with the situation a quarter century ago. However (and there is always a "however"), in this day and age they have a different but equally nontrivial challenge to face: Are business school faculty members spending their time and efforts as effectively as possible? Are quality faculty being deployed, and deploying themselves, to best advantage to meet the needs of students, the university, and the profession?

6

TEACHING*

In this and the next chapter we discuss the two major activities of any faculty: teaching and research. Since most faculty members are engaged in both these functions, at least to some degree, the treatment of one without considering the other at the same time might seem somewhat arbitrary and artificial. We considered combining the two into one chapter, and even folding both into the chapter on faculty, but we concluded that each of these two important activities was sufficiently discrete to merit separate treatment—hence an individual chapter devoted to each. However, we want to emphasize that these two chapters need to be considered as closely complementary.

In this Project, teaching was examined primarily from two perspectives: how well it is—or is perceived to be—performed, and what is—or should be—the relative attention devoted to teaching, compared to the other professional roles, especially research, in which faculty members can be involved. In addition, we also will review some of the criticisms voiced in recent literature and will identify some pedagogical issues which the literature suggests deserve attention. To begin with, we examine the changes that have occurred in teaching over the span of the last (nearly) three decades in business/management schools.

THE PAST 25 YEARS

Consistent with the general format throughout our report, we set the stage by presenting a summary of the scenario in the late 1950s as described in the Ford and Carnegie reports.

*The initial draft of this chapter was prepared by Douglas Kiel.

148

The Situation Circa 1958

As was the case with the curriculum, students, and faculty, as described in the preceding chapters, teaching came in for its share of criticism in both the Gordon and Howell and the Pierson reports. Gordon and Howell lamented that while they encountered notable exceptions, the typical undergraduate programs they examined relied predominantly on the lecture/textbook approach, with course content "weighted too heavily toward the description of existing institutions, procedures and practices," while students received scant exposure to "the analytical, and the managerial-clinical" (Gordon and Howell, 1959, p. 360). They did see some improvement occurring, especially in graduate programs, but they were less than enthusiastic in their overall evaluation, as demonstrated by this comment: "While a number of schools and a good number of faculty members give much time and thought to improving the quality of their teaching, and while the situation generally is tending to improve, the overall quality of teaching is not high" (p. 359). A good example of damning with faint praise!

Pierson, likewise, cited the preponderance of the "lecture method with heavy reliance on textbook recitations...[with] the tendency to stress exposition by the instructor, not active participation by the student" in programs with a heavy first-job orientation (Pierson, 1959, p. 286). He contrasted this type of school with those offering a "managerial approach...[with] more emphasis on participation, discussion, and investigation by the individual student" (p. 287). He cited teaching as the critical variable: "The difference between these two groups of schools is bound up with their methods of teaching, not with subject content as such" (p. 287). Perhaps his most scathing comment captures the essence of his concerns about the quality of teaching in general: "Undergraduate business schools almost without exception fail to challenge the more promising students" (p. 293).

Pierson, attributing much of the problem to what he termed "teaching conditions," was particularly concerned with faculty course loads and increasing student/faculty ratios. Reporting that "nearly two-thirds" of the undergraduate and graduate programs studied maintained a "standard work load of 12 hours per week or more," he observed, "it is obvious that faculty members would have little opportunity under these circumstances to pursue their own research interests and would even find keeping abreast of current developments difficult" (p. 284). His survey also revealed that of the 112 business schools examined, 62% had student/faculty ratios of 25:1 or more, leading him to comment that, "taken together with the information on standard work loads, it appears that business faculties at most schools must be hard pressed to keep up with their teaching responsibilities" (p. 284).

The composite picture emerging from the Foundation reports portrayed a large number of business schools, especially at the undergraduate level, with a rather uninspiring classroom environment: passive, unparticipating, unchallenged students in large classes being lectured to by an overburdened faculty.

On the bright side, there were definite exceptions to this dismal prototype, and change was in the wind, especially among leading graduate schools.

Developments over the Past 25 Years

While our study was not designed to elicit detailed information on current teaching methodologies, our visits to over sixty campuses left us with the impression that considerable improvement has occurred in business school teaching since the Foundation reports were published. A number of other studies in recent years also provide bases for making inferences about how the current scene has changed since 1959.

The faculty teaching loads cited by Pierson as a factor contributing to poor teaching no longer appear as a problem. As noted in the preceding chapter, in our interviews with both faculty members and deans we found very few individuals who expressed dissatisfaction with their teaching loads. One probable contributing factor was the introduction in the 1960s of specific quantitative limits on teaching course loads and faculty/student ratios in the AACSB Accreditation Standards. Twelve-hour loads were specified as the maximum, with the further provision that "assignment of responsibilities for graduate instruction, research direction, and thesis supervision...should result in *downward adjustment* [emphasis added] of the teaching load" (Standards, 1986–1987, p. 28). We did not gather data on teaching loads, but our impression is that the standard load for most Category I schools is 6 hours, whereas for Category II schools the load would be close to 9 hours and for the majority of Category III schools it would be 12 hours, except for those with graduate programs, in which case the load would typically be around 9 hours. The Standards also limited the student/faculty ratio by specifying the maximum number of student credit hours per full-time-equivalent faculty member (i.e., 400 for undergraduate and 300 for graduate level work).

Business schools also seem to have responded to the criticisms concerning the unparticipative nature of teaching described in the Foundation reports. They appear to have heeded well Gordon and Howell's advice (p. 365):

> Above all, techniques and materials should be avoided that leave the student merely a passive observer. The very first condition of good teaching is that the student must become an active participant in the learning process.

One report summed up the progress in business school teaching with these comments:

> Probably nowhere in four-year colleges has the stronghold of the lecture method diminished more than in schools of business, as innovative teachers have searched for more realistic ways to make the learning experiences of their students more meaningful, more realistic, and more lasting. (Fields, 1979, p. 100)

Developments in instructional techniques in business schools have largely centered on directly involving students in actual or simulated business situations. The two dominant techniques employed are case studies and simulations (or games). Both techniques place students in decision-making positions. Case studies, of course, are hardly new—but what has changed significantly is the relative pervasiveness of their use across a broad spectrum of business schools and a broad array of classes, not as the dominant mode, but salted throughout many course syllabi which would formerly have been geared to a pure lecture approach. Business simulations were first employed in business schools in the middle to late 1950s. In most instances, these exercises require students to take on roles and interact with their fellow students in lifelike business settings. As early as the 1960s their use had become fairly widespread in a variety of subject areas, ranging from economics to business policy.

Technology also has had an impact on the classroom, with many visual aids products which either did not exist or were prohibitively expensive in the fifties now readily available to instructors. The one aspect of teaching and instruction that obviously has changed most dramatically in recent years is the incorporation of the computer as a fundamental component of instruction. This is, of course, a response by business schools to provide instruction for students relevant to a business environment increasingly dependent on the computer. The relatively low cost and ease of use of microcomputer technology have expedited its introduction into the business school. Many MBA programs require their students to use microcomputers as a business management tool throughout their course of study; others use them in the majority of their required courses. In many respects, the computer is becoming as common to business students as the ubiquitous slide rule was, in years past, to engineers. It should be noted that whereas the national publicity engendered by a number of significant grants—awarded with considerable fanfare—might suggest that computer technology is used extensively by only a limited number of elite schools, in fact, we found that business schools throughout the entire spectrum were conversant with computer technology and were employing it broadly in their programs. We were, in fact, somewhat surprised to find, in our visits to several smaller rural schools, very well-equipped—both in size and in technological quality—microcomputer laboratories. While not all schools were at the cutting edge, our interviews with deans and faculty members certainly indicated an awareness of the availability of technology—especially computer technology—and in those cases where there was a perceived deficiency, efforts were underway to obtain more equipment.

Obviously, the mere existence and availability of technology does not ensure its use. Our interviews revealed that many faculty members and deans viewed the integration of computer use across the entire curriculum—as opposed to being confined only to the obvious areas, such as information systems and accounting—as one of their schools' immediate goals. The development and availability of user-friendly software would appear to make that goal realistic.

In summary, the preponderance of evidence, both from our campus interviews and from the current literature, suggests that substantial progress has been made in recent years in addressing the major shortcomings in business school teaching cited by Gordon and Howell and by Pierson. Students are more actively engaged in the learning process than they were in the 1950s and are becoming more so, especially with the advances in computer technology; faculty are far less dependent on lectures as the dominant teaching mode. In general, teaching has moved toward a more applied approach with direct participation on the part of students. Also, the second major problem—that of faculty overloads—generally appears to have been addressed, with AACSB standards playing a major role.

Have we reached nirvana? Hardly. Despite considerable progress, the current system is not without its problems and its critics.

CURRENT CRITICISMS OF BUSINESS SCHOOL TEACHING

Our review of the relevant literature suggests that current criticisms of business school teaching fall into two basic categories. One line of criticism is directed at the content of business courses, or what is taught. (We dealt with that in Chapter 3.) The second category concerns the incentive/reward system in business schools. Critics charge that the quality of teaching is adversely affected by the absence of adequate incentives for effective teaching, causing professors at many schools to concern themselves principally with research and scholarly activity, to the detriment of their teaching responsibilities.

The perception that the faculty reward system is causing poor teaching is premised on the belief that there is an imbalance in the relative value assigned to the various activities in which the faculty are engaged, with teaching being underappreciated relative to research and scholarly activity. In this view, faculty members are perceived as being rewarded with promotion and tenure for producing scholarly publications while receiving little benefit, if any, for effective teaching, with the result that they invariably are driven to consider teaching as a secondary rather than a primary professional concern. Representative (although perhaps an extreme version) of this line of criticism is this commentary by two university professors:

> Universities generally recognize three criteria upon which pay, promotion, and tenure are based—teaching, service, and research. In reality, these translate to research, research, and everything else. Teaching is usually given lip service, sometimes emphatically. In reality, however, good teaching rarely helps a career, although bad teaching sometimes hurts it. Even worse, an outstanding teacher is often rewarded with less teaching so "he/she can get his/her research up to speed." We have known cases where extra teaching loads were heaped upon marginal performers as a punishment. The message, then, is that teaching is a bad thing. (Giaque and Woolsey, 1981, p. 31.)

The implication is that the professor seeking tenure, promotion, and professional recognition must always know, albeit perhaps subconsciously, that time spent on teaching might be better spent on research. To put it another way, the opportunity cost associated with teaching can be high—effective teaching may be personally rewarding and a service to the student, but a quality (some would say quantity) research record pays greater dividends. Is this criticism justified? Is underappreciation of teaching relative to research a pervasive phenomenon? Much of our inquiry on teaching, both in the interviews and the survey questionnaires, focused on the role of teaching as well as its evaluation. While we did not deal directly with the rewards and incentives employed, we did attempt to assess the relative importance accorded teaching vis-à-vis other activities. We turn now to the findings.

PERCEPTIONS OF TEACHING

One way to gauge the role of teaching in the typical business school is to compare its emphasis relative to that of the other major faculty activity—research. Therefore, in our interviews and survey questionnaires we attempted to assess the campus community's perception of the relative amount of attention given to each of these activities. In addition, we sought opinions on how well the job of teaching was being done in business schools.

The University Perspective

Role of Teaching   University respondents were asked to express their views concerning the relative emphasis on teaching in their (own campus) business school with respect to (1) the current situation, (2) what they think "should" happen, and (3) what they "expect" to happen in the future (10 years from now). The responses to these questions for faculty, deans, provosts, and graduating MBA students are presented in Table 6.1. As the table shows, faculty members across all schools surveyed (over 400 schools) indicated that there currently is somewhat more emphasis on teaching than on research: 54% of all

TABLE 6.1
RELATIVE EMPHASIS ON TEACHING AND RESEARCH AS SEEN BY FACULTY, DEANS, PROVOSTS, AND MBAs IN THEIR OWN SCHOOLS
(Expressed as a Percentage of the Respondents Who Indicated Teaching or Research as Having the Greatest (or Equal) Emphasis in Their Own Schools)

	Relative Emphasis								
Respondent Category	Current			Should Be			Expect to Be		
	Teaching	Equal	Research	Teaching	Equal	Research	Teaching	Equal	Research
Faculty	54%	9%	37%	48%	30%	22%	38%	18%	44%
Deans	74	11	15	64	25	11	61	21	18
Provosts	77	10	13	63	30	7	59	31	10
MBA students	45	21	34	48	42	10	n/a	n/a	n/a

faculty members surveyed report greater emphasis on teaching than on research in their schools, compared to 37% who report the reverse. These proportions, however, are much more pronounced among deans than among faculty members. That is, a higher percentage of deans than faculty members are convinced that their schools place more emphasis on teaching than research. For deans (as compared to faculty), 74% said teaching was emphasized more than research in their schools, compared to only 15% who saw it the other way. Of course, the responses vary dramatically by type of school, as shown in Table 6.2. Category III school deans, as was to be expected, saw their schools emphasizing teaching; deans of Category I schools saw research as the primary faculty activity.

Provosts, in their answers to the same question on teaching versus research emphasis, responded similarly to deans overall. About three-fourths (77%) of them believe that currently in their own schools teaching is accorded higher priority than research. However, graduating MBA students were much less likely to see such a widespread teaching-over-research emphasis, with 45% viewing it that way, compared to 34% who saw the reverse. The student reactions are obviously quite different from those of provosts and deans, but somewhat similar, though not identical, to faculty views.

To recapitulate, across the total set of all schools, teaching is widely seen by deans and provosts as emphasized more than research, but these percep-

TABLE 6.2
RELATIVE EMPHASIS ON TEACHING AND RESEARCH AS SEEN BY FACULTY, DEANS, AND PROVOSTS BY CATEGORY OF SCHOOL
(Expressed as a Percentage of the Respondents Who Indicated Teaching or Research as Having the Greatest (or Equal) Emphasis in Their Own Schools)

	Relative Emphasis								
Respondent Category	Current			Should Be			Expect to Be		
	Teaching	Equal	Research	Teaching	Equal	Research	Teaching	Equal	Research
Category I schools:									
Faculty	10%	13%	77%	11%	32%	57%	8%	15%	77%
Deans	8	25	67	10	40	50	8	38	54
Provosts	28	27	45	17	55	28	14	41	45
Category II schools:									
Faculty	55	10	35	48	33	19	36	20	44
Deans	69	16	15	57	34	9	53	26	21
Provosts	71	14	15	52	39	9	47	42	11
Category III schools:									
Faculty	80	5	15	71	22	7	60	17	23
Deans	91	4	5	80	15	5	79	13	8
Provosts	92	2	6	81	18	1	76	21	3

tions are more muted for students and faculty. (However, it is important to stress that in Category I schools research is seen as receiving the predominant emphasis by the majority in each respondent group.)

Next, we examine what various relevant university groups think *should be* the relative role of teaching versus research. As was illustrated in Table 6.1, when their questionnaire survey responses are considered, a number of faculty members indicate a desire to move toward a more balanced teaching/research emphasis than now exists. The percentage of faculty who believe there should be an "equal" stress on both increases from 9% in the "currently" response category to 30% in the prescriptive "should be" category. Deans also advocate a more balanced emphasis, although more of them give an edge to teaching as the major priority than do faculty. For deans, as for faculty, the desire for relatively more equal attention to both teaching and research is expressed in terms of a reduction in the percentage checking either extreme alternative ("significantly more emphasis on") compared to the more moderate alternatives. A large percentage of provosts similarly express a preference for more balance than presently exists, but this comes about through a sharp reduction (from 56 to 24%) in the number who said teaching is currently significantly more emphasized than research. MBA graduating students, however, who also go along with a desire for a move toward balance, want to achieve this through a reduction in the faculty's research emphasis.

While all four of these university groups seem to be saying that they want a generally more equitable emphasis between teaching and research than is currently occurring, they want this to be accomplished by a reduction in what they view as overemphasized—and that differs from group to group. As might be expected, when the schools are divided by category, more deans from Category I schools move toward the equality response alternative from research than from teaching, and the reverse is true of Category III deans. Some of this is probably a simple "ceiling effect," since it would be difficult for a much higher percentage of Category I deans to move to a stronger research emphasis when "should be" is compared to "current," and vice versa for Category III deans. However, our interview data would seem to indicate that there is more involved here than a mere statistical artifact: Faculty and (especially) deans at some of the schools toward the most extreme ends (very high emphasis on either teaching or research) stated that they think their schools should move to some kind of greater (although in most instances not necessarily equal) balance. Furthermore, since there currently are many more teaching-oriented compared to research-oriented business schools in the total AACSB membership, the majority of our interview respondents (deans, faculty members, and provosts) indicated that they thought this better balance should be achieved through a heavier emphasis on research than is now the case.

What various groups expect to happen, as opposed to what they think should happen, presents an interesting picture. Referring again to Table 6.1, we can see that faculty and deans believe that in the future research will, in fact, be emphasized even more than they think it should be. This is especially true for faculty who, across all schools, expect that research will be stressed more than teaching (44% expect this versus 38% who expect the reverse). Deans, on the other hand, think teaching will be emphasized more than research, by a margin of 61 to 18%. While the 18% of deans who expect a greater research than teaching emphasis seems small, an even smaller number (11%) indicated that they wanted this particular form of imbalance. Provosts want and expect a decrease in an extreme relative emphasis on teaching—i.e., they want more research but with the balance still weighted toward teaching.

Evaluation of Teaching Quality   We surveyed four groups (graduating students, undergraduate and graduate, and alumni 5 to 10 years out, undergraduate and graduate) to determine how they evaluate, on a scale of 1 to 10, the quality of instruction in business schools. Current students were asked to rate the quality of the instruction they had received thus far in their own programs, and alumni were asked to rate the quality of the instruction they had received in their own respective programs. The results are shown in Table 6.3.

The median rating accorded teaching by current undergraduate students is 7.6, and that by MBAs is 7.3; both BBA and MBA alumni rate the overall quality of teaching they received at 7.3. We interpret these ratings to mean that students (present and past), the primary customers of business schools, feel that they have had a satisfactory overall instructional experience themselves and that the system in this respect is performing reasonably well. They are not giving rave notices, but they certainly are not giving low ratings to the quality of teaching they are receiving or (in the case of alumni) have received in the past.

The Corporate Perspective

Data were collected from corporate respondents regarding their perceptions of (1) the degree of emphasis that should be placed on teaching in business schools, and (2) how well business schools are performing their role of teaching as compared to other activities, such as research and executive education.

TABLE 6.3
STUDENT/ALUMNI RATINGS OF BUSINESS SCHOOL
TEACHING

Respondents	Median Rating
BBA students	7.6
MBA students	7.3
BBA alumni	7.3
MBA alumni	7.3

Note: Rating Scale: 1 to 10 (low to high).

TABLE 6.4
CORPORATE RATINGS OF BUSINESS SCHOOL TEACHING

Respondents	Median Rating
Chief executive officers	6.8
Senior corporate executives	6.9
Vice presidents of human resources	6.8
Operating managers	6.8
Directors of management development	6.4
College relations managers	7.1

Note: Rating Scale: 1 to 10 (low to high).

To determine their perceptions of the relative importance of the functions that faculty typically are expected to perform, we asked SCEs and CEOs how they thought faculty effort should be apportioned among a number of activities—teaching, research, service, building relations with the professional business/management community, and executive education. Their responses clearly showed that in their view teaching is, by a wide margin, the most important activity. They would have the average faculty member devote between 50 and 55% of his or her effort to teaching, versus between 10 and 15% for research, with the remainder of the time being divided fairly evenly among the other activities.

We also attempted to determine corporate views of the quality of business school teaching. The entire set of corporate respondents was asked to rate, on a scale of 1 to 10, how well, overall, business schools are doing their job with respect to teaching. The median responses in each category are shown in Table 6.4. The data presented here do not portray resounding support by the corporate respondents for the teaching efforts of business schools, but they are certainly not highly critical either. Our interview responses were along similar lines—on the whole, the corporate world expressed reasonable satisfaction with the teaching job being done in business schools. Perhaps the best characterization of corporate views is to say that from this vantage point teaching is regarded as the most important function to be performed by business schools, and faculty members should be devoting at least half their total professional effort to it. Overall, business schools are currently seen as doing a good, but not outstanding, job of teaching.

COMMENTARY

As we indicated at the beginning of this chapter, teaching is a complementary activity to research/scholarship, and we will therefore expect the reader to consider this section and its counterpart in the next chapter as essentially one piece. Much of our attention, when discussing research (in Chapter 7), deals with the fact that most of our academic respondents see a movement—drift?—toward more balance between research and teaching. Those schools with a high commitment to research (mostly Category I schools in our taxonomy) see themselves as placing more emphasis in the future on teaching, and the predominantly teaching-oriented schools see themselves as moving toward a greater emphasis on research. Given the fact that our data show that, across all respondent categories, teaching is perceived to be the most important function, the issue is whether any general move to increase research will come at the expense of effort devoted to teaching and, if so, whether such a shift is justifiable or desirable.

The movement toward greater balance between teaching and research may appear reasonable enough, on the surface. Certainly there is a need, in our view, for those (few) schools who place such overwhelming emphasis on research as to denigrate the teaching function to concern themselves with the improvement of their teaching performance—the market is demanding it, if nothing else. Furthermore, a shift in emphasis toward teaching by (mostly Category I) schools can probably be accomplished without much impact on the output of their research; their research ethic is so pervasive that it seems unlikely that their faculties would downgrade its importance, even if administrators were to attempt to coerce them to do so. (One of the main reasons for this is the importance of research to professional mobility; a faculty member makes his or her reputation in the larger academic community as a researcher, not as a teacher, generally speaking.) Regardless of whether faculties in some schools may resist moves to increase emphasis on teaching in their schools, we believe that there will be increasing pressures in coming years—coming from students, alumni, the corporate world, and the general public—for better teaching.

Although an increased emphasis on teaching in the research-oriented schools seems desirable—and not likely to impact adversely their research efforts in any event—the reverse may not hold true for those schools whose traditional orientation is primarily toward teaching. There is some risk that increased emphasis on academic research will in fact cause a deemphasis—albeit unintended—on teaching in these schools. It is a question of a balance of activities being appropriate to the mission of the institution. Once a strategic balance is struck, and faculty members know what is expected of them, there needs to be a reward system which motivates behavior toward the desired objectives—that is, a reward system consistent with the objectives. As we observed earlier in this chapter, critics charge that overemphasis on research is pervasive. While this is no doubt true in some schools, we did not find this to be an important issue among the preponderance of our interviewees. Those who expressed serious concerns were generally from schools which were near the threshold level of accreditation—either seeking to become accredited or newly accredited. These schools complain that the AACSB accreditation process places too much emphasis on "scholarly productivity." The Accreditation Standards pertaining to scholarly productivity do raise an important question: For predominantly teaching institutions, are these standards reasonable, or do they unduly emphasize research at the expense of teaching?

A defender of the Standards would point out, accurately, that there is considerable emphasis on teaching. The Standard on Personnel requires that "the faculty...shall demonstrate...instructional performance...essential for over-all high quality." Instructional performance is then interpreted to include "...teaching effectiveness...curricula development...and other meaningful efforts to improve the instructional program." Further (to demonstrate compliance with this Standard), "a plan for the evaluation of teaching activity should be in place and be of significance in the annual evaluation of each faculty member." However, the Standards explicitly require more research from those institutions with graduate programs: "The scholarly productivity of a faculty offering a graduate program should exceed that of a faculty offering only an undergraduate program" (Standards, 1986–1987, p. 25). This requirement, coupled with "downward adjustment of the teaching load" (p. 28) for those faculty teaching graduate courses, unquestionably drives some institutions—especially those seeking to attain accreditation for the first time and those already accredited but close to the margin of disconformity with this Standard—toward doing more research than they would if they were not influenced by accreditation. The issue here is whether the time released by the downward revision of the teaching load for graduate instruction is being optimally allocated in those schools that are more committed to a teaching rather than a research mission. For faculty in such schools, might the time and energy made available through a reduction in course loads be better spent in pursuits directly aimed at the improvement of teaching?

We believe that there is a positive relationship between scholarly research and the quality of teaching, but there may well be a greater impact on teaching quality in many cases if faculty in predominantly teaching-oriented environments were to spend their time and energy (currently devoted to academic research) in other forms of professional development activities designed specifically to enhance teaching skills. The Standard on scholarly activity, while designed to improve the quality of graduate level teaching, may in some cases instead cause misallocation of resources by diverting teaching effort into research of dubious value. What is needed is scholarly activity which prepares the faculty member to do better teaching; this does not necessarily imply publication in academic journals.

The AACSB's efforts to develop output measures seem to us to offer a potential solution to the problem of misguided preoccupations with research (at the expense of teaching) for the sole purpose of attaining accreditation or peer recognition. If schools can demonstrate that they have added significantly to the level of skill and knowledge of their students, i.e., that they can measure outputs rather than inputs independent of faculty credentials or numbers, then they will be able to claim teaching effectiveness. An excellent start has been made: The AACSB has recently concluded a 10-year effort—the Outcome Measurement Project—which resulted in the development of two sets of measurement tools "intended to assist business schools in assessing how well they are meeting their educational objectives in terms of the students' acquired knowledge and personal skills and characteristics" (AACSB Newsline, June/August 1987, p. 1). The new instruments, made available to business schools for the first time (outside the experimental project setting), when once validated through the test of time and use, hold great promise, in our opinion, for assisting schools in measuring teaching quality. While there are some risks—instructors "teaching to the tests"—we believe that outcome measures in one form or another are likely to become widely used tools of assessment.

Another dimension having an impact on teaching effectiveness, of course, is the amount of formal training and development provided for faculty. This has been dealt with in Chapter 5.

In the final analysis, we feel that if teaching is going to be improved, more attention must be given to the measurement of performance, the structure of incentives, and the training and development of faculty. Accreditation standards which focus on output measures may help, but the principal impetus must come from within the institution—recognition and reward of good teaching and allocation of resources to develop teaching skills. We also believe that market forces and the rapidly rising costs of education, both public and private, along with a generally rising public insistence on accountability in all institutions, will drive business/management schools in general to give more serious attention to their teaching practices and commitments—whether they want to or not—than has been true in the past. This will occur, in our view, despite the countervailing pressures within the university—across a wide spectrum of institutions—for a greater emphasis on research.

CHAPTER 7

RESEARCH
AND SCHOLARSHIP

Certainly one of the most controversial of all topics relating to university business/management school education is research. The controversy revolves around three basic issues:

• The role of research in business/management schools in general and in a given school in particular
• The type of research being carried out
• The quality and impact of that research

Later in this chapter, after reviewing the history of business school research for the past 25 years and the criticisms of that research today, we will address each of the preceding issues in turn. In so doing, we will interpret the term *research* (defined as "systematic inquiry...into a subject in order to discover or revise facts, theories, applications, etc.") fairly broadly. In other words, we will not confine our consideration only to a strict interpretation of research as the discovery of *new* knowledge, but rather will also include that activity which is subsumed under the more general designation of *scholarship* ("learning; knowledge acquired by study"). In any case, it is clear that for our purposes in this chapter, research/scholarship is an activity distinct from teaching, service, consulting, and other types of functions typically engaged in by faculty members, even though research may have —and often should have—strong connections with them.

THE SITUATION 25 YEARS AGO

As almost any faculty member over the age of 50 knows, the role of research in business schools was made one of the central themes in the Foundation reports. This issue was succinctly summed up by Gordon and Howell (1959, p. 377):

> There is a critical need to develop in the business schools a more stimulating intellectual atmosphere and to generate within their faculties the capacity to ask more probing questions and to engage in more significant research.

This view of the situation at the end of the 1950s was predicated on the assumption by Gordon and Howell (with which we strongly concur) that "if the business school belongs in the university, then research belongs in the business school" (p. 377). They found that at that time, "most thoughtful observers are agreed that the research performance of the business schools has so far been unsatisfactory" (p. 379). In elaborating on that conclusion, they stated (p. 379):

> Much if not most research in the business schools attempts merely to describe current practice or, going a short step further, to develop normative rules which summarize what is considered to be the best of prevailing practice. The business literature is not, in general, characterized by challenging hypotheses, well-developed conceptual frameworks, the use of sophisticated research techniques, penetrating analysis, the use of evidence drawn from relevant underlying disciplines—or very significant conclusions. A substantial amount of the publications now emanating from the business schools represents activities that scarcely qualify as research. . . . In many schools, no more than lip service is paid to the need for research. . . . It is also true that many deans have little conception of what might be significant lines of research.

This assessment was echoed in Pierson's study for the Carnegie Corporation (1959, p. 311):

> From every side—judging from the comments of university leaders, faculty members in other fields, business executives . . . , business faculty members, and even the deans themselves—comes the common complaint that business schools have seriously underrated the importance of research. Specific evidence . . . could be cited in support of this well-nigh universal opinion, e.g., data on time business faculties give to research, the proportion of a typical school's budget allocated to this purpose, the extent to which business looks to business schools for significant research ideas, the types of activities and publications which the schools define as research, the research training and equipment of business faculty members, and the like.

Taken together, these statements added up to a rather powerful—and certainly blunt—indictment of how well business schools were carrying out their research functions. Business schools of that time were, based on the results of these two studies, engaging in a high percentage of "low level" descriptive investigation in relation to a low percentage of "high level" analytical research. Thus, as the authors of those two studies viewed the contemporary scene, the problem was not simply the *amount* of so-called research activity—although that was certainly a problem in many schools—but also the *quality*. In the words of Gordon and Howell (p. 384), "It is clear that business research needs to become more analytical, to develop a more solid research underpinning, and to utilize a more sophisticated methodology."

Given their views of the nature of the problem, Gordon and Howell (and also consistent with the views of Pierson) believed that there were two primary steps that needed to be taken by the business schools of that era: (1) an improvement in the intellectual climate (of the schools), and (2) the development of closer relations with relevant underlying disciplines in addition to economics (i.e., the behavioral sciences and mathematics and statistics, in particular). To bring about these changes, they suggested that schools adopt several related approaches: increase the level of "scientific curiosity" of faculty members, update faculty members with "recent developments in their fields and in the related underlying disciplines" in order to "increase their technical competence," and "find ways of releasing faculty time for scholarly activity and formal research." Of course, the latter suggestion meant more time for the "right type" (i.e., more analytical-based) research in order to generate "a larger volume of significant research results" (Gordon and Howell, 1959, p. 392).

In summary, at the end of the decade of the 1950s, Pierson and Gordon and Howell by and large found the status of research in business schools to be woefully weak. Research as an activity and obligation of business schools was not sufficiently emphasized in most schools, and what activity there was often consisted of mere descriptions of current business practices that were masquerading under the label "research." These authors believed—to put the matter directly—that a research revolution was needed in business schools of the time.

DEVELOPMENTS DURING THE PAST 25 YEARS

In many important ways, the research scene in business schools in the mid-1980s is vastly different from what it was at the end of the 1950s. In some other equally important ways, however, the situation may not have changed as much as some observers might think. We will have more to say on the latter point subsequently in this chapter, but for the moment we will attempt to summarize some of the major changes that did in fact take place—largely, but certainly not totally, as the result of the two highly influential Foundation studies.

The strongly negative evaluations of the status and quality of research in business schools conveyed by Gordon and Howell and by Pierson in their reports did not fall on deaf ears at the beginning of the 1960s. They were heard by college presidents, provosts, some business school deans and faculty members, and the AACSB itself. Business school research had been held up to rather harsh mirrors, and the picture was not very flattering. Clearly, many people, in and out of business schools, thought that something fairly drastic needed to be done in this area. However, it seems fair to point out that the two Foundation reports did not, by themselves alone, bring about the significant changes that took place in business school research in the decade of the 1960s. There were at least two other developments that played major roles in the research revolution: (1) the highly visible examples of certain business schools whose faculty already were turning out high-quality, academically respectable research, and (2) the financial support provided by the Ford Foundation—following completion of the Gordon and Howell report which it had commissioned—to upgrade the quality of higher education for business in general and especially the quality of research and scholarship emerging from business schools. Let us briefly look at each of these other factors in turn.

The fact that, at the end of the 1950s, at least several well-known business schools already were focusing on highly analytical research meant that the two Foundation reports did not actually *start* a revolution in this area, but they were enormously influential in providing momentum for an incipient one that had been underway for several years. In the words of James Howell,

> We didn't cause [the] revolution [of helping schools to raise standards in all areas], Gordon and I; we were part of it, and we were catalysts, but it was going on before our report. Part of the reason the Foundation funded our study was because they sensed change was beginning. They wanted to accelerate it.... What we really did was help the revolutionaries, wherever they might be. (*Schmotter,* Spring, 1984, p. 9.)

As we stated, by the end of the 1950s several prominent business schools were already putting strong emphasis on superior academic research as a major goal of their schools. Other business schools—often located in universities of some renown—who had had sluggish or virtually nonexistent research programs began to attempt to emulate these few leading research schools. In other words, the research part of the revolution was being led by certain pace-setting models.

The other factor that helped bring about a fundamental change in the research atmosphere in business schools was the funding supplied by the Ford Foundation. Money talks. Nowhere was this more apparent than in the American business school landscape in the decade of the 1960s. The Ford Foundation poured some $35 million into business education in an attempt, in the words of Howell, to "bribe schools into doing what the survey [Gordon and Howell study] thought they should do." The money was granted to a number of individuals and institutions for a variety of purposes, but certainly one of the chief intended outcomes was to raise the level of business school scholarship. To that end, certain leading schools were given unrestricted funds to support basic research, doctoral dissertation fellowships (and dissertation prizes) were sponsored, faculty members were sent for updating and upgrading of their research skills to selected university research centers, schools received grants to help recruit outstanding faculty from ancillary discipline areas, and the like. Probably seldom in the history of higher education has the infusion of large amounts of money had such substantial and direct impacts on both the amount and level of research being carried out in a particular academic field. The Ford Foundation "bribe," coupled with the report the Foundation sponsored, worked well—too well, some might argue later (i.e., the contention of some critics that business schools now put *too much* emphasis on research).

What were the major changes in the next two decades after 1959 with respect to business school research as the result of efforts spurred on by the Foundation reports, by the examples of several research-oriented schools, and by the Ford Foundation's money? Probably first and foremost was the fact that a number of the larger public university and leading private university business schools began to stress the development of a strong research climate within their schools as a major objective. This meant that they gave explicit attention to developing the research skills and capabilities of their faculty members and to an increase in the volume and quality of the faculty's research productivity. Thus research typically was moved from a somewhat peripheral and secondary activity to front and center and given equal or even greater emphasis than the school's previous primary—often almost exclusive—mission of teaching.

Making the goal of improved and increased research a central function of many schools had a number of far-reaching effects. Among the most important, it led to the second major change that took place: increasing existing faculty members' motivation and capabilities to do research and giving these traits high priority in the hiring of new faculty. As we discussed in Chapter 5, those already on the faculty at many schools found themselves having to adapt to the new research atmosphere or else ending up on the way out—physically, if they were nontenured, and psychologically, if they were tenured. Those schools attempting to move up in status and prestige were doing so by hiring top researchers away from their sister competitive institutions or, failing to do so, at least trying to generate more research activity among the faculty members already there. And, indeed, the research capabilities of the faculty did increase, due to such factors as gradually improving quality (as far as research was concerned) of doctoral programs, participation in skill-building seminars such as those sponsored by the Ford Foundation, and increased funding and more released time for research.

The third significant development relating to research that began to occur in the early 1960s was the seeding of some of the larger business school faculties with a few experienced (typically) members from so-called underlying disciplines other than economics. Principally, this meant the recruitment of industrial or social psychologists from psychology departments (and occasionally other types of behavioral scientists, such as sociologists or political scientists) and applied mathematicians or statisticians from mathematics departments or other highly trained quantitatively oriented professors from related departments (such as engineering). This trend, of course, was directly in line with Gordon and Howell's recommendation in this area, and it had the intended effect: It brought an increase in research emphasis in certain areas (e.g., the behavioral side of management, managerial decision making, etc.) that previously had not been firmly research based. The plus was that a contribution was made to the goal of "improving the intellectual climate." The minus was that many schools found that it was not easy to integrate some of these former outsiders into their overall array of faculty, and certainly some early mistakes were made by both schools and individual faculty members from these other disciplines who did not always find the business school a congenial home. By the beginning of the 1970s, however, the "shakedown cruise" in this respect was largely over, and the research agenda for most schools looked rather different than it had in the 1950s, both in amount and character. If a full-scale revolution had not occurred, at least it was a large-scale evolution for many schools.

CRITICISMS OF BUSINESS SCHOOL RESEARCH

As we look at the situation in the mid-1980s, what can be said about this major change in a key activity of university business schools? Before we examine the data collected for the current Project, it is useful to review briefly the chief criticisms leveled at business school research in the past few years by various observers—in and out of academia. These criticisms can be grouped into three overall categories: (1) quantity of research has become more important to business schools than quality, (2) the intended audience of most business school research is the academic community rather than the combined professional community of scholars and practitioners, and (3) owing to the effects of the first two tendencies, there has been a proliferation of arcane, trivial, and irrelevant research. Without at this point attempting to evaluate the validity, or lack thereof, of these three sets of criticisms, we can briefly elaborate on each.

Overemphasis on Quantity in Relation to Quality

The first charge against the research programs of business schools—that they focus on volume of publications rather than on the quality of the research—obviously reflects a substantial increase in the number of articles published in scholarly journals. Many new research journals relating to various areas of business and management were started in the last 25-year period, and some of the previously-existing journals have expanded the number of articles published per year. Clearly, the overall volume of published research articles has increased—and increased rather dramatically. In large part, of course, this is due to the fact that because the number of business school students has increased by a factor of 5 or more (see Chapter 4), the number of business school faculty members has also increased. Even if the output of research articles per faculty member had not increased since 1959, the overall number of published articles would have increased with the sheer growth in faculty size. In addition, however, the increased emphasis on research in many schools caused the average output per faculty member to increase. Thus, the increase in total volume was influenced by both factors.

There is one other point that should be made about this increase in research volume, and that is that there has been a concomitant spread in most business fields (with the possible exception of accounting) in the number of schools represented in published research articles in a given year in a given journal. This means that research is being carried out in a much wider range of schools in the 1980s than was the case in 1959. The research revolution hit more than just the so-called top schools. All this leaves unanswered, however, the crucial question implied by criticism 1: Has the increase in volume been accompanied by a proportionate increase in quality? Many critics, in fact, would contend that the answer is a decided "no."

Too Much Focus on the Academic Community as the Audience

The second criticism centers on the *audience* for business school research. The critics' premise here, basically, is that research in a professional school should be directed to the profession, which includes practitioners as well as scholars. They argue that faculty researchers in business schools, however, are writing only (or at least primarily) for other academics rather than attempting to generate research useful to both groups. An example of this type of criticism is the statement of Behrman and Levin in their 1984 *Harvard Business Review* article (p. 141):

> Most academic business journals have...become in-house (within discipline) organs rather than a means of communicating with those involved in management procedures and business leadership. The serious policy issues management faces tend not to be addressed in "academic" journals. Managers must get their help from other quarters.

Most who share this criticism would probably go on to posit that the target audience of other academics is an intended one. That is, the argument is that most business school professors are purposely aiming their research reports toward their academic brethren and that they do not *care* whether such publications are comprehensible to practicing managers or not. They would cite a number of reasons for this, most notably that the tenure and promotion systems throughout universities, and not just in business schools, reward this type of behavior. In effect, they would contend that publications intended for and acceptable to other academics "count," while publications intended primarily for the practitioner "don't count." For many universities, this would be a reasonably accurate description of the reward system. Furthermore, at least some critics would maintain that this issue is even broader: Many business school professors would not know how to write effectively for a managerial audience *even if they wanted to*. The argument would be that because many professors (especially those younger ones who have gone through doctoral programs in the last decade or so) have had so little contact with the "real world" of business, they would not know how to communicate their research findings and results in such a way that would be meaningful and useful for the manager. Thus, the problem, as seen by the critics, is some combination of an inability to reach a professional audience and a lack of motivation to do so.

Too Much Research that Is Irrelevant

The third fundamental criticism of current business school research builds on the first two and is, arguably, the most telling: Research being turned out by business schools is largely trivial and irrelevant. It does not, say the critics, address very well or at all the most important problems and issues faced by business. In other words, and most damning, it can be safely ignored with little loss to the manager or executive. To quote Behrman and Levin again for a typical version of this criticism (1984, p. 141):

> For the most part, given the thousands of faculty members doing it, the research in business administration during the past 20 years would fail any reasonable test of applicability or relevance to consequential management problems or policy issues concerning the role of business nationally or internationally.

This particular accusation against business school research zeroes in on the types of problems chosen for investigation. It says, in effect, that it does not really matter whether a lot of research is being turned out or that much, if not most, is being directed toward an academic audience, because it will not have any impact anyway. Or, to state the case in the extreme (and in Shakespearean terms): It is much ado about nothing. Only if its basic nature is changed—the magnitude, scope, and pertinence to key business and management issues of the problems chosen for study—will business school research begin to be taken seriously by the profession, claim the critics.

THE ROLE OF RESEARCH IN BUSINESS SCHOOLS

With these criticisms in mind, but not at this point either accepting or rejecting them, we turn to data obtained for this project. We begin with a consideration of the role of research in the business school of the mid-1980s, examining first the perspective from the university and later looking at the corporate view.

The University Perspective

A critical fact that pervades the entire issue of business school research, and especially that part of the issue relating to the *role* of research, is the diversity that exists across schools. Some schools are clearly, explicitly, and deeply immersed in a research environment primarily because of the kind of universities within which they are located. This can be seen vividly in how the deans from the three categories of schools (see also Chapter 6) responded to the question of how they would rate the "degree of emphasis on research" in their respective schools. Eighty-five percent of deans in Category I schools rate that emphasis at 7 or above on a 10-point scale, whereas only 35% of Category II deans (recalling that these are all *accredited schools*) and 14% of Category III deans say that the emphasis is that high in their schools. (These differences are, obviously, highly significant statistically.) Thus, in talking about the role of research in the business school, one must be acutely conscious of the type of school being considered. Of course, a major factor creating these differences is the fact that all Category I, some of the Category II, and virtually none (two, to be exact) of the Category III schools have doctoral programs. By their nature, doctoral programs attempt to build a certain level of research competence in their students, and hence schools having such programs ordinarily will put more faculty and financial resources into this type of activity. Nevertheless, the point is that there is no modal degree of research emphasis around which most schools cluster. Since there are no directly comparable data from the 1959 reports, it is not possible to determine objectively whether the average amount of emphasis across all schools has increased. It almost certainly has, but it may be more accurate to say that an emphasis on research has increased greatly at some schools—compared to 25 years ago—and hardly at all at other schools (see Chapter 5).

Expectations for an increased emphasis in the future on research, which came from both interviews and questionnaire responses, are shown in Table 7.1. In response to a survey question about whether they expected a change in emphasis on research—*regardless* of whatever emphasis was placed on teaching— faculty, deans, and provosts gave surprisingly similar patterns of answers: About 70% of each group expected an *increase*, about 25% thought there would be no change and only 5% or so expected a decrease. There seems little doubt about the anticipated trend during the next 10 years!

The Corporate Perspective

Corporate respondents were asked about two issues pertaining to the role of research in business schools: what knowledge the business world has of the research process and product of business schools, and how the relative teaching/ research emphasis is viewed. The chief business community respondent sets for these purposes were CEOs and executives (typically upper-middle or top-level executives) who were members of schools' business advisory councils (BACs).

TABLE 7.1
EXPECTATIONS REGARDING CHANGES IN EMPHASIS
ON RESEARCH IN THEIR OWN SCHOOL:
BY FACULTY, DEANS, AND PROVOSTS
(Percent Checking One of Three Alternatives)

	Faculty	Deans	Provosts
Expect no change	25%	20%	26%
Expect *increase*	69	75	73
Expect *decrease*	6	5	1

Note: All columns add to 100% within rounding.

The degree of acquaintance that the business world has with the research coming out of business schools seems limited at best. Stated otherwise, as far as we could tell, many key managers and executives pay little or no attention to such research or its findings. The direct impact appears nil. When asked on the questionnaire survey, only 5% of some 400 BAC members rated their knowledge of their own school's (i.e., the school on whose advisory council they were serving) research as "large." Another 26% rated their knowledge as "moderate." Exactly 70% of the BAC members rated their knowledge of their school's research program as either "slight" or "very little/almost none." These individuals, it should be kept in mind, are among those executives in the business community who are probably the most interested in, and knowledgeable about, business schools and business school education. Furthermore, they were being asked about the research of the school with which they were directly affiliated, not about business school research in general. The survey findings were reinforced by the results of our interviews with both BAC members and CEOs. We found few in either group who claimed any knowledge of, or even any interest in, the research of business schools. This should not be interpreted, however, as a denigration of the *role* of research in business schools. More than a few volunteered the view that it was quite appropriate for quality business schools (usually meaning the ones on whose advisory councils they were serving or the ones from which they had graduated) to be undertaking research and that they were not advocating less of an emphasis. They were only making the point that that research had seemed to have little impact on them or their organizations and that they knew little about what research was being turned out by business schools. They seemed firm in this latter belief, although they often appeared to regret this state of affairs.

TYPE OF RESEARCH

The position or role that research occupies in business school activities is only one of the central issues surrounding this topic. A second major issue concerns the nature of the research carried out—more specifically, the extent to which research is "pure" or basic versus applied or practice-oriented. The notion of *relevance* becomes crucial here. When critics claim that one of the problems with business school research is that most of it is of interest only to other scholars, they are implying that it is too abstract and thus not oriented enough in an applied direction and consequently not relevant to the "real" problems of business. Relevance, of course, exists in the eye of the beholder, and what seems irrelevant to a manager may be quite relevant to the researcher, and vice versa. Also, who is to say that what appears irrelevant and of little use today (e.g., study of a mold in a laboratory dish) may not be highly relevant/practical tomorrow (e.g., discovery of penicillin)?

The issue of basic versus applied research was explored by means of both interviews and questionnaires with faculty, deans, and provosts. In particular, the focus was on whether each of these groups thought that business school

TABLE 7.2
FACULTY REPORTS OF DIVISION OF THEIR
RESEARCH TIME BETWEEN BASIC AND
APPLIED RESEARCH:
BY CATEGORY OF SCHOOL
(Percent of Research Time Allocation)

	Category of School		
	I	II	III
Basic research	60%	47%	40%
Applied research	40	53	60

research *should* move in a more basic or more applied direction than it is now. First, though, we take a look at how much time faculty members currently devote to research. Across our sample of over 2000 faculty members from several hundred schools, the median amount of their total work time they report spending on research is 22%. Obviously, this varies greatly by type of school. For Category I schools the median time is about 40%, for Category II schools it is 22%, and for Category III schools it is 15%. Of the total amount of time spent on research, faculty members across all schools report a fairly even split of their time between "basic" and "applied" research: about 47 to 53%. Here again, however, this varies considerably by type of school. The figures for the three categories are shown in Table 7.2. In terms of the future, the key survey question asked was, in the next 10 years, do you expect to shift the type of research you do (on a basic/applied dimension)? For all faculty members, about 60% answered "no." Of the remainder, the ratio of those planning to shift to more applied compared to more basic research was about 2:1. (For Category I schools, about 65% said they were not planning to change the type of research they do, but the ratio of those who were shifting was about 3:1 in the direction of more applied versus more basic research. The comparable figures for Category III schools are 60% "no change," and a ratio of 2.1 shifting to more applied versus more basic.)

Now, we can return to the question of what the several university groups think *should be* the direction—in basic/applied terms—of business school research. For both faculty and deans, there was a strong majority favoring a move to more applied research within business schools, as shown in Table 7.3. Roughly 45% of deans and faculty favored more applied research than is now the case, whereas only about 15% wanted to move in a more basic research direction. Provosts, however, were about equally divided in their opinions. (The interview data for all three respondent groups were consistent with the survey results, except that preference for a move to a more applied emphasis was even stronger than appears in the questionnaire data and was equally true of provosts as well as deans and faculty.)

What is especially fascinating, however, is that when the questionnaire responses of deans were broken out by types of schools, the preference to move

TABLE 7.3
OPINIONS CONCERNING WHETHER THE FACULTY'S RESEARCH
(WITHIN OWN SCHOOL) *SHOULD* BECOME MORE BASIC
OR MORE APPLIED:
BY FACULTY, DEANS, AND PROVOSTS
(Percent Checking One of Three Alternatives)

	Faculty	Deans	Provosts
Should become *more basic*	18%	15%	27%
Should become *more applied*	45	47	31
Should be *no change* in basic/applied ratio	37	38	42

Note: All columns add to 100% within rounding.

in a more applied research direction was virtually as strong for Category I schools as for Category II and III schools. As we see in Table 7.4, only 2% of Category I deans wanted their schools to move in a more academically oriented research direction, whereas 45% wanted to have the school's research become more applied. This latter figure compared to nearly identical figures of 47% for Category II deans and 46% for Category III deans. Considering all the data concerning where relevant university groups think business school research should be heading, there seems to be a generally strong push for more emphasis on applied research—which is consistent with how faculty reported they were heading if they were going to change their research mix at all—but provosts are not as united (relatively) as deans and faculty in this view.

PERCEIVED QUALITY AND VALUE OF BUSINESS SCHOOL RESEARCH

Our primary sources for addressing the quality/value of business school research were interviews with provosts, CEOs, and BAC members. Much of what we learned on this topic was indirect rather than direct, i.e., what members of these

TABLE 7.4
DEANS' OPINIONS CONCERNING WHETHER THE FACULTY'S
RESEARCH (WITHIN OWN SCHOOL) *SHOULD* BECOME MORE BASIC
OR MORE APPLIED:
BY CATEGORY OF SCHOOL
(Percent Checking One of Three Alternatives)

	Category of School		
	I	II	III
Should become *more basic*	2%	16%	18%
Should become *more applied*	45	47	46
Should be *no change* in basic/applied ratio	53	38	35

Note: All columns add to 100% within rounding.

groups did *not* say as much as what they did say about research originating in business schools.

Starting with the view from within the university, about 40% of the forty-three provosts interviewed indicated that their business schools needed to put *more* emphasis on research than they were currently. This belief, of course, reflects some combination of both quantity and quality of research, since "increased emphasis" can encompass either or both. However, it was our impression that when those provosts who wanted to see more of a research emphasis made this point, they often were not just talking about more quantity, but also more quality from their perspective. We did not delve extensively into how they would define quality, but that certainly varied by school—at some this meant more research that could be published in top academic journals, and at other universities this meant research that would be seen as more important by the business community. Of additional interest, perhaps, is that when each of the more than forty provosts interviewed was asked to name the greatest strength and the greatest weakness of their respective business schools, only four mentioned research as a major strength and none labeled it a significant weakness. One could infer, therefore, that while frequently (in 40% of the cases) provosts wanted to see their business schools place more emphasis on research, this was not a highly salient issue (regarding their business schools) either in a positive or negative sense.

A similar conclusion could be reached regarding our interviews in the business community. Not a single CEO or BAC member who was interviewed cited the research of business schools as either their most important strength or their major weakness. Four presidents or CEOs did, however, explicitly mention research when asked what advice they would give business schools regarding how best to meet the challenges of the future. Three of those stressed that business school research should become more relevant to the business community, and one felt strongly that research was out of balance with teaching (i.e., that the research part of the balance should be reduced). As one CEO put the relevance issue—which would probably gain concurrence with a large number of other top executives—"we need more blockbusting research out of the business schools." Our overall impression from all our corporate interviews (with all categories of interviewees, not just CEOs and BAC members) was that current critics are correct in at least one respect: The business world is, generally speaking (and omitting a few very specific exceptions such as certain areas of corporate finance), *ignoring* the research coming from business schools. The business sector is neither very irritated nor very upset by business school research or its quality, but most business executives certainly do not laud it either. The total perceived impact is, judged by what we learned in some 200 interviews in the business sector, virtually nil. The business world is not very aware of what research is being carried out, and when managers and executives are aware in specific instances, they typically report that they do not pay much attention to it.

COMMENTARY

In this section we discuss four issues pertaining to business school research efforts: the relative degree of emphasis placed on research now and likely to be exhibited in the future, the nature of that research, corporate knowledge—or the lack of it—of business school research, and its quality and impact.

Emphasis on Research

One fact seems crystal clear when business school research in the 1980s is compared with what it was in 1959: There *is* a stronger overall emphasis on research and scholarship in business schools now compared to 25 years earlier. The Foundation reports and other associated events of the early 1960s had a discernible—even profound—impact: Research is a central goal of more schools, and there seems to be an irrefutable increase in the amount of research activity. (We will address quality later.) Furthermore, as our data seem to indicate, this trend toward research becoming a higher priority within business schools generally is highly likely to continue. We saw no evidence whatsoever of a retrenchment in research. Quite to the contrary, we frequently encountered in our campus interviews a desire to make a greater push in this area. If Gordon and Howell and Pierson helped the research genie to escape from the business school bottle (bottleneck, some might argue) 25 years ago, the genie is, and is likely to be in the foreseeable future, growing and expanding and not at all headed back into the bottle.

The trend toward a heavier research emphasis appears to be strongly focused in Category II and III schools, especially the former. Since most Category I schools already have established what they consider to be a strong research emphasis, their attention seems to be focused on issues other than expanding its role in their schools. In Category II schools, however, as well as in some Category III schools, we frequently encountered explicit statements that this—increasing the emphasis given to research in the school—is a top priority. The reason for this was often (not always) attributed to extrinsic, not intrinsic, goals: to increase the (national) status, prestige, or "ranking" of the school, or to raise its stature within its own university setting, rather than simply to fulfill what the school considered to be a proper function of a professional school in an institution of higher education. Thus, increasing the role of research in a school was an objective often tied up with the school's visibility/recognition aspirations, either internally or externally. For some schools, it is seen as much as (or even more than) a means as it is seen as an end in itself.

Is it a "good thing" that so many business schools apparently want to strengthen their research emphasis? In one sense, it is hard to argue otherwise. For a school to want to develop new knowledge and to advance theory and fundamental concepts would seem to be an undeniably worthy objective. However, we detected what we considered to be some uncritical acceptance of this as a goal for the (particular) school. To put the matter differently, some schools (both deans and faculty) seemed not to have adequately thought through the *strategic* role that research should play in their school. That is, there was almost universal agreement about the potential *gains* from a greater research emphasis—increased respect within the university and more recognition/visibility outside of it (especially in the wider academic community, if not the business community)—but very little attention was paid to the possible *costs*. At least two potential costs come to mind: the financial and other resources needed in order to do this at a high level of quality, and a negative impact on the teaching function. Neither is inevitable, but both are possible.

With respect to resource costs, there is the question of whether current—and always limited and frequently scarce—dollars should be reallocated to this activity, in comparison to other functions of the school. Of course, the resource base in terms of dollars can be increased, through contributions or extramural research grants, for example, but typically there would be costs in administrative and faculty time in augmenting existing financial resources for this purpose. However, the "resource cost" issue is broader. For example, how easy will it be for some schools either to develop additional research capabilities in faculty already in place and/or to recruit those talents in new faculty? If a Category II school is considering attempts to move into the major national research visibility stream, for example, is there enough high-quality research talent (for business schools) around the country for all the schools that want to do this—and our interviews indicate that a number do—to be able to do this? To use an analogy, is there enough superior baseball talent to double the number of major league teams?

The other significant potential cost is the possible effect on the quality of a school's teaching program (see Chapter 6). Many would argue, of course, that as a school's faculty becomes more involved in research and scholarship, this would *improve* their teaching—they would be closer to the "cutting edge," more attuned to the latest research findings, etc. Under the right circumstances, this would be a very valuable result indeed. This consequence, though, does not appear to be inevitable. It is at least conceivable that under some circumstances the research efforts might actually dilute the attention to teaching and especially to the improvement of teaching. In the worst-case scenario, which is not outside the realm of possibility, the school gains poor research and loses good teaching. A considerable amount of the right kind of resources and effort, in fact, are required to ensure that this kind of result does not happen.

We want to make it clear that we are not arguing against schools (in general) putting more emphasis on research. It should not be necessary here to say the obvious: We are *for* research. What we do want to raise as an issue, however, is the question of whether all or even most schools should move in this direction. Are business school students, the university, and the professional business community always served better by more research—regardless of its quality—by any school? In answering this question, we believe that more schools (and their universities) need to give more careful consideration than they have up to now to the purposes for doing so, to how this will be accomplished, and to what the range of possible consequences are. Perhaps schools need to re-search the issue of research more than some appear to be doing.

There is one other issue relating to the emphasis that some schools (espe-cially some Category II and III schools) recently have been putting on research—and on hopes of increasing that emphasis even more in the future: the impact of the AACSB Accreditation Standard that relates to research. That Standard (the impetus for which was strongly influenced by the findings reported in the two Foundation studies) currently states: "The faculty as a whole shall... demonstrate [among other aspects of performance]...scholarly productivity." This part of that Standard is officially interpreted to mean that "scholarly pro-ductivity includes the quality and extent of research and publication." The key question to ask is: Has this Standard possibly generated some unintended con-sequences?

Since those schools that see themselves as somewhat near (but currently above) the margin with regard to AACSB accreditation—as well as those schools that believe they have a reasonable chance to attain accredited status—want to make sure that they retain (or obtain) accreditation, they often develop and structure all aspects of their programs to meet the several different Standards. In the case of Standard IIIB, which includes faculty engaging in "scholarly pro-ductivity," this means some sort of research effort—whether or not this fits in with other parts of the school's overall mission within a given university (with its own overall mission and characteristics). As we have said previously, in principle this part of the Standard is laudable. In practice, however, for some schools it may result in a set of faculty activities that have the surface appear-ance of "scholarship," but which in reality are not very scholarly and contrib-ute little to the fund of knowledge in various fields relating to business. In point of fact, we felt this was the case in some of the business schools we visited. "Research" (putting that term in quotation marks deliberately) was being pushed in the school not because it was central to the school's educational objectives, but only because it was perceived as necessary to meet Standard IIIB. Some of that activity and resultant output we did not believe met very high criteria of quality. The letter of this Standard may have been met, but not the intent or spirit. In some instances, we believed that both the school and the AACSB may have been, in effect, deluding themselves that research and scholarship that met defensible quality standards were actually taking place. We raise the question, then, of whether that part of Standard IIIB relating to research is serving the AACSB, some schools and their students, and the professional busi-ness community well, or whether it would be possible and desirable to recast this particular section of that Standard in a way that would motivate schools to engage in scholarly activities more directly appropriate to their mission.

Nature of Research

Our interview and questionnaire results showed that there was a moderately strong trend among faculty members, and across schools, to shift the balance of the type of research being carried out from so-called basic to applied research. A fairly substantial proportion of faculty members (25%) report that they plan to do this; many deans (46%) and faculty members (45%) across all categories of schools believe that this shift *should* take place, and they expect such a shift. It seems apparent that business schools have, indeed, "heard" the criticism that a high proportion of business school research is too abstract and not, therefore, sufficiently applied. But what does "more applied" mean? For many of the faculty and deans we talked with, it means doing research that is of more interest to the business community and thus more relevant to that particular audience. It means, as a number told us, being somewhat less concerned with aiming research toward other academics and somewhat more concerned with directing it toward managers and executives.

The relevancy issue, however, is not simply one of where a particular research project falls on a basic/applied scale. It has as much or more to do with the choice of problem to be investigated. Thus, if faculty members are in fact going to attempt to shift their research in a somewhat more applied direction, they will need to give as much attention to the problems on which they choose to do research as they do to the approach to carrying it out. If the problems selected are fundamental and important, then basic research which can lead to eventual applications is as relevant as more applied research that appears to have immediate practical implications. If the problems selected for study are not seen as significant or important, however, then no amount of applied veneer will make them so.

In considering the nature of business school research, it is necessary to distinguish between the relevance of the research problem, which we have been discussing above, and the import of the reported findings. The latter concerns the issue of how comprehensible the results are for managers and executives. It is possible—and certainly seems to happen frequently if we can read between the lines of our interviews—that business schools are in many instances already conducting research that has a fairly high potential for applicability except that the professional managerial audience does not grasp the underlying relevance. To the extent that this happens, some of the blame for failure to see applicability undoubtedly can be placed at the feet of the typical executive. However, business school faculty members would be greatly remiss, in our opinion, if they "let the buck stop there." The cause of the breakdown in the application of research findings often can be placed squarely on the shoulders of those producing the research. Faculty many times appear either unable or, as is more likely the case, unwilling to frame their findings in such a way as to highlight managerial applicability.

There are some encouraging recent signs that this is changing, however. An example would be the new journal—*Academy of Management Executive*—being started by an organization of academic scholars (The Academy of Management) that formerly published two journals strictly oriented to a professorial audience. It will take some time to tell whether this new journal will achieve its objective of communicating academic (largely basic) management research successfully to practicing managers such that they both see and understand how such research findings can be applied. There is also the question of whether academic recognition—on a par with that achieved by publication in a strictly scholarly journal—will be earned by a contribution to this type of outlet. Nevertheless, the mere establishment of a publication of this nature indicates that some academic groups in business schools are becoming more aware of, and concerned about, the goal of making their findings relevant to professional practice.

We leave this section with one other question: Can researchers in business schools become *too* concerned about relevance? Will an overfocus on relevance, if that should happen, move schools back toward the situation of the 1950s, where the concern (strongly stated by Gordon and Howell) was that "there has been a flood of applied research, but most of it has been observational, descriptive, or at a low analytical level." We believe that there is a real danger that the "rush to relevance" perceived in some schools (and as indicated to an extent by our questionnaire answers) could lead to a high percentage of largely trivial, although overtly applied, research if schools and their faculty are not careful. We do not think that this is an inevitable result, by any means—because *relevant* does not have to mean "nonrigorous"—but the danger is there if insufficient attention is given to stringent scrutiny (by the researchers themselves and their peers) of the kinds of problems being investigated—their scope, centrality, and depth. If this is not done, the desire to be relevant may well prove to have an unintended downside.

Corporate Knowledge of Business School Research

By and large, our data show that the business community knows relatively little about the kinds of research being carried out within business schools and the findings being obtained from that research. Even those who might be expected to have a fair degree of knowledge—members of schools' business advisory councils, for example—typically report otherwise. Again, the extent to which this state of affairs is a problem cannot be made the exclusive responsibility of either the schools or members of the business community. It is apparent, however, that whatever the reasons, the potential for impact of business school research on business executives is being vitiated by the fact that the relevant information seldom gets through in the first place.

In our interviews with deans and faculty members, we found a rather consistent pattern of responses about how well (or poorly) a school was doing in getting the word out to the business community about the research efforts and findings of its faculty. That response pattern indicated that, typically, the school had not made concerted efforts to keep the corporate community systematically informed about the research program of the school. If anything was done at all, it usually consisted of the routine distribution of a reprint series to supposedly interested parties. The school's efforts ordinarily stopped there—if they went that far. Furthermore, individual faculty members reported very little, if any, involvement of practitioners in helping to formulate problems and even to react to particular sets of findings. Of course, such involvement would be impractical and perhaps even counterproductive for some kinds of research issues and problems, but it is our view that—on the whole—business school faculty members are remiss in not taking greater advantage of informed practitioner input at various stages of their research. This, if done in specifically targeted instances (i.e., with some advance planning and thought), could provide a double advantage: The likelihood of more information reaching the business community about the school's research would be increased at least somewhat, and the quality and impact of some of the research itself might be improved. In sum, stronger and more insistent efforts to inform the corporate sector about business school research would seem to be a joint responsibility of the school as an organization and faculty members as individual (or as groups of) researchers.

The responsibilities, however, as we noted earlier, do not lie only with the university. Those in key managerial and executive positions have to ask themselves to what extent they and their colleagues are in a "learning mode." To use an analogy that we think is appropriate here, many physicians seem eager to learn about the latest research results coming out of medical schools and laboratories. Such physicians (many of them) exhibit a strong motivation to keep up with research developments in their particular fields. Can the same be said of practicing managers in the business world? We do not have the data to answer this question, but we raise it here simply to suggest that there would seem to be some responsibility on the part of potential consumers of business research, as well as on the part of producers of that research, to be informed on what research is going on and what findings are emerging from it.

Quality and Impact of Business School Research

All that we have said previously in this commentary leads up to this final issue: Has business school research improved in quality and has it had (and does it have) a substantial impact on the management profession? There are no accurate gauges that we know of to provide an unequivocal answer to the first part of this question: whether the quality of business school research has improved over the years since the 1959 reports. We think that a fair assessment would be that, on the whole, it has. However, the qualifier to our judgment, "on the whole," indicates that we do not think that the record is one of across-the-board accomplishment or that quality has been consistently better everywhere such research is carried out. We do not believe that business schools, for the most part, have a strong basis for developing self-congratulatory feelings about the quality of their research programs.

On the positive side, our data do indicate that business school research has ceased to be the highly visible target it once was. It is not strongly criticized either within the university (as shown by the general lack of such comments from provosts) or within the corporation (where most executives have little to say about it at all). This does seem to be a definite change from 25 years ago,

when so many people were lamenting the very low quality of research emanating from business/management schools. On the other hand, relatively few
knowledgeable observers inside or outside the university are explicitly and enthusiastically praising such research either. It was almost never, in any of our
university or corporate interviews, mentioned as one of the major strengths of
business schools. Overall, then, it seems that the quality of business school
research definitely has moved out of the position of being an object of derision
but has not yet moved into a position of being the focus of unstinting respect.
Those who have high aspirations for it believe that there is still substantial
progress to be made. For example, we endorse the views of Clark Kerr, former
president of the University of California and former chair of the Carnegie Commission on Higher Education, who stated (in an interview for this study):

> I would like to see business schools become intellectual leaders on campus. Even
> though business schools have been the great success story of professional schools
> since the end of World War II, I had hoped that they would be more successful than
> they have in helping to bring a *unity* to the social sciences—a unity among social
> sciences, and unity between theory and applications.

Finally, we come to the ultimate question: What is the impact of business
school research on the practice of business and management? The apparent
answer—based on data provided in earlier portions of this chapter—is: not
much. If impact is measured in terms of whether managers are directly influenced in their day-to-day actions by the latest research articles and scholarly
books, then one would have to conclude that such effects are virtually nil. Since
the executives we interviewed and surveyed on this issue claimed almost no
knowledge of what business schools were turning out by way of research, such
a conclusion is almost inescapable. However, the situation is considerably more
complex than meets the eye, and the actual impact is probably greater than
many managers in business realize, though also probably less than most academic researchers assume—or hope. The reason is that much of whatever impact there is is indirect and, in a sense, disguised. For example, some of the
knowledge of newly-hired managerial employees, especially recent business
school graduates, may have been directly affected by the research of faculty
members, but that link is not obvious to superiors or senior colleagues. Similarly, consultants hired by a company may themselves be quite up-to-date on
contemporary research findings in their area of expertise and are using those
findings in their practice, yet the bases of some of their approaches to business
problems are not identified as originating from research carried out in business
schools. Other examples could be cited, but the point is that, as we stated above,
business school research overall is probably having a greater effect than is recognized even though such impact is not highly visible. Regardless of the true
state of affairs, however, we believe it is incumbent on deans and faculty members everywhere to address the issue of how to increase the impact of business
school research on the practicing profession. How can, in effect, business school
research *lead* business practice?

8

BUSINESS SCHOOL RELATIONS

There are at least two sets of "publics" with which the typical business/ management school has relations: the university community in which the business school is housed, and the professional management/business community external to the university. In this chapter we examine the relations between the business school and each of these two major sets of institutions.

The business school, with rare exception, operates within the structure of a larger university community; it is strongly affected by the culture of that community and has only limited freedom to diverge from the mainstream of the formal as well as the informal norms and customs of the university. The wider institutional policies affect the selection, promotion, tenure, and salary decisions that pertain to business faculty, limit the degrees of freedom to set standards of admission and graduation, typically set limits on the extent to which the business school can engage in fund-raising, prescribe the amount of time a faculty member can devote to consulting, and often constrain the school's nondegree-program activities.

Since the business school is dependent on the larger university to provide at least 40 and as much as 60% of the course work for the 4-year undergraduate business degree, the quality of that degree depends in large measure on the quality of those courses taught by colleagues across the campus. While the nonbusiness component for graduate degrees is smaller, the intrinsic quality of the MBA (or other equivalent degrees) can nonetheless be significantly improved if nonbusiness faculty are utilized as supplementary and complementary resources in the design and delivery of business programs and courses. Clearly, therefore, the strength of the working relationships between the business faculty and the campus at large can be a factor influencing the overall quality of business school degree programs.

Quite aside from the direct impact on the design and delivery of degree programs, the interactions by business school faculty members with the university have other important implications. The latitude allowed the business school to determine its own destiny is determined, at least in part, by the level of prestige and influence that the business school has within the university community and the relationships it has with key elements—the provost, faculty in certain related areas, continuing education units, development officers, the alumni director, the placement office, and others. The level of integration (or lack thereof) and harmony between the business school and other elements of the university community can enhance or diminish the quality of business school programs.

The business school typically also has a significant impact on a number of other academic programs within the university structure. It contributes service courses to the university community at large and can play a strong role in helping to determine the general education requirements for all (undergraduate) students while contributing important electives to significant numbers of graduate students in other disciplines.

The business school also has important linkages to the business community. The business community is a major stakeholder—among other things, business firms hire the graduates, are a source for part-time and visiting faculty, use faculty as teachers in executive development programs and as consultants, utilize research findings, and make major financial contributions to the business school. Gordon and Howell made reference to the importance of relationships with the business community in the context of business schools' evaluation of their own operations, "taking stock." "Stocktaking should extend beyond curricula, course content, standards, and teaching methods in the school's regular degree programs. It should encompass also the scholarly activities of the faculty *and the school's relations with the business community*" (Emphasis added). (Gordon and Howell, 1959, p. 427).

As with other chapters, we first review the situation 25 years ago, describe the evolution of relationships during the last two and a half decades, report on the results of our interviews and surveys, and present our commentary based on these findings.

THE PAST 25 YEARS

In assessing the progress—or lack thereof—in the patterns of relations between the business school and its internal (to the university) and external constituencies, we need to examine how things were at the start of the decade of the sixties. How was the business school perceived by other academics and by the business community, and what patterns of interaction were prevalent at that time?

The Situation at the Beginning of the 1960s

Since the internal relationships are of a different nature and have different consequences compared to relations with the business community, we will deal separately with the two areas. First, we examine the relationships with the academic community (but this order of presentation should not be construed as implying that the academic relationships are necessarily more important than those with the business community).

Relationships with the Academic Community At the time of the Ford and Carnegie reports, business schools apparently were not held in the highest esteem on campus. Gordon and Howell described the business faculties of the late 1950s as generally inferior, in academic terms, to those of other university units. "The intellectual atmosphere in the business school frequently compares unfavorably with that in other schools and colleges on the same campus" (Gordon and Howell, 1959, p. 356). Students, likewise, were (on average) of lower quality—as measured by test scores—than those of most other units. Pierson summed up the prevailing perception: "[Business] schools have come to be rather generally identified with students of limited academic ability" (Pierson, 1959, p. 72). Moreover, there apparently was not a great deal of administrative zeal for upgrading the status or intrinsic quality of the business school: "Sometimes, it is our impression, the university administration offers little support to significant improvement in the business school" (Gordon and Howell, 1959, p. 357).

The quality of research in business schools was of particular concern. To upgrade the quality of research in business schools, Gordon and Howell recommended increased involvement with other academic units, asserting that "improving the quality of business research...calls for closer cooperation between research workers trained in the business fields and economics and those whose backgrounds are in...other fields....This implies seeking to interest more behavioral scientists, mathematicians, and statisticians in business problems" (p. 392).

In sum, the typical 1960 business school was held in relatively low esteem on campus, both faculty and students were seen as inferior to most other academic units, there was little significant interaction by the business school faculty with those in other disciplines, and the university administrative apparatus was not overly supportive.

We turn now to an examination of the relationships between the business school and the business community.

Relationships with the Business Community The business school's interaction with the business community in the 1950s consisted predominantly of two sets of relations: First, the business community was a major source of part-time faculty, and second, it provided consulting opportunities for full-time faculty. A few schools provided regular service to the business community through their bureaus of business research, which supplied regional and local economic statistical data on a regular or contract basis, but these efforts did not typically involve regular, full-time, academic research-oriented faculty.

The part-time faculty, while being in a position (theoretically) to provide valuable state-of-the-art expertise, in fact were seen by many as weakening the overall quality of the business school. According to Gordon and Howell (p. 351), "There is general agreement that the use of businessmen [sic] as part-time teachers is an expedient to be avoided as much as possible, particularly in the regular day program of the business school. The use of such part-time instructors should be confined, if at all possible, to evening courses not carrying degree credit."

While decrying the excessive use of business people in the classroom, the importance of practical experience for the regular faculty was recognized: "While the business schools should probably not rely to any significant degree on former or present businessmen to man [sic] the business school's regular courses, most faculty members should have a significant amount of responsible business experience, whether obtained through an interlude of full-time business practice or through consulting activity" (Gordon and Howell, 1959, p. 352). Thus consulting was seen as a positive means for faculty to obtain experience; however, the need to control and direct the activity was deemed important also. As Gordon and Howell pointed out (p. 435), "Too often . . . 'consulting' work consists of routine jobs that absorb the time and drain the energies of business school teachers without adding much if anything to their professional competence." The concern for control of the amount and kind of faculty involvement outside the university was also expressed by Pierson (p. 277): "One of the difficult issues confronting business schools is how much emphasis they should put on part-time teaching, practical experience, and faculty consulting work. . . . Business schools should hold part-time teaching within very severe bounds."

Given the rather extensive involvement of the business community, through part-time teaching by business people and through the consulting activities of faculty, one might have expected that relations would be close enough for business executives in general to be quite familiar with what was going on in business schools. Not so, apparently, at least insofar as research done by business school faculties was concerned. As Gordon and Howell observed (p. 380): "The lack of familiarity with the research activities of the business schools was quite striking." (The latter observation should not have been at all surprising; as we pointed out in Chapters 5 and 7, this issue still remains very relevant today.)

In sum, from the evidence presented in the foundation reports, relations between the business school and the business community were far below what would have been considered ideal.

Developments during the Past 25 Years

The Foundation reports appear to have had some influence in moving business schools toward a greater understanding of and interaction with other elements of the university—particularly mathematics and the social sciences—and toward more extensive and systematic relations with the business community—beyond merely hiring part-time instructors and taking advantage of consulting opportunities for individual faculty members, but the strength of these relationships has not yet improved to the degree that many deans would like to see.

The business school, in moving to adopt some of the Foundation reports' recommendations on curriculum—particularly those concerning the infusion of quantitative methods and the social science disciplines—necessarily had to become more involved with academic departments outside the business school than had hitherto been the case. The movement from specialized provincialism was not total, however. More often than not, the adoption of the quantitative and social sciences was accomplished not so much by interaction between the business school and other academic units, but rather through hiring Ph.D.s from those disciplines and then acculturating them into their new environment in splendid isolation from their root disciplines. Psychology, sociology, industrial engineering, and other relevant academic units (and in some cases even departments of economics) seldom have become linked formally and systematically with the business school.

We see some evidence that the business school is somewhat more interactive today than it was in 1960; however, it is far from the interdisciplinary unit that might be envisioned, given the complex, diverse nature of the subject matter which comprises business. Not only do business faculty typically appear to have little direct interaction with relevant counterparts across campus, but there is less communication among the parts (departments) within the business school itself than we believe ought to be the case.

As we pointed out in Chapters 5 and 7, the business school has become at least a peer, and on many campuses, a leader, among academic units doing research; hence we believe that those university relations which are a function of academic respectability have indeed improved considerably. And as we have seen (in Chapter 5), campus administrators (e.g., provosts) have become more respectful of the business school.

In summary, over the span of 25 years, the business school has gained considerable respectability on campus, has hired doctorates with training in disciplines other that the functional areas of business—especially from the social sciences, mathematics, and statistics—and has gained stature with the central administration of the university. It has not, however, become as interactive with other campus units as might have been envisioned or as many would like to see.

Relations with the business community appear to have improved substantially since the early sixties. Business advisory councils are now the mode, not the exception. With the expansion of the AACSB to the assembly format, (described in Chapter 9), business organizations were admitted to membership, with the result that direct influence could be brought to bear on the setting and administration of standards. There is an increased awareness, in some of the functional academic areas, of the need to disseminate research findings to practitioners, as evidenced by the emergence of a few academic-edited journals aimed at a nonacademic audience.

As will be pointed out in Chapter 12, the number of institutions engaged in postdegree and nondegree executive education has increased, as has the overall volume of such activities. This implies greater interaction and potentially better relations between industry and business schools, although only a small fraction of the faculty is (typically) involved. The growth of executive MBA programs, where the students are company-sponsored and have considerable work experience as a prerequisite to admission, is another phenomenon suggesting closer interaction between business school faculty and the business community, inasmuch as such programs put a premium on faculty work experience. Since it is difficult for a faculty member who has no empathy for actual real-world conditions to be effective in a classroom comprised of students who want to learn—from the professor—how to cope more effectively with their current managerial environment, schools will either have to hire faculty members with the requisite background, or their existing faculty will have to acquire such experience through increased interaction with business, either through consulting, case writing, research, serving on boards, or other means.

We turn now to the direct data from our interviews and questionnaire surveys to see how deans, provosts, and business executives assess current relationships between academia and business.

PERCEPTIONS OF RELATIONS

We gathered data concerning perceived relationships between the business school and the university community through interviews with provosts and deans. The survey instruments directed to provosts and deans included questions designed to elicit their perceptions on relationships within the university community. Likewise, we inquired from provosts, deans, and faculty members about relationships with the business community, and on this topic we, of course, also solicited opinions from corporate executives.

Perceptions of Intracampus Relations

In our interviews with provosts and deans, we probed for their evaluation of the business school in relation to other units on campus. We were especially interested in the provosts' evaluations, because they are in a position to judge the business school in comparison with other academic units. In view of the low regard with which business schools had been held before 1960, we wanted to determine their status today. Were they deemed important and influential, and were they perceived as playing important roles in the development of the institution as a whole?

Our interviews with deans and provosts left us with a number of impressions:

- Business schools feel rather good about themselves; deans perceive their schools to have reasonably high status on campus.
- For many academic institutions, there is a constant battle for resources; the typical business school regards itself as overburdened—too many students—and underfunded.
- While there are exceptions, the typical school sees itself as pretty much a "stand alone" operation; there is little interaction—or perceived need for interaction—with other academic units on campus.
- Provosts think highly of their business schools; they believe business faculties are academically competent; but they decry the isolationism of the business school; they do not see campus-wide academic leadership coming from the business school.

The survey results generally support our interview observations. Deans were asked to assess their campus administration's rating of the business school in terms of its importance (relative to other academic units). Only 3% said that the business school was considered one of the less important units on campus, while 85% felt that it would be considered one of the more, if not one of the most, important units on campus (see Table 8.1). There were, interestingly, no significant differences among categories of schools on this question.

High ratings of a business school's importance could, of course, be merely a reflection of the size of the operation. After all, business schools account for close to a fourth of all undergraduate degrees granted; hence they could hardly be classified as unimportant. We were, therefore, interested in knowing how the business school's intrinsic quality was perceived, as compared with other academic units. Here too, the deans felt that their campus administration would rate their school highly. Only 2% thought that their school would be consid-

TABLE 8.1
DEANS' PERCEPTIONS OF ADMINISTRATORS' RATINGS OF THE RELATIVE IMPORTANCE
OF THEIR OWN BUSINESS SCHOOLS

Rating	Category of School			
	I	II	III	Total
One of the most important	45%	51%	49%	49%
One of the more important	40	36	37	37
Average importance	8	10	11	11
One of the less important	5	3	3	3
One of the least important	2	0	0	0
	100%	100%	100%	100%

TABLE 8.2
DEANS' PERCEPTIONS OF ADMINISTRATORS' RATINGS OF THE RELATIVE QUALITY
OF THEIR OWN BUSINESS SCHOOLS

Rating	Category of School			
	I	II	III	Total
One of the highest-quality units	40%	50%	34%	41%
One of the higher-quality units	48	35	35	36
Average quality	10	13	27	20
One of the lower-quality units	2	1	4	3
One of the lowest-quality units	0	1	0	0
	100%	100%	100%	100%

ered one of the lower-quality units, while 77% believed that their school would be rated one of the higher- or highest-quality units on campus. There were significant differences ($p=0.05$) between categories of schools on this dimension: 88% of Category I and 85% of Category II deans thought their schools would be rated one of the higher- or highest-quality units, versus 69% for Category III schools (see Table 8.2).

Provosts rated their business schools more highly, in terms of importance, than the deans predicted they would, with 64% opting for the response "one of the most important units on campus" (see Table 8.3). There were significant differences, however, between the types of schools, with only a third of the Category I provosts rating the business school on their own campus in the highest category, whereas two-thirds of Category II and III provosts accorded their business schools the highest echelon of relative importance. This pattern of results is understandable when one takes into account the research nature of Category I institutions: Most universities with doctoral programs in business are likely to have many units (notably in the sciences) with extensive research involvement, large investments in equipment, and long historical commitments to scholarly research. The business schools, in these institutions, are not likely to be perceived as of higher importance than other units with longer (and probably stronger) records of research—and especially funded research. It is notable, however, that no Category I provost rated his or her business school as merely average or below average in importance.

In terms of academic quality, provosts were not quite as generous with their ratings as they were in assessing the business school's importance, but they were nonetheless supportive (see Table 8.4). Only 3% of the provosts rated their business school as one of the lower-quality units on campus, 24% assessed it as of average quality, and 73% said the business school was either one of the most or the most important unit. There were no statistically significant differences among categories of schools. Notably, however, only 18% of Category I provosts rated their school as average in quality, and none said their school was below average in quality. It seems safe to assume that these results are

TABLE 8.3
PROVOSTS' PERCEPTIONS OF THE RELATIVE IMPORTANCE OF THEIR OWN BUSINESS
SCHOOLS

Rating	Category of School			
	I	II	III	Total
One of the most important units	34%	67%	66%	64%
One of the more important units	66	25	27	29
Average importance	0	8	7	7
One of the less or least important	0	0	0	0
	100%	100%	100%	100%

TABLE 8.4
PROVOSTS' PERCEPTIONS OF THE QUALITY OF THEIR OWN BUSINESS SCHOOLS

Rating	Category of School			
	I	II	III	Total
One of the highest-quality units	21%	35%	27%	29%
One of the higher-quality units	61	41	42	44
Average quality	18	22	27	24
One of the lower- or lowest-quality	0	2	4	3
	100%	100%	100%	100%

vastly different than what would likely have been obtained had our questionnaire been administered in the same manner by the Ford and Carnegie researchers in the 1950s.

Perceptions of Relations with the Business Community

We dealt quite extensively with faculty relations with the business community
in Chapter 5. There the issue was the degree of the faculty's involvement/
experience with the real world of business. Here we consider the business/
management school as a whole and its interaction patterns with the business
community. Within the university community we inquired of deans, provosts,
and faculty members, both in our interviews and in the questionnaire survey,
about their schools' relations with the business community: how well they were
performing in this regard and what advantages or caveats they saw as pertaining to the relationships. We followed a similar line of inquiry with senior corporate and human resources executives concerning their perceptions of how
well business enterprises in general and their own organizations in particular
related to business schools and how they perceived business schools relating
to the business community in general and their own organizations in particular.

Our findings are presented below; we first report on the perceptions of the university, with the corporate views to follow.

University Perceptions   Our campus interviews left us with the overall impression that the university perceptions could be summed up by saying that relationships with the business community are "good, but could—and should—be better." No one waxed superlative about their own school's relationships, although most could point to some specific activities involving direct linkages which suggest fairly pervasive and consistent relationships, including business advisory councils, internships for students, well-organized placement functions, consulting by faculty, visiting lectureships and part-time faculty from the business community, executive development activities, etc. They could also point to financial support from the business community as evidence of a fairly close relationship, although, of course, there are wide divergences among schools on this dimension. While most felt that the relationships ought to be improved, few, if any, seemed to have any definite idea of what, precisely, ought to be done, other than "more of the same."

The survey data support our interview observations. Provosts, deans, and faculty members all see their own school's relationship as being reasonably strong (the median rating of the strength of its current relations was between 6 and 7 on a 10-point scale, with virtually no differences among the three groups of respondents), but needing improvement—82% of the deans said their school should "make very strong efforts to increase such relations" in the next 10 years. Business advisory council (BAC) members gave almost the same ratings as their academic associates. Interestingly enough, deans, faculty members, and BAC members saw the collective relationships of all schools as decidedly lower (5.1 versus 6.2) than their own school. Only provosts did not perceive a major difference between the relationships enjoyed by their own school versus those of the system (all business schools) as a whole; they rated the relations for all schools at a fairly respectable 6.3 (versus 6.7 for their own school).

We also attempted to determine whether the campus community perceived any particular advantages or disadvantages in their relationships with the business community, and if so, what the nature of the advantages or concerns was. When asked whether there were major advantages, there were surprising differences among the categories of schools in the strength of their affirmative responses: 97% of Category I and 90% of Category II schools chose to answer "yes, definitely"—the strongest choice available—but only 13% of Category III schools chose the strongest "yes" and 87% opted for the more equivocal "yes, somewhat."

There also were significant differences among categories of schools concerning the nature of the advantages of close relationships. Category I deans see income (40%) as the principal advantage, with contacts for the school and its faculty members a close second (38%). For Category II schools, nonfinancial support and contacts shared equal billing, while income rated further down the line and almost equal in importance to placement. Nonfinancial support was clearly the dominant benefit seen by Category III deans.

Were major disadvantages seen? The majority (81% of provosts, 78% of deans, and 68% of the faculty) said no, while 19% of the provosts, 22% of the deans, and 29% of the faculty responded, "yes, somewhat." Almost no one opted for the stronger reservation, "yes, definitely." For those who do have concerns, the major disadvantage seen is a potential for undue influence on academic programs.

While not evidencing undue concern about the urgency of the matter, fully 92% of the deans nonetheless felt that their own faculties should have more interaction with the business community than they have currently. Overall, deans rated the interaction of schools in general—i.e., all schools, not just their own—with the business community at a full point lower than the rating of teaching performance but slightly higher than the rating for executive education. The same general balance of perceptions was true for provosts and faculty members. Clearly, business school academics as well as provosts see business schools overall as performing much less well in those activities dealing with the business community than they do in the primary areas of teaching and research, and they believe more interaction should take place.

Corporate Perceptions   Our impressions gathered through the interview process are that corporate executives, in the aggregate, feel themselves quite distant from the university. There is interest on their part, but that interest is most intensely focused on the recruitment of graduates, not on influencing the operations of the business school, except in isolated instances. There was general agreement that relations ought to be improved, but there were few concrete suggestions about how that might be done.

The corporate survey data, across the board, give a rather low report card to business school relations. Almost all the categories of executives polled—CEOs, SCEs, directors of management development, and operating managers—could rate the quality of relations no higher than 5 on our 10-point scale (as compared to 6 or 7 ratings for teaching and research). Of all the activities of the business school, relations with the business community ranked lowest as viewed by corporate respondents.

COMMENTARY

We will discuss, first, the relationships—or lack thereof—between the business school and other elements of the university in light of the foregoing findings. Then we will, in a similar fashion, comment on the relations with the business community.

Relations with the University

Clearly, business schools have improved their image with the larger university community since the time of the Foundation reports more than two decades ago. They have more power, partly because of increased numbers, but they also have earned a higher level of respect, largely on the strength of the faculties' scholarly capabilities vis-a-vis the rest of the university. While the overall stature of the business school faculty has risen, the quality of their relationships with the rest of the university community has improved very little, if at all. A number of provosts, in our interviews, expressed serious concern about the business school faculty's lack of integration with the larger university community.

There are probably good explanations for this relative isolation. The business school (as is true in the case of a number of other professional schools) is to a large extent a stand-alone operation; it typically has a definable market constituency which not only provides jobs for its graduates, but also is a source of direct financial support. Its relative independence has been reinforced in recent years by differences in the supply and demand for faculty, causing severe strains in the relationships, in many institutions, between the business school faculty and those in other academic units, particularly the humanities. Pay levels currently are significantly higher for business school faculty than for their counterparts in many other sectors of the university, a fact which causes understandable discontent among nonbusiness faculty and provosts on many campuses. In our interviews, a number of provosts commented on the difficulties caused by the relatively high pay scale for business faculty; they understand the supply and demand factors which force up these salaries, but they rather resent having to acquiesce to these forces. When one imputes the income derived by business school faculty members from consulting—something seldom, if ever, available to humanities faculties—one can readily see how far apart incomes on the same campus might be.

Invoking the unseen hand of free-enterprise economics, while justification enough for the average business school faculty member, hardly suffices as an acceptable explanation for those who are near the low end of the salary range. We certainly do not wish to suggest that the laws of supply and demand be suspended; rather, we offer the observation, unpalatable though it may be, that business school faculty relationships with their peers in the humanities and social sciences are likely to continue to be strained until there is at least some semblance of economic parity between the various faculty groups. In the final analysis, the faculty pay issue may well influence the ultimate size constraint on the business school. If demand were to continue to escalate while the faculty supply remained the same, the upward pressure on salaries for professionals could become intolerable, in organizational terms, so that there would have to be a ceiling on the proportional size of the business school. The degree to which these forces, in fact, are ultimately brought to bear on the business school is, at least in part, influenced by the quality of the relationships between the business school and the rest of the university.

One of the most important factors influencing attitudes toward the business school is the degree to which it engages in suboptimizing behavior by being parochially concerned only with its own academic turf and not paying enough attention to the opportunities for enrichment of programs for business students that are available in other areas of the university. There are two aspects to this issue: First, there is the concern for the breadth, or well-roundedness, of the business student, and second, there is the question of whether some areas of the business curriculum might not be taught as effectively, or perhaps better, by faculty outside the business school. Both these objectives require close working relationships with colleagues across the campus. The broadening, general education objective can only be reached with the collaboration of a wide range of faculty who help to identify, prescribe, and jointly control the quality of non-business courses for business students; and, of course, this requires the business school to be willing to limit the amount of required work in business relative to the total curriculum requirements. Suboptimization can occur when the business school fails to analyze the courses taught by its own faculty in terms of the alternatives—refuses, in effect, to consider a make or buy decision. There may well be—and we are convinced this is a rather common phenomenon—cases where business school faculty are assigned to design and teach courses which might well be taught elsewhere in the university, either less expensively or more effectively, or both. For example, ethics might be taught at least as effectively, if not more so, by philosophers as by business school professors, government relations by political scientists or historians, communications by creative writers or journalists, international business by area studies experts jointly with economists, etc. In our view, then, the business school should seriously consider ways to subcontract, as it were, certain courses (often taught in the business school) to other departments in the university with the active participation of business faculty in the selection or design and specification of these courses. Obviously, for this to be effective, the business school will have to generate more collegial interaction patterns than appear—according to our interviews—to be the mode among faculties today.

Relations with the Business Community

While faculty and deans do not give themselves as poor a report card as do corporate executives, both academia and the business world feel that there is a great deal of room for improvement in the current pattern of relationships. Both groups believe that interaction between the business school and the business community should be encouraged. However, as we pointed out in Chapter 5, the nature of the interactions need to be managed with care—there are some risks, the main one being that of business having too much direct influence on the academic programs of the university. Universities, if they are to do their job of research and development of new knowledge, must necessarily remain somewhat detached. With this caveat, we endorse the consensus view that relationships should be improved.

Executives gave both their own firms' relationships, and the perceived relationships of all firms with business schools a low rating—less than 5. They did not seem ready, however, to lead a charge to change those relationships.

Most firms seem content to preoccupy themselves primarily with the recruitment process while providing business schools with an occasional member of an advisory committee, some part-time faculty, and modest financial support. We did not find them bursting with ideas—or expressing keen interest—about becoming involved in designing the curriculum or in participating in faculty development. In fact, overall, there seems to us to be relatively little empathy or understanding of the internal operations or culture of a business school.

Deans, likewise, while expressing the conviction that more should be done, did not volunteer many ideas on what should be done or how. Relations are "generally OK," says the typical dean, "should be better," but it is not really highest on the priority list of things to do, except perhaps as it relates to fund-raising. We believe that relationships will not get better unless deans make it happen. The initiative is unlikely to come from the business community (or, for that matter, from the faculty).

CHAPTER 9

ACCREDITATION

Accreditation in the United States is the "primary communal self-regulatory means of academic and educational quality assessment and enhancement" (Millard, 1983). It is the process by which institutions and programs are measured to determine whether they have met certain standards. Ideally, the process not only measures quality, but also drives the system to improve quality.

American accreditation may be unique in that it is self-regulated, i.e., administered and controlled by member institutions, not by government. The higher education system in the United States, while subject to governmental constraints—each state has its own unique system of educational charters and control—has relied primarily on private associations to set minimum standards of quality and to inform the public as to whether particular institutions are in compliance with these standards. There are two categories of accreditation, and it is important to recognize the differences between them. Institutional accreditation, as the name implies, refers to the institution as a whole; specialized, or programmatic accreditation, on the other hand, focuses on specific professional, academic, or occupational programs normally located within larger institutions.

Six regional commissions provide institutional accreditation for colleges and universities. Each consists of the member accredited institutions in its geographic region. Often, therefore, this kind of accreditation is called regional accreditation. Most colleges and universities that are authorized by their respective states to grant degrees are accredited by these regional associations.

However, associations consisting of member schools of a discipline or profession conduct specialized accreditation. It is typically national, rather than regional, in scope. Schools of education, business, library science, music, law, engineering, medicine, and many others have their own national organizations which accredit their member institutions. These associations, in turn, are accredited by an umbrella organization, the Council of Post-Secondary Accreditation (COPA), which provides technical assistance and recognition to its members. The AACSB is the official accrediting agency (recognized by COPA and the U.S. Department of Education) for collegiate schools of business in the United States. (Canadian institutions also may choose to be accredited by the AACSB.)

Our inquiry included an examination of the overall AACSB accreditation system and the reaction of various groups to it. We queried deans, provosts, faculty members, and business executives with a view toward assessing the effectiveness of AACSB accreditation. We asked, in effect, a basic bottom-line question: In an era of increasing deregulation and greater reliance on entrepreneurial initiative, is accreditation an anachronistic concept which might well be scrapped in favor of free-market competition as the primary regulator of academic quality?

As with previous chapters, our point of departure is the situation 25 to 30 years ago, with great reliance on the Gordon and Howell and Pierson reports as the basis for setting the scene. We will then describe the changes that have taken place since that time and report survey and interview data that assess the attitudes of our respondents toward accreditation and its probable future. Finally, we will add our own observations based not only on the analysis of the data, but also on our own experiences with the system over a considerable period of time.

THE PAST 25 YEARS

Trends established during the quarter century comprising the immediate past may be the most prescient for shaping the future. We first outline the situation at the beginning of the period and then analyze the issues and directions that seem most relevant to the future.

The Situation at the Beginning of the 1960s

Both the Gordon and Howell and the Pierson reports criticized the AACSB and its accreditation activities as the latter were conducted in the late 1950s. In their views, the AACSB had set insufficiently demanding Standards, and moreover, there had been virtually no enforcement of the Standards. To understand the situation and to put things in perspective, it may be useful to review briefly the history of the organization.

The AACSB was formed in 1916 not for the purpose of accreditation, but to provide a forum for the systematic exchange of information among institutions and to establish common curricular themes among the sixteen members which comprised the original organization. From the the outset, one of the major objectives was to increase recognition and prestige for its member schools. The first annual meeting included in its agenda the issue of honor societies for business students, perhaps reflecting the relatively low prestige of business schools on liberal arts–dominated campuses. (The most notable honor society, Phi Beta Kappa, did not induct members from business programs.)

Early on, and throughout the first several decades of its existence, one of the AACSB's major criteria for admission was the independence of the business school and its comparability to other professional schools within the university structure. While the Association's stated purpose was "the promotion and improvement of higher business education in North America" (Standards, 1946), recognition within the academic community remained an important issue. Membership criteria precluded admission of units without sufficient autonomy to have a dean with clout in his or her own institution. Exclusively part-time operations were discouraged: "It is expected that the school or college will be primarily interested in full-time day students and that it not be primarily an evening school" (Executive Committee Interpretations, August 1949). Further, "it is also felt at this time teachers colleges will seldom qualify for membership." The members carefully nurtured their academic image.

It is noteworthy that not until 1961 did the AACSB officially make reference to Standards in the context of *accreditation;* until then, they were Standards for *membership.* However, while formally structured and operated as an Association, the organization had nonetheless evolved rapidly into the de facto accrediting association for programs in business administration and management. By the late fifties, the AACSB consisted of approximately 100 fully accredited members, plus a half-dozen associate members. (Associate members were those who met the membership Standards in all respects save the autonomy of the business unit.)

Nonmember institutions in 1959 offering business degrees numbered some 400. The latter for the most part were housed in institutions which had regional institutional accreditation and could thus claim to be accredited even though they did not belong to the Association. Therein lies a problem: How does the general public—even the relatively more informed professional public—distinguish from among schools which claim—truthfully—to be accredited but yet are not so designated by the professional body, the AACSB? More on this issue later.

While the more than a hundred members of the AACSB in 1959 represented only about one-fifth of the number of schools granting degrees in business, they did represent, essentially, "the Establishment" of the system. The membership accounted for roughly three-fourths of the total number of undergraduate degrees in business and included the most prestigious universities, both public and private, with leadership and guidance provided predominantly by the large midwestern ("Big Ten") institutions. Apropos of the times, there were no women deans.

Although clearly acknowledged by this time as the accrediting agency for programs in business and management, the AACSB operated rather like a gentlemen's club—a club comprised of business school deans. The organization's small size provided an atmosphere of intimacy—most of the member deans knew one another personally. Getting in was the key factor. Expulsion or, for that matter, probation, while provided for in the AACSB's constitution, was essentially unheard of for a member school.

It should not be inferred that the AACSB had been an entirely ineffectual organization. Indeed, the Association had played a strong role in "stirring the pot," so to speak, of inquiry and discontent within its membership. Earnest introspection had been the mode for annual meetings during the decade of the fifties; the business school establishment was ripe for reform. Thus, the Gordon and Howell and Pierson reports, backed by the prestige (and money!) of the Ford and Carnegie Foundations, had a ready audience which had been "softened up" to accept and act on recommendations. The reports, in essence, recommended tightening up of admissions requirements, increasing the full-time component and commitment to research of the faculty, reduction of the number of courses and introduction of more rigor and more nonbusiness subject matter (breadth) into the undergraduate curriculum, and limitation of specialization in the graduate curriculum.

The stage having been set, as it were, by a number of years of turmoil in business school academia, culminating in the two major, highly publicized reports which presented a rather specific list of things to do to fix the system, the question remained: How should the prescriptions be administered, and by whom? Accreditation offered one avenue. A set of Standards, rigorously enforced, was seen as a way of shaping up the system for the growth that was to emerge in the 1960s and beyond. The AACSB was the logical organization to carry out the mandate.

Developments during the Past 25 Years

In this section we will first discuss the principal changes in the membership composition and structure of the AACSB (because these changes had important implications for accreditation). We will then focus on changes in the Accreditation Standards, changes in the processes for Standards enforcement, and the introduction of separate Standards for degree programs in accounting.

Changes in the Membership Structure of AACSB   In 1968, the AACSB changed the rules of admission to the organization: Membership was opened up to unaccredited American schools (who met the autonomous degree-recommending test), to international schools, and to business, government and other institutions with relevant interests in education for business and management. The first word of the name was changed from *Association* to *Assembly;* accredited members comprised an Accreditation Council within the Assembly. The Accreditation Council retained the same powers and responsibilities that members had earlier as an Association, i.e., it was the body responsible for the setting and the enforcement of Standards.

This development gave an immediate boost to membership (in the Assembly). Whereas in 1960 the total membership consisted of 98 domestic, accredited institutions, by the end of the first year of the new configuration (1968), 2 international, 42 nonacademic, and 169 nonaccredited academic members had joined the ranks with 126 accredited schools. Of the total membership of 337, only 37% represented accredited institutions. That proportion remained fairly stable through 1986, while the total membership grew to 830, comprised of 655 domestic and 65 foreign educational institutions and 110 business, government, and professional institutions. Of the 655 domestic educational institutions, 245 (37%) were accredited and 410 (63%) were nonaccredited. Member schools accounted for approximately 80 to 85%, while accredited schools produced 50 to 55% of all business degrees granted in 1986.

Changes in the Standards As has been discussed in previous chapters, the Ford and Carnegie reports had a significant impact on the accreditation standards during the decade of the sixties and beyond. In particular, the development of a core curriculum, both for undergraduate and graduate programs, and the specification of quantitative measures for Standards—such as the number and proportion of doctorally qualified faculty and their distribution across academic fields and programs and test scores as a prerequisite for the admission of graduate students—were doubtless due directly to the influence of these reports. Perhaps the most important factor was the shift from a purely undergraduate focus to accreditation for graduate programs as well.

Master's program Standards had been introduced in 1958; however, schools could choose to ignore them with impunity. Not only were there no meaningful enforcement procedures, but since mere membership in the AACSB constituted accreditation—and undergraduate programs were the criteria for membership— there was little incentive to shape up (for accreditation purposes) graduate programs. There certainly was no public notice given that an accredited school (undergraduate) might be offering at the same time a very unaccreditable graduate program.

If graduate programs were to be influenced through accreditation, clearly they had to be singled out for focus. In May of 1961, the AACSB moved to put the spotlight on graduate programs by enacting a rule providing that "listing [in the AACSB membership roster] shall constitute accreditation for professional collegiate education for business at the masters level." (Public listing was to commence in 1963.) This meant that those member schools with unaccredited master's programs were unmasked, as it were—there were now two levels of accreditation, and failure to be listed at the graduate level meant either that a school did not have master's programs or had unaccredited ones.

Later, in 1976, in recognition of the difficulty of inducing public awareness of unaccredited master's programs housed in schools accredited at the undergraduate level only, measures were introduced to require schools to meet Accreditation Standards simultaneously at both master's and undergraduate levels as a requisite for membership in the Accreditation Council (if programs were offered at both levels). By 1981 this rule was in full effect; accredited schools continuing to offer unaccreditable master's programs would lose their undergraduate accreditation.

Accreditation Enforcement   The Association (later the Assembly) took to heart the criticisms of the Foundation reports concerning the ineffectiveness of the enforcement process. Changes in the Standards themselves were, of course, a prerequisite to enforcement—it was deemed necessary to set standards which could be measured objectively. Under the old (pre-1961) Standards, the constitution provided that

> He [the secretary] shall...make such inquiries of members and associate members...as will show whether Association standards are being maintained. When in the opinion of the Executive Committee a school is not maintaining these standards, an inspection committee shall be appointed to investigate and report.

Naturally, this provision was difficult to implement, since there was no provision for the systematic gathering of information with which to determine the need for inspection committees.

To rectify this shortcoming, a regular, mandatory revisitation schedule was set up on a 10-year basis and self-study reports by all accredited institutions were required every 5 years. Such reports detailed the institution's mission and provided data on its faculty, admissions policies, curriculum, and other pertinent areas of concern for all programs that could reasonably be construed as business administration or management, whether organizationally administered by the business school or not. The latter provision was to deal with those programs—quite prevalent, especially in urban institutions—organizationally housed in evening divisions, continuing education units, or off-campus operations not under the jurisdiction of the business school but offering degrees that sound very much like business degrees—with titles such as Bachelor of Commerce.

To administer the continuing reaccreditation process, staff support was needed along with a group of volunteer deans and representatives from business members (nonacademics) to serve as on-site campus visitors. During the first several years of the process, the self-study reports and the reports from visitation teams were reviewed by the Standards Committee. In 1974, a Continuing Accreditation Committee (a standing group of deans and corporate representatives) was formed to do this review and to recommend action on reaccreditation matters to the Operations Committee (later the Executive Committee and now the Accreditation Management Committee) of the Accreditation Council.

By the end of the decade of the seventies, considerable dissatisfaction with the reaccreditation process was being voiced by the membership. Some schools complained that the quantitative requirements for accreditation were inappropriate to their situations—a plea which came rather frequently from urban schools with large part-time populations both of students and faculty. Perhaps the most strident voices of dissent came from prestigious schools, who viewed the reporting and visitation requirements as especially onerous. There was enough dissonance among some of the leading members of the AACSB to warrant the establishment of an ad hoc Accreditation Standards Review Committee, in 1980, to review the entire process. The committee's charge was to go back to "square one," as it were, to redesign the Standards and process from the ground up. After about a year's deliberation, the committee essentially reaffirmed the basic philosophy and direction of the Standards and the process by which they were being administered (Report of the Accreditation Standards Review Committee, 1981). The committee made recommendations which laid the groundwork for revisions in the Standards in 1982 which were intended to "increase flexibility, place more reliance on qualitative assessments and decrease reliance on the quantitative, and rely more on output" (Accreditation Council Meeting Minutes, April 30, 1982).

In 1984, a Task Force on Reaccreditation was formed to review the process of revisitation. The work of this task force led to a process designed to enhance the consultative aspects of visitations while still determining the maintenance of quality and compliance with the Standards. The new procedures, adopted in 1985, allowed the school being visited to recommend persons to be on their visitation team and to designate areas of special emphasis for the visit. These measures addressed one of the major complaints of the more prestigious schools, namely, that they got no benefit from the accreditation process.

Accounting Accreditation   Largely because of pressure from the accounting profession—most notably the American Institute of Certified Public Accountants (AICPA) and the American Accounting Association (AAA)—and influenced also by a number of schools or departments of accounting, the AACSB in 1981 agreed to take on the task of accrediting bachelor's and MBA programs with concentrations in accounting and master's of accounting programs. This was a radical departure from tradition and was not undertaken without a great deal of debate, if not serious differences of opinion, within the organization of deans. Before this move, the emphasis had been on accrediting entire business units as a whole, with levels—master's and undergraduate—being evaluated separately as discrete units, but without making distinctions among academic areas of concentration.

Many deans felt strongly that too much fragmentation and dysfunctional specialization existed already; there were fears that the creation of a special, separate accreditation process would lead to other groups wanting the same distinction—if it is good for accountants, why not for marketing, finance, or other groups? Others resented the influence of the professional accounting associations and felt that the AACSB would be taking on accounting accreditation for the wrong reasons—not so much for the purpose of improving the quality of accounting education, but as a defensive measure to prevent some other organization from doing the accrediting. Reasons for supporting the initiative included: to keep accreditation in the hands of educators rather than professional practitioners, to blunt a movement toward freestanding schools of accountancy (which was perceived to have been a threat to the integrity of business schools), and (an argument for acquiescence rather than active support) to emphasize the fact that accounting accreditation would be entirely voluntary, i.e., to be entered into independently of other bachelor's and master's level accreditation. In any event, the AACSB membership voted affirmatively, if not entirely enthusiastically, for separate accreditation for accounting programs. By July of 1986, sixty-one schools had received accounting accreditation.

Our investigation elicited very little commentary on accounting accreditation from either the academic or the corporate communities; there were few expressions of concern, and we found no evidence of any sentiment toward separate accreditation for other fields. We believe it is reasonable to presume that the process is proceeding smoothly and that the worst fears of those who were opposed to it have not been realized.

In summary, by 1986 the system of accreditation for business and management had grown tremendously; the focus had shifted from exclusively undergraduate accreditation to a school-wide, multiprogram approach, with master's and undergraduate programs having to be accredited simultaneously. Accounting accreditation had been added as a separate (voluntary) option, and a systematic review process to evaluate compliance with Accreditation Standards had been put into place. In addition, significant progress had been made toward a consultative, as opposed to a legalistic, approach to the accreditation process.

PERCEPTIONS OF ACCREDITATION

Deans and provosts from the academic community and corporate recruiting officers and executive development officers were our target informants on accreditation. We wanted to learn how they perceived accreditation as a factor influencing business school quality. Our findings are presented below.

Deans' Perceptions

In general, we found the deans we interviewed to have more burning issues on their minds than accreditation. The exceptions were those whose schools either were recently accredited, expecting a visitation for reaccreditation, actively seeking accreditation, or planning to do so in the near future.

The vast majority of our interviewees did not volunteer complaints about the process or the Standards themselves. The few exceptions were of two varieties: There were some (from prestigious schools, typically) who did not see anything particular to be gained from accreditation for their own schools and who saw the process as too burdensome and costly, and there were a small number of others (mostly from unaccredited schools seeking accreditation) who felt that the Standards were unrealistic or unfair. But—and we must stress this—there was no mandate for significant change in either the Standards or the enforcement process.

The survey data reinforced our interview observations. In answer to the question, What is your school's current attitude toward accreditation? none of the Category II and only 8% of the Category I schools indicated that accreditation was unimportant or had been a hindrance to the school, while 88% of Category II and 54% of Category I schools said accreditation had been of at least some direct value to them (see Table 9.1).

The unaccredited school deans also supported AACSB accreditation in general. As shown in Table 9.2, only 17% of the respondents said that accreditation was not important, while 56% indicated that not only was accreditation important, but also that they were making active efforts to be accredited.

In response to the question, What do you predict your school's orientation toward accreditation to be in the next 10 to 15 years? 99% of Category II and 98% of Category I deans indicated they would probably maintain accreditation; only one Category I dean suggested that there was more than a slight possibility that his school would let its accreditation lapse.

Another bit of evidence indicating deans' supportive attitudes toward accreditation: When asked to indicate the constraints or limiting factors in reaching their school's 10- to 15-year goals, accreditation was mentioned the least number of times (by only 6% of the deans responding) among the ten choices given them. Clearly, of all the potential impeding factors, accreditation was the least threatening in the minds of these deans.

The survey also solicited attitudes toward the accreditation process. Here the respondents were more critical. A mere 3% (see Table 9.3) gave the process an excellent rating and only 41% felt that it was "reasonable and appropriate," while 12% said that it was "unduly burdensome" and 44% damned with faint praise by checking the response "generally OK, but somewhat cumbersome." There were no significant differences among the categories of schools.

As for attitudes toward the Standards themselves, Table 9.4 shows that there were (perhaps predictably) significant differences in the reactions by catego-

TABLE 9.1
ACCREDITED SCHOOL DEANS' CURRENT ATTITUDES TOWARD AACSB ACCREDITATION

Importance/Value	Category of School	
	Category I	Category II
Important and of great value	31%	50%
Important and of some value	23	38
Important but of little value	38	12
Not important or a hindrance	8	0
	100%	100%

TABLE 9.2
NONACCREDITED SCHOOL DEANS' ATTITUDES TOWARD AACSB ACCREDITATION

Accreditation important and active steps being taken to become accredited	56%
Accreditation important but steps *not* being taken to become accredited	27
Accreditation unimportant	17
	100%

TABLE 9.3
DEANS' EVALUATION OF THE AACSB ACCREDITATION PROCESS

	Category of School			
Rating	I	II	III	Total
Excellent	0%	5%	2%	3%
Reasonable and appropriate	33	49	35	41
Generally OK, but somewhat cumbersome	54	39	47	44
Unduly burdensome	13	7	16	12
	100%	100%	100%	100%

TABLE 9.4
DEANS' ASSESSMENT OF THE RIGOR OF AACSB STANDARDS

	Category of School			
Level of Standards	I	II	III	Total
Too high	0%	6%	36%	20%
About right	58	81	63	70
Too low	42	13	1	10
	100%	100%	100%	100%

ries of schools: 36% of Category III deans felt the Standards were "set too high," while 42% of Category I deans thought the Standards were "set too low." The Category II deans, generally speaking (81%), said they were "set about right." None of the Category I deans and only 6% of the Category II deans felt the Standards were set too high.

When queried about the appropriateness of individual Standards, again there were differences. Category I deans saw no problem with the Standards pertaining to faculty, while Category III deans were rather critical of these. They thought the Standards on research and doctorally qualified faculty were inappropriate or unreasonable. As might be expected, the most disaffection was expressed toward the Standard on research, especially by those (Category III) schools which see themselves as predominantly teaching institutions (reflecting the view that too much emphasis is placed on research as a prerequisite to accreditation).

While the majority of Category I and II deans had no problem with the Curriculum Standard, about a third of the Category I deans indicated some dissatisfaction. For those who are uncomfortable with the Standard affecting the curriculum, the question is principally one of faculty and school prerogatives—a form of academic freedom. A number of deans see the curriculum as a matter to be determined by each school in its own way, not something to be dictated by outsiders. They see the quality issue as one ultimately dependent on the competence of the faculty; if the faculty is competent and is involved in the design and implementation of the curriculum, it should follow that (within broadly defined parameters) the curriculum should be acceptable to the accreditors.

In general, all things considered, deans support AACSB accreditation, both the Standards and the process. The survey data reinforce the impressions we formed from our interviews—that there is some mild dissatisfaction, but little pressure for wholesale change.

Provosts' Perceptions

Provosts are the chief academic officers who deal directly with business school deans and faculties. They are in positions of power and influence in setting budgets and determining faculty rewards. Moreover, they have (typically) had experiences with other accrediting agencies, both regional and professional, and should therefore be able to judge AACSB accreditation by comparing it with other specialized types of accreditation. Hence we felt that their attitudes would be especially important.

During our interviews with provosts we assiduously invited opportunities for criticism, but we received very little. Some, in fact, were especially complimentary, particularly when they compared the AACSB with other accrediting agencies. The general attitude toward professional accreditation seemed to be "we wish it weren't necessary to have accreditation of professional schools, but there are a lot of cheap, low-quality programs out there, and we need accreditation to differentiate our product."

The survey data, as was the case with deans, support our interview conclusions. Less than 3% of the 133 provosts who had had experience with AACSB accreditation and who responded to these items on the survey indicated that they thought accreditation was not important or had been a hindrance to their school's development, while 90% said that it was important and had been of value to the university and its business/management school. Only 11% saw AACSB accreditation standards as among the top three constraints or limiting factors affecting the school's ability to reach its goals during the next 10 to 15 years. None volunteered accreditation as one of the factors they would use to measure the school's progress.

The process was thought to be reasonable and appropriate or even excellent by 60%, while only 9% thought it unduly burdensome. Among unaccredited school provosts, 74% of 140 respondents indicated that they thought AACSB

accreditation was important to their university and that the school should be
making active efforts to be accredited. Only 14% thought that it was not important and that the school need not seek accreditation, while 13% said that it
was important but that the school need not make active efforts to become accredited.

Provosts, as the data indicate, are even more supportive of AACSB accreditation than business school deans, a finding which, again, argues for basic continuity rather than revolutionary action.

Corporate Perceptions

In our interviews with corporate managers, we detected very little awareness
of, or sensitivity to, AACSB accreditation. With the exception of those who
are active participants as members in AACSB, few showed any knowledge of
what this form of specialized accreditation entails.

Certainly the key corporate decisions which might be affected by accreditation—recruitment, tuition reimbursement, the use of faculty consultants, contract research done by universities, executive development contracted to universities, and financial support—seem not to be influenced significantly by the
school's accreditation status, except in rare instances.

Summing up, the perceptions of AACSB accreditation by the academic community are generally favorable, with a few notable exceptions, while the corporate world is generally unaware and indifferent.

COMMENTARY

It seems clear that the overall quality of business schools has improved since
the time of the Ford and Carnegie reports. An issue is whether accreditation
was a help or a hindrance in the process. There is little question in our minds
that at least some of the improvement can be attributed to AACSB accreditation—that the imposition of specific Standards together with a systematic audit
review process indeed pushed many schools beyond where they might have
gone voluntarily.

In the academic community we encountered attitudes more positive toward
AACSB accreditation than we had expected. These attitudes were widely expressed by deans, faculty members, and provosts alike. We were particularly
surprised by the reactions of provosts. On the whole, they were quite complimentary. Since they are beset by so many groups making demands on their
institutions, we anticipated encountering antipathy toward accreditation in general, and we had no reason to believe their attitudes toward business school
accreditation in particular would be anything but hostile or, at best, ones of
grudging acceptance.

While the assessment of AACSB accreditation was on the whole favorable
enough to tempt us into suggesting that "it ain't broke, so don't try to fix it,"
there were enough questions raised among our academic colleagues and—per-

haps more disturbing—so much ignorance about or irrelevance accorded to AACSB accreditation by the business community that we have to conclude that either the system needs further improvement or it needs to be marketed more effectively (or both).

Before discussing possibilities for change, it seems appropriate to analyze AACSB accreditation in terms of what we believe to be its three main functions: to assess the quality of business school education, to improve the quality of that education, and to inform relevant publics about its quality.

Assessment of Quality

AACSB accreditation is based on the threshold concept. A school's programs are evaluated to determine whether minimum Standards have been met. At least three questions immediately might be raised: Do the Standards relate to quality? Are the level and rigor of the Standards sufficiently high to differentiate—on quality grounds—accredited from unaccredited schools? And, is the audit process reliable enough to ensure that schools seeking accreditation are fairly judged and that accredited schools continue to maintain conformity with the (minimum) Standards?

Perhaps the most troublesome of these questions is the first: Are the Standards really a yardstick for the measurement of quality? Some Standards are expressed in quantitative or other objective terms, such as the number of faculty required for a given volume of operations—the number of student credit hours—or specified topic areas to be included in a curriculum; others require subjective judgments, such as the quality of scholarly work done by a faculty or the adequacy of coverage of, say, the international dimension of an MBA program. We are quite comfortable with a process which relies on judgment calls to determine quality if those calls are made by competent evaluators who are reasonably consistent in their assessments. We are somewhat less confident about the appropriateness of those Standards that are expressed in purely quantitative terms, such as the number of doctorates or the proportion of full-time faculty required for a given student load.

Although the quantitative Standards employed in AACSB accreditation are intended to be used as guidelines and not absolutes, with judgment prevailing when the numbers do not support a case for quality (a school may meet all the quantitative Standards but still be deemed to be unacceptable, or vice-versa), in practice it is always possible for numbers to become (unreliable) surrogates for the yardstick of quality. However, notwithstanding our misgivings concerning the possibility of their inappropriate use, on balance we believe that the application of quantitative Standards has been useful and probably has been fair and accurate in the vast majority of cases. It is a matter of probability—that is, although the presence of, say, doctorates on a faculty will not guarantee high quality of performance, on the whole it seems reasonable to presume that a faculty with the minimum prescribed number of doctorates will perform better than one that does not meet this standard.

While the Standards themselves, quantitative as well as qualitative, seem appropriate enough as yardsticks—i.e., they do appear to relate, however imperfectly, to "real" quality—the question remains as to whether the rigor and level of the Standards are high enough. Have too many institutions been granted, or permitted to maintain, accreditation status too easily? Some critics argue that a set of well over 200 heterogeneous—both as to their mission and their quality—institutions does not discriminate well enough to be at all useful as an index of quality. There are clearly vast differences among the institutions within the accredited set; the range is from highly prestigious, graduate-only programs which serve broad, international constituencies to small, relatively unknown undergraduate programs which serve limited local environments. Some schools do not see any market advantage in belonging to this large conglomerate set, except in the negative sense—they feel obliged to maintain accreditation for fear of negative publicity if they were to lose it. They would like the opportunity to belong to a somewhat more exclusive club.

What needs to be emphasized here is that current AACSB accreditation certifies only that a school has met a threshold set of Standards; it is not designed to rank schools in order of hierarchical quality. It does signify, however (and herein lies its principal value, in our view), that the school has undergone a self-study and has been examined by outsiders—that is, that the school's programs have been reviewed to determine conformity with a set of criteria which have been established by professionals in the field of higher education for business.

Some schools argue that the AACSB criteria for accreditation—especially the quantitative Standards on doctoral qualifications and part-time faculty—inhibit creativity and innovation. Leaving aside the question of whether or not the current Standards and processes for administering them do tend to stifle new initiatives—we have no conclusive evidence one way or the other—it seems appropriate for a school to be expected to measure the results of its "innovations" in some reliable manner and to communicate the results to relevant outside parties. Mere departure from convention is not necessarily innovative—it may simply produce shoddy merchandise. If not AACSB Standards, what criteria would a nonaccredited school be willing to accept as legitimate indices of performance?

Of course, some nonaccredited (by AACSB) schools argue that proof of quality for their programs is vested in regional accreditation. By implication, their view is that the AACSB is demanding something unreasonable in its Standards if a college or university is acceptable for regional accreditation but not for AACSB accreditation. However, AACSB members contend—and we agree—that regional institutional review is so general as to be relatively meaningless for the professional school; virtually no collegiate business school is excluded from the set of regionally accredited institutions.

Ironically, while some outside the system of AACSB accreditation argue that AACSB Standards are inappropriate and do not accurately measure quality or promote innovation, there are complaints, especially from leading member schools, that the Standards are too low—that too many borderline institutions are accredited. These critics would like to see the threshold raised. We are not prepared to argue that current Standards are as rigorous as they ought to be, but we can say that we encountered, in the interview process, a broader base of quality (as determined subjectively by us) among lesser-known institutions than we had expected. Those schools near the margin of accreditability—especially those aspiring toward accreditation or who feel threatened by the potential loss of it—appeared to place a great deal of value on accreditation and were strongly motivated to attain or maintain it. Would raising the threshold for such institutions improve the overall quality of the system? We doubt it— the greater likelihood would be, in our view, disillusionment and abandonment of quality goals among many threshold-level schools, perhaps with the result of driving some institutions toward cheapening their educational product, with cash flow and volume as the major criteria of success.

Another issue relating to accreditation's role in assessing quality is the reliability of the audit process. Can one be confident that an institution that has been judged to have met certain Standards, however modest, on a certain date will maintain those Standards over the full span—currently 9 years—of the term between audits? In the corporate world the public would hardly accept unaudited financial statements for other than brief interim periods. Is the academic system that much more trustworthy? For those institutions that are significantly above any threshold, 9 years may well be a reasonable enough time period between accreditation reviews—such institutions typically have a large cushion of resources along with internal quality-control mechanisms that may well be sufficiently reliable to ensure ongoing maintenance of quality. Many schools, however, have barely edged over the threshold; for them, there is considerable risk of slippage. In principle, therefore, frequency of audit should vary with the risk of noncompliance. (Currently, AACSB has a shorter review cycle—6 years—only for newly accredited members.) Thus, we believe that the AACSB should consider some system of variable interval schedule of reviews to reflect the differences in the probability—assessed as part of the accreditation process— of an institution's ability or commitment to maintain standards.

In summary, our assessment is that AACSB accreditation does measure reasonably well an institution's threshold level of quality within the context of its mission, but it is not designed for assessing the quality of schools above the threshold level of performance. Another concern is the reliability of the process—the frequency of visitations may well be inadequate for some schools. We are confident that the majority of AACSB-accredited member schools are ahead of where they were 25 years ago. The floor has indeed been raised, but what about the ceiling? We now turn to the second function of accreditation, that of improving the quality of business education beyond the threshold.

Raising Quality: The Improvement Function

As we suggested earlier, the evidence appears overwhelming in favor of the conclusion that AACSB accreditation has had a significant impact on the performance of those schools clustered around the threshold level of accreditation. However, has it affected quality in those institutions which, for a variety of reasons, including market forces and their own traditions, are significantly above the minimum levels required for accreditation? The impact has been very mixed, in our view.

Unquestionably, there is a set of schools—call them "tier 1" or "top 10" or "elite institutions"—which have been essentially impervious to AACSB accreditation. (Incidentally, it is difficult to define with precision this elite set of schools. As one dean—of a school which would surely qualify for inclusion—said, "There are at least 35 schools in the top 10.") Some of these see accreditation as a necessary but benign nuisance, the cost of which is to be minimized; a few see the process as intrusive, burdensome, and unnecessary—they would like to see it eliminated altogether, at least as it applies to them. The AACSB has moved to resolve this problem by making reaccreditation a consultative—as opposed to an audit—process, with schools having a great deal of influence in the selection of visitation teams and the issues that will be addressed during the visit. This will undoubtedly make the process much more palatable; however, there is some risk, in our view, that in order to placate the very elite schools, the legitimate audit function of accreditation might be ignored or relegated to secondary importance. An audit has in and of itself a useful function— and no institution ought to be able to claim exemption from going through a process of periodic outside review.

It might be well to note, somewhat parenthetically, that while the predominant influence of accreditation has been on the threshold schools, there nonetheless has been considerable impact as well on elements of some of the more prestigious AACSB members. The so-called distribution requirement—the insistence on looking at faculty deployment across all programs, not just the principal one—has had significant leverage on overall quality in a great many institutions, including some of the very elite. A school's reputation is generally built on its principal programs—typically the full-time degrees (BBA and MBA) offered on the main campus. Off-campus, night school, and other part-time programs were originally not a factor in accreditation—indeed, those schools with predominantly part-time programs were traditionally precluded from AACSB membership. With the spotlight of accreditation broadened to include all programs within the purview of the business school, it became apparent that even some schools of the highest repute had "bargain basement," "cash cow," or similar programs designed to "serve the public," often without the concomitant assignment of faculty and other resources at levels generally deemed necessary for accreditation. Night school programs in major cities were common offenders. Accreditation raised the floor for these programs, which traditionally had been marketed by some schools under the umbrella of the more prestigious full-time degree programs but without commensurate resource deployment or devotion to standards of excellence.

Similarly, an additional impact on schools that were well above the threshold level for accreditation has been the specification of elements of the core curriculum in the standards. An example is the requirement for integration, which has come to be widely interpreted as being met through a business policy course. There is little doubt that policy as a subject would be far less ubiquitous than it is if it were not specifically required for accreditation.

In our opinion, quality above the threshold will be influenced most if the accreditors concentrate on evaluating the professional and academic quality of a faculty and then look at the internal mechanisms employed to make sure that the faculty participates in the design as well as the delivery of the curriculum. We believe that a strong faculty, highly motivated and involved in the ongoing operations of a school, is the best insurance of overall high quality. We are not confident that the accreditation process has consistently placed enough emphasis on the quality of the faculty resources and the manner in which they are deployed—as opposed to counting the numbers of doctorates and full-time staff.

Incidentally, in recent years the AACSB has relied less exclusively on the traditional audit process of accreditation—imposing Standards and reviewing for conformity—as the means for raising the overall quality of most schools; it has supplemented this process with a number of educational, information-sharing, faculty-development programs. An example would be the series of summer workshops to educate faculty on information systems and the efforts to internationalize various functional areas of the curriculum. The selection of topics for these programs is influenced by needs assessment, which is a significant by-product of the accreditation process. We applaud these efforts and are convinced that they are making major contributions to the improvement of education for business and management.

We did not encounter, in our visits to sixty campuses, any evidence that accreditation per se was an influence of consequence in motivating schools to achieve excellence beyond minimum requirements. Schools at the margin were indeed striving to reach the threshold, but was accreditation prodding the already-accredited school toward greater heights? No, as far as we could determine. While some very positive strides have been taken since the time of the Foundation reports—Standards have been imposed and enforced and a consultative process has emerged—we believe that accreditation could have greater influence in the improvement of education for a significant number of schools which are well above the threshold level. The system is moving in the right direction, but much more needs to be done if its full potential is to be realized. We will amplify this point in Chapter 15.

Educating the Public: The Information Function

The third element of the trilogy of accreditation objectives is informing the public about the quality of individual institutions. On this dimension, the AACSB has underachieved, in our opinion.

There is abundant evidence that AACSB accreditation has little influence outside a certain set of business schools themselves. The corporate world seems to pay little attention to it as a factor in its recruitment and tuition-reimbursement programs, there is no evidence that students choose to attend a particular school because of its AACSB accreditation status, and the elite schools certainly do not appear to see major advantages accruing to them from accreditation.

Why is accreditation so impotent outside the AACSB membership? Ignorance is a factor. An understandable confusion exists between AACSB (professional) accreditation and regional (institutional) accreditation. If an institution is regionally accredited, the public is quite likely to assume that all programs within the institution are accredited. However, sophisticated buyers of the educational product—business firms—might be expected to know the difference. Why, then, are corporations so indifferent to a school's AACSB accreditation status?

The answer to this enigma may well lie in the ambivalent way the corporate world looks at education for business. On the one hand, a great deal of care is exercised in the active recruitment of graduates from (what one assumes to be) top programs, with only a few schools targeted (by each firm) for this time-consuming and expensive process. On the other hand, corporations spend millions on tuition-reimbursement plans for employees to attend part-time, night programs, often without any attention whatsoever to their AACSB accreditation status or any other explicit criterion of quality. Part-time programs apparently are regarded as a convenience good—logistical convenience, ease of admission, length of program, and cost would seem to be much more important variables in the selection of schools than AACSB accreditation.

Our interviews with corporate officials clearly demonstrated that the corporate world is not insensitive to quality, but they do not see AACSB accreditation as a reliable indicator of quality for recruitment purposes. The corporate world, in its recruitment practices, seeks to differentiate schools on quality grounds to a fault. Recruiters are often supersensitive to public ratings, surveys, opinion polls, and other indices, however unreliable, that might identify a limited set of schools which they can then target for recruitment. We became convinced that we could develop a profitable business by going into the ratings business ourselves; corporations seem willing to buy into virtually any ratings scheme.

Prospective (full-time) students also appear to play close attention to ratings. On university campuses, the most dog-eared reference works in the library are volumes that claim to rank academic programs. It would appear that the national psyche has been infused with the "we're number one" syndrome which is so prevalent in athletics. If a school is not in someone's "top 20," it feels disadvantaged; in the marketplace, it may well be. Accreditation obviously does not help one's ranking. There are over 200 accredited schools. "We're in the top 200" does not help to market the institution, but if a school could find even one poll that identifies its accounting, marketing, or whatever program as "in the top 10 in the country," that really commands attention.

In our opinion, accreditation does have the potential to contribute to overall high quality; while there undoubtedly are individual exceptions, the set of schools that is accredited is on average almost certainly of higher caliber than the set that is not. And those schools which are striving for accreditation are in all likelihood better than they would have been if they had decided to eschew AACSB accreditation. Logic dictates that the AACSB should aggressively market professional accreditation to the corporate world and to the general public so that they would more clearly understand and therefore appreciate the value of AACSB accreditation and the difference between it and regional accreditation. The marketing task would be made much easier, however, if the AACSB could find a way to provide information which would enable the public to gauge the level of quality of an institution in terms more definitive than mere threshold-level compliance provides.

EXECUTIVE EDUCATION AND MANAGEMENT DEVELOPMENT

CHAPTER 10

LIFELONG LEARNING NEEDS OF MANAGERS

In today's world, and most definitely in the world of tomorrow, a person's management education cannot stop with the completion of a formal bachelor's or master's degree program in business or any other relevant subject. If it did, such an individual would rapidly become obsolete and relegated to the "also rans" rather than continuing to be a member of that group expected to provide leadership—at whatever organizational level—in the management sectors of our society's institutions, including, but not limited to, business firms.

This has not always been the case. In the early decades of this century, many companies regarded management development as purely and simply a matter of providing someone who possessed apparent ability and motivation with a chance to learn from performing a succession of supervisory and managerial jobs. (As we learned from some of our interviews, this viewpoint is not entirely absent even in the 1980s.) To the extent that explicit educational activities were even considered relevant, they were usually thought of as something that a person did *prior to* joining a firm. From then on, on-the-job experience was expected to take over and provide whatever additional development was needed. It was not until after World War II, with relatively few exceptions, that companies began to recognize that perhaps something more was needed to facilitate the development of managers. That "something" was explicit management development programs. (Bridgman, writing in the Pierson report in 1959, reported that "management development programs...have had almost all of their growth since the end of World War II....In 1935, some 3% of about 2,500 companies and, in 1946, some 5% of about 3,500 companies stated in response to general surveys...that they had 'executive training programs.'" By the end of the 1950s, however, Bridgman was able to cite a survey showing that "77% of about 350 large companies stated that they were carrying on management development activities.")

Returning to the current situation in the 1980s, any assumption on the part of organizations that all that their managers need for the successful performance of their jobs indefinitely into the future is some type of formal educational degree program at the beginning or early on in their careers—plus additional on-the-job experience—would seem to be, in this age of rapid change and expansion of knowledge, an absolutely disastrous policy. Thus, when one is considering the postdegree educational needs—the lifelong learning (LLL) needs—of managers, there is a clear mutuality of interests: those of the corporation or firm and those of the individual.

The needs that managers or would-be managers have for lifelong learning can be categorized roughly and broadly into two major components: (1) knowledge and (2) skills. The former refers to basic sets of facts, principles, and information relevant to different aspects of management; the latter refers to proficiencies in applying knowledge and aptitudes in carrying out management activities. It is obvious, of course, that the particular types of knowledge and skills needed in management will vary depending on where individuals are located in the organization—on both the vertical and horizontal dimensions—and on where they are in their own managerial careers.[1] Therefore, it seems appropriate, as we indicated above, to view managers' lifelong learning needs from two explicit perspectives: that of the organization and that of the individual manager.

From the point of view of the firm, one can identify several potential stages of a manager's *organizational* career, approximately as follows:

1 Entry level
2 First supervisory assignment
3 Manager of a particular functional unit
4 General manager: manager of a set of different functional units
5 Executive level

At each of these stages, different types of knowledge and skills would be emphasized.[2] For example, at the entry-level stage the organization would want to provide basic information about the person's job and functional area as well as about the organization and its values and ways of conducting its operations; skill building would presumably relate to those skills necessary to carry out particular functional activities (in marketing, production, finance, etc.). As the

[1]We are indebted to Boris Yavitz, professor and former dean of the Graduate School of Business at Columbia University, for a number of ideas relevant to the introductory section of this chapter on the lifelong learning needs of managers. Prof. Yavitz' thoughts on this topic were contained in an informal paper prepared for the use of AACSB's Futures Committee prior to the initiation of the present project.

[2]Conceptualizations of the types of knowledge and skills needed at different levels of management have appeared in the literature at least as far back as Katz's classic article on this topic in the *Harvard Business Review* in 1955.

person progressed to the next level, the organization would work on broadening and deepening the person's knowledge base, probably still mostly pertaining to the particular functional area within which he or she was operating, as well as on building interpersonal skills relating to working with others as both peer and supervisor. To skip (in our discussion) to the executive level, knowledge building would presumably be heavily weighted to learning about complex aspects of the external environment, and skill building would focus on such activities as the formulation of long-range strategies. Of course, at this level the distinction between knowledge and skills is often blurred, especially when the intent is to develop comprehensive perspectives as much as it is anything else. The point to be made here is simply that—viewed from an organization's objectives—management development is not some blunt instrument to be wielded indiscriminately, but rather is to be thought of more as a precise tool to be tailored to the particular needs that the organization has for a given manager related to where he or she is located both functionally and by level of management.

Viewed from the individual manager's perspective, needs for management development will also vary with the person's career stage. In the early stage, the person most likely will want to develop additional knowledge and depth in a specialized area. As the manager finds that he or she takes on new job responsibilities such as supervising and directing the work of others, then the apparent or felt need for skill building in these areas is likely to increase. The manager's self-determined needs for development and those needs that the organization deems necessary will likely coincide in many instances. However, this is not always the case. For example, in early career stages a manager (or would-be manager) might want to acquire various types of knowledge and/or skills that would not be seen as particularly necessary by the organization at that point but which (from the individual's view) would provide the manager with additional versatility in case he or she should move to a different organization. Similarly, late in a manager's career—if that person has not progressed to the highest levels of the organization—the organization could well take the stance that further explicit developmental activities are unnecessary in that particular person's case because he or she is not viewed as someone likely to advance to any higher level. However, for a variety of reasons, the individual may believe that additional developmental programs would be useful for both the firm and himself or herself. Thus, while in general there is, as we noted earlier, a strong commonality of interests on the part of both the organization and the individual manager in management development activities, it cannot be casually assumed that their interests and views will be *identical*. The individual has certain personal career goals and objectives, and those may not always fit with what the organization would like to plan for him or her.

In the remainder of this chapter, we will present data from our questionnaire surveys and interviews regarding the needs of managers for development programs. Consistent with our preceding discussion, the findings will be divided into data relating to the organization's perspective and those from the point of view of the individual manager (i.e., the potential recipient of management development). We will look at such issues as the perceived need of the organization to carry out management development activities, the types of needs seen as existing at various levels, and some of the particular topic areas of need identified by managers themselves.

THE ORGANIZATION'S PERSPECTIVE

The Organization's Need for Management Development

In interviews with three categories of our corporate respondents—CEOs, VPHRs, and directors of management development (DMDs)—and on the questionnaire for DMDs, we explored the general issue of how important formal management development activities are to one's own particular organization. The directors of management development, who could be regarded as having an obvious vested interest in the topic, were asked on their survey specifically, "What degree of need does this organization have for formal management development activities?" Their answers showed that two-thirds responded "a large amount" and another 29% said "a moderate amount." Only 5% indicated that the need was "slight" or "almost none" in their companies. Also, and perhaps more revealing, virtually none of the CEOs and presidents we interviewed regarded management development activities as unimportant. To the contrary, we encountered numerous emphatic and spontaneous statements about how critical such activities were to the particular organization in question. For example, one CEO, whose views were fairly typical of his counterparts at other companies, stated, "Management development is not a luxury; it is necessary to move the organization ahead." A VPHR from another firm noted that in his company "management development activity had doubled in the past 10 years." Several VPHRs indicated that they felt that their companies were clearly behind in management development (MD) activities and needed to catch up. Said one, "There is a great need for more to be done [in MD] in this company." Another confessed, "[This company] is not doing enough in management development."

More crucial than basic statements about how important management development activities are to their companies were the *reasons* that various executives gave about *why* such endeavors are essential and why they expect (in most cases) even more emphasis on them in the future. To take some CEO views, first:

"Management development is the absolute glue that holds the corporation together."

"It [MD] is important because it is important for managers to develop their people."

"We can't rely only on job assignments for management development."

"Management development is important because we are dealing with fewer differences between managers and those managed."

"We're in a more competitive environment."

Vice presidents of human resources (VPHRs) also talked about why, from their roles as heads of this functional area, they regarded MD activities as important. Paralleling the views of some of the CEOs cited above (who were from firms different from his own), a VPHR of a highly visible and well-regarded company indicated the following concerning his firm: "In the past in [this company] the focus was on 'on the job' development. Now, . . . [this company] has recognized that there needs to be more of a systematic approach to management development." This is a pivotal point and one that we will want to return to in our Commentary section.

Other reasons cited by VPHRs and DMDs for the need to continue and increase the emphasis on management development were many and varied. Some examples (taken from different companies) would include the following:

"We have increased needs for nonauthoritarian leadership and the ability to work in matrix-type situations" (a VPHR).

"We need to put a heavy focus on the development of the next cadre of top managers" (a VPHR).

"The major reason for more attention to MD in [this company] in the last 5 years is the increasing 'sophistication' of our clients. The [changing] marketplace is driving our needs" (a DMD).

"Our needs have changed dramatically in the past few years. Until recently there was no attention paid to management development for those who have been here 3 years and beyond. Recently, senior management is much more management development–oriented primarily because the business environment has changed [so rapidly]" (a DMD).

"The structure of [our company] will flatten [in the coming years], and our managers must learn to deal with a more flexible system" (a DMD).

Summarized, most of the reasons that top human resource executives—and many line executives—give for what they see as the imperatives for why their organizations will need to devote increasing attention to MD in coming years revolve around one phenomenon: *the pace of change*—both in the external environment and within the internal environment. If the pace of change were slower, the needs would be less.

Nowhere did we find this general conclusion—especially with regard to the need to cope with the changing nature of the work force—better stated than in the words of one of the executives we interviewed, a veteran director of management development:

Things are moving and that is part of the complexity. . . . Things are moving so much faster today than they were before and that means that we cannot necessarily get all of those experiences internally (through job experiences) that meet today's needs.

There are things that we are going to have to do for which we don't have the particular backgrounds (within the company) or knowledge....The rate of change and the increasing complexity of the economy are not just a national but an international phenomenon....It's the changing employee, the changing workforce....The employees want more and expect more than they did before. Lately [line] managers have begun to recognize the need to be able to respond to the needs, the higher expectations of these employees. They have to learn to manage these employees differently. It is not a cut and dried thing of just checking on them [employees] and reading reports. It's more of a relational kind of thing and more of a developmental kind of thing....When I started we just did what we were told. This change has been a real thing and it is not just a superficial change. It is hard for some of us old timers to recognize it.

Approaches to Determining Needs

If an organization is convinced it should provide an array of management development programs and activities (no matter from what source), it would seem logical that it should first make a determination of what those needs are. In other words, it should carry out some form of "needs analysis." To find out the extent to which such needs analyses—of a systematic type—are being conducted, and also to obtain information about the general approach that corporations use to assess their management development needs, DMDs were asked in the survey to identify "the primary means" by which their respective organizations determine those needs. The results are shown in Table 10.1. As this table demonstrates, nearly 30% of the responding DMDs indicate that their organizations have "*no* formal, systematic means of needs assessment for management development." For the remaining 65 to 70% of the companies, there was a fairly wide dispersion of types of approaches to needs assessment. About 30% answered that the needs were primarily determined by line management

TABLE 10.1
METHODS COMPANIES USE TO DETERMINE THEIR
MANAGEMENT DEVELOPMENT NEEDS: BY DMDs
(Percent Checking "Primary Method"; N = 249)

Percent	Method
11%	By top management
20	By all levels of line management
16	By human resources staff, with participation of top management
26	By human resources staff, with participation of all levels of line management
27	Company has no formal needs assessment for management development

with assistance from the human resources staff. The other 40% indicated that the lead was taken by the human resources staff with assistance from line management. Thus, there does not appear to be a predominant general approach that organizations use in assessing their management development needs.

Our interviews with DMDs also documented that a wide range of specific methods are being used to assess needs. These methods include the following:

- Questionnaire survey data (from managers)
- Information gained from performance appraisals
- Ideas generated by top management's strategic planning
- "Sensing" carried out within each unit of the organization
- Specific analyses by the human resources staff
- Assistance from an outside consulting firm

The interviews, collectively, revealed that there is no single specific method that is used universally. Some organizations clearly take a rather centralized approach, usually involving top human resources management and top line management, and others take a much more decentralized approach with heavy participation by individual units. The former typically seems to lead to the generation of management development programs that are applied more or less uniformly (at particular levels) throughout the organization, while the latter capitalizes on the divergent needs of individual units and gives relatively high degrees of autonomy to each unit to design the particular programs that would be most useful to it.

Location of Needs by Level of Management

Both interview and questionnaire findings indicated that most organizations believe that management development (of one type or another) is needed at all management levels: lower, middle, and upper. The DMDs in several of the companies in which we interviewed reported that in the past their organizations' management development activities had been focused more on lower to middle levels but that in the future there would be more of a shift to middle and top levels. However, this was by no means a consistent viewpoint across a wide range of companies, depending to a large extent on what the approach of a given company had been in the past. (At some companies, for example, management development activities for top management had for some time been a prominent feature, and thus these companies obviously did not believe they needed to give more attention to this level of management; at other firms, the situation was exactly the reverse.) To reiterate, if there was one generally consistent viewpoint that we encountered—often stated with a great deal of intensity—it was that some sort of (formal) management development activities are essential at *each* level of management. Some companies are already implementing this policy, but for other organizations it is merely a hoped-for plan to be initiated sometime in the indefinite future.

Specific Types of Management Development Needs

Two sets of top corporate line officers—CEOs and SCEs—and one group of human resources staff managers (the DMDs) were asked on the survey forms to "list the most important developmental needs during the next 10 years" for each of three different levels of management: lower, middle, and upper/top.

Analysis of the tabulated frequency of responses for needs perceived to be most important at "*lower* management levels" are shown in Table 10.2. (The two open-ended responses of each survey participant were content analyzed and coded into a set of some twenty different content categories that emerged from the raw data. Such classification is to an extent arbitrary, since it is impossible to establish precise boundaries among the categories, but it does provide at least a rough indication of the trends of the responses.) From this table it can be seen that there was relatively close agreement between the two groups of top line officers (CEOs and SCEs) about the MD needs they thought were most important at the lower management levels. Clearly, "interpersonal/people management skills" were seen as the number 1 need for this level of management. In second place were "communication skills," followed by "supervision skills." The human resources staff "experts," the DMDs, however, saw the situation somewhat differently: They had the need for "supervision skills" in first place, followed by "management skills" (planning, organizing, staffing, etc.) and "interpersonal/people management skills."

The picture actually changes very slightly for developmental needs seen as most important at the *middle* management levels. As Table 10.3 shows, "interpersonal/people management skills" and "communication" skills were seen

TABLE 10.2
DEVELOPMENT NEEDS SEEN AS MOST IMPORTANT
FOR *LOWER* LEVELS OF MANAGEMENT:
BY CEOs, SCEs, AND DMDs
(Ns = 120, 162, and 233, Respectively)

CEO views:
　　Number 1 Need: Interpersonal/people management skills

　　Number 2 and Number 3 Needs (tied): Communication skills
　　　　　　　　　　　　　　　　　　　　　　"Specialized" task skills

SCE views:
　　Number 1 Need: Interpersonal/people management skills

　　Number 2 Need: Communication skills

　　Number 3 Need: Supervision skills

DMD views:
　　Number 1 Need: Supervision skills

　　Number 2 Need: Management skills (organizing, staffing, etc.)

　　Number 3 Need: Interpersonal/people management skills

TABLE 10.3
DEVELOPMENT NEEDS SEEN AS MOST IMPORTANT
FOR *MIDDLE* LEVELS OF MANAGEMENT:
BY CEOs, SCEs, AND DMDs
(*Ns* = 118, 164, and 230, Respectively)

CEO views:

Number 1 Need: Communication skills

Number 2 Need: Interpersonal/people management skills

Number 3 Need: Management skills

SCE views:

Number 1 Need: Interpersonal/people management skills

Number 2 Need: Communication skills

Number 3 Need: Management skills

DMD views:

Number 1 Need: Communication skills

Number 2 Need: Leadership skills

Number 3 Need: Planning skills

as about tied in importance by CEOs and were definitely number 1 and number 2 in that order as seen by the SCEs. This parallels the answers of these two groups when they were listing needs for lower levels of management. "Management skills" were seen by both these top line groups as the third most important need for middle managers. Again, directors of management development varied somewhat from CEOs and SCEs in how they saw the needs for middle-level managers. The DMDs regarded "communication," "leadership," and "planning" skills about equally tied for most important for this management level.

There was a high degree of unanimity across the two groups of senior line officers (CEOs and SCEs) and the human resources staff group (DMDs) concerning the most critical development need for executives at the top levels of their organizations, namely, "strategic planning/thinking" (see Table 10.4). Interestingly, the respondent group that put this need in first place by the widest margin was the directors of management development, rather than either group of top officers themselves. The second most frequently cited need by CEOs was "leadership skills," followed by "communication skills." Senior corporate executives rated "interpersonal/people management skills..." and "communication skills" as second and third most important.

The importance of particular management development needs was frequently discussed—often with fervor—in our interviews. Roughly categorized, the thoughts expressed generally seemed to focus on two major areas of needs: the need for development of *people skills* and the need for managers to develop greater *breadth of perspective and outlook*. To provide the flavor of some of these viewpoints, we quote several of them below (with occasional slight para-

TABLE 10.4
DEVELOPMENT NEEDS SEEN AS MOST IMPORTANT
FOR *UPPER/TOP* LEVELS OF MANAGEMENT:
BY CEOs, SCEs, AND DMDs
(*Ns* = 117, 162, and 231, Respectively)

CEO views:
    Number 1 Need: Strategic planning

    Number 2 Need: Leadership skills

    Number 3 Need: Communication skills

SCE views:
    Number 1 Need: Strategic planning

    Number 2 Need: Interpersonal/people management skills

    Number 3 Need: Communication skills

DMD views:
    Number 1 Need: Strategic planning

    Number 2 Need: Communication skills

    Number 3 Need: Leadership skills

phrasing to smooth out the informal syntax of interview-type conversation, but with no change of any key elements of the person's ideas). First, the importance of the necessity for managers (once they are hired by the organization) to further develop their *people skills:*

The CEO of a Service Organization

We really do need effective team interaction. The whole problem we have with the younger guys is to teach them to be good project leaders—to help them understand how you get the most out of a highly talented, highly motivated group of competitive people.

The CEO of a Service Organization

You know, we just routinely expect people coming in will be able to handle the work, but it's handling the clients that gets to be the problem....It's people skills and the ability to reason and to keep your cool and not to be dogmatic and [instead] to be able to see someone else's viewpoints.

President of an Industrial Company

I think the importance of people skills has increased appreciably [in this organization], and I hope that those skills will continue to be important because that's where the real challenge is.

The Director of Management Development for a Financial Organization

Perhaps the skills [we need most] in the future to maintain our [competitive] position in this [new] environment are a whole set of different skills...and I think more and more the people skills and management of people as a resource is beginning to tell the tale on organizations that survive....In the past we managed either money or we managed risk or we managed something that allowed us to rise to the top and the organization succeeded, but now in order to maintain that we are totally dependent upon the people who work for us and we're not managing them very well.

The following were some representative views on the need for managers (at all levels) to increase their *breadth of thinking and perspective:*

A Senior Line Executive of an Industrial Company

The most demanding aspect [of my job as a senior executive] is to get people to think beyond their own functional area....For example, we need our managers to think broader than their own function in communicating so that everyone understands their part in the total scheme of things...to think about how they have to support people in other functions to get their own job done.

The Director of Management Development for an Industrial Company

I think the biggest need [we have around this organization] is to be able to work cooperatively and collaboratively within a multifunctional environment.

The Director of Management Development for a Service Organization

Our managers learn [relatively easily] how to manage operations, but when it comes to making the leap from operations to a broader business management, which is very different, that is very, very difficult for them....It's a huge problem....It means that, quite frankly, right now there is no internal person [within this organization] to take over [a particular] major division just because working in that division does not produce a broad-based business executive.

Director of Management Development for an Industrial Company

I think we've got a lot of need for—how am I going to phrase this—changing or expanding or looking more creatively at the ways we measure our successes and failures....We tend to be pretty conservative in the ways we measure things—we use traditional measures which tend to be pretty short term—yet we're in businesses that I think are longer term in nature.

Finally, in this section we report on the perceived developmental needs for a set of managers of particular relevance to the general focus of this project: *recent business school graduates.* Directors of management development were asked the following question (on the survey): "With respect to bachelor's-level business/management graduates (BBAs): for *recent* graduates, does this organization find it necessary to provide management/professional development activities in their first few years in areas that should have been covered more adequately in their business/management school undergraduate programs?" (The exact same question, with appropriate modification of terms, was asked about recent MBA graduates.)

The data show that 71% of the DMDs answer "yes" (the organization *does* find it necessary to provide such developmental activities) for BBAs, and just as high a percentage—72%—answered "yes" for MBAs. Those responding "yes" were further asked to indicate "those areas in which remedial-type work is required." From a list of fourteen alternative answers that were provided, the first three needs most often checked for BBAs were (1) organizational behavior/human resources, (2) business communications, and (3) general management. For MBAs, the same exact three areas also were the most frequently checked needs. Again, interview responses from several categories of executives provide a useful elaboration of this set of findings, particularly as they relate to people skills:

President of a Service Organization

We have a less intuitive, judgmental group [of business school graduates] who are more prone to study than to move....We've got a person [graduate from a business school] who is infinitely stronger [than in previous years] in the functional skills but not as good a leader.

Senior Executive of a Consulting Firm

If I look at the people in my client organizations who are the most effective executives, this ["people skills"] is where they are good....On the other hand, I can find dozens of people in client organizations [to hire] who can do the hard analytic stuff and will never lead anything; they will do great staff work, they will be writing reports till the day they die, but they will never get any kind of institution behind them, they will never get any kind of program off the ground, they don't know the difference between what people can and can't do, they don't know how to marshal support and they sure as hell don't know how to deal with ambiguity because they are trained to get rid of ambiguity. Well, I don't think those are the guys who make much of a difference in corporations, and I would argue that not only from a consultant's point of view—but also from from a general business standpoint—if you want your product to end up being effective, you [business schools] have got to do more.

The Director of Management Development for a Service Organization

We don't find ourselves doing "hardside" training in accounting, computers, analytical skills, etc. So, apparently whatever the business schools are doing must be working....We do find deficits, however, in the "softside." We're trying to provide softside feedback earlier [in a manager's career], so that they will know if they don't interact with people very well. And, if they want to do something about that, we've got some suggestions for them.

INDIVIDUAL MANAGERS' PERSPECTIVES

In this section we shift from the perspective of organizations regarding the needs of their managers for development to the views of the *managers themselves* about their needs. The respondents consist of three basic groups: operating managers at middle or lower levels of their organizations, some of whom are business school graduates (65%) and some of whom are not, and bachelor's degree alumni and master's degree alumni of business schools. The data come from responses to survey questions. First, we look at what each of these groups considers its most important needs for development; second, we examine the issue of the amount of time that these managers say they spend in attending formal management development programs versus the amount of time they think they *should* spend in such programs.

Most Important Needs for Development

Operating managers (whose average age in this sample is approximately 43, with about 13 years' experience in a management position) indicate four major developmental needs above all others (as determined by content analysis of their open-ended responses on the questionnaires):

1 Leadership skills
2 Computer skills
3 Communication skills
4 Planning and strategy

Business school alumni (who were from 5 to 10 years beyond their degrees)—both BBA and MBA alumni—singled out two major areas of developmental needs for themselves: computer/management information systems (MIS) skills and communication. (No doubt the former need reflects the fact that most of these alumni graduated before the recent intensive use of personal computers in a variety of business school courses and the associated rise in the number of MIS-type courses in the curriculum. It is likely that a similar survey question within the next 10 years would *not* indicate that this is a major developmental need for recent business school graduates.) Other frequently mentioned needs, but ones which were well below the first two in number of tallies, were finance and human resources.

Time Spent in Attending Formal Management Development Programs

As a general indication of the importance that organizations attach to "formal management development programs of some type," DMDs were asked whether "each manager in this organization is *required* to spend a minimum number of workdays per year" attending such programs. Over 90% answered "no."

Consistent with the preceding finding, operating managers and business school alumni (both BBA and MBA alumni) were asked to indicate for the past several-year period "the average number of workdays (away from your job) in a typical year, that you *actually spent* in attending formal management development programs," as well as to indicate—in a separate question—the number of workdays "you believe you *ought* to spend" attending such programs. The results are presented in Table 10.5, where it can be seen that the number of days managers (operating managers and business school alumni in managerial positions) report they actually spend (about 3.0 days for operating managers, 2.4 days for BBA alumni, and 2.0 for MBA alumni) is considerably *less* than the time they think they ought to spend in such programs (5.1 for operating managers and 5.0 for both alumni groups of managers). Or, to put this another way, 44% of operating managers report that they spend *two or fewer* workdays per year attending management development programs away from their jobs, but only 8% think they *ought* to attend only this much (or this little).

Even more interesting than the discrepancies per se in the amount of time reported being spent in management development programs versus the time managers believe they ought to spend are the reasons given for this discrepancy. Of those operating managers reporting discrepancies, roughly half (52%) indicate that they are "too busy to take sufficient time away from my job." However, and rather revealingly, nearly 25% (22% to be exact) check the following as the reason for the discrepancy: "I think I ought to spend more time on MD programs than the organization thinks I ought to spend." Only 2% check the reverse ("The organization thinks I ought to spend more time on MD programs than I think I ought to"). (Similar results—28 to 2% for BBAs and 31 to 1% for MBAs—were obtained for the two alumni groups.) It seems fairly obvious that managers perceive a different—and greater—amount of need for man-

TABLE 10.5
NUMBER OF WORKDAYS PER YEAR THAT MANAGERS REPORT SPENDING IN MANAGEMENT DEVELOPMENT PROGRAMS: "CURRENTLY" AND "OUGHT TO SPEND"
(Percent of Each Group Checking One of Five Alternatives)

Workdays per year	Operating Managers (N = 596)		BBA Alumni (N = 212)		MBA Alumni (N = 291)	
	Currently	Ought	Currently	Ought	Currently	Ought
0	10%	2%	25%	4%	23%	6%
1–2	34	6	28	8	37	9
3–5	39	48	26	44	25	43
6–10	13	39	11	33	13	35
11+	4	5	10	8	2	7

Note: All columns add to total of 100% within rounding.

agement development programs compared to what they think is their organizations' perception of this need.

COMMENTARY

Viability of the Traditional Approach to Managers' Lifelong Learning Needs

The findings obtained from our interviews were quite convincing, we believe, in sounding the death knell to any lingering beliefs that anyone might have that the hoary and traditional method of developing managers—namely, depending *solely* on on-the-job experiences—would be sufficient in the 1980s, let alone in the world of the 21st century. When the vice president of human resources of a large, influential company that is highly respected for the quality of its management states that (as we quoted earlier) "Now [i.e., recently], [this company] has recognized that there needs to be more of a systematic approach to management development [than] 'on the job' development," we regard this as a significant statement about this issue. Equally significant, in our opinion, was the statement by a VPHR of a company at the other end of the "progressive management" continuum, who said, candidly, "There is not much management development currently being done in this company. There is a great need for more to be done." If ever there were a company that appeared to us to typify (until recently, at least) the traditional sole reliance on on-the-job training, that was it. Yet, even here in this company, where many of the winds of change in the business world seemed not to have penetrated very far, there was a reluctant recognition that the past approach to managerial lifelong learning was not sufficient.

We want to be clear that we are not belittling the utility of job assignments for providing extremely valuable developmental experiences for managers. They obviously can (at least they have the potential for doing so) and should. (We return to this topic later in this section.) The point, however, and one that we consider vital, is that job experiences are simply *not enough* these days to provide the necessary degree and rate of development. They must be supplemented—and supplemented fairly continuously. The reasons, as we stressed earlier and as documented extensively in our interviews, revolve around the magnitude and especially the speed of changes taking place that have an impact on the world of business. Time and again in our interviews we were struck by the almost tangible awe with which middle-age (let alone older-age) and even youngish managers in their late thirties were viewing the rapidity with which their work environments—both outside *and* within the organization—were changing. It is this phenomenon—both actual change and the perception of that change—which is the driving force behind the strongly held view by organizations (i.e., those responsible for determining the policies of organizations) and individual managers themselves that there needs to be increased emphasis on planned and designed management development activities. We expected to find some of this point of view, but we were surprised by its extent and its evident intensity.

Organizations' Approaches to Needs Analysis

We encountered (in our interviews) a number of firms that were quite deliberate in their approach to determining just what needs their managers had for development. We also encountered a number that were not. This apparent divergence across companies in terms of how much attention they were giving to careful and systematic needs analysis was confirmed by our questionnaire findings, where almost 30% of the responding firms (and the figure might be expected to be somewhat higher for nonresponding firms, especially those without someone in a position specifically designated as director/manager of management development) reported that they have no formal means of needs assessment for management development. We do not find this particularly surprising, but we do view this as an important indicator that a fairly sizable proportion of companies probably do not give more than superficial attention to management development.

As we noted in the previous section, it is possible to categorize the approaches of those companies that do carry out systematic needs analysis along at least two major dimensions:

1 Centralized/decentralized
2 Primary role for human resources staff/primary role for line management

It was our view that on the basis of the type of information we obtained in this study it would not be possible to state that either of these approaches is better than the other. Probably each can be made to work effectively *if* the organization has given sufficient attention to the entire area of management development and to the specific task of determining needs. It is the *amount of attention* to needs analysis in particular and to management development in general that is most important, not whether needs are determined centrally or by individual units or whether the primary responsibility rests with line managers or human resources staff. In particular instances these latter decisions may well be critical, but only if they are undertaken in a context or climate where the larger decision has already been made that management development will have a high priority.

Types of Management Development Needs

Our survey findings supported the logical assumption that different needs would be seen as important for different management levels. However, there was not as much variation as might have been expected, especially between lower- and middle-management levels. For *both* these levels, top corporate line officials saw "interpersonal/people management" skills and "communication" skills as

the two most important needs for the development of managers in their organizations. "Management skills" (planning, organizing, etc.), although secondary (actually tertiary) to these two needs, did become more important at the
middle levels than at lower levels. The largest change in needs seen as most
important occurred between middle and upper levels, with "strategic planning/
thinking" being regarded as clearly the most critical development need for top-
echelon executives. However, even for this level, "interpersonal/people management skills" and "communication" skills still were ranked high in importance
by senior line executives.

The net import of these sets of findings would seem to be that: (1) people-
type skills and communication-type skills (the latter to be interpreted in their
broadest sense, not in some micro sense of writing grammatically correct let-
ters, for example)—as areas for management development—really cannot be
ignored at *any* level of management; and (2) certain particular types of skills
and knowledge—such as so-called "management skills" and a strategic perspective and knowledge about how to do strategic planning—emerge as most important at specific levels of management. This latter conclusion reinforces the
notion that organizations should attempt to anticipate the needs that their best
managers will have in advance of the time when those individuals will move up
in the organization and thus should target their development activities accordingly. From our interview findings with both line managers and human resources
staff experts, we would infer that a not insignificant portion of companies are
not doing very much of this in any sort of proactive fashion. On the other hand,
there are some specific firms that serve as outstanding models of how to go
about doing this. In our view, such firms are obviously developing a long-range
competitive advantage.

One interesting aspect of our findings was that although the needs that top
line executives see as being most important for the development of managers
at lower levels in their organizations were relatively similar to the needs seen
by those lower and middle managers themselves, they did not always match
precisely. In particular, for example, these managers see a strong need for improving their computer skills, whereas this was given a lower priority by top
executives when viewing the developmental needs for those (lower and middle) managers. The reverse appeared to occur with respect to "developing a
breadth of perspective." In the interviews, as we noted, top line executives
and human resources staff personnel frequently mentioned this as a major
developmental priority for line managers as they advanced up the organization. The managers themselves seldom pointed to the need to obtain such
breadth. One gains the impression, therefore, that, left to their own devices,
so to speak, many managers would concentrate on their immediate and more
short-range developmental needs. In contrast, those company officials responsible for overall management development policies and approaches
would like to have a relatively (and we stress the word *relatively*) stronger
emphasis on less tangible skills and knowledge that perhaps might have
longer-lasting impact.

The needs, or lack thereof, for development of recent business school graduates were accorded special attention, given the objectives of this particular research project. The results, as we indicated, showed that nearly three-quarters of the directors of management development believed that their organizations *do* need to provide remedial-type development activities for these individuals *"in areas that should have been covered more adequately"* in business school *(BBA and MBA) programs*. Such needs, as identified in both the survey and in the interviews, were clearly not in analytical or basic functional (accounting, marketing, etc.) areas. They were in people skills and communication areas. Thus, one obvious conclusion is that developmental needs for business school graduates parallel those for lower and middle managers in general. The second conclusion is that, as we discussed at some length in Chapter 4, there is a fairly high degree of consensus across companies about the strengths and relative weaknesses of business school graduates, whether from undergraduate or master's programs. Some of the implications we see for business/management schools from this finding will be addressed later in Chapter 15. In the meantime, suffice it to say that we believe that this is a nontrivial issue.

Meeting Management Development Needs

Many managers believe that they ought to be participating in more developmental activities (of an organized, planned type) than they are now doing. As our findings demonstrate, one obvious reason that they are not doing so is simply that they are (by self-report, at least) too busy doing their current jobs to take more time off to take part in such development. The other reason, as attested to by almost 25% of these (middle- and lower-level) managers, is an apparent difference of opinion between the organization and the managers about how much time they should be spending on such activities. This perceived "developmental gap" should, in our opinion, become the focus of discussion in at least some organizations (i.e., those where the gap is relatively pervasive). We are not assuming that individual managers are necessarily correct when they say they ought to be spending more time in developmental activities, only that the issue may need exploring. Development is costly in money and in other resources. Organizations, for their own good, as well as in the interests of their managers, need to consider the cost/benefit trade-offs of providing additional development. This should—it seems to us—involve assessments of long-range as well as short-range consequences and should involve some form of participation by those who would be affected by any decisions reached.

If organizations are going to consider how best to meet the lifelong learning needs of their managers, they will need to focus on the two primary vehicles for development: job experiences and MD programs. Both have a potentially important role to play, especially in interaction with each other. Neither, by itself, guarantees successful development. Merely having someone perform a particular job or set of jobs does not ensure that that person will *learn* something from those experiences. If development of a manager is one of the explicit objectives of job assignments, then an organization will have to give attention to how a person can best learn something from those particular assignments that will make him or her an improved manager in the future. Merely hoping this will happen and leaving such on-the-job learning to chance will not likely produce a great deal of significant development. Coordinating formal development activities with particular job assignments is probably one major way that an organization can increase the odds that development will in fact occur. This, of course, requires more than a glancing dab at planning and implementing a systematic approach to such activities. It also, in turn, implies some not insignificant resources. This is not a perfect world where all managers can obtain all the training and development they desire, and organizations cannot provide all that they might ideally like to. They will have to make some difficult choices, but at least they should be deliberate and not incidental choices.

As we conclude this chapter, we want to point out that being able to meet effectively the lifelong learning needs of managers involves the *joint* responsibilities of four sets of individuals:

1 *Top line officials* The organization's policymakers who will have to determine the priority and strategic role to be given to management development activities and to the broad approaches that will be utilized throughout the organization.

2 *Human resource staff specialists (either inside the firm, in the case of large companies, or outside of the firm, in the case of smaller companies)* Those who should have the technical expertise to help determine the needs and provide guidance about how best to implement effective developmental activities.

3 *Providers of management development* Those who actually conduct the programs, whether they are in-house, from consulting firms or other external professional associations or vendors, or from universities.

4 *The individual manager* Those who potentially will be directly benefiting from any developmental activities and without whose involvement, motivation, and effort any such activities will have little or no effect.

In short, meeting management development needs requires the combined efforts, judgments, and expertise of a number of people. Furthermore, it is no small task and it is not one to be undertaken lightly. To meet such needs effectively and in a consistent and, should we say, persistent manner is not easy. However, those organizations that succeed in this endeavor are probably the ones most likely to do well in the future—indeed, they are the ones most likely to *have* a future.

We are now ready in the following set of chapters to consider the roles of various categories of "providers" of such development programs.

CHAPTER **11**

EXECUTIVE EDUCATION/ MANAGEMENT DEVELOPMENT: CORPORATIONS

In this and the following two chapters, the focus will be on formally planned executive education/management development (EE/MD) activities. Thus (in this set of three chapters), we are making a distinction between "formal," explicit, and classroom-type EE/MD activities, and (generally) less formal and noninstructional developmental activities such as experiences gained from job assignments and routine mentoring. The latter type of activities are extremely important from a developmental standpoint, as discussed in the previous chapter, but are beyond the scope of this Project which has specifically limited objectives.[1]

In the present chapter we shift our attention to how a major set of societal institutions—business firms and corporations—go about attempting to meet those needs. That is, we will focus on corporate EE/MD programs, programs that are, in effect, designed to answer the following question: What learning activities can a company add to normal job experiences to improve and accelerate the development of its managers? Answers to this basic question involve viewing corporations as *both* "consumer" and "provider" of EE/MD activities.

Business firms are the primary "consumers" of management development because it is *their* managers and executives who have the *needs* described in the previous chapter. Corporations and companies of whatever size are faced

[1]We should add, at this point, a note about terminology: With respect to the terms *executive education* and *management development*, some would view the former as aimed at top-level managerial personnel only and the latter as aimed more at middle and lower levels. For simplicity sake, however, and for a change of pace in wording, we will (as is often done elsewhere) use the terms interchangeably. At those points where we are talking about MD programs specifically designed for upper-level executives, we will make that clear.

236

with the issue of how to satisfy or meet those needs which are directly generated by the types of job responsibilities they expect their managers to fulfill currently and in the future. In other words, business organizations, by their very nature, create the needs to which they then must proceed to respond. In their role as consumers of management/executive development, companies, as is typical with most consumers in other markets, have a choice about where to "buy" from among several types of potential "providers": themselves, universities, or "other" providers (commercial vendors, consultants, professional associations, etc.). They also have other choices, such as whether to utilize courses which are developed exclusively for managers from their own company or ones which are open to participants from a variety of companies. Additional consumer choices would involve such issues as content, length, depth (intensity), cost, and other factors that would determine the exact nature of specific courses or sets of courses. The ultimate choice, at least for smaller firms, is whether to have any sort of recognizable overall management development program of activities at all.[2]

Corporations and firms not only buy EE/MD services, but some are themselves major "providers" for their own needs. Obviously, the larger and more affluent a company is, the more likely it is to be able to have the resources to be a provider. However, many firms of lesser size and smaller assets can still choose to be at least a limited provider, if so inclined. As potential providers, just as in their role as consumers, corporations face an array of choices. For example, with respect to instruction, they have the option (for specific courses) of having it provided by their own personnel (whether human resources staff members or line managers), by outside "experts," or by some combination of the two. Another decision involves the question of facilities. Should the corporation utilize its own existing facilities (often not well designed for classroom instruction involving different presentation formats), construct new facilities or remodel old facilities for this specific purpose, or use off-premises facilities (hotels, universities, etc.)? Taken together, these and other questions boil down to a fundamental decision that every corporation of any size ought to make: What is the extent and intensity with which the corporation should be involved as a direct provider itself of management development activities? Answering this central question obviously involves consideration of a number of cost/benefit trade-offs.

---

[2]The word "program" can be somewhat confusing when used in a discussion of EE/MD. Often, the term is used to refer to a company's entire set of activities in this area. Thus, for example, one could speak as follows: "The management development program of the XYZ company consists of the following types of activities, from those for first-level supervisors on up to those for the top echelon of executives." On the other hand, the term "program" is also frequently used to refer to a specific classroom-type course put on by the corporation or some other provider. For example, "XYZ corporation provides a program on 'supervisory responsibilities' for any newly appointed manager." Although the term can have either of these two meanings when the topic is executive education and management development, we will not attempt to substitute some other more awkward or less common term. Rather, we will depend on the context of the sentence to assist the reader in determining in which sense we mean the term in a specific instance.

In the remainder of this chapter, we first look at what corporations were doing 25 years ago in the management/executive development arena and what has happened in the intervening decades. This is followed by an examination of our survey and interview data relating to the EE/MD activities of corporations, first in their role as consumers and second as providers. The chapter concludes with a Commentary section that will consider especially the connection between EE/MD activities and corporate strategy.

THE PAST 25 YEARS

Management development activities of corporations have a history extending back at least 40 years. As in other chapters, we begin by reviewing the scene as it existed 25 years ago, followed by a brief synopsis of developments since then.

Situation at the Beginning of the 1960s

For a picture of the extent and nature of corporate management development activities at the beginning of the 1960s, we will rely on an extensive report by Bridgman, who provided a detailed review in a specially prepared chapter for the Pierson volume (Pierson, 1959). As Bridgman noted, "management development programs, including higher as well as the lower echelons of supervision...had almost all their growth since the end of World War II" (p. 537). As he went on to point out (in the terminology of the times):

> Although not often recognized, a real foundation had been laid for [management development programs] over the previous quarter century [prior to 1946] through the growth and extension in scope of foreman training programs. While such training was confined to production departments and originally dealt mainly with the specific day-to-day work, it came to include more and more material concerning the...effective handling of men, broad principles of organizing work, and company policies, now [at the end of the 1950s] primary elements in management training. The point of view gained by foremen through such training invariably had its impact on their relations with their own supervisors and was one of the factors in breaking down the time-honored assumption that natural ability and ambition would provide competence needed by the higher supervisory levels and even more clearly by executives, currently and in the future. (Pierson, 1959, pp. 537–538.)

Aside from the "often not recognized" consequences of foreman training in "breaking down the...assumption that natural ability and ambition would provide [managerial] competence," other factors cited by Bridgman that influenced the growth of corporate management development activities between 1945 and 1960 included the following: the changing nature of labor/management relations, the "explosive growth of the country's population, national product, and technological knowledge," and the fact that "business has been able to draw upon an increasing body of organized knowledge concerning the science and art of management for use in its development programs."

Data cited by Bridgman indicate that at the beginning of the postwar era in 1946 about 5% of companies surveyed had some sort of management development program activity, with this figure rising to somewhere above 50% of larger firms by the end of the 1950s. In the words of Bridgman:

> Four or five years ago [prior to the publication of the chapter in 1959] at least, only a small proportion, even of the companies large enough to justify them, had formal programs. Today, it can be assumed that a majority of the leading organizations in their fields are giving major attention to this matter, but *the programs of many are quite limited in scope* [italics added]. (Pierson, 1959, p. 540.)

Thus, it can be seen that corporate management development efforts flourished in the 1950s, and by the end of the decade many companies, especially larger ones, had initiated at least a rudimentary, if not comprehensive, set of such activities.

What can be concluded in addition is that—as one reviews Bridgman's descriptions of activities of specific companies and his characterization of the overall picture of such activities throughout the business world—by 1960 corporate management development programs and the types of courses included in them already had acquired the basic shape they have today in the 1980s. Although the picture was one of "an extremely uneven area" (p. 574), certain essential components had been put in place in at least some of the more "progressive" (insofar as management development activities are concerned) companies:

First, training and development were extended across the range of management levels, even though "the number of companies with...[such programs across levels] or with comprehensive courses for management above the first or second level is distinctly small" (p. 574).

Second, a variety of types of courses designed to meet different objectives had been developed in a number of companies. As enumerated by Bridgman, these included "courses for the primary purpose of increasing competence in the present job or level" (including "general courses" for "first-level supervisors," for "middle management," and for "higher management"), "courses to assist in providing highly qualified management personnel for the future," and "courses covering specific topics provided for groups or individuals on either a company recommended or elective basis" (p. 548).

Third, the content of at least some of the courses and programs would be quite familiar to managers of today. For example, Bridgman (p. 561) notes the amount of attention given to what he calls "human relations problems" (today, the phrase *human resources* would more likely be used):

> The extent of the concern about human relations problems in industry is especially well illustrated by the number of specific courses devoted to this area and the emphasis given to it in the comprehensive courses for lower-level management. In such courses for the middle and higher levels, there is less direct attention to it, but rec-

ognition of the importance of its principles underlies the approach to discussion of management skills generally, particularly those of supervision and communication.

With substitution of the word *leadership* for *supervision,* that description would not be too far off the mark in characterizing many programs in the 1980s. Furthermore, as is true today, a number of the more comprehensive programs at the end of the 1950s did not concentrate only on "human relations" issues. The following brief excerpts from Bridgman sound almost as if they had been written 25 years later:

> Company organization, policy, and future development are major topics in practically all the comprehensive courses for middle and higher management and constitute the dominant theme in several of them.... Although on the basis of relative time, discussions of the economic, social, and political environment receive less emphasis in practically all of the comprehensive courses than management skills or company policy and problems, this area is a significant one in most of those above the first level and receives greatest attention at the higher levels. (Pierson, 1959, p. 561.)

Fourth, and finally, the instructional format and conduct of courses in such programs, particularly at the middle and upper levels, also appear not materially different from their current counterparts. A few comments from Bridgman are again illustrative of the relative resemblance of "then" to "now":

> The courses in human relations given to middle management...in companies of moderate size frequently are led by university teachers. In the comprehensive courses at the middle and upper levels, a reasonable generalization is that company executives, executives of other companies, and university professors all appear as speakers or discussion leaders....Top company executives, including presidents, are convinced of the need to give time to talks or to lead discussion in these courses and appreciate the values to themselves of such participation. Certainly the greatest care is used in securing speakers from universities and other companies, and it has proved possible to attract outstanding individuals....The usefulness of special techniques, such as role playing,...[has been examined by company staff]. Wide differences have been developed in the extent to which the case method is used, based on strong differences of opinion concerning its value. A major purpose of the methods adopted, such as discussion in small groups and, in some courses, individual and group projects, is to stimulate active participation in the course program. (Pierson, 1959, p. 562.)

Taken together, these four sets of similarities appear to make a strong case for arguing that the essential foundations of today's management development programs were constructed by the "pioneers" in this field in the decade of the 1950s. As Bridgman stressed, the national scene was "uneven," but at least some companies were already showing the way in executive education for at least the next two decades, if not longer.

Developments during the Past 25 Years

An examination of the "developments" in corporate management development activities during the past quarter century would appear to point to the conclusion that what changes there have been were more evolutionary than revolutionary. While hard, factual data with respect to such changes are difficult to come by, several general trends can be identified. One, clearly, is the general growth of such programs, both *outward* (to a larger percentage of companies) and *upward* (to include a relatively greater percentage of middle- and upper-level managers). The former type of expansion probably has resulted in a comparatively higher percentage of middle- and smaller-sized organizations instituting some type of management development program compared to 25 years ago. Since most large companies had initiated at least some degree of involvement in management development by 1960, the percentage growth among this size of firm has been less.

The upward expansion of management development is again a relative change, since the programs of some companies by 1960 already were aimed at all management levels. The change has been that more companies (than before) appear to believe that development activities should be aimed throughout management rather than only at the lower levels (with younger and newer managers). The reason, of course, is an increasing recognition of the fact that (as noted in the previous chapter) in this era of rapid change a mere dose of management development early in a person's career (i.e., at a lower management level) will *not* be sufficient to keep that person at the forefront of all the organizational, economic, societal, and demographic factors that affect decision making and other actions in key middle- and upper-level positions. In other words, there has been more sensitivity—if at times grudging—to the needs for lifelong managerial learning.

Interestingly, there appear to have been relatively few major changes in the *type* of content (as distinguished from specific content elements or particular details of knowledge and facts) comprising many EE/MD programs, especially at lower and middle management levels. This was shown, for example, in a study published by Middlebrook and Rachel (1983), who compared data on middle management programs in the early 1980s with those of the early 1960s. As summarized by the two authors, "the data revealed little, if any, significant trends or new developments in middle management development over the past 20 years" (p. 30). With respect to "subject matter areas deemed most important...there appears to be very little, if any, change in the selection of...subject areas between 1963 and the present." Further, the authors note that "this situation finds further support in a study accomplished by Prentice-Hall for the American Society of Personnel Administration [*Employee Training,* 1979].... There were no new developments [as shown in these two studies] in training and development program topics that would indicate significant trends" (p. 31).

Probably one content trend that has occurred—again more of an evolutionary development than a radical change—is the relatively increased emphasis, in programs for upper-level executives, on formulating and, especially, implementing corporate strategy. This topic was not entirely absent in 1960-vintage comprehensive programs, as Bridgman documented in his review, but it was probably not as prominent a feature then as it appears to be now.

One other change which appears to have occurred in some companies is the relatively stronger involvement of top executives in the design of management development programs. This change, for example, was highlighted in a recent article by Bolt (*Harvard Business Review,* 1985, pp. 168–175), who stated that (based on "a survey of many of the nation's most highly regarded corporations") "senior executives are playing a more directive role in shaping management training and development courses and curricula" (p. 168). Again, however, we must stress the relative nature of such a conclusion from two respects. First, this degree of involvement by top executives was not entirely absent in programs of the late 1950s, as Bridgman noted. Second, while there is probably a wider extent of intensive top management involvement than was the case 10 or 20 years ago, it is certainly not a uniform feature across a high percentage of companies, as we discovered in our interviews. In many firms, management development still appears to be regarded as a specialized area to be delegated (by top management) to the human resources unit. Consequently, a number of human resources staff members with whom we talked indicated a strong desire to have considerably more upper-level management involvement than currently exists in their companies. This is especially true in terms of formulating a corporate strategic approach to management development, a point to which we will return in our Commentary section.

CORPORATIONS AS CONSUMERS
OF EXECUTIVE EDUCATION/MANAGEMENT DEVELOPMENT

In this section we will present survey and interview data obtained primarily from directors of management development (DMDs) (or those with equivalent titles/responsibilities), that is, from those human resources staff members specifically responsible in companies and firms for implementing their organization's overall approach to EE/MD activities. Their responses will enable us to examine the distribution of the types of such activities within firms, the relative intrafirm extent of such activities, and corporate attitudes toward the use of different types of providers. The section concludes with observations of DMDs regarding possible future changes in their own firms' management development programs.

Types of Corporate EE/MD Activities

Table 11.1 presents the percentages of responding firms reporting the use of one or more of six different types of EE/MD activities. As can be seen from the table, there was not a large amount of variation in utilization across these several types, whether between "in-house" and "external" programs (i.e., courses) or between "live-in" (i.e., residential) and "non-live-in" programs. The percentages of firms using each type varied from around 50 to about 65%. It

TABLE 11.1
TYPES OF CORPORATE MANAGEMENT DEVELOPMENT ACTIVITIES
(Percent of Companies Utilizing Each Type of Activity: By DMDs; N = 250)

Percent	Type of Activity
11	Reimbursement for *full-time* MBA degrees, but only for *selected* universities
15	Reimbursement for *part-time* MBA degrees, but only for *selected* universities
16	Reimbursement for *full-time* MBA degrees, for any university
63	Reimbursement for *part-time* MBA degrees, for any university
64	*In-house live-in* management development programs offered by *this organization* solely for its own managers
64	*External live-in* management development programs offered by *universities* for managers from a variety of organizations
53	*External live-in* management development programs offered by *nonuniversity vendors* for managers from a variety of organizations
69	*In-house major non-live-in* management development programs (i.e., programs of 3 or more working days)
52	*External major non-live-in* management development programs at *universities* (i.e., programs of 3 or more working days)
57	*External major non-live-in* management development programs at *nonuniversity vendors* (i.e., programs of 3 or more working days)

must be noted, though, that these responses are from firms large enough to have someone designated as specifically responsible for EE/MD activities, and thus the percentages of utilization could be expected to be lower overall for smaller firms. In any event, the main conclusion to be drawn from the data in Table 11.1 is that companies of moderate to large size as a group do not concentrate their EE/MD activities primarily in any one type of program, but rather spread their efforts across a range of types of programs. Of course, however, any single company may utilize only one or two of the various possible types of programs.

Given the overall objectives of this Project, we also asked about a particular type of management development activity, namely, reimbursement for employee enrollment in MBA programs. Responses from DMDs indicated that only 15% of firms would reimburse for enrollment in *any full-time* MBA program, but more than half (63%) would provide "reimbursement for part-time MBA degrees from any university." Only about 15% of responding companies reported that they would restrict reimbursement only to "selected universities" for part-time programs. Of those (15% of) companies restricting their reimbursement to "selected" programs, about half (i.e., about 7% of the total sample) would base such selectivity on "AACSB accreditation" of the particular business school. Overall, these particular findings relating to reimbursement for MBA programs indicate that: (1) many firms (roughly 50% in our sample) are willing to provide reimbursement for part-time MBA programs (presumably located in geographical areas in close proximity to their plants, offices, or other units) *without regard to any criteria relating to the quality of a given program;* and (2) in the total set of all firms in the sample, AACSB accreditation is a negligible factor in determining a basis for reimbursement.

Extent of Corporate EE/MD Activities

There are a number of potential measures of the extent of management development activities in firms, but the one utilized in this study was a survey question that asked DMDs to indicate "the total number of workdays (away from the job) in a year the typical manager in this organization currently spends attending formal management development programs." The DMDs were also asked to indicate what they expected the situation to be "10 years from now." The results are shown in Table 11.2, where it can be seen that some two-fifths (41%) of the DMDs report that the typical manager in their company spends 2 *or fewer* workdays per year on EE/MD programs and only 14% indicate that their managers take more than 5 workdays per year away from the job for this activity. Predictions regarding 10 years hence provide exactly the reverse picture: Only 10% expect that the typical manager will spend only 2 or fewer workdays on development, whereas exactly half (50%) expect that 6 or more days will be spent in this activity. Clearly, there is a statistically significant difference between the currently reported situation and that expected in another decade. The present situation is one where a substantial number of managers (more than 40%) apparently receive minimal development, since it amounts to 2 days or less per year. This is confirmed by the finding reported in the previous chapter that only 10% of DMDs report that their company "requires" managers to spend a "minimum number of workdays per year" attending development programs. The situation projected by the DMDs for 10 years from now is so substantially different that it leads one to the conclusion that either these directors of management development are naively optimistic about how much development will actually be taking place in their organizations *or* they in fact have their fingers on the pulse of a powerful and important trend. Probably, there

TABLE 11.2
NUMBER OF WORKDAYS PER YEAR THAT MANAGERS SPEND
IN MANAGEMENT DEVELOPMENT PROGRAMS: "CURRENTLY"
AND "EXPECT 10 YEARS FROM NOW," AS REPORTED BY DMDs
FOR THEIR ORGANIZATION
(Percent of DMDs Checking One of Five Alternatives; $N = 245$)

Workdays per Year	Currently	Expect in 10 Years
0	8%	1%
1–2	33	9
3–5	46	40
6–10	13	40
11+	1	10

Note: All columns add to total of 100% within rounding.

are some elements of both factors contributing to this particular set of expectations regarding the future.

Corporate Utilization of Different EE/MD Providers

Table 11.3 presents data from the responses of DMDs regarding the current usage of three different types of providers of management development programs: the corporation itself (i.e., in-house programs), universities (i.e., business/management schools) and others (professional associations, commercial vendors, etc.). As shown in this table, the vast majority of companies represented in the sample use all three vendors at least "occasionally," but the most extensive use by far is made of programs provided by the firms themselves, their own in-house programs. Interview data tended to confirm that most companies (not all) prefer to use in-house programs to the extent they believe they have the resources available within the firm to mount quality programs. (For the reasons, see the following section.) In such cases, university and other third-party external programs are utilized to fill in those niches which could not otherwise be covered by the array of in-house programs. Examples would be a university-based course at a prominent business school for top-level executives from a variety of companies, or a highly specialized program where a particular consultant or vendor organization could provide a unique instructional service.

Future Changes in the Corporate Consumer Role

One major predicted change is one that we have already reported: DMDs expect a much higher participation rate (workdays spent per year) in EE/MD activities by managers from their organizations. Aside from this projected development, our interviews elicited a wide variety of responses to queries about "likely major changes" in this area in the DMD's own organization. Certainly one change that a number of these human resources staff members wanted, but were not at all sure would happen, was for their top management to take a more systematic and comprehensive approach to management development.

TABLE 11.3
CORPORATE UTILIZATION OF DIFFERENT PROVIDERS:
AS REPORTED BY DMDs
(Percent Checking One of Three Alternatives; N = 246)

	Providers		
	In-House	**University**	**Other External**
Do not use	2%	10%	4%
Use occasionally	31	80	80
Use extensively	67	10	16

(This is a topic we will address further in the Commentary section.) Examples of other changes predicted by particular companies—but changes about which there seemed very little consensus across companies—included more emphasis on "the articulation of the corporate culture," on "shorter-term business objectives," on "product skill training," on "top management awareness of strategic implications," on "development of people skills," and on "how to modify and impact the environment." Clearly, the lack of consensus in the nature of these predictions about the future reflected the variety of types of companies and firms represented in the sample and the diversity of their particular competitive and environmental (internal and external) circumstances.

CORPORATIONS AS PROVIDERS OF EXECUTIVE EDUCATION/MANAGEMENT DEVELOPMENT

This section will focus on why there is high utilization of in-house courses; how different sets of corporate personnel rate the effectiveness of in-house programs, especially in relation to university and other external programs; the relative advantages and disadvantages of in-house programs as seen by DMDs; and views regarding the future use and nature of such programs.

Utilization of Corporate In-House EE/MD Programs

As we saw previously in Table 11.3, the companies in our sample reported using in-house programs more heavily than programs provided by other sources. Sixty-seven percent of DMDs said in-house programs were used "extensively," and another 31% said at least "occasionally." The reasons for this relatively high use of programs provided internally, as indicated by our interviews, involved a number of potential factors. Largely, however, (as will be shown below in the discussion of advantages and disadvantages of in-house programs) these reasons revolved around the ability to tailor content precisely to the needs and objectives of the corporation. Partly this is due to the fact that those running these programs, and often a high percentage of those instructing in them, are familiar with the particular company, its culture, its problems, its terminology, and the like. Thus, there is the potential for maximizing content relevance and credibility in programs provided in-house. All this depends, as we noted earlier, on a company deciding to invest in the necessary personnel and other resources to put on its own programs.

Effectiveness of Corporate In-House EE/MD Programs

Four different categories of corporate respondents—two line groups (CEOs and SCEs) and two human resources staff groups (VPHRs and DMDs)—were asked to rate the effectiveness of in-house EE/MD programs, as well as those provided by universities (business schools) and by other external sources, on a

TABLE 11.4
EFFECTIVENESS OF PROGRAMS OF DIFFERENT PROVIDERS
(Median Rating, on a 10-Point Scale, of Extent to Which Programs Have "Met Corporate
Training Objectives" and, in Parentheses, Percent Checking that Programs Have a "Wide
Variation in Quality")

Raters	Providers		
	In-House	University	Other External
CEOs $(N = 122)$	5.9 (35%)	5.3 (57%)	5.6 (68%)
SCEs $(N = 149)$	5.9 (34)	5.5 (45)	5.6 (59)
VPHRs $(N = 203)$	6.1 (35)	5.6 (51)	5.6 (61)
DMDs $(N = 225)$	6.8 (23)	5.3 (41)	6.3 (45)

10-point scale. These corporate respondents also were asked to indicate whether or not they thought there was a wide variation in the quality of programs produced by each provider source. The combined results of these questions are presented in Table 11.4. It can be seen in this table that the four sets of corporate respondents generally rated in-house programs as slightly more effective than either university (business school) or other external programs, but the differences are not of great magnitude. As might be expected, among the corporate groups the DMDs were clearly the most positive about in-house programs, while the two top line groups (CEOs and SCEs) were somewhat more reserved about "how well" such programs "have met corporate training objectives." Since 5.5 is the midpoint on a 10-point scale (i.e., a scale running from 1 = low to 10 = high), the mean ratings of 5.9 by CEOs and SCEs for in-house programs appear to indicate that executives in those types of positions believe, rightly or wrongly, that there is still room for improving the effectiveness of these programs (and, even more so, as Table 11.4 shows, for programs put on by the other two types of providers). With respect to their views about variation in quality (across programs from a given source), all four of the corporate respondent groups believed that there was *less* variation among in-house programs compared to those from other providers (especially the nonuniversity external providers). Chief executive officers, in particular, saw distinct differences in uniformity of quality between in-house programs (where more uniform quality was perceived) and those provided by the other two sources.

Perceived Advantages/Disadvantages of Corporate In-House EE/MD Programs

In the following subsections we review the perceived advantages and disadvantages of corporate in-house programs as seen by directors of management development (DMDs). Other groups of corporate respondents might or might not have similar views about the strengths and weaknesses of this category of program.

Advantages   Table 11.5 presents the responses of DMDs to a survey question in which they were asked to indicate for each of a fixed list of alternative features whether that feature represented a "major advantage" of in-house programs. As is shown in the table (and as generally supported by our interview data), three program attributes received the higher percentage of "major advantage" responses: "program content related to the specific needs of the organization" (83%), the fact that "participants interact with other managers from their own organization" (65%), and "cost-effectiveness" (65%). It is also interesting to note the two potential advantages that received the relatively lowest (and also fairly low in an absolute sense) percentages of respondents checking "major advantage": "highest-quality instruction" (21%) and "maximum input of new ideas" (17%).

Disadvantages   The DMDs, as shown in Table 11.6, cited "insufficient number of instructors within the organization who are technically competent in the subject matter" and "insufficient number of instructors...who are effective teachers" as the two most frequent "major disadvantages." However, the absolute percentages (26% in each case) checking these two alternatives were relatively small, indicating that most DMDs do not see many important disadvantages to in-house EE/MD programs as long as resources are sufficient. Of course, since they themselves usually are directly responsible for the effectiveness of these programs—and hence their organizational careers often depend on their firms' willingness to continue conducting in-house programs—it would not be expected that they would believe that these programs have a large number of serious drawbacks. (Unfortunately, because of the necessity to keep surveys as brief as possible, it was not feasible to ask these same questions about "advantages/disadvantages" of in-house programs on the survey forms for other categories of corporate respondents. The percentages of respondents in these other groups checking "major advantage" or "major disadvantage" might or might not have paralleled those of DMDs.)

TABLE 11.5
PERCEIVED ADVANTAGES OF CORPORATE IN-HOUSE EE/MD
PROGRAMS
(Percent of DMDs Checking "Major Advantage"; $N = 247$)

Percent	Advantage
83	Program content specific to needs of the organization
65	Cost effectiveness
65	Participants interact with other managers from own organization
53	Convenience, logistics, etc.
21	Highest-quality instruction
17	Maximum input of new ideas

TABLE 11.6
PERCEIVED DISADVANTAGES OF CORPORATE IN-HOUSE EE/MD PROGRAMS
(Percent of DMDs Checking "Major Disadvantage"; N = 247)

Percent	Disadvantage
26	Insufficient number of instructors within organization who are technically competent in subject matter
26	Insufficient number of instructors within organization who are effective teachers (in Executive Education/Management Development programs)
13	Overemphasis on current way of doing things within the organization
11	Participants do not get exposed to enough breadth of content
9	Lack of appropriate facilities within the organization
6	Participants interact only with other managers from their own organization
4	Lack of sufficient number of participants from the organization for a program to be cost-effective
3	Overpriced

Future Changes Relating to Corporate In-House Programs

The DMDs were asked to estimate the changes in usage of in-house programs by their own organizations during the next 10-year period. The results for this survey question are shown in Table 11.7, where it can be seen that 87% of DMDs expect an increased use during this period, including 44% who expect the increase to be "substantial."

Another survey question relating to the future of EE/MD programs provided by different sources asked DMDs to indicate what they "expect will be the major source of programs to meet the most important management development needs of 'this organization' in the next 10 years," for each of three management levels: lower, middle, and upper/top. Table 11.8 reports the percentages checking one of the three sources (in-house, university, and other external providers) for each of these three levels. The results appear to show that, relatively speaking, at lower and middle levels in-house programs would be used

TABLE 11.7
EXPECTED INCREASE/DECREASE IN USE OF EE/MD PROGRAMS
FROM DIFFERENT PROVIDERS IN NEXT 10-YEAR PERIOD:
AS VIEWED BY DMDs
(Percent Checking Each of Five Alternatives; N = 242)

	Provider		
	In-House	University	Other External
Increase substantially	44%	10%	14%
Increase somewhat	43	55	43
Maintain at present level	11	30	31
Decrease somewhat	2	4	10
Decrease substantially	0	0	2

Note: All columns add to total of 100% within rounding.

TABLE 11.8
EXPECTED MAJOR SOURCES OF PROGRAMS IN THE FUTURE TO MEET MOST
IMPORTANT CORPORATE EE/MD NEEDS: AS VIEWED BY DMDs
(Percent Checking One of Three Possible Providers for Each Management Level; N = 230)

	Provider		
	In-House	University	Other External
Lower management levels	84%	3%	13%
Middle management levels	63	13	24
Upper/top management levels	24	36	40

Note: All rows add across to total of 100% within rounding.

the most, by a considerable margin. At the upper levels, DMDs expect in-house and nonuniversity external sources to be used the most. Again, it must be kept in mind that the respondents to this question are corporate directors of management development and thus come from firms large enough to have this specialized type of position. Undoubtedly, were a sample to be composed mostly of smaller firms, it would show much lower percentages for in-house programs as a major source and much higher percentages for both university and other external programs.

Future predicted changes in in-house programs, as gained from interview comments, tended to revolve around additional attention to how to make them relate as effectively as possible to company objectives. This was seen as part of the larger effort to relate the total program of EE/MD activities—both internally and externally provided courses—to long-range corporate strategic planning. In some instances this would involve expanding in-house capabilities; in other cases it would involve creating a more effective combination of use of internal and external programs. The specific direction for the future use of in-house courses (as well as those provided by university and other external agencies) in a particular company appeared to depend on: (1) the extent of current and expected resources available for in-house programs; (2) the effectiveness of the current in-house array of EE/MD activities; and (3) the views of the DMD and other senior human resources executives about what would be the most appropriate mix between internal and external programs (courses). When these three factors, especially the latter, are considered together, different organizations in our sample arrived at rather different conclusions, although there was a general tendency—on the part of both line and staff executives—to want to do as much in-house as seemed feasible and appropriate. Nevertheless, almost none of the firms we encountered wanted to rely exclusively on their own courses and instructional personnel.

COMMENTARY

Since corporations are involved in executive education and management development as both buyers and producers, there are potentially a relatively large number of issues that could be discussed. In this Commentary section we will concentrate on three of them: the consumer role of corporations; the provider role of corporations; and, the decisive issue, do companies take EE/MD seriously? For all three of these issues we will be drawing especially heavily on impressions we gained in our corporate interviews, as well as on the specific (largely survey) data reported in the preceding sections of this chapter.

Corporations in the EE/MD Consumer Role

As we discussed in the previous chapter, for management development to be most effective it should be anchored in some type of a substantial needs analysis. However, as we also reported in that chapter, almost 30% of the companies in our survey sample stated that they do not undertake a formal needs analysis. We suspect, moreover, extrapolating from our interview impressions, that the degree of thoroughness of such needs analyses in the other 70% of companies varies considerably. This lack, at least until fairly recently, of much attention to conducting any sort of systematic assessment of managers' developmental needs in many companies, in turn, seems to lead to a considerable amount of wasted effort—and certainly wasted costs—in the EE/MD area. In our judgment, a not insignificant portion of the companies with which we talked appeared to be putting on various types of management development activities— whether internally or externally provided—without having any basis for knowing whether those activities were (1) meeting the most important needs and (2) meeting them in an effective manner. Money and valuable time were being "tossed" at presumed needs with the *hope* that something would "hit." Thus, although other data we collected (see the following chapter) indicate that some companies are definitely becoming relatively more sophisticated consumers and purchasers of management development courses than they have been in the past, there still seems to be substantial room for improvement in this regard on the part of many firms. More of them need to develop a sound basis for implementing an appropriate *caveat emptor* policy.

In this connection, we cannot refrain from commenting on company policies in some organizations regarding tuition reimbursement for MBA programs. Such policies (in these particular companies) seem to involve a curious anomaly: On the one hand, the company reports that it *recruits* MBA graduates only from a very restricted list of schools (often a set of the so-called tier 1 schools) and would be very unlikely to hire in directly (for positions or training programs specifically requiring an MBA degree) anyone with an MBA from outside this short list. On the other hand, that same company has a tuition reimbursement plan that will pay totally or partially the fees of any employee attending *any* MBA program—irrespective of quality. Various explanations for this apparent inconsistency can be suggested (e.g., tuition reimbursement is simply a company benefit like health insurance and hence the would-be part-time MBA student is at liberty to choose his or her "own doctor," so to speak). Nevertheless, it appeared that at least some of the companies had not thought through whether they in fact should be financially supporting any MBA program without attempting to gauge its quality—especially in light of the fact that such great efforts go into determining the quality of the programs from which they are recruiting MBAs. Since the process of obtaining an MBA degree can be thought of as a form of management development, more attention to the quality of programs employees are attending—under auspices of the company's tuition reimbursement program—might be thought of as one way of increasing corporate consumer sophistication. Likewise, such action might also exert pressure on business/management schools to pay attention to factors other than merely making their programs convenient—and easy—for students to enter and complete.

Corporations in the EE/MD Provider Role

As clearly indicated by both interview and questionnaire data presented earlier in this chapter, many companies are enamored of the idea of becoming (or continuing to be) their own providers of management development courses to as great an extent as possible. This is understandable because, as we noted previously, in-house courses—at least in principle—can be targeted to focus directly on identified corporate needs and concerns. Ideally, they can be designed and implemented in ways that not only provide highly relevant company-specific information, but also serve to reinforce overall corporate goals and objectives. These obvious advantages of in-house courses need to be assessed against two questions: (1) can in-house courses be implemented effectively in order to maximize the potential advantages, and (2) what are the costs involved in doing so? Put differently, the overriding issue is: Are in-house courses always the best answer for corporate management development needs?

With respect to the first question, much depends on the available resources within the company—especially the presence of qualified instructors. *Qualified,* in this sense, refers to both technical/content knowledge *and* the capabilities and skills to relate that knowledge effectively in classroom and development sessions. Often, the latter qualification requirement represents a more difficult implementation problem than the former because many line executives used in courses for middle- and upper-level managers do not have the training and experience in these types of presentational skills. (In addition, there is the additional issue of the "opportunity cost" of their time if they are used on a repeated and regular basis in EE/MD courses.) Of course, companies—if they are willing to pay the costs—can supplement their own employee teaching resources by hiring external consultants (including university professors) to meet instructional needs for particular sessions or topics in in-house courses. However, this latter solution has its own set of potential problems. The external resource person, no matter how capable an instructor and how expert in a given subject matter area, may not be highly knowledgeable about the company and its specific objectives, issues, and problems. Thus, one of the major potential advantages of in-house MD courses (vis-à-vis externally provided courses) is attenuated somewhat when noncompany individuals are included as part of the set of instructional personnel.

The second major question concerning in-house courses relates to the issue of costs. If a company provides a limited number of such courses mostly for lower-level junior managers, then the marginal costs probably will not be especially high. Often, these courses can be conducted effectively by those human resources staff members who have responsibilities for training and development programs as part of their overall set of assigned tasks. However, when courses are to be designed for more senior and higher-level managers, this relatively simple and low-cost solution becomes much more problematical. Different types of both training and development sophistication and subject matter expertise are often needed. Such personnel requirements, particularly if they involve permanent staff resources, can increase costs considerably. To put on a comprehensive in-house EE/MD program that includes an array of courses for all levels of management represents a substantial investment, even for a large and prosperous company. For smaller and less well endowed companies, the proportional investment is greater.

In looking to the future, many corporate directors of management development want and expect to see a large increase in the use of company-provided EE/MD programs. However, in our opinion, an exclusive or very high reliance on in-house sources probably will not become a viable long-range solution for meeting management development needs in most companies. Although there are some distinct and important advantages connected with such an approach to management development, there are also some potentially serious problems. Costs and implementation capabilities are only two of them. The other significant, and perhaps more serious, disadvantage is the inbreeding problem. Company-provided courses are extremely effective for helping managers get acquainted with other managers from their own organization and for allowing such managers to learn about company approaches to dealing with managerial issues. Also, though, they are, by their very nature, much less effective in providing managers with the type of fresh insights that can come from interacting with managers from other companies. In short, company-provided components have a definite place in any mix of courses in a comprehensive approach to executive education and management development, but by themselves they do not constitute a panacea.

Do Most Companies Provide Real Substance to Their Management Development Efforts?

Throughout all our several hundred corporate interviews in some fifty-plus different companies we found almost universal endorsement of the value and importance of (planned) management development activities. Indeed, (as discussed in the previous chapter) many of those with whom we talked in a variety of middle- and senior-level line as well as staff positions expressed the view that such activities should be expanded and strengthened in their own particular organizations. On the surface, therefore, it would appear that there is a large reservoir of support for increased corporate efforts to meet the lifelong learning needs of managers—for the presumed benefit of both the organization and the manager. Executive education/management development very nearly falls into the category of parenthood and apple pie: It is regarded as a "good thing" for the organization to do—everybody comes out ahead.

Nevertheless, we would like to raise this question: Do most companies and firms provide more lip service than real substance to their efforts in management development? One indication was provided in the previous chapter, where some 40% of managers reported spending 2 or fewer workdays per year attending EE/MD programs and about 50% (of the total sample) reported that they think they should be spending more time on this activity than they actually do. The former finding was corroborated in this chapter in Table 11.2, which shows that 41% of DMDs agreed that the typical manager in their companies spends 2 or fewer workdays per year attending formal management development programs. A second indicator, reported previously, was the fact that only 10% of DMDs stated that each manager in their organizations was *required* to spend a certain number of workdays per year attending such programs.

Considering these findings together, the following question has to be asked: If only one in ten organizations requires their managers to participate in EE/MD activities for a certain number of days per year, and if the typical manager in more than 40% of reporting firms (which tend to be the larger and more management development–oriented firms at that) spends no more than 2 workdays per year in such participation, does this constitute evidence of serious attention by most firms? Our answer, clearly, is "no." Our interviews left us with the view that some companies are, indeed, very serious and have done a remarkable job in both designing and implementing a comprehensive approach to management development. Other firms, however, in our opinion, do not support their encouraging words about the importance of management development with a great deal of concrete action and follow-up. In essence, the corporate management development scene—as viewed across a wide spectrum of companies—in the mid-1980s seems much like Bridgman described the picture 25 years earlier: "an extremely uneven area." It may be less uneven today, but it is certainly not level.

Another type of indicator of the role that management development actually plays (as opposed to the role that it could play) in organizations emerged from our interview discussions regarding how much attention was given to comprehensive corporate planning for management development. Each firm about whose EE/MD activities we were able to develop sufficient information seemed to fall into one of three categories in this regard: (1) firms that had well-entrenched, comprehensive approaches that had been in place for some period of time; (2) firms that very recently (within the past 5 years) had decided to take a more thorough approach to planning exactly where management development would fit into overall company goals and operations, but where not enough time had elapsed to gauge the effectiveness or the durability of these more systematic approaches; and (3) firms that did not seem to have engaged in any sort of basic planning for the types and amounts of management development activities that should be carried out and how they should relate to larger corporate strategies. The total set of firms interviewed ($N = 50+$), in our estimation, seemed to be about equally divided among the three categories.

Interestingly, the DMDs of several very prominent companies, including one or two firms that had been nominated by a nationwide set of human resources experts as having superior management development programs, confessed (in confidence, of course) that, in effect, "our company's EE/MD program [i.e., overall approach to management development] is in reality not nearly as good as its reputation." The following direct quotations from four of these firms (i.e., their DMDs or top human resources executives) were typical:

> I would characterize our management development [program] as a kind of smorgasbord approach—we offer lots of seminars and short kind of stuff on the assumption that people are going to make [the right] choices, but there hasn't been much systematic [guidance] from the top regarding "this is what we want our managers to know and do."...We've been pretty lackadaisical about management development for the last 10 years.

> I think [this company's] development activities have changed radically in the last 5 years....We had a training and education department that offered, in effect, a smorgasbord of training programs that was very much up to the individual or their boss to select the appropriate program....I think as we came out of the 1970s, [this company] recognized that that simply wasn't enough. We had to shift gears to give people management development in a much more structured [systematic] way.

> Top management support for management development activities is "spotty"—when the economy is going down, management development gets an early axe. But, can we [this company] afford to keep operating this way?

> Internal MD is a major weakness [of this organization]....We just haven't paid that much attention to it in the past. We have always had very good front-end training [for new management-level employees] but subsequent development was not systematic.

As the first two of these quotes (from two distinctly different companies) illustrate, "smorgasbord" seems to be an apt label for describing the character of management development programs that emerge as the product of a lack of systematic planning in this area in a number of major corporations.

Companies in the first category identified above—those that have firmly established, highly coordinated, comprehensive programs—were benefiting from their EE/MD programs in several ways. First, of course, their managers and executives appeared to be obtaining quality developmental experiences that supplemented their job experiences in systematic ways at appropriate stages of their organizational careers. These organizations thus gained something directly from their managers' accelerated learning. Additionally, however, a few of these companies were also capitalizing on another potential benefit—though a benefit largely unrealized even in most of the companies in this first category—that can result from well planned EE/MD programs: the facilitation and reinforcement of overall corporate strategy. In other words, a comprehensive management development program can become a very effective means for ensuring the communication and understanding of significant corporate objectives. To show how one company is attempting to do this, we cite below a portion of its stated mission for its overall EE/MD program:

> To be a major catalyst in revising, disseminating, and fostering the development of the leadership characteristics...and shared values...of [this company]...[and] to be an instrument for cultural change as well as part of the cultural glue of [this company].

If this company is successful in actually achieving this objective, it will, it seems to us, have gained a significant competitive advantage that other companies would be advised to attempt to emulate. Utilizing a total management development program as a very explicit part of implementing corporate strategy marks a quantum advance in this activity compared to its humble beginnings 40 years ago. Unfortunately, some companies still seem to regard management training much as it was back at the end of World War II: not much more than upgraded foremen's training.

CHAPTER 12

EXECUTIVE EDUCATION/ MANAGEMENT DEVELOPMENT: UNIVERSITY BUSINESS SCHOOLS

University business/management schools constitute one of three major "producers" of nondegree executive education (EE) and management development (MD) programs, along with other external (to the corporation) providers of such programs and companies and firms themselves. University business/ management schools are similar to the former and differ from the latter in that they operate only on the "production" side and are not also consumers. They are, however, also quite different from most commercial vendors of EE/MD programs because these programs are not their primary educational/instructional focus but rather a secondary-level endeavor. Indeed, many business schools (about one-third of the AACSB member schools) do not have any such programs at all, and another 50% (47% to be precise) are involved in only a minor way (according to their own self-descriptions). Thus, at the present time, only about one-fifth of the nation's business/management schools are active in this type of education in a major way, and even for them such efforts are invariably subsidiary to the schools' degree programs. Nevertheless, as will be seen, there are strong indications from our interview and survey data that such activities will become an increasingly important object of attention for a significant number of schools in the decade ahead.

In this chapter, as in most of the previous chapters, we will begin by reviewing the EE/MD situation as it existed at the time of the Foundation reports some 25 years ago. This will provide a baseline to compare current business school efforts in this area, as viewed from both the university and the corporate perspective. Thus, in subsequent sections of the chapter, we will look at such issues as the current level of emphasis placed on this activity, the missions/ goals that schools see for themselves in this type of educational undertaking,

257

the kinds of programs currently offered, their effectiveness as assessed by corporate consumers, the advantages and disadvantages that university-offered programs are seen as having versus those from other providers, and finally, views about where university EE/MD programs are heading—and should be heading—in the future.

THE PAST 25 YEARS

This section reviews the situation at the beginning of the 1960s and the developments that have occurred during the intervening years as they relate to university business/management schools' efforts in EE/MD.

The Situation at the Beginning of the 1960s

University-based nondegree executive development programs for practicing managers had their birth as far back as 1931, when the Massachusetts Institute of Technology initiated its Executive Development (Sloan) Program (Gordon and Howell, 1959, p. 294; Pierson, [Andrews] 1959, p. 578). However, this activity was hardly a growth industry before World War II. In fact, no other such programs were instituted until the middle of the war, when, at the government's request, executive education programs were started at Harvard, Stanford, and the University of Chicago. These were discontinued when the war ended in 1945, and the first postwar programs of this type were launched by the University of Pittsburgh and Harvard. Other programs soon followed, and by 1953 there were seventeen such programs. By 1958 the number (of residential programs of 2 or more weeks duration and aimed at developing general management competence) had expanded rapidly to about forty (Gordon and Howell, 1959, p. 294; Pierson, [Andrews] 1959, p. 579).

By the beginning of the 1960s, executive development programs already could be classified into several major types that are still predominant today. As Andrews (writing in Pierson, 1959) noted, three key dimensions formed the basis for categorizing these different types of programs: (1) whether a program was residential or nonresidential, (2) whether it focused on general management and "a broad approach to the administrative process" or on some specialized functional area or industry, and (3) its length. (Andrews also listed a fourth dimension—whether the subject matter was business/management or liberal arts.) Using these dimensions, EE/MD programs of that day could be placed into several distinct types, of which three tended to be most common: (1) residential general management–oriented programs of at least several weeks' duration, (2) nonresidential programs of the same type as the first (involving, for example, a half day or day per week for a period of weeks), and (3) specialized courses, either residential or nonresidential, and usually of shorter duration (i.e., typically 2 weeks or less).

There is little doubt that at the beginning of the 1960s the first type—the residential programs oriented at developing breadth and general management competencies and perspectives—was the dominant and most visible form of university-based executive education. As Gordon and Howell noted then (p.296): "This [is the] type of program that is usually meant when the term 'management development' or 'executive development' is used, and most of the university programs for executives fall into this category." These programs, then as now, put particular emphasis on "broadening the executive's mental horizon" and were designed on the "common assumption...that the most important single problem in management development has to do with how to convert capable specialists into even more capable generalists" (Gordon and Howell, 1959, p. 296). They were also based on another assumption which would seem to be somewhat outdated today: "It is our impression," stated Gordon and Howell, "that most university programs are based on the assumption that the participants have not had the equivalent of much formal training in business administration" (p. 307). With a good deal of foresight, however, they also added: "This assumption will become less justified as the years go by."

The content of such programs 25 to 30 years ago, as described in the Ford Foundation report, was quite forward-looking by today's standards and might even surprise some recent faculty entrants to the business education scene who view anything that far back as truly old-fashioned. According to the report (p. 298), three topic areas "tend[ed] to be emphasized" in such programs: (1) financial management and control, (2) "management of human resources in an organizational context," and (3) a "firm's nonmarket environment" (usually including "some material on national income and related topics, the place of business in society...and the responsibilities of business to the community").

The two Foundation reports noted several potential problems that faced business schools at the beginning of the 1960s in their efforts to implement effective management development programs, and these are issues that clearly are still with us nearly three decades later. For example, Andrews (in Pierson, 1959, p. 596) identified "two major dangers which imperil the quality of the courses being offered" (and, presumably, that would face those schools anticipating offering such programs): (1) "distraction from [the school's] principal mission" (this primarily refers to "inroads into the time of [the] faculty" that would dilute the faculty's attention to the basic undergraduate and graduate degree programs; it also refers to the more indirect but nevertheless important administrative and other overhead costs that can put a strain on important resources), and (2) "superficiality," specifically, "the...superficiality which must occur when tasks undertaken exceed resources." In particular, Andrews (in 1959) was concerned about such things as "the concept that a short course can do a big job,...the way in which courses are conducted,...[and] faddism [in topics] " (Pierson, 1959, p. 599). In addition to these two major dangers, Andrews also expressed serious reservations about the possibility of what we would now call "contract" or tailor-made courses put on by business schools for managers from a single firm: "Trouble lies ahead if companies decide that they should specify the content and length of the courses they will support or if they expect schools to conduct courses especially designed to their specifications" (Pierson, 1959,

p. 600). Here, the cause for concern was the possible "loss of independence" for the school and the possibility that the particular company would not be willing to provide the kind of "substantial support...which meaningful executive education may require."

In looking to the future, the Foundation reports at the end of the 1950s were optimistic that executive education was here to stay as part of the business school landscape. Gordon and Howell, for example, said, "Little doubt can remain that the business schools have a considerable opportunity for useful service in the field of adult business education" (p. 318). Andrews, in his chapter on this topic in Pierson's report, was even more emphatic (and also prescient):

> It would be unwise to conclude that we are considering a temporary phenomenon like miniature golf....it is probable that business education will one day be permanently altered by the concept that there is no natural end to learning and by the expansion of the business school's sphere of influence to the whole executive career....It is quite possible that the swift expansion of education for managers has a greater promise than most of the other changes which have taken place since business education began in 1881. (Pierson, 1959, p. 585–586.)

Both reports were not only positive in their expectations about the role that executive education could play in the future of business schools, but they also laid out similar agendas for that future which stressed the importance of schools choosing and setting their objectives carefully in this area. Their similar views were summed up in the following comments by Gordon and Howell (p. 319):

> The most important need at the moment is for the universities to take stock of what they are doing in the field of adult business education—to develop a clear-cut philosophy and set of objectives and to appraise the needs to be served and the resources available for meeting them....We also hope there will be a greater insistence that, for a particular program of adult business education to be offered, reasonable evidence be given that the university can provide the kind of training desired better than any other available agency and without serious conflict with the other (and prior) claims on the staff and resources available.

Developments during the Past 25 Years

In the more than 25 years since the two Foundation reports, considerable change—as with other areas of management education—has taken place in executive education programs offered by university business schools. These changes can be categorized roughly under the following six headings: (1) growth, (2) types/diversity of programs, (3) content of programs, (4) structure and process of programs, (5) participants, and (6) purchasers. In the remainder of this section we will discuss each development in turn.

Growth   As predicted by both the Pierson and the Gordon and Howell reports in 1959, there has been substantial absolute growth in university-based nondegree EE and MD programs. This growth is summarized in Table 12.1 from data published in 1986 by the Bricker Executive Education Service. The table shows the expansion in the period from 1962 to 1985 in the number of institutions offering major EE programs, the number of such programs—both general management and functional management—and the number of participants. As can be seen from Table 12.1, the number of schools involved in a major way (as defined by the Bricker publication, meaning that schools offer residential courses of 1 week or more in duration) has about doubled, the number of general management programs has more than tripled, the number of functional management programs has increased by more than eight times, and the total number of participants in both types of programs together has multiplied by a factor of about eight. This growth, up to now, has been fairly steady, but it has differed by type of program (see following paragraphs).

Types/Diversity of Programs

General Management   The number of residential general management programs of (typically) several weeks' duration has continued to grow at a relatively constant pace over the past couple of decades. However, some see the market for such programs as "maturing," with relatively few schools starting this type of enterprise in recent years. Furthermore, traditionally this has been a field dominated by a small number of nationally visible schools. For example, the Harvard and Stanford business schools together account for over one-third of this market (S.A. Pond, as cited in *UNC/Business*, 1985). The focus and content of such programs continue to be as in the past: to emphasize breadth and to develop managers with functional experiences into more broadly oriented general managers for upper-level executive positions. (A variant of this type of program, as was the case in 1960, is the nonresident general management program which managers attend once a week for some period of weeks—e.g., 12 to 16 weeks.)

Specialized Programs   Although this type of program—aimed at providing an in-depth exposure to a particular functional area of business or to a particular industry or set of managers (e.g., women executives)—also has been around since the 1950s, it has shown relatively more rapid growth in that time in num-

TABLE 12.1
GROWTH IN UNIVERSITY EXECUTIVE EDUCATION: 1962–1985

	1962	1985
Academic institutions	39	73
General management programs	39	139
Functional management programs	9	77
Total number of participants	1,900	14,600

Source: Bricker Executive Educational Service, *Bricker Bulletin*, vol. 5, no. 1, 1986.

bers of programs and participants than have the general management programs. Undoubtedly, this is due to the fact that more schools have the capabilities and faculty resources to mount such programs, which tend to be shorter in length and less complicated compared to the latter type of program.

"Contract" Programs   A relatively recent phenomenon, at least insofar as the rate at which such programs are being conducted is concerned, is the tailor-made or "contract" program put on by a business/management school for managers of one particular company. These "private" programs have increased rapidly in recent years; in fact, for those schools that offer them, they now "equal or exceed executive education in the form of public programs offered by the same set of institutions" (*The Bricker Bulletin,* vol. 3, no. 3, 1984). However, as Pond (cited in *UNC/Business*, 1985) notes, they are "a controversial area of university education." Some schools like the links that such programs provide with particular firms of special interest to the school and also the economic and resource security (at least for a guaranteed period of time) that a contract for specified executive education services provides. Other schools abjure such arrangements precisely because of the potential "strings" that may be attached and because this may restrict their opportunities to develop contacts with a larger number of companies through their executive education programs.

Programs Offered by Institutions outside the United States   Although this Project is limited to coverage of management education and development activities in the United States, it is worth noting in passing that in contrast to the situation existing a quarter century ago, this country does not have a monopoly on providing comprehensive university-based executive education programs. Whereas U.S. educational institutions were virtually the sole supplier of such programs at the beginning of the 1960s, they now can be found in almost every major country in Europe, Asia, and other parts of the world. (See McNulty, 1985, for a listing of such programs.)

Executive MBA Programs   This chapter is focused on university-based *non-degree* executive education programs, so, strictly speaking, a discussion of degree-based "executive MBA" programs might not be appropriate here. However, since such programs have characteristics that cut across both regular MBA degree programs and nondegree executive education programs, they deserve a brief mention here—especially in relation to a discussion of developments that have occurred in the last 25 years. As noted in the Andrews chapter in Pierson, at the end of the 1950s the University of Chicago Executive MBA program was virtually the only one of this type being offered anywhere in this country. About a quarter century later, there were at least eighty-five such programs in existence and at least that many more schools were contemplating adding them to their roster of degree programs (Nohl, in GMAC *Selections,* 1986, vol. 2, no. 3, p. 20). It seems obvious that for certain schools and companies (i.e., those companies that financially sponsor the managers attending these programs), this type of hybrid program that combines elements of the typical MBA degree and general management executive education program is fulfilling a useful service. Whether, as more and more managers obtain the regular MBA degree, there will continue to be a relatively strong demand for these programs in the future is another question. Certainly, though, the rapid expansion of this type of offering has been a significant post-1960s development, particularly during the last decade.

Content of Programs   The content of executive education programs—particularly general management–oriented programs—has changed over the years to about the same extent as degree (especially the MBA degree) programs. That is, as new advancements in knowledge are made in various areas, such as finance or marketing or organizational behavior, these have been reflected in the changing content of EE programs (including specialized MD programs focusing on those or similar specific topic areas). Probably the largest thematic changes that have occurred since the time of the Foundation reports have been: relatively more emphasis on the external environment of the corporation and an increasing focus on international aspects of business ("the global economy").

Structure and Process of Programs   The major structural change that has occurred in executive education activities has been a trend toward programs of shorter length. This trend, mentioned in a number of our interviews with schools' executive education directors, has come about primarily through pressure from firms who (for the most part) do not wish to see key managers and executives taken away from their jobs for periods much longer than several weeks. Our interviews with various managers also confirmed this conclusion of the EE directors. As one human resources executive of a fast-growing service organization explained (with only slight hyperbole), "If one of our managers was away from the job for more than a month, not only would he or she not recognize their job when they got back, they wouldn't recognize the company—because things are changing so fast around here."

The other significant structure/process change that has occurred gradually over the years in EE programs has been a strong tendency to use more "participative" approaches with respect to how programs are "delivered" in the classroom. Although straight lectures have always tended to be deemphasized in MD programs in favor of case studies, small group discussions, simulations, and the like, this tendency has become more firmly entrenched in the leading programs during the past two decades. It is still somewhat of an open question, however, whether there is—even today—a wide enough recognition among faculty members across a wide range of schools that are offering or thinking of offering MD programs that a different style and approach to teaching mature adults compared to teaching young adults in their twenties is probably required. We will have more to say about this subject in the Commentary section.

Participants   One development in executive education that almost certainly has been taking place in the past 20 years or so—although we have no direct objective data on this point—is the *increasing sophistication* of the participants.

Given the remarkable growth in enrollments in undergraduate and master's degree business/management programs since the early 1960s, this means that a much higher percentage of those attending EE programs is likely to have had at least some formal education in business subjects. This, coupled with the increasing emphasis on in-house MD that companies themselves have been supplying, has provided a typical manager with a much stronger background at the time she or he enters a university EE program. This has increased the challenge—upped the ante, as it were—for university-supplied programs to "teach me something I don't already know."

Purchasers   Just as managers attending EE programs have become (on average) more sophisticated over the years, so have the corporate purchasers of such programs. A director of EE programs at a major university, in thoughts echoed by a number of his colleagues at other universities, explained this point as follows (in paraphrased form): Ten or fifteen years ago corporations tended to confine most of their MD activities to the lower-management level. *Now,* MD activities in many corporations are found throughout *all* levels of the organization. Therefore, this has meant that the corporate director of MD is at a higher level within his or her own organization and much more competent and more influential within the organization than used to be the case.

Given this development over the last decade or so, corporations and firms have become more knowledgeable and demanding buyers and have thus changed—at least to a degree—the balance of power between the university producer of EE and the corporate consumer. The effect, as with more sophisticated participants, has been to increase the challenge to business/management schools to provide the types of programs that meet the needs of potential corporate purchasers.

UNIVERSITY PERSPECTIVE

In this section we review interview and survey data collected from university respondents regarding several aspects of EE/MD activities provided by business/management schools: the amount of involvement schools see themselves having in this domain, the mission they see for such activities, the nature of the programs they are offering and believe they should be offering, issues relating to the instructional/faculty resources for such programs, and their general views of the future in this particular area.

Involvement of Business/Management Schools in EE/MD Activities

Of the more than 400 deans responding to our survey, exactly one-third reported that their schools were not involved in EE/MD activities in any way, 47% indicated that they were involved in a "minor way," and just over one-fifth (21%) answered that their schools were involved "in a substantial way."

These percentages varied statistically by category of school. The percentages of deans reporting "substantial" involvement were as follows:

Category I: 53%
Category II: 25%
Category III: 11%

If we extrapolated the overall results to all 620 AACSB member schools (the total membership at the time of survey), the number of schools (444 x 21% = 93) reporting "substantial involvement" would probably not increase appreciably because most (dean) nonrespondents were from small schools which typically (as confirmed by our interview data) do not have such programs. Therefore, in the mid-1980s it appears that roughly 100 business/management schools in the United States are involved with executive education in a major way (insofar as their own views of what they do are concerned).

Even for those schools that are involved, both our questionnaire and interview data indicate that the emphasis currently being placed on nondegree EE/MD programs is clearly *secondary* to the emphasis on degree programs. More specifically, the various categories of respondents (e.g., deans, provosts, and faculty members) indicate that the ratio of emphasis is about 90% to 10%. When asked whether they think this relative emphasis *should* change in the future, there is a small shift in all respondent groups and in each of the three categories of schools to something approximating an 80% to 20% split. Therefore, it appears that there is a general consensus (although with a large segment of individual dissenters) of those directly associated with university business schools that the balance between types of programs provided by the schools should be altered in favor of slightly more emphasis on nondegree programs than is now the case.

Mission of EE/MD Programs

All relevant university groups—deans, faculty, provosts, and executive education directors—believe that the primary purpose of a school's EE/MD activities should be to provide appropriate service to the business community. In other words, it seems clear from both questionnaire and interview responses that almost all schools already involved in this type of activity believe that their mission here should be to meet the legitimate needs of firms and corporations for postdegree education of their managers and executives.

However, there are also other purposes served by these kinds of programs, as seen by the various sets of respondents. Deans and provosts, for example, put particular emphasis on how such activities could provide increased opportunities for faculty members to develop contacts with business organizations. They also stressed the potential for increased visibility of the school in the business community by offering such programs.

Faculty members agreed that these additional purposes (beyond providing service to the business community) could be achieved by EE/MD programs, but they also indicated (in their survey responses) that—as might be expected—they believe another element of the mission for such programs should be to provide discretionary income for the faculty. Such an extrinsically oriented motivation probably cannot be taken lightly as a means to generate faculty interest in this type of activity.

The directors of executive education endorsed all the preceding goals for EE/MD programs and also (in interviews) suggested several other objectives that such programs could help the school attain, e.g., assistance in faculty recruiting (by the prospect of being able to supplement income by participating in these programs) and the generation of "instantly influential" alumni for the school (who might otherwise not have any connection with it) in the business community. The directors of executive education were also queried in the survey regarding their views about whether the basic mission (serving the business community effectively) of EE/MD programs in their respective schools was being achieved. Their answers were generally on the positive side, with about one-quarter indicating "to a large degree" and another 50% checking "to a moderate degree." However, that still left a sizable minority of about 25% who felt the mission was being met only "slightly" or "not at all." Thus, this latter portion of EE directors believe there is still considerable room for improvement—as seen from the perspective of someone with a decidedly vested interest.

Comparative Advantages of University EE/MD Programs

Deans and EE directors were asked (in interviews) how they viewed the role of university-based MD programs versus those offered in-house by companies and those provided by commercial vendors. Many points were mentioned, but they could be grouped into the following categories that capture what these respondents (using their own representative terms) thought were the comparative advantages of programs designed and offered by business/management schools:

   1 *Credibility* The legitimacy of the university and the lack of vested interests
   2 *Cutting edge* Programs based on the latest research-based knowledge
   3 *Forum for different companies to come together* Respondents exposed to a variety of company experience
   4 *Well-designed and integrated programs* Programs that capitalize on a breadth of perspective
   5 *Quality instruction*
   6 *Relatively low costs*

Later in this chapter, when we examine the corporate perspective, it will be instructive to see whether others outside the university see the same comparative advantages for university business school programs.

Nature of University-Based EE/MD Programs

Table 12.2 shows how deans and provosts describe the type of jurisdiction and responsibility business schools currently have for sponsoring EE/MD activities on their respective campuses and what they believe should be the nature of that jurisdiction in the future. As this table illustrates, a wide variety of arrangements are utilized by those schools that have at least minor levels of EE/MD activity: About 60% of the schools (according to the deans) have either exclusive (especially in the case of Category I schools) or predominant jurisdiction over their executive/management education programs, while the other 40% must work in conjunction with the campus's continuing education (CE) (often called extension) units and thus do not have major control over what is done in this area. As might be expected, a number of deans would like to see these programs become more under the control of the business school in the future. Provosts, on the other hand, tend to show the opposite trend: If changes are to be made in the future, they would like to see more cooperative ventures between the business school and the campus CE unit than is now the case.

In our survey, directors of EE/MD programs (including those who were located in campus CE units but responsible for the business school's activities in this area) divided about 50–50 in their description of their current programs as emphasizing either "broad" or "specialized" management topics. With respect to the level of management (of participants) toward which their programs were targeted at the present time, 41% reported "lower and middle" levels, while 29% indicated "middle and upper" levels. (Nine percent reported focusing exclusively on lower levels, 19% on middle levels, and 3% on upper levels.) About one-fourth of these directors indicated that their business schools currently "tailored" programs "frequently and regularly" for specific companies or industries.

Instructional Staff for University-Based EE/MD Programs

Directors of business school EE/MD programs were asked several questions regarding the composition and performance of the instructional staff in their

TABLE 12.2
VIEWS OF JURISDICTION OVER UNIVERSITY-BASED EE/MD PROGRAMS
(Percent Checking One of Four Alternatives; By Deans: $N = 297$, and Provosts: $N = 222$)

	Deans		Provosts	
	Now	Should Be	Now	Should Be
Exclusively by business school	39%	46%	30%	16%
Predominately by business school	23	33	24	28
Partly by business school/partly by university continuing education	17	16	25	36
Predominantly by university continuing education	21	5	21	19

Note: All columns add to total of 100% within rounding

programs. They report that full-time faculty members from their own business/ management schools typically comprise about 60% of the instructors utilized in such programs. Of course, this will vary from 100% in some of the larger schools with considerable faculty resources to less than 50% in some smaller schools. Across the entire set of schools, part-time business school faculty and faculty from other universities each account for about 10% of the instructors and nonuniversity personnel (practicing managers, consultants, etc.) make up the other 20%. When asked whether they expected these ratios to change much in the next decade, half the directors answered "no" and most of the others indicated that if there is a change, it will be to increase the percentage of instructors drawn from the roster of full-time faculty members in the business school.

About two-thirds of the EE/MD directors indicated that previous full-time practical experience in industry was a *major* requirement for someone to be an instructor in these types of programs. On the rather crucial issue of what percentage of current business school faculty members could be considered as capable of "performing effectively" in such programs, the median answer for junior (i.e., assistant professor level) faculty was 25% and for senior faculty 45%. As to whether their particular business school made "explicit efforts" to develop the capabilities of junior faculty for MD/EE programs, 60% of the directors indicated "little" effort (i.e., individuals are left to develop these skills on their own), about 30% indicated "some" effort (e.g., providing opportunity to develop skills in lower-level courses, but with minimal feedback and coaching), and only about 10% reported that their schools provided considerable effort in this regard. If the EE directors' views can be accepted as a relatively accurate reflection of the current state of affairs, it would appear that most business schools do not consider the development of the talents of their faculty in instructing managers and executives in EE/MD programs to be a high priority.

Views about the Future of EE/MD Activities in Business Schools

Whatever else deans, faculty members, and provosts may disagree about, they are virtually united in their belief that business schools should put *increased* effort into management development activities in the future (i.e., in the next 10 years). This belief (that such activities of their school should be increased) is held by 88% of deans, 73% of faculty members, and 83% of provosts. Only 1% of deans, 2% of faculty members, and 1% of provosts think such activities should be decreased; therefore, also, only about 10 to 15% of deans and provosts and 25% of the faculty members think that the degree of emphasis in this area should remain as it is. If ever administrators of business schools felt they needed a mandate to give more attention to executive education activities, these findings (which were independently and strongly confirmed in the interviews) should provide sufficient reinforcement to proceed.

When questioned about why EE/MD activities should be increased, deans and faculty members were strongly of the opinion that their schools ought to be responsive to the needs of the business community and to the general increased emphasis in the business world on the necessity of lifelong learning for managers and *not* to the possibility that such an increase could serve to offset any potential loss of revenue from a decrease in demand for regular degree programs. (Many deans, in fact, were skeptical that EE/MD programs would raise any net revenue at all.) Of course, if there were rather drastic drop-offs in demand for degree programs, this probably would become a much more salient reason for increasing EE/MD emphasis. For now, however, this is not the ostensible reason most deans and faculty members would like to see more aggressive actions by their schools in this type of activity. Furthermore, most deans are convinced that the demand for such nondegree programs to be provided by their respective schools will moderately or greatly increase in the next 10 years.

In terms of program changes expected in the next decade, the views of deans and EE directors reflect recent and current trends that were summarized earlier in this chapter: more tailor-made "contract" programs, more programs on specialized management topics, a modest shift to programs aimed at relatively higher levels of management (than particular schools have served in the past), and the possibility (which appears to occur infrequently at the present time) of EE teaching counting as part of the regular teaching load (which would, in effect, alter the current reward system for this type of activity). Also, in interviews many deans expressed a need to obtain "greater faculty involvement" in MD activities than is currently the case. Executive education directors also expressed the same point, especially with respect to trying to attain a higher *percentage* of faculty involved in their programs. In addition, they urged their schools to place greater emphasis on assisting the typical faculty member (as opposed to a small set of select senior faculty members who seem to have a natural talent for instructing in executive programs) in learning how to become effective in teaching adults—i.e., managers and executives.

THE CORPORATE PERSPECTIVE

This section examines how the corporate world views executive education programs offered by business schools. We begin with data on the extent to which companies and firms say they utilize such programs. This is followed by ratings of the effectiveness of university-based programs compared to those offered in-house by companies and those provided by "third party" commercial vendors. The next part of the section deals with what corporate personnel—particularly those in charge of MD programs for their firms—believe are the relative advantages and disadvantages of university programs, and we conclude with corporate views about how much they expect to use such programs in the future.

Current Utilization of University Executive Education Programs

Table 12.3 (comparable to Table 11.3 in Chapter 11) indicates the extent to which directors (also often called managers) of management development (DMDs) in corporations say their firms currently utilize university EE/MD programs compared to in-house and commercial vendor programs. As noted in the previous chapter, the overwhelming majority of these respondents say that their companies use all three types of programs at least occasionally. The frequency of reported extensive usage, however (and not surprisingly), is much less for university programs compared with those provided in-house (and somewhat less than for third-party programs). Thus, by this criterion, business schools definitely are not at the present time the dominant supplier of management development programs for business firms, although they would have to be judged one of the significant "players."

Corporate management development directors were asked in the survey whether there are "topic areas needed by their organization but which are not currently offered by university MD programs." About three-quarters of these respondents answered "no," which would indicate that for the majority of companies represented in the sample the reasons for not using university programs more extensively do not involve a lack of appropriate coverage of topic areas. For the other 25% or so of the sample that answered "yes" (i.e., that there *are* needed topics not being covered in university programs), the follow-up question asking for a listing of such topics demonstrated a wide diversity of specific needs across a sample of companies.

A survey question about the types of university programs utilized by corporations revealed that about 65% of the responding companies reported using university residential executive programs (versus 65 and 50% using in-house and commercial vendor programs of this type). (Since length of the residential program was not specified in this question, these percentages obviously reflect the use of short-duration residential programs as well as those of several weeks or more in length.) Use of nonresidential programs of 3 or more days was fairly similar across the three types of providers: 52% for university programs, 69% for in-house programs, and 57% for commercial vendors.

TABLE 12.3
CORPORATE UTILIZATION OF DIFFERENT PROVIDERS:
AS REPORTED BY DMDs
(Percent Checking One of Three Alternatives; $N = 246$)

	Providers		
	University	**In-House**	**Other External**
Do not use	**10%**	2%	4%
Use occasionally	**80**	31	80
Use extensively	**10**	67	16

Note: This table presents the same data, rearranged, as in Table 11.3.

As our interviews in the corporate sector repeatedly indicated, the most pervasive use of universities in the provision of MD programs was, in effect, indirect: the employment of individual university professors (especially, in the case of the largest and most prestigious corporations, nationally and internationally recognized academic "stars") in programs offered in-house and usually (though not always) designed by corporate personnel. In other words, many companies admitted "cherry picking" one or two individual faculty members from a particular business school but never (or at least very infrequently) using a *set* of that school's faculty in a program *offered by the school*. As one director of development in a large, high-visibility company put it bluntly, "Our company would rather deal with individual moonlighting faculty, and business schools as schools should concentrate on degree programs." In such arrangements as these, the individual faculty member benefits directly, but the school that provides that person's basic job and salary does not receive any direct benefits (although there may be some indirect benefits from the "prestige" of having one of its faculty members associated with a major company). In effect, the corporation is receiving the services of the faculty "star" at marginal cost.

One other type of usage of university programs is the relatively recent effort of some companies, as we noted earlier in this chapter, to contract with business schools to provide a program tailor-made just for managers from their specific companies. When asked how frequently this type of university-provided program was used at the present time, only 3% of the MD managers said "frequently and regularly," 31% said "sometimes," and the other two-thirds responded "rarely" or "never." Thus, to the extent that such programs represent any sort of a "trend," it does not appear to be a trend that is as yet strongly established, at least as viewed by corporate DMDs.

Effectiveness of University Executive Education Programs

Several different categories of corporate respondents—CEOs, SCEs, VPHRs, and DMDs—were asked to rate the effectiveness of university-based, in-house, and vendor programs on a 10-point scale. They were also asked to indicate whether or not they thought there was a "wide variation" in the quality of each type of program. The combined results of these questions are presented in Table 12.4 (which is comparable to Table 11.4 in Chapter 11). As can be seen, the effectiveness of university programs offered by business schools was rated slightly lower than the other two types of programs by two of the four groups of respondents and moderately lower by DMDs. However, in terms of how frequently these groups perceived there to be "wide variation" in the quality of programs, university programs were seen as having somewhat more uniform quality than programs of vendors but less than in-house programs.

TABLE 12.4

EFFECTIVENESS OF PROGRAMS OF DIFFERENT PROVIDERS

(Median Rating, on a 10-Point Scale, of Extent to Which Programs Have "Met Corporate Training Objectives" and, in Parentheses, Percent Checking that Programs Have a "Wide Variation in Quality")

	Providers		
Raters	University	In-House	Other External
CEOs $(N = 122)$	5.3 (57%)	5.9 (35%)	5.6 (68%)
SCEs $(N = 149)$	5.5 (45)	5.9 (34)	5.6 (59)
VPHRs $(N = 203)$	5.6 (51)	6.1 (35)	5.6 (61)
DMDs $(N = 225)$	5.3 (41)	6.8 (23)	6.3 (45)

Note: This table presents the same data, rearranged, as in Table 11.4.

Perceived Advantages/Disadvantages of University Executive Education Programs

Advantages   Corporate DMDs were asked to respond to a fixed-alternative survey question regarding what they viewed as the major specific advantages and disadvantages of university EE/MD programs. Taking "advantages" first, the responses of the DMDs are shown in Table 12.5, which displays the percentage checking "major advantage" for each listed alternative. As this table demonstrates, the biggest plus (as seen by 54% of the respondents) attributed to programs offered by business/management schools is the opportunity for participants to interact with managers from other organizations. This was referred to in several of our interviews as the benefit of "cross-pollinization" occurring in university programs. The second most frequently cited advantage (checked by 41% of the DMDs) is that recipients receive "maximum input of new ideas." "High-quality instruction," which might be expected (at least by those within universities) to be a major advantage, was seen as such by only one-fourth of the DMDs. "Cost-effectiveness" and "convenience" were definitely *not* regarded as major pluses.

TABLE 12.5

PERCEIVED ADVANTAGES OF UNIVERSITY EE/MD PROGRAMS

(Percent of DMDs Checking "Major Advantage"; $N = 246$)

54%	Participants interact with managers from other organizations
40	Maximum input of new ideas
26	Highest-quality instruction
23	Prestige associated with university affiliation
7	Ambience of campus setting
3	Cost-effectiveness
3	Convenience, logistics, etc.

Other advantages of university programs were noted in interviews by various members (e.g., VPHRs, operating managers) of the corporate community. The most frequently mentioned one was that programs offered by business schools tend to bring a "breadth of perspective," or, as one executive phrased it, they "help keep us from becoming 'insular' in thinking about our problems." In a similar vein, a vice president stated that campus-based programs "teach things that corporations can't do for themselves." One operating manager voiced the view that university faculty members are "experts at education compared to corporate managers," and another line manager offered the opinion that university programs are "a good way to keep up with what academics are thinking." In a more pragmatic assessment, a DMD at a large company said that "a 'certificate' from a university adds another stripe" to the records of managers in his organization.

Disadvantages　The survey instrument also offered DMDs the opportunity to register views about disadvantages as well as advantages of university programs. (It should be stressed that the particular questionnaire item—as with the corresponding "advantage" item—did not force DMDs to check any "major disadvantages" if they did not believe they existed.) The findings for this question are presented in Table 12.6, where it can be seen that about 35% of the DMDs believed that a "major disadvantage" of university programs is that "managers (participants) don't get exposed to enough information specific to their own organization's needs." This, in a sense, is somewhat of a mirror image of what many DMDs believe is the chief advantage of university programs: the opportunity for participants to interact with managers from other companies. Clearly, the latter essentially precludes the possibility of providing "information specific to the needs" of a particular organization. Some 35% also said that "overpricing" was a major disadvantage of university programs, and an additional 55% rated this as a "moderate disadvantage." This finding seems to be at some variance with the views of many deans, although perhaps this reflects merely the classic difference in perspective between buyers and sellers.

TABLE 12.6
PERCEIVED DISADVANTAGES OF UNIVERSITY EE/MD PROGRAMS
(Percent of DMDs Checking "Major Disadvantage"; $N = 247$)

36%	Managers (participants) do not get exposed to enough information specific to their own organization's needs
35	Overpriced
15	Insufficient number of instructors (for EE/MD programs) within a given university who are effective teachers of adults
15	Inconvenience, logistics, etc.
10	Insufficient number of instructors who are technically competent in the subject matter
4	Universities lack appropriate facilities

(Of course, it should be recognized that there is a wide range of pricing; the over-pricing perception may be due to the disproportionate influence of only a few very high-priced programs.) In any event, it would seem a fairly safe conclusion that corporations use some university programs for reasons other than perceived low costs.

The set of corporate interviews brought out some other disadvantages occasionally felt by some firms. A view that was heard more than once—although it could not accurately be said that it was a widespread opinion—was summed up by a CEO who stated that "our use of university executive education programs would increase if we could find enough top quality programs." A director of management development put this same idea in another way: "Many business schools lack the 'bench strength' to mount successful MD programs." Several interviewees also questioned whether some faculty members they had encountered in executive education programs "really knew the latest" or had sufficient "real-world" experience to be serving as instructors in these types of programs.

Expected Future Use of University Executive Education Programs

Those who direct corporate management development programs (the DMDs) were asked whether they expected that their own organization (not organizations in general) would increase or decrease their use of university EE/MD programs in the next 10-year period. The results are shown in Table 12.7. The expectations on the part of most business school deans that corporations and firms will increase their use of university executive programs in the coming years generally appear to be borne out by the data in Table 12.7. Over 60% of the firms (according to their DMDs) indicate that they expect to increase their use of such programs. (As noted in the other corresponding chapters on management development, this compares with about the same percentage indicat-

TABLE 12.7
EXPECTED INCREASE/DECREASE IN USE OF EE/MD PROGRAMS FROM DIFFERENT
PROVIDERS IN NEXT 10-YEAR PERIOD: AS VIEWED BY DMDs
(Percent Checking Each of Five Alternatives; $N = 242$)

	Provider		
	University	In-House	Other External
Increase substantially	10%	44%	14%
Increase somewhat	55	43	43
Maintain at present level	30	11	31
Decrease somewhat	4	2	10
Decrease substantially	0	0	2

Note: All columns add to total of 100% within rounding. This table presents the same data, rearranged, as in Table 11.7.

TABLE 12.8

EXPECTED MAJOR SOURCES OF PROGRAMS IN THE FUTURE TO MEET MOST
IMPORTANT CORPORATE EE/MD NEEDS: AS VIEWED BY DMDs
(Percent Checking One of Three Possible Providers for Each Management Level; $N = 230$)

	Provider		
	University	**In-House**	**Other External**
Lower management levels	3%	84%	13%
Middle management levels	13	63	24
Upper/top management levels	36	24	40

Note: All rows add across to total of 100% within rounding. This table presents the same data, rearranged, as in Table 11.8.

ing an expected increase in use of commercial vendors and about 85% who anticipated greater use of in-house programs.)

As reported in Chapter 11, DMDs were asked what they expected would be the "major source of programs to meet the most important management development needs of 'this' organization in the next 10 years," for each of three management levels: lower, middle, and upper/top. Table 12.8 (comparable to Table 11.8) shows that, relatively speaking, the heaviest expected use of university programs will be for managers at upper levels of organizations. Even here, however, the DMDs do not expect universities to be the provider of first choice.

Finally, on the question of whether business schools *should be* providing "contract" tailor-made programs, DMDs answered emphatically in the affirmative. Some 80% said that this "should happen" (for their organization) at least "sometimes" or "frequently and regularly," while, it will be recalled from data presented earlier, only about 30% believed that this was currently happening. Those deans and university executive education directors who see contract programs as a potential future market for their EE/MD programs would seem, on the face of it, to have realistic expectations. Corporations appear to want this type of arrangement, and each business school and its administrators and faculty will need to decide whether this is an appropriate activity to undertake.

COMMENTARY

In this section we discuss several of what we consider to be the most important issues pertaining to the involvement of business/management schools with executive education/management development. These include the growth in emphasis on EE/MD in business schools, the role and involvement of business schools in these programs, the types of programs that can be offered by business schools, and maximization of instructional quality.

Growth in Emphasis on Executive Education in Business Schools

The high promise that business school executive education and management development programs represented 25 years ago has been only partially fulfilled. A much larger number of schools, to be sure, offer major programs in this area than was true then—about 100 versus 40. However, given the rapid rise in number of business schools during this same period, the increase in the number of schools offering substantial EE/MD programs is not commensurate with the overall growth of the system. Likewise, if one uses the measure of number of participants in general and functional management programs then (1962) and now, the increase of about eight times compares with an increase of about twelve times in the number of MBA graduates. The point is that what business schools are doing in executive education by way of numbers of managers served and number of schools "serving" has reached fairly impressive figures, but it by no means has outdistanced the increase that has taken place in degree programs and MBA students and has perhaps even fallen behind that pace a bit. Thus, although it has shown considerable absolute growth, its proportion of the efforts of the total national business school enterprise has probably remained essentially constant over the past quarter century.

Several other basic conclusions relating to the degree of emphasis that executive education activities currently have, or can be expected to have, seem warranted by our data. First, for almost all schools, degree programs remain—and, in our view, should remain—absolutely paramount, and they seem likely to continue to do so in the foreseeable future. This is in a context, however, where many deans and faculty members predict at least some relative (to degree programs) increase in emphasis on nondegree executive education activities by the school.

Second, the need for postdegree continuing education for managers and executives from the business community (as well as from nonbusiness organizations) is likely to increase markedly in the future. (Demographic factors—as discussed in Chapter 2—if nothing else, would seem to be a significant force in this direction for the next several decades.) Therefore, the demand from the business sector for management development programs also seems certain to expand substantially in the future. For example, over 60% of the corporations (i.e., those managers responsible for their firms' management development activities) surveyed expect to increase their use of university-based EE/MD programs in the coming decade. This would, on the surface at least, suggest a clearly larger market for such programs in the future.

Third, however, programs put on by business schools are by no means the only available source of executive education. They face, and will increasingly face, in our opinion, stiff competition from in-house programs and those provided by other (than university) external vendors. This means that business schools decidedly cannot *assume* that they will automatically keep getting their portion of an anticipated expanding executive education "pie." The pie may indeed be getting larger, but the business school slice could actually get smaller—both relatively and absolutely.

With respect to this latter point, it should be emphasized that corporations now, and in the future, have a relatively large number of potential options available to meet their executive education needs. To illustrate some of the *non-university-based* choices: Larger companies have the luxury, in many cases, to provide for almost all their needs by in-house programs put on by their own management development staff and often utilizing selected managers as instructors for specific topics. Also, in such programs they have the choice of adding an academic perspective on particular subjects by hiring one or more carefully selected professors from a university or several universities on a consulting basis. This, however, does not involve the business school as a school and certainly does not make use of its executive education programs. Companies of somewhat smaller size, but still large enough to have a full-time professional human resources manager or small staff, can still mount an in-house program (i.e., a program put on only for its own managers) by using a set of instructors from various sources (from within the company, from one or more universities, or from commercial vendors, including individual consultants). Often a business school faculty member may be involved in helping to design such a program, but again, a *school's* program is not used. The smallest and least sophisticated (from a human resources management perspective) companies can—as is obviously the case with larger companies too—utilize various external vendors, of which a university business school program is only one. Typically, such companies often use individual consultants to talk with their managers on specific topics or send their managers to brief 1-day programs put on by a wide variety of sources rather than using longer and more elaborate university programs.

The bottom line for business schools is that they cannot take for granted that—in the future—the business sector will be forced to use their executive education programs. Business school EE/MD programs will be compared to those from alternative sources and will be chosen only to the extent that they offer distinct advantages. Therefore, unless deans, faculty members, and those responsible for a school's executive education programs pay a great deal of attention to issues of program design, content, and the quality of instruction, firms and corporations will look elsewhere to satisfy their increasing management development needs. This, in turn, raises a critical strategic planning issue for every school: What should be the specific role of EE/MD in the school?

Role of EE/MD Programs in the Business/Management School

Both the Foundation reports, as far back as 1959, stressed the need for schools to examine, from a strategic perspective, where (if at all) and how executive education fits into a school's overall objectives. Gordon and Howell, in words that are just as valid today, stated (p. 319), for example, that

> The most important need at the moment is for the [business schools] to take stock of what they are doing in the field of adult business education—to develop a clear-cut philosophy and set of objectives and to appraise the needs to be served and the resources available for meeting them.

This was the need then and, in our opinion, is still the most important need now. The strong impression we gained from our interviews was that in many schools—certainly not all of them—the school had *not* given comprehensive and *strategic* consideration to the role of EE/MD programs. Partly this was due to the fact that in a number of schools relatively little attention had been given to detailed long-range planning for the school as a whole. Thus, not much fundamental consideration had been given to the particular element of executive education. However, the lack of overall long-range planning by some schools was only part of the reason why little systematic strategic attention (as opposed to short-term tactical attention) had been directed to this area. The other reason was that some schools which exhibited planning with respect to other programs seemed (to us, at least) to regard EE/MD activities as so secondary or peripheral that they did not really deserve much concerted attention. This, we think, is a nontrivial mistake.

To be able to consider the strategic role of EE/MD, a school must first *know itself*. Planning for the kind of EE/MD activity that will serve effectively both the school and managerial participants should, we believe, be built on a foundation that takes into account the school's distinctive mission and accompanying long range plans for its basic academic programs. Only then can effective plans be developed for *how* executive education fits into, and supports, the school's overall goals and objectives. If a school does have a good sense of where it is heading, then three key questions need to be asked: (1) how involved should a school be in EE/MD activities, (2) what types of EE/MD programs should a school offer, and (3) how can the instructional quality of EE/MD programs be maximized?

How Involved Should a School Be in EE/MD Activities?

A number of schools—roughly 100—as we noted, already have made a definite decision and consider themselves to be involved in this activity in a major way. Another 200 or so report being involved in only "a minor way." All these schools, even those schools reporting that they already are firmly enmeshed in executive education, need to ask themselves whether they should be even more involved in the future or, perhaps, less involved. For many of the remaining schools that are not now involved (one-third of our sample of schools), the issue is whether to begin at all.

A critical first issue to address is: How will other existing and planned programs of the school be affected? Will beginning or expanding executive education programs take critical resources away from the (presumably) basic degree programs such that the school ends up gaining a mediocre set of EE/MD programs and losing the sharp edge of good or outstanding undergraduate and/ or master's programs? Will adding new or expanded programs of a continuing education type for managers fundamentally change the school's "product mix" in such a way that its central mission (including research activities) will be affected adversely? Phrased more cynically and metaphorically, will a school's executive education programs' tail somehow wag its academic programs' dog?

These are legitimate concerns that need to be addressed by any set of school administrators and faculty contemplating more extensive involvement in EE/ MD. However, it is our considered opinion that—properly planned and conducted—executive education can make *substantial positive contributions* to a school and its core teaching and research activities. First and foremost, for the faculty it develops additional interaction with the world of practice in a potentially healthy way. It offers a meeting place, as it were, for theories and research findings to engage real-world problems and issues. It imports reality into the classroom, and it exports concepts and ideas out to the boardroom and office—to the benefit of both environments and their respective organizations (i.e., business schools and companies). Second, for both the school as a whole and for individual faculty members it provides a source of contacts that can be useful in a variety of ways, e.g., obtaining sites for research studies, locating potential guest lecturers for class sessions, and expanding the number of people in the management community who have direct knowledge of the school and its faculty resources. Third, and not to be discounted, it offers the potential for (but not the certainty of) increased external financial support for the school and extra remuneration for faculty members.

All the preceding are fairly obvious positive outcomes that in theory can be gained—but which in practice are not always fully actualized—from a school's executive education activities. However, there is another potentially very significant advantage of offering EE/MD activities that is not so obvious: using them as an "instrument of constructive change" in degree programs. That is, the experiences that faculty members have in executive education programs— even when those experiences might from time to time be somewhat painful— can sometimes have powerful effects both on what is taught in undergraduate and MBA classes and, especially, on *how* such teaching is carried out. It is unlikely that someone who has taught practicing managers and executives will ever teach "regular" students in exactly the same way in the future. Thus faculty participation in EE/MD programs has the potential for improving instruction in degree programs.

What Types of EE/MD Programs Should a School Offer?

Once a school has made a decision about how heavily (if at all) it wants to go into, or stay involved in, executive education, it must then consider what types of programs it wants to offer in the future. Here, the basic issue is: What will, or can be, the school's *comparative advantage* in this kind of activity? How can it maximize its potential assets and minimize its potential liabilities for conducting such programs?

Obviously, large and prestigious schools start with a major advantage. They have the quantity and often the quality of faculty to put on a broad range of programs and attract participants from large and equally prestigious companies. They have the luxury of a great deal of choice, although even they can end up overextending themselves or misallocating faculty resources. For relatively smaller and less well known schools, options are a great deal more limited in the kinds of programs they can offer. Does this mean, however, that there is little left for them to do after the large school elephants, so to speak, have decided where to stake out their ground in the executive education forest? In our view, hardly. While it is virtually impossible for medium-level schools to attract top executives from the IBMs, GEs, and Citicorps of the business world to any executive program, there are other potential target audiences that can be served: for one, lower- and middle-level operating managers from local or regional units of larger firms; for another, middle- and upper-level executives from smaller firms; still another would be programs tailor-made for the needs of local individual companies. In essence, any school needs to search for an appropriate match of its faculty resources with the needs of specific elements of the business sector. In our study, we found some schools that were doing this well and others that appeared not to have grappled effectively with developing productive congruence.

Probably the complaint we heard most from companies regarding business school–based executive education and management development programs was that some of them could not *deliver* what they advertised and promised in the way of faculty expertise and instructional strength. As mentioned earlier, we encountered a fair degree of skepticism that many (more than a couple of dozen or so) business schools could really mount a high-quality general management program for upper-level executives using only their own faculty. Of course, if a school is willing to "borrow" faculty "stars" from other schools, then it can expand its resources for a particular program and partially or totally counter this particular concern. The point remains, however, that it is absolutely incumbent on a school to decide not only what audiences it wants to reach, but also whether it can deliver quality programs to those specific audiences with the faculty resources it has available or can put together.

A variety of other decisions must follow, relating to specific content and structure of programs. The increasing desire of many companies for shorter programs makes it somewhat more difficult to carry out thoughtful general management programs for upper-level executives, but on the other hand, it opens up more opportunities to develop innovative and imaginative specialized programs—programs that probably do not require as extensive a range of faculty resources. Thus, this trend in corporate preferences regarding program length actually could turn out to be a blessing for a number of business schools wanting to get more involved in MD activities.

How Can Instructional Quality Be Maximized in EE/MD Programs?

It should already be apparent that we believe that if a business/management school is to be involved in executive education activities to a significant degree, it will take more than a token commitment. One test of that commitment is the extent to which a school and its leaders encourage a critical mass (rather than just a few) of its faculty members to get involved and the extent to which the school is willing to spend resources and effort in *developing* faculty and rewarding them specifically for this type of instructional activity.

If a school decides to become serious about improving the quality of instruction in its executive education programs, it could follow several non-mutually exclusive courses of action: One simple step would be to make assessment of talent for teaching managers (as contrasted with typical undergraduate or graduate students) more of a factor than it is now in the selection of new faculty members. Of course, a school would have to decide how to weight this against other obvious selection criteria (potential for scholarly contributions, potential for teaching in degree programs, etc.), but even for most of those schools already involved in executive education any weight greater than zero would represent a fairly radical change in the approach to faculty selection.

A second step—perhaps the most important—would be to provide early and systematic developmental opportunities for faculty to begin to get involved in such programs at least in a minor way (e.g., participating in programs for lower-level managers in their functional area). Pursuing this approach would be in marked contrast to the typical situation, where a school waits to see who has sufficient natural talent for EE/MD work such that they emerge without any particular developmental efforts on the part of the school.

A third approach would be to involve executive education "gurus" or "stars"—whether members of a school's own faculty or that of some other school—in coaching and working as advisors to those faculty (junior or senior) who want to develop or improve their skills in this arena. Quite likely a school would have to invest some financial resources to encourage this process if it were to be more than a superficial exercise.

Still another approach, utilized at some of the leading schools in executive education, is to involve faculty members together as teams in designing, planning, and implementing parts of general management programs or shorter programs on specific topics. It was our impression that in most schools faculty members did not seem to be involved in this way in executive education but rather worked more as individuals (frequently in conjunction with the school's director of executive education) in planning course content and approach. We would suggest that if more teamwork were encouraged in this area, there would be a number of beneficial outcomes, but again, much depends on whether there is a concrete incentive system set up to reward and recognize this type of activity.

Finally, we believe that business school faculty members teaching in EE/MD programs probably need to give more concentrated attention to some of the principles of *adult learning*. These tenets would include giving priority to efforts to tap the learner's experience, acting on an up-front assumption that the learner is capable of a considerable amount of self-directed learning and wants to take more personal responsibility for what is to be learned, and orienting teaching efforts toward developing immediately applicable skills and knowledge. The point is simply that if instructors view adult learners (managers and executives, in this case) as simply "just another typical student," it is likely that their effectiveness will fall far short of what it potentially could be. It is a matter of attitude as well as aptitude and action.

Concluding Observation

The findings from the corporate sector clearly indicate that business schools have, collectively, an excellent opportunity to make major contributions in the realm of postdegree management development and executive education. However, since companies and firms do have a number of alternative sources of such programs from which to choose, it behooves business schools to approach this type of activity with as much sophistication on their part as the "buyers" are rapidly developing on theirs. To do so requires, as we have tried to emphasize, serious commitment to developing programs that take advantage of some of the unique features that a university-based program has to offer and an equally deep commitment to making sure that the instruction in those programs is at a high level of quality. Without that, many business school executive programs could go the way of the dodo, which is (according to the dictionary) "a large flightless bird, now largely extinct."

CHAPTER 13

EXECUTIVE EDUCATION/ MANAGEMENT DEVELOPMENT: OTHER PROVIDERS

In the previous two chapters we presented data on two major categories of providers of executive education and management development: corporations/ firms themselves and university-based business schools. In this chapter we turn our attention to a third and significant category: nonuniversity external providers. As we will discuss shortly, this is a very large, amorphous, and difficult to define category. Its boundaries are not easy to identify, but that in no way should minimize the current and potential importance of this set of providers.[1]

In any discussion of this collectivity of providers of EE/MD, terminology looms as a somewhat troubling issue. Many view these external providers—whether they be individuals or organizations—as vendors (i.e., as sellers), which, of course, they are in the broad sense of that term. However, there are those among this category of providers who, while agreeing that the selling connotation is not inappropriate, would prefer to have the term *professional associations* (or *professional firms*) applied to this category to emphasize that there is a professional (i.e., an advanced level of specialized skill qualifications necessary to do the providing) component involved. From our perspective, either term is satisfactory, although *vendor* seems simple, generally appropriate, and was the term most often used by corporate officials (in our interviews) to refer to this category. Also, the term *professional association* can get confused (at least for academics) with nonprofit organizations of peers in a particular field

---

[1]Nonprofit trade and professional associations that put on programs for their own members or industry—e.g., the American Bankers Association—could be considered a fourth category of providers of EE/MD programs or as a major subset of other providers, but they will not be further discussed in this report owing to the fact that limitations of cost and time prevented us from gathering information and data about their activities in this arena.

of expertise, such as the American Economics Association. [During the course of the project, we adopted the arbitrary term *third-party provider* as a shorthand way to distinguish this category from corporations (first party) and universities (second party) as providers. Throughout the remainder of this chapter we will use these several terms interchangeably.]

This chapter will be able to give only limited coverage to this group of providers. The reason is that the cost/time resources of the Project, as well as its general focus, required us to concentrate most of our attention on universities and corporations. It was not possible, for example, to survey a large number of these providers by means of questionnaires. We were, however, able to interview officials of several major such organizations, which gave us some insights from the point of view of this category of provider. Also, we included several questions about this type of provider in four versions of the corporate questionnaire (those for CEOs, SCEs, VPHRs, and DMDs), as well as in our interviews with relevant corporate executives. Thus, while our data base is neither extensive nor complete, it does permit some analysis of the role of this set of providers in the EE/MD arena, including views from corporate consumers about how well they are fulfilling this role.

ROLE OF NONUNIVERSITY EXTERNAL PROVIDERS

As is the case with corporations and university business schools as providers of executive education and management development, it is possible to view the role of the third-party providers in a historical context. Therefore, before examining the part that this category of providers plays in the management development scene of the mid-1980s, it is worthwhile to take a brief look at the situation 25 years ago, as we have done with other areas covered by this Project.

Then: 25 Years Ago

At the beginning of the 1960s, there already had been for some time a number of individuals and organizations in the business of providing EE/MD courses and programs for managers. Although the 1959 Ford Foundation report gave no mention of the work of such nonuniversity, noncorporate providers (because the report focused specifically only on higher education for business), the Carnegie report of the same year did spend several pages (pp. 564–567) noting then-existing EE/MD activities from this source.

In the Carnegie report, Bridgman (in a chapter entitled "Company Management Development Programs") stated:

> Undoubtedly, the organization with the most comprehensive and widely used program in this field is the American Management Association, which, in addition to its conferences, courses, and seminars in the major functions of business, offers several courses and seminars specifically in the management development field. The most comprehensive of the courses is the AMA Management Course, first offered six years ago. (Pierson, 1959, p. 564.)

Bridgman also went on to cite several other types of major executive development programs offered by such organizations as the National Educational Association (through its National Training Laboratories), the Menninger Foundation, and the Aspen Institute for Humanistic Studies. Virtually no mention was made of programs provided by consulting organizations specifically in the business of conducting EE/MD courses for managers and executives. Probably a safe conclusion is that the American Management Association (AMA) had, at that time at the end of the 1950s, a virtual monopoly (at least when viewed from a national perspective) on the provision of substantial nonuniversity external (i.e., external to the corporation) management development programs, except for the few programs put on by the other above-mentioned organizations.

Given the prominence of AMA's role at the beginning of the 1960s as *the* major third-party provider, it may be instructive to sketch briefly the history of this organization's pioneering involvement in EE/MD programs.[2] Prior to World War II, the AMA's activities in this area were limited to about a dozen conferences per year held in different parts of the country, each dealing with a particular functional area (e.g., marketing, finance, personnel). Although managers and executives came together in these conferences to talk about topics and issues in a designated functional area, there was no formal instruction as such. It was not until 1949 that the AMA developed workshops lasting 2 to 3 days that were conducted by a "leader," a practicing executive in a given functional area. The AMA's 4-week "Management Course," as Bridgman noted, was developed about 1953; other, shorter courses on more specific topics were also instituted by the AMA during the latter part of the 1950s. Thus, what had originally started out as get-togethers of managers from a variety of companies talking about common interests gradually evolved into courses with specific leaders (almost always practitioner instructors in the AMA's case) who delivered *instruction* on a topic or area of management. The needs of business organizations in the EE/MD area were clearly changing—and expanding—and the AMA, as the chief external provider of the 1950s, had to keep up with these rapidly unfolding developments.

Now: Mid-1980s

The third-party provider scene has changed considerably in the past 25 to 30 years. No longer does the AMA have a near monopoly as a nonuniversity external supplier of EE/MD courses. Owing to both the growth of business since 1960 and the concomitant, even greater, growth in companies' needs for managerial development programs, the number of such providers has mushroomed. There are, in other words, many competitors for companies' EE/MD business, but no single supplier dominates the field in the mid-1980s.

[2]We are indebted to Dr. Thomas Horton, the current president and chief executive officer of the AMA, for providing us with the basic information about his organization's history in the management development field.

In understanding the current collective role of third-party providers, it is useful to try to identify the several major *types* of such suppliers: First and foremost are the firms and organizations (e.g., the AMA, Wilson Learning, Forum Corporation) for whom conducting executive education and management development courses and programs is either their exclusive activity or one of their primary consulting activities. Usually such firms operate on a for-profit basis, either independently or as a subsidiary of a much larger company (conglomerate), but there are also a few nonprofit organizations, such as the Center for Creative Leadership, that function in much the same manner. These firms/ organizations/professional associations typically include a number of professional-level specialists in adult-education approaches to instructing in particular subject matter areas relating to management. In essence, these firms provide a specialized type of service, and in this case the service is putting on EE/MD programs (either public programs for managers from a number of companies or customized or packaged programs for individual companies). It is also interesting to note that a number of these firms specializing in EE/MD activities formed a kind of "trade association" in 1975 called Instructional Systems Association for the purposes of sharing information, improving their methods and practices, and (as one of our interviewees put it) "helping to raise the standards for the training industry."

A second significant category of nonuniversity external providers is comprised of companies and firms that have their primary activity in areas other than EE/MD, but which have the personnel and other resources to provide management development programs for their own managers as well as managers from other companies (e.g., client companies). Examples would be several of the "big eight" accounting firms.

A third—and vast—category is comprised of individual consultants who either spend almost all their time offering management development courses or who include this as part of their repertoire of consulting activities. Often, such consultants specialize in one particular, sometimes quite narrow, topic relating to management. They have, in the vernacular, their "shtick," a talk or seminar on a specialized topic that they have honed to perfection by repeated presentations to a wide array of managerial audiences.

An important point to be made about external providers of EE/MD is not the categorization scheme per se, but rather the great *diversity* in the total set of third-party providers. The fact that there are many variations within and across the three types described above only serves to emphasize the point. This diversity also leads to a second key point: Generalizations about the total set are very difficult to make and frequently can be highly inaccurate when talking about the activities of any single organization, firm, or consultant. Nevertheless, it is probably worthwhile to attempt to assess the significant role that they collectively play in management development, as seen by both themselves and by current or future corporate "buyers."

EXTERNAL (NONUNIVERSITY) PROVIDERS' OWN PERSPECTIVES

The small number of interviews conducted with third-party providers for this Project allow for only a limited exploration of the views of this very large and diffuse set. Nevertheless, certain key points did emerge that are worth reporting. We first look at what these providers believe are their distinctive advantages vis-à-vis in-house corporate efforts and university-based business school (nondegree) programs. Second, we note their own assessments of possible relative disadvantages associated with this type of provider compared to other providers (as they view the needs of the potential EE/MD "purchaser").

Comparative Advantages

Probably the number one comparative advantage nonuniversity external providers of EE/MD programs see for themselves is simply the fact that they offer companies an alternative—in the training and development area—to maintaining a large in-house training staff. That is, by using commercial vendors on a spot basis for particular needs, they maintain, companies can limit their investments in the fixed costs of a permanent management development staff. In this sense, then, such providers fill a role much like temporary-help agencies do when companies have certain accounting or secretarial needs.

The second major comparative advantage that these providers believe they possess is specialized expertise. Such expertise, from their perspective, can take a number of forms depending on the specific type of provider (firm specializing in offering management development courses, individual consultant, etc.). For example, as noted earlier, the expertise could be in some specialized content area where the firm or consultant has had the opportunity to develop a level of knowledge beyond that typically found in a company or on a university campus. (Of course, it would be recognized that such an advantage would only apply to particular content areas and not necessarily to other subject matter areas that would clearly be more in the realm of the in-house or university-based program.) Related to the advantage of special expertise in certain subject matter areas would be, in the views of third-party providers, expertise in the delivery of that content that is developed and sharpened through repeated presentations on a much more frequent basis than typically would be the case with those who make presentations in company or university programs.

Other kinds of expertise that commercial external providers cite as a potential advantage in particular situations (and for particular providers) would be in areas relating to the design and "packaging" of programs. Packaging—really prepackaging—would include such items as audiovisual materials, standard forms to be completed by participants (where the data that would be collected could be compared to other samples), and various methods for conveying the content. None of these design/packaging elements of expertise would be unique to commercial firms or consultants, but such providers would argue that their expertise is more routinely developed when those involved in planning and delivering presentations and courses are doing this every day as a full-time job. In other words, they see themselves as experts in how to "put on" or conduct highly effective management development courses and programs.

One other comparative advantage, as seen by these providers, would be that by working with a large number of companies over a given span of time, they are able to adopt a very practitioner-oriented approach which is usually reinforced by the fact that the course leaders are themselves former practitioners. This would be seen, by them, as a distinct advantage compared to university-supplied programs. In-house company programs would, of course, also have a practitioner orientation, but with one significant difference: practice (usually) confined to one company's experiences. The commercial vendors would aver that by the nature of their activities they are able to bring to bear knowledge about practices from a wide variety of companies and select the best approaches in their management development programs.

Comparative Disadvantages

The one significant problem or issue that concerns third-party providers when looking at their peers collectively is that of "quality control." In part, this is due to the fact that, as one of them put it in an interview, "anybody can be in this business." By that this person meant that a single individual can start a consulting operation in the EE/MD field with virtually no capital and with very few overhead expenses. Thus, there are few barriers to entry for individuals or small groups with minimum qualifications as well as for highly qualified professionals. This situation allows those of lower quality to "stay in business" for a considerable length of time before the market weeds them out. In turn, this also leads to a wide variation in quality across the total group of commercial vendors, whether they are firms or individual consultants. Those vendors who perceive that they are providing a quality EE/MD service are (correctly, in our opinion) worried that those offering inferior courses or programs will generate negative reactions toward all commercial external suppliers from any company that has been "burned" in this manner. It is for this reason, among others, that a number of commercial vendors and consultants formed an association a decade or so ago (as described earlier) to help raise "industry standards" by exerting more voluntary quality control.

THE CORPORATE PERSPECTIVE

In this section we report corporate views—obtained from both interviews and questionnaire data—on the role of nonuniversity external providers. These opinions come from several different categories of corporate respondents: CEOs, SCEs, VPHRs, and DMDs. We first look at current corporate usage of programs provided by this source, followed by corporate perspectives on the relative advantages and disadvantages of third-party programs and their overall effectiveness. In the final part, expected future use of these programs, as seen by DMDs, will be compared with the expected use of programs from the other two primary sources (corporations and university business schools).

Current Usage

Table 13.1 (comparable to Table 11.3 in Chapter 11, but with the figures for other external providers highlighted) shows that DMDs report that courses and programs provided by third-party sources are used slightly more than those provided by university business schools, but—as would be expected—not nearly as extensively as in-house programs/courses. Interviews with the DMDs in our sample clearly indicated that programs/courses from these nonuniversity providers ordinarily are used by the corporate consumer to meet specialized types of EE/MD needs, such as developing specific skills or techniques, improving sales management, and the like. In other words, external EE/MD consultants and providers are seen primarily as "niche players" by the corporate personnel who hire them. Generally speaking, in most of the corporations in which we interviewed, the typical provider in this category was not seen as particularly appropriate for a wide range of management development needs, but rather as a potential resource to perform in fairly narrowly specified roles and to meet spot needs.

Relative Advantages/Disadvantages of This Type of Provider

Advantages As viewed from the perspective of chief corporate human resources officers (VPHRs), interviews showed that the relative advantages of this type of provider are related to the characteristic we noted above: the ability to fill certain well-defined niches and meet specialized needs (which sometimes were described as "needs for low-level special skills" or "needs of local units"). Not surprisingly, this also represented the view of most of the DMDs we interviewed, as well as being confirmed in the larger sample of DMDs who

TABLE 13.1
CORPORATE UTILIZATION OF DIFFERENT PROVIDERS: AS REPORTED BY DMDs
(Percent Checking One of Three Alternatives; $N = 246$)

	Providers		
	Other External	**In-House**	**University**
Do not use	4%	2%	10%
Use occasionally	80	31	80
Use extensively	16	67	10

Note: This table presents the same data, rearranged, as in Tables 11.3 and 12.3.

TABLE 13.2
PERCEIVED ADVANTAGES OF OTHER EXTERNAL PROVIDER
PROGRAMS
(Percent of DMDs Checking "Major Advantage"; N = 244)

41%	Offer a level of expertise unavailable elsewhere
34	Participants interact with managers from other organizations
21	Program content specific to needs of the organization
19	Maximum input of new ideas
17	Highest-quality instruction
15	Convenience, logistics, etc.
4	Cost-effectiveness

responded to a questionnaire item pertaining to third-party providers (where the highest checked advantage was that "these providers frequently offer a level of expertise unobtainable elsewhere"). The other advantage most frequently indicated (relatively speaking) by DMDs on the applicable survey item was the capability of these external providers—as with universities—to bring together managers from a variety of companies in "public" programs. The percentages of DMDs indicating this and other potential attributes as "major advantages" of nonuniversity providers are shown in Table 13.2. As this table also makes clear, "cost effectiveness" was seldom seen as one of the major advantages (see the following paragraph).

Disadvantages   By far the most critical relative disadvantage of third-party providers, as cited by DMDs in questionnaire survey responses, is the cost of their services. As shown in Table 13.3, 42% of the DMDs listed "overpriced" as a "major disadvantage" of programs offered by such vendors. (This compares—as noted in Chapter 12—to a figure of 35% for programs provided by

TABLE 13.3
PERCEIVED DISADVANTAGES OF OTHER EXTERNAL PROVIDER
PROGRAMS
(Percent of DMDs Checking "Major Disadvantage"; N = 244)

42%	Overpriced
18	Managers do not get enough information specific to their own organization's needs
16	Lack of long-term stability of vendor organizations
14	Limited/specialized approach/technique
9	Lack of appropriate facilities
7	Instructors not technically competent
7	Instructors not effective teachers
7	Inconvenience, logistics, etc.
7	Managers do not get to interact with other managers from their own organization

TABLE 13.4
EFFECTIVENESS OF PROGRAMS OF DIFFERENT PROVIDERS
(Median Rating, on a 10-Point Scale, of Extent to Which Programs Have "Met Corporate
Training Objectives" and, in Parentheses, Percent Checking that Programs Have a "Wide
Variation in Quality"

| | Providers | | |
Raters	Other External	In-House	University
CEOs (*N* = 122)	**5.6 (68%)**	5.9 (35%)	5.3 (57%)
SCEs (*N* = 149)	**5.6 (59)**	5.9 (34)	5.5 (45)
VPHRs (*N* = 203)	**5.6 (61)**	6.1 (35)	5.6 (51)
DMDs (*N* = 225)	**6.3 (45)**	6.8 (23)	5.3 (41)

Note: This table presents the same data, rearranged, as in Tables 11.4 and 12.4.

university-based business schools.) As Table 13.3 also shows, no other potential disadvantage (listed as possible responses to the specific survey question) was regarded as "major" by more than 20% of the DMD respondents. In addition, and somewhat surprisingly, given the views of some key providers in this category, which were cited earlier in this chapter, interviews with both VPHRs and DMDs elicited some—but not a great deal—of concern about the potentially troublesome issue of wide variation in quality of programs across the range of vendors. If such a concern was there, it was not highly prominent.

Perceived Effectiveness of This Type of Provider

The overall effectiveness of programs provided by nonuniversity external firms was rated by CEOs, SCEs, VPHRs, and DMDs. As depicted in Table 13.4 (which is the same as Tables 11.4 and 12.4, but with the column for third-party providers highlighted), such programs were generally rated by these four categories of respondents as slightly more effective than university-based programs and slightly less effective than in-house programs. Directors of management development were especially inclined to rate the programs from these nonuniversity providers as more effective than those from universities (a mean rating of 6.3 versus 5.3). When asked explicitly about *variation* in quality across programs, however, somewhat higher percentages of corporate respondents did report "wide variation" from this particular external source, as Table 13.4 shows, than from programs provided in-house or from university business schools. However, consistent with our interview findings, the frequency of respondents indicating wide quality variations for third-party providers was not dramatically higher than for the other category of external providers, i.e., universities, but clearly higher than for in-house programs.

Future Use of Programs from This Type of Provider

As with the other two types of providers (corporations and universities), corporate DMDs project an increased use of third-party provider courses and programs during the next 10-year period. Nearly 60% of DMDs report that they expect that their companies will increase their use of nonuniversity external providers during this period, and only 12% project a decrease. The percentage of DMDs predicting an increase is about in line with the percentage (65%) predicting an increase in use of business school EE/MD programs, but it is lower than for in-house programs (where the comparable figure is 87%).

A surprising finding, to us at least (but perhaps not to the nonuniversity providers themselves), showed up in DMDs' answers to the question, "What do you expect will be the major source of programs to meet the most important management development needs of this organization in the next 10 years?" As seen in Tables 11.8 and 12.8, third-party providers were checked most frequently by DMDs as the major source—among the three types of providers—for meeting the developmental needs of "upper/top management" levels. (The figures were 40, 36, and 24% for third-party programs, university-based programs, and in-house programs, respectively). Since the most prominent need identified for this top level by DMDs (as reported in Chapter 11) is "strategic planning/ thinking," this clearly identifies one of the future specific opportunities for this category of provider (regardless of the extent to which such firms already are providing this type of program). Nonuniversity external providers were seen as more likely than university sources, but less likely than in-house sources, to be the major provider of programs for lower and middle management levels (again, as previously shown in Tables 11.8 and 12.8).

COMMENTARY

There are three issues relating to nonuniversity external providers of executive education and management development that we would like to discuss in this section: the role for this type of provider in EE/MD activities, quality control in their programs and courses, and future use of programs/courses from this provider source. Given the somewhat restricted nature of our data concerning this category of provider, our comments will be relatively brief.

Roles for Third-Party Providers

There is little doubt that the corporate community currently views third-party providers, collectively, as an important nontrivial source for meeting highly specific EE/MD needs. This is the "niche player" role referred to earlier. In this sense, then, such providers can be thought of as supplemental to a company's own in-house management development resources. For firms large enough to have their own human resources staff that can supply most of the organization's developmental efforts, external vendors can be used for specialized spot assignments to round out a complete array of programs across a variety of topics and subjects. For smaller firms unable to afford full-time specialists in management development on their own payroll, commercial providers can be used to supply most developmental needs through programs tailored individually for the company or through sending managers and executives to public programs.

The two primary factors inhibiting greater corporate use of commercial vendors of EE/MD programs are the perceived (by many companies) relatively high costs of such services and the possibility of being "burned" by a low-quality program that does not justify the cost. However, most companies we interviewed did not seem overly concerned about the latter factor because they felt they usually could avoid low-quality programs in the first place (through checking with other companies or by general "grapevine" knowledge) or simply not using them again if they were once tried and found deficient. The costs of programs and courses, even when of very high quality, put on by third-party providers seemed to be much more of a sensitive issue.

If the primary role for third-party providers is to offer EE/MD programs and courses that can serve as adjuncts to, or substitutes for (depending on the size of firm), in-house programs, then in this regard that role does not differ from that of university business schools in their nondegree program activities. To state this more directly, business schools and third-party providers are often direct competitors for supplying these types of corporate EE/MD needs. In the previous chapter, we indicated some of the particular strengths and advantages that business schools often have in undertaking these activities. Here, we will note that many nonuniversity external providers have their own particular assets in attempting to capture a larger share of an expanding EE/MD market. Often, commercial vendors can respond much more rapidly than business schools to particular corporate needs that must be fulfilled on short notice. In addition, for a variety of reasons, many of these vendors have greater flexibility than the typical business school in adapting program content, delivery, or packaging to specific corporate requirements. As noted earlier, some third-party providers would claim that another advantage they have is that they can provide specialized expertise often unavailable elsewhere; however, leading business schools would dispute this as a typical advantage and claim that often their own faculty members have expertise on leading-edge topics that cannot be matched by the typical commercial vendor. In any event, though, it seems clear that—because of some unique capabilities that many of them possess—third-party providers can and do play a highly significant role in satisfying certain types of corporate EE/MD needs that cannot be met either by in-house staff resources or by university business schools.

Quality Control

The one potential dark cloud hanging over commercial vendors of EE/MD programs is the relative ease with which unqualified individuals can enter the field and put on low-quality courses and programs that serve to give the industry a mixed reputation. In recent years, as we described earlier, a number of vendors formed an association designed to promote quality and raise standards for providers of such programs. This is, from the point of view of both the providers themselves and their corporate consumers, a positive step. Such efforts should help provide companies and firms with useful guidelines for determining what they should reasonably expect from programs from this category of external provider. Nevertheless, the problem remains that many vendors and consultants will choose to ignore those standards and continue to operate as they see fit—and, sometimes, quite expediently. Thus, when it comes to any EE/MD program/course provided by an external source, whether a business school or a commercial vendor, nothing will substitute—as we stressed in Chapter 11—for companies taking a heavy dose of *caveat emptor* before purchasing.

The Future for Third-Party Providers in EE/MD

The total set of data we collected and impressions we gained from carrying out this Project lead us to believe that nonuniversity external providers of management education and executive development programs, in toto, will gain an increasing share of the market (relative to in-house and university business school programs) for these kinds of activities. Certainly, in the past 25 years, such sources already have made great inroads into this market, and we see little on the horizon that is likely to reverse this trend or even slow it appreciably. We would predict that many medium-sized firms in the future will decide to "contract out" most or all of their management development needs to such suppliers rather than keep additional human resources staff members on the permanent payroll. Even some large companies may find it less expensive to fill an increasing share of their EE/MD requirements in this manner. While certain business schools undoubtedly will get some portion of this increased "action," by and large there are simply not enough faculty resources within most business schools to be able to meet the aggregate demand for this kind of nondegree education. Thus, commercial vendors appear to be the major available source of supply on a large scale. The only question is which vendors will meet this opportunity and challenge successfully and which will be found wanting. There will, we predict, be great variability in the fate of particular third-party providers, but, in general, they should fare extremely well in the latter years of this century if they can generate and sustain a reputation for offering quality products.

PART FOUR

OVERVIEW
AND CONCLUSIONS

OVERVIEW
OF THE FINDINGS

This chapter presents a summary of university and corporate perspectives on management education, a comparison of the similarities and differences in these perspectives, and a summary assessment of the validity of recent critiques of management education.

THE UNIVERSITY PERSPECTIVE

This section provides an overview of how the current and future state of management education and development is appraised from the perspective of those operating in the university context, whether at the level of the campus (i.e., provosts), the business/management school (i.e., deans, faculty members, etc.), or the school's immediate external environment (i.e., members of business advisory councils). We first consider the general perspective—across all university-affiliated respondents—regarding present conditions, outlook for the future, and key concerns and issues relating to that future. This is followed by a summary of comparisons of viewpoints across different categories of schools and across different subsets of respondents.

Overall Perspective

Our data-collection efforts from university respondents involved obtaining their

• Assessments of current conditions and circumstances relating to management education and development activities in their own schools.

• Views about what they *expect* the future for management education in general and in their own schools in particular to be like, *and* what it *should be* like.

• Thoughts about key concerns and issues that would determine the nature of this future.

Assessments of Present Conditions and Circumstances By many standards (e.g., the large numbers of students applying for admission to BBA and MBA programs, the high salaries paid to MBA graduates), business/management schools in recent years have been quite successful. Therefore, it should come as no surprise that—generalizing across all our more than 300 interviews at the more than 60 universities we visited—we observed that there is a high level of satisfaction *within* schools about the quality of the job they are doing in educating students for productive careers in the business world and advancing the knowledge and practice of business and management. In one sense, this could be construed as a positive sign, since, after all, an appropriate degree of pride in one's accomplishments can be conducive to continued effective performance. Nevertheless, in this instance we do not regard it as a particularly positive state of affairs, and we came away from our university interviews concerned that there may be too much overall *complacency and self-satisfaction*. It is important to stress, however, that what we are talking about is a general level of complacency that would not necessarily describe any particular school or any individual dean or faculty member. We did encounter a number of specific exceptions to our generalization, but not enough to (in our opinion) invalidate it. In short, business/management schools and those associated with them think they have been doing well—maybe, as we see it, *too* well.

The consequence of this self-satisfaction is that currently within universities and their business/management schools there is little perceived need for major changes in the way in which collegiate management education is carried out. There was scant overt evidence of serious and comprehensive thinking about, or support for, the types of significant changes and innovations that are always necessary if an important endeavor—in this case, the total set of university-based management education and development activities—is to move ahead and do as well or better in the future as it has done in the past. Failure to make significant changes while the environment is currently benign but demonstrably and continually changing could lead to unpleasant consequences—such as perceived irrelevance—later on.

Outlooks for the Future Consistent with the above-reported general level of satisfaction with the job that they and their schools have been doing, most deans and faculty members appear to have strongly optimistic views of the future relating to their own respective business/management schools. This is especially so with regard to a school's goals in general and its prospects for increasing its national or regional ranking relative to other comparable schools. In fact, across the sample of all sixty-plus schools at which we interviewed, the primary goal or aspiration of schools was exactly this: to increase their relative ranking or visibility in the set of schools with which they compare themselves. This was particularly the case with most Category I and II schools; for Category III schools the primary aspiration typically took the form of "obtaining AACSB accreditation."

The second most frequently cited goal across the sample of schools was to "increase our research efforts and output." This was mentioned by many deans and faculty members, but especially by those in Category II schools and some other schools in the other two categories that had strong desires to "move up" or increase their ranking. The third most frequently reported goal—which was strongly present in some schools but almost totally absent in others—was to find or continue to develop "our niche"—what "this school can do best" given its particular environment and set of circumstances. Other goals that were mentioned more than a few times across the sample of schools were to "increase our emphasis on executive education/management development," to "attract better-quality students," to "develop better relations with the business community," and (by faculty members) to "provide a better mix or balance between theory and applications in the classroom."

We also queried deans and faculty members about their schools' plans for the future. What we found in response was an extremely wide variance across schools in the amount of their long-range planning. In general, there did not appear to be extensive planning of this nature. Instead, there seemed to be a considerable amount of ad hoc or spur-of-the-moment planning. Also, this typical (but certainly not universal) situation was accompanied by frequent reports from faculty that previously agreed-on "plans" were often ignored in subsequent actions or decisions, and thus these observers imputed "lack of commitment to the plans" on the part of those responsible for implementing them.

Concerns/Problems/Issues   Our interviews revealed two key problem areas that deans and faculty members thought would be the most critical obstacles to their schools' efforts to improve in the future. The issue most frequently identified was—no surprise here—funding, especially the capacity to obtain external (nonuniversity) financial support. Even most of the wealthier schools (although there were one or two exceptions in our sample) regarded this as the area of their greatest concern with regard to factors that could inhibit their progress. The second area most often mentioned as constituting a problem for achieving a school's goals was the (perceived) limited supply of qualified faculty members and the ability of the school to attract the best ones. Much less often mentioned as problem areas that could block future plans were the campus administration, the school's own administration (as seen by faculty), and in a very few cases, a possible decline in student demand. All these latter issues, however, paled in comparison to the near universal concern about how well a school would do in the future in obtaining extramural funds.

Major Similarities/Differences across Categories of Schools

In this section we review our findings from the university sector as they relate to similarities and differences *across* types or categories of schools. As will be recalled from Chapter 1, the schools in our survey and interview samples were divided into three categories based on a set of four criteria (AACSB accreditation status, Ph.D. program, primarily full-time master's program, and self-rating in top quartile of all business/management schools). In their responses to a number of survey and interview questions on a variety of topics—curriculum, students, faculty, teaching, and research—deans and faculty members in Category I schools, as a group, answered differently from those in Category III schools, with respondents from Category II schools typically (but not always) in between. On other questions, however, there were essentially *no* differences across the category groups. Thus, type of school was strongly correlated with viewpoints about some issues but not others.

In general, the largest differences that did occur reflected the overall stronger research and scholarship orientation of the Category I schools. Deans and faculty members in these schools believed that research was much more strongly emphasized than teaching in their schools, while exactly the reverse was true for respondents in Category II and III schools. However, deans (and, to a lesser extent, faculty) in all three types of schools *expect* that in the future their schools will move to more of a research/teaching balance—by increasing the emphasis on teaching in Category I schools and on research in Category II and III schools. Also, there was no essential difference of opinion across categories of schools as to the *type* of research that deans and faculty members think there *should be* more of in the future, namely, *applied* research.

In curriculum matters, there was a clearly stronger preference in favor of curriculum *breadth* and a substantial liberal arts background for students by faculty and deans in Category I schools compared to those in Category II and, especially, Category III schools. The latter, in fact, appeared to be concerned about whether there was *enough* specialization, particularly in the MBA curriculum. Category I deans and faculty members also relatively more frequently believed that there is currently some degree of overemphasis on quantitative subject matter and that the amount of emphasis on the international component of the curriculum should be increased. Category II respondents, on the other hand, most often wanted more attention paid to management information systems in the curriculum.

Major Similarities/Differences by Types of Respondents

Respondent groups associated with universities consisted of business/management school deans and faculty members, directors of placement and executive education in these schools, provosts (academic vice presidents), members of a school's business advisory council (BAC), and BBA and MBA current students and recent (5 and 10 years out of school) alumni. However, most of our overview comments in this section will focus on comparisons between deans and faculty members, with other groups' responses noted where relevant.

Deans were generally more optimistic than faculty members about their schools, as might be expected, since they are the ones who have their names most closely associated with the schools as a whole. Put differently, faculty members we interviewed were generally (although there were numerous individual exceptions) somewhat more critical of the state of affairs within their schools—for example, in their views of the effectiveness of their schools' long-range planning—and were more guarded in their projections of their schools' future than were deans. They also were not as positive as deans about the degree of "strengths" possessed by graduates from their schools and about how well prepared those graduates are for "eventual positions of significant leadership." Faculty also differed from deans in their views of the amount of relative attention given to research versus teaching now and expected in the future. They believed that their schools focused more heavily on research as a criterion for hiring and promotion than did their deans. (Our data, of course, do not permit us to determine which group was more *accurate* in their perceptions, only that those perceptions differed.)

The differences in overall views between business/management school deans and faculty members should not be overstated, however. Many of the differences were in degree only and were not differences in kind. This tended to be true, for example, on issues pertaining to the curriculum, although faculty members were moderately more positive toward quantitative-oriented subject matter than were deans. Furthermore, on many issues the two groups were in quite close agreement. For example, deans and faculty members, across the total sample of schools, tended to agree that research is likely to receive increased emphasis vis-à-vis teaching in their schools in the future. Also, both groups were in agreement that in the future faculty research should become relatively more applied. In this they both differed somewhat from the views of provosts. In addition, deans and faculty members (as well as provosts) seemed to be in strong agreement that their own business/management schools should give more attention (compared to what is given currently) to postdegree executive education and management development activities. Finally, deans and faculty members were in very close agreement about how well business schools nationally were doing in various areas: research, teaching, executive education, and the like. Both groups agreed that U.S. business schools are strongest in teaching and research and weakest in executive education and interaction with the business/management community.

Both undergraduate and MBA students tended to rate themselves considerably (in the case of the BBA students) or moderately (in the case of MBA students) higher on positive attributes than did their faculty mentors. The BBA students also rated themselves higher than deans rated them, although MBAs tended to evaluate themselves fairly similarly to how deans viewed them.

With respect to evaluations of the quality of the faculty in their own schools, ratings by provosts and members of business advisory councils were remarkably similar. Considering that these two groups have quite different roles in relation to their respective business schools and thus interact with faculty members in very different ways, this concurrence of opinion is noteworthy. Interestingly, both groups rated the quality of business school teaching, nationally, somewhat *higher* than did faculty members and deans themselves. They gave roughly equivalent ratings to business school research, on a national basis, ratings which were very similar to those from deans and faculty. Provosts, perhaps out of lack of direct knowledge, rated the quality of U.S. business schools' interaction with the business community more favorably than did BAC members, deans, and faculty members.

Business school alumni, both BBA and MBA alumni, gave substantially higher ratings than either deans or faculty members to the quality of the job that business schools do, collectively, in the area of teaching. Their ratings of other business school activities, on a national basis, were fairly close to those of deans and faculty members. In fact, on a rating of the "total set" of activities of business/management schools, alumni were somewhat more positive than either of the latter two groups. Either their experience since receiving their degrees has provided them a basis for relatively positive evaluations or, perhaps, they simply need to find reasons to justify having invested time, energy, and money in earning business degrees. However, it must be noted that these ratings (cited above) were not ratings of the quality of a respondent's own school's activities, but rather assessments of how "business/management schools are doing their job today in the United States."

THE CORPORATE PERSPECTIVE

Information on the corporate perspective on management education and development issues came from six key respondent groups: CEOs, senior corporate executives (SCEs) at the vice-presidential level in areas other than human resources, vice presidents/directors of human resources (VPHRs), middle/lower-level operating line managers, directors/managers of corporate management development activities (DMDs), and directors/managers of college relations. As with university-based respondents, interviews and survey questionnaire responses provided the basic data for analysis.

Overall Perspective

Members of the corporate world, by and large, are neither highly satisfied nor highly dissatisfied with the quality of university-based management education in this country. Their view, overall and generalized across all respondent groups, is one of moderate satisfaction with the job that today's business/management schools are doing in their total set of activities: teaching, research, executive education, and interactions with the business community. Among these four activities, the business community is most satisfied with the quality of teaching provided by business schools and least satisfied with their relations with the business community. They praise the quality and effectiveness of teaching provided by business/management schools more than they do the quality and impact of the research they turn out, and they are more satisfied with business schools' research than they are with their postdegree executive education efforts. The latter, in turn, are regarded more favorably than the quality of schools' interactions with the corporate community. These general conclusions about corporate-sector views, however, do not accurately convey the very wide range of opinion from respondent to respondent—some individuals were extremely dissatisfied with the performance of business schools and others were highly laudatory. Most were in the middle, slightly toward the positive side. The overall conclusions also mask some important corporate-sector concerns in certain specific areas relating to business schools and the education they provide.

Based on our interview findings and responses to open-ended survey questions, it seems safe to conclude that the type of change that the various members of the corporate community—from CEOs to VPHRs to operating managers—would most like to see in business education from *their* perspective is to make it more "realistic," "practical," and "hands on." Whether this in fact would be best *for* the business community is (in our opinion) quite debatable, but there is no question that this is the number one concern currently that the business world has about BBA and MBA degree programs. The next most frequently mentioned specific concerns were the need for business schools and their faculty to have closer interactions with the business community, the need for a higher percentage of business school professors to have "real-world" work experience, and the need for more emphasis in the curriculum on the development of students' "soft" skills (i.e., leadership/interpersonal skills).

We have previously elaborated on these and some other issues in earlier chapters, but it is useful to recapitulate briefly some of the highlights of corporate viewpoints in certain topic areas as follows.

Curriculum   Most high-level corporate executives think that behaviorally oriented subject matter should be emphasized more in the curriculum. Most think that the amount of current emphasis on quantitative-oriented subject matter is about right, although there is a fairly sizable minority that think that this emphasis should be reduced. There is considerable and widespread support for maintaining what is perceived to be a current strong emphasis on developing students' analytical skills.

Students/Graduates   Corporate respondents are moderately positive (about 6.8 on a 10-point scale) about the quality of the BBA and MBA graduates they see being turned out by business/management schools. Vice presidents of human resources (VPHRs) do not believe MBAs have lived up to their companies' expectations for them as well as have BBAs. Corporate executives and managers are not nearly as impressed with students' (especially MBAs) "soft" skills as they are with their analytical skills, motivation, and content area knowledge. In fact, according to corporate directors of college recruiting, the number one ranked basis for making differential hiring decisions among MBA graduates—the principal characteristic they are seeking—is leadership/interpersonal skills. Many corporate respondents also were concerned that many students, particularly MBAs, have "unrealistic expectations" when they enter the business world.

Research   Interview data indicated that most corporate respondents pay relatively little attention to research being produced by business schools, even research directly relevant to their own areas of expertise. Members of the corporate community generally support the idea that research should be one of the major missions of business schools, particularly those regarded as "top level," but they report that to date they have not noticed much impact of this research on them or their companies. In effect, they typically claim that they can safely ignore most business school research with impunity.

Relations with the Business Community   These are seen as having improved considerably in the past decade or so, but they are still regarded as somewhat weak and in need of further attention.

AACSB Accreditation   The business community appears to pay very little attention to the AACSB accreditation status of a business/management school. As one concrete indication of this, whether a school is accredited (by AACSB) or not is not a factor in where companies choose to recruit or in whether an employee will be reimbursed for part-time enrollment in degree programs.

Executive Education/Management Development   Most companies appear to give a great deal of "lip service" support for this type of activity, whether carried out in-house or provided externally by a university business/management school or other organization. However, other data from this study raise questions as to whether such activities are, in fact, supported as extensively as many managers think they should be. With regard to EE/MD provided by business schools, corporations see the major advantage as the fact that their managers can interact with those from other companies and the major disadvantage as the lack of information relevant to company-specific issues.

Similarities/Differences across Categories of Corporate Respondents

In general, there were not large differences of opinion across the six sets of corporate respondents (CEOs, SCEs, operating managers, etc.). While individuals within categories often differed greatly from one another—even within the same company—there were few large or systematic differences among *modal* (i.e., the most typical) responses for these various groups. Perhaps the area of greatest difference occurred in questions about the types of business school graduates that companies most want to recruit. Operating managers more often reported—compared to higher-level executives—that their companies were seeking those who could carry out the "first job" most effectively. The latter were more inclined to the view that their companies were focusing their recruiting not so much on ability to do the first job as on assumed capability to fill eventual positions of significant leadership. Aside from this particular difference of opinion, corporate groups of respondents were more similar than they were different in how they viewed various components of university-based management education and development.

COMPARISON OF CORPORATE AND UNIVERSITY VIEWS

Any comparison of corporate and university views on management education and development must look at both similarities and differences. While differences may be the object of most interest, it is the similarities that put those differences into a meaningful context. We did find a number of important differences between the views of corporate respondents and those from university settings, but we also found some significant areas where they did *not* differ. We begin with those major similarities.

Similarities

At the most all-encompassing level of opinion—a rating of "how well overall are business/management schools doing their job today in the United States on their total set of activities,"—the responses from key groups within each sector were nearly *identical*: ratings (on a 10-point scale) of 6.1 and 5.9 from deans and faculty, respectively, and comparable ratings of 6.1, 6.2, and 6.2 from CEOs, SCEs, and VPHRs. Clearly, the corporate sector (currently) is *not less positive* than business school deans and faculty themselves, and, in fact, in the important area of teaching is actually *more positive*.

Both sectors are moderately well satisfied with the student "product" being turned out by U.S. business/management schools. Although there are specific areas where they are not, overall they are basically positive about the educational experience students are receiving at both the undergraduate and master's degree levels. Respondents from both sectors are in close agreement that the greatest strengths of contemporary business school graduates are their high motivation level and their relatively well developed analytical skills. In other areas, both the business and the academic world concur that they would like to see closer relations in the future between the business community and business/management schools. They also are in accord in believing that executive education/management development activities will—and should—become increasingly important in the future.

Differences

Corporate respondents tended to differ with their academic counterparts on several important issues pertaining to the curriculum and the educational process. For one thing, as a group, they were much more convinced of—and consequently more forceful in articulating—the need for stronger emphasis on development of "soft" (people) skills in the curriculum than were faculty and deans. They also expressed more concern than business/management school academics about whether students were acquiring sufficient knowledge of the "real world" of business, and they considerably more often endorsed the view that students were not obtaining enough of this type of information. Likewise, corporate respondents were markedly less convinced than deans and faculty members that MBA graduates possess "realistic expectations" when they enter the work force following completion of their business/management school education. On the matter of the type of BBA graduate that companies prefer to hire, the prevalent corporate view is that it is the individual with "a broad background and knowledge base" and the potential for future positions of leadership that is most wanted, whereas the typical academic viewpoint is that companies prefer to focus on hiring the person who has "a well-developed area of specialized knowledge" and is particularly "well prepared to perform effectively in the first job."

Some other key areas of differences between the two sectors included such issues as the value of academic (business school) research, the importance for a school to be or become AACSB accredited, and the role of the university in executive education/management development. With regard to the research products of business schools, managers and executives (especially in their comments during interviews) evaluated the impact and relevance of this research as much lower than did faculty members and deans. As to the significance of AACSB accreditation, most (although not all) either pleaded ignorance or said it was not a critical factor in the relationship of their organization to particular schools. This was decidedly not the view from most (not all) business schools. In the area of EE/MD, corporate respondents were less likely than deans and other academic officials to credit the university with special or unique advantages in providing superior programs. They were positive about business/management schools' current activities in this area, but they were not as optimistic about their future role in this area as were those representing the university sector.

CRITICISMS OF UNIVERSITY-BASED MANAGEMENT EDUCATION IN RETROSPECT

Throughout previous chapters in this report we have discussed a number of the specific criticisms directed at various components of the education currently being provided by business/management schools and what light our data shed on the degree (if any) of their validity. Here we provide an overview of the status of those criticisms, from the perspective of the total set of information—interviews, surveys, and our own observations—collected during the entire study.

A number of the criticisms appear to be relatively well founded. On some others, we were able to obtain little direct data and, in fact, believe that it would be very difficult for any research investigation to prove or disprove these claims convincingly. There were some criticisms, however, that we believe were not well supported by our data and our observations and should be rejected.

In the first category, i.e., those criticisms that appeared to have at least some degree of validity, we would put the following (we should note that several of them will be discussed in more detail in Chapter 15):

• There is a lack of meaningful integration across functional areas. While direct data were difficult to come by, all our indirect evidence pointed to a serious deficiency by business schools in this regard. We believe that this is one of the most critical issues for business/management schools to face in the future.

• Insufficient attention is paid in the curriculum to managing people and the development of leadership skills. As we have documented extensively, a significant segment of the business community believes this to be the case.

• Insufficient attention is paid to the "international component" of the curriculum. Our interview discussions with deans and faculty members—and certainly our own personal biases on this point—would lead us to this conclusion. However, it is important to note that this was *not* a strongly voiced concern by most of our corporate interview respondents *and* did not emerge as a highly ranked concern on our corporate survey responses.

• Business school graduates have overly high expectations about how they will be treated and what they will receive (in terms of challenging jobs, rapid advancements, etc.) when they begin their corporate-sector careers. The business community strongly believes that this is so, *especially* with regard to MBA students. Whether this "expectations gap" is a function of unrealistic expectations on the part of graduates of business/management schools—or of the failure of some companies to provide the kinds of tasks and opportunities that would challenge a highly motivated, bright person—is, however, another question and not one that can be answered in any direct way by our data. We suspect that the truth probably consists of both phenomena, but certainly business/management schools need to address more than they seem to be doing now the issue of students' perceptions of the value of such early career activities as "getting your hands dirty," "learning the business from the ground up," and the like. We agree with many business critics that the latter types of activities and experiences should be something to be valued by new graduates rather than something to be avoided. These are values that would seem to be amenable to influence in the business school setting.

• New, younger faculty members (i.e., those who have recently completed their doctoral education) are too narrowly educated in a functional specialty. Our observations and discussions would lead us to agree strongly, but we did not collect direct objective data on this issue.

• Faculty members lack "real-world" business experience. From our interviews with over 150 faculty members and more than 60 deans, we would conclude that this criticism is only partially true. Or, to state it differently, it is a very apt criticism of a certain portion of faculty members of U.S. business/management schools, but it misses the mark completely on a large segment of faculty. Our impressions gained from interviews lead us to conclude that there is a distinctly bimodal distribution of faculty on this dimension: A not insignificant percentage have had, and continue to have, a close relationship with the business community and thus considerable contact with the "real world" of business. In fact, at certain schools we found deans and faculty colleagues worried about the fact that some faculty members were spending *too much* time on their business-world contacts and not enough time on their academic responsibilities. Contrariwise, in other schools deans and some faculty members were concerned that there was not enough "practical business experience" represented on their faculty. Thus, insofar as this specific criticism is concerned, it is *not* valid in general, but it is quite apropos with regard to some schools and with respect to particular individual faculty members.

• Faculty research is too heavily oriented to the academic community as an audience and its products are largely irrelevant to the business community. This is a criticism that generates a wide variance of opinion. The academic community, by and large, disagrees. The business community, for the most part, is inclined to agree. As in some other popular criticisms of business schools and their educational and research activities, the "truth" is extremely difficult to discern. We are inclined to believe that the business community has a point, *but* that this point is often grossly overstated. Furthermore, we see signs in recent years that this possible overbalance is being redressed. The real danger, though, is that the pendulum will swing too much the other way and business school research will become very applied, but at a trivial level. In our opinion, it is better to have high-quality basic research that does not seem to have immediate applications than to have low-quality applied research that has pretensions of importance but in fact makes trifling contributions.

• Business schools, and their faculty, do not interact enough with the business community. There seems to be general agreement in both the academic and business communities that this criticism has a certain degree of merit. It obviously is an area for *both sides* to work on, and, consequently, it is not exclusively a challenge for business schools. Expectations in this area, on both sides, may always be somewhat unrealistic, but there seems to be some degree of consensus that it—stronger relationships—is an objective worth additional effort in the future.

Now we turn to some criticisms that have been voiced but which we think are not well supported by our data:

• Business schools place too much (instructional) emphasis on analytical techniques. Not only do we not agree, but we found that the corporate world generally found such skills of graduates to be a very positive attribute. Perceptive individuals in the corporate sector with whom we talked seemed in near unanimity that this was a strong point of business education and that, whatever else might change in the future, they did not want this competence to be diminished. They wanted other abilities to be added, but not at the expense of this one.

• Business schools do not develop their students' communication skills sufficiently. Our interview and survey respondents fell far short of raving about the skills of business school graduates in this area, but they were not particularly disparaging. In fact, the level of other attributes (e.g., leadership and interpersonal skills) came in for considerably more condemnation. Also, a number of our corporate interviewees commented on what they thought was a definite improvement in this area in the past 5 years or so.

• Faculty, in their classes and teaching activities, do not pay enough attention to the real world of business. From all the information we could obtain, this is not a generally valid criticism. The issue, it seems to us, is not whether instructors in business/management schools focus enough on what is "really" happening in the business world, but rather whether they expend enough effort on how to *improve* the functioning of business organizations. Simply reproducing in the classroom what is taking place currently in business surely should not be the primary goal of all business/management schools. What *should* be a goal is to challenge current practices in order to make them better and more productive for not only business organizations themselves, but also—*particularly*—society at large.

• AACSB accreditation standards rely too much on quantitative ratios and not enough on basic quality; furthermore, the process is unduly cumbersome and expensive. This is a criticism that originates not in the corporate world, but in the academic community. While there are certainly individual deans, faculty members, and provosts who agree with this assessment, the general consensus of those with whom we talked—and we pressed this issue intensively— was that there did not seem to be serious problems with either the accreditation standards or procedures at this time. A number of deans explicitly applauded recent efforts to move away from strict (and, in their view, sometimes petty) numerical ratios to broader-based evaluations of quality. Their major concern seemed to be that this might be only a passing phenomenon and that the AACSB might slip back into approaches that were judged (by these respondents) to be dysfunctional. Overall, there seemed to be much more of a feeling of general satisfaction with the AACSB accreditation system than we had anticipated.

CHAPTER 15

CONCLUSIONS

This final chapter presents our concluding views on the challenges and opportunities that confront management education and development. These conclusions are derived principally from the data collected for this research, but draw as well on our own personal observations and experience as professors and former deans. If casual drift is to be minimized and purposeful thrust maximized, we believe that those individuals and institutions responsible for delivering management education and development in the United States in the next 10–15 years must address the fundamental issues that we set forth below.

1 THE CHANGING ENVIRONMENT FOR BUSINESS EDUCATION IN THE UNITED STATES: THE NEED FOR STRATEGIC PLANNING

Business schools insistently include strategic planning as a subject in their curricula; however they do not always practice what they teach. Relatively little planning for anything beyond next semester's classroom schedule (so to speak) really takes place in a great many schools. Inertia of tradition, inadequacy of marginal resources, strength of continuing market demand, and especially, lack of incentive systems with which to reward change in academia all combine to inhibit strategic planning.

There can be no denying that, in the aggregate, business schools have been extremely successful (in market terms) since the 1950s. This is probably the most cogent explanation for the fact that very few of our respondents saw any reason to believe that they needed to think about significant new directions or thrusts. The most descriptive operative word in the mid-1980s in business schools has been *complacency*. The overriding concern seems to be how to get more resources to "keep on doing what we're doing." The pervasive attitude might be described as "I'm all right, Jack."

Perhaps our most disturbing finding was the general absence of concern for, or even expressions of awareness of, looming changes in the environment in which business schools will be operating in the next 10 to 15 years. We believe, however, that there are a number of increasing expectations and societal trends which business schools will need to take into account *if* they are to avoid aimless drift and possible eventual irrelevance. Among the more important are the following:

- Greater accountability demanded of all institutions
- Higher costs and a shift in the burden of who pays
- The increasingly important role of universities in regional, national, and international economic development
- International relationships and the globalization of management
- Changing pedagogical methods through developments in communications technologies
- Increasing emphasis on entrepreneurial activities
- Changing demographics

This list is by no means intended to be exhaustive; rather, it is illustrative of the dimensions that need to be taken into account if business schools are to avoid institutional ossification (if not outright obsolescence) as we approach the beginning of the 21st century.

Of overarching importance, in our view, in charting the business school's course for the next decade and beyond, is a trilogy of changing factors: (1) supply/demand patterns for business education, (2) societal expectations of institutions, and (3) employer expectations.

Supply/Demand Patterns for Business Education

There are three major areas of domestic (U.S.) demand for business education:

- Business majors—for those who want degrees in business, either undergraduate or graduate
- Majors in other subjects who want courses (perhaps minors) in business
- Executive education

For graduate business degrees, especially the MBA, we found no evidence to lead us to expect an imminent decline in the overall demand. For undergraduate business degrees, we see two factors that will, in all probability, inhibit further growth of significant proportions. First, the surge in demand by women, which fueled much of the growth in business enrollments during the decades of the sixties and seventies, can be expected to level off. Second, the overall saturation level for business degrees in most universities has probably been reached or is at least very close to the limits of acceptability. We do not see many universities—especially the better ones—tolerating an untrammeled growth pattern in business enrollments much beyond the current (approximate) 25% level since the very essence of a university is diversity and breadth, not a concentration in any one subject matter area. Moreover, for business schools themselves the prospect of capping enrollments in business represents an opportunity to increase the quality level of BBA graduates while at the same time protecting the basic academic integrity of the university. We believe that this opportunity for quality improvement will not, and certainly should not, be foregone.

We expect the demand for courses in business for nonmajors to continue to rise, partly as a direct consequence of the limits which will be placed on the number of undergraduate degrees in business, but also because the business minor, or some variant of a minor, is likely to become more highly regarded in the marketplace for its own intrinsic worth. The corporate sector respects the well-rounded graduate with communications and verbal reasoning skills, but one who also can demonstrate some knowledge of, and empathy toward, business.

In the area of executive education, we strongly believe that a significant number of business schools can and *should* develop the expertise to be major suppliers of high-quality education of this type not just because there will be a market demand (see Chapters 10 and 11), which there is likely to be, but also because such involvement keeps the faculty in closer touch with the profession about which they are teaching and in which they are doing research. The question is whether a given university business/management school will have the acumen, skills, and, especially, motivation to respond to this demand. To date there is little evidence to suggest that, in the total picture, many business schools will be anything but dilettantish in the executive education field, but we believe that the opportunities for significant involvement will be there for those who incorporate this type of education into their strategic plans and then develop the faculty resources to deliver a competitive product.

We referred above, quite deliberately, to *domestic*—U.S.-based—demand. However, we are aware that a growing number of business schools are becoming involved in the development and marketing of educational products for international consumption. These take the form of institution-building projects involving U.S.-based universities assisting in the creation of new schools, expanding and improving existing ones, or establishing branch campuses abroad (with degrees actually issued by the parent institution in the United States). We expect an increase in the number of such "offshore" entrepreneurial academic exercises, especially in the Pacific Rim countries, which have both high-volume student demand and the economic means to support local (in-country) business schools. A special and intriguing case is that of China, where recent political accommodations, the huge population, and developmental needs portend a high eventual demand for business education at all levels.

Quite apart from the emerging patterns of supply and demand for management education, both domestic and worldwide, we believe that important changes in American societal expectations are taking place that will affect the nature of this education and what business schools are called upon to do. We turn now to some observations on this issue.

Increasing Societal Expectations

One of the most important variables affecting the future of business schools is the set of changing societal expectations concerning the role of institutions in general and educational institutions in particular. There is a growing belief, thrust upon the United States by increasing international competitiveness (manifested most dramatically by the recent success of the Japanese in international trade), that the American higher education establishment has not lived up to its obligations to produce highly competent, productively proficient, and ethically responsible graduates. America is seen by some to have lost its competitive edge, and business schools are seen as at least partly culpable.

There also appears to be a growing expectation that the business school should be held accountable for its activities. The societal demand for greater accountability is reinforced by the shifting patterns of funding for education. Gone are the days when education—and particularly university education—was essentially a free good for a large proportion of the population. With the shift from a primary base of tax support to a system in which the students or their sponsors pay an increasing share of the costs directly, accountability for value added is bound to be demanded more insistently than has ever been the case before. With an increasing share of the cost being borne directly, public institutions will be expected to become rather more like their private counterparts, i.e., more responsive to market demand.

American society is also expanding its expectations concerning the scope of the activities of its major institutions. Thus, the university as a whole is seen more and more as an important resource that can influence the rate of growth of the socioeconomic system in which it is a part. Silicon Valley in California, Route 128 in the Boston area, and North Carolina's Research Triangle are often cited as prime examples of the influence of higher education in the attraction and formulation of new enterprises. Therefore, in addition to its time-honored task of preparing new entrants for the managerial workforce, the business/management school will increasingly be called upon to play a direct role in the economic development process of its city, region, or nation. We believe there will be growing insistence from agencies of government and its elected officials that university business schools (especially those located in institutions that are directly supported by taxpayers) be held accountable for services in this area—research, technical and economic information, consultation, and education. We were struck by the fact that this issue was infrequently mentioned by our interviewees or survey respondents. In our view, however, the business/management school, if it is to expect a full measure of support from its constituencies in the future, will need to examine carefully the degree to which it ought to become an active participant in the economic development process.

Changing Employer Expectations

Along with growing societal expectations of accountability and value added, employers are also changing their expectations of business schools. One of the most insistent pleas from many of the interviewees in the corporate sector was for more broadly educated people who not only can learn to cope (quickly) with the financial and market vicissitudes of the business world, but who also can operate effectively in diverse managerial and societal settings.

At the same time, however, the typical corporation *also* expects business school graduates to "hit the ground running" and to be able to *do* something immediately upon graduation. This poses a difficult, but not insurmountable, challenge: how to prepare students not only for their first job, but also for future growth as managers. This is hardly anything new—the balance between narrow vocational interests and longer-run personal development and societal goals has always been difficult to strike. What has served to accentuate the issue are the rising costs of education and the increasing complexity of the business world that impinge with greater urgency than ever before on the tasks of business schools. The consequences will be greater demands for efficiency in the design and delivery of programs that are simultaneously cost-effective and relevant to both the short- and long-term needs of employing organizations and graduates themselves.

2 BUSINESS SCHOOL MISSIONS AND NICHES: CAPITALIZING ON DIVERSITY ACROSS THE SYSTEM

At first glance there appears to be a wide variety of types of business/management schools—large–small, public–private, etc.—among the more than 600 collegiate members of the AACSB. However, the deeper issue is whether there is *real* rather than apparent diversity and whether the differences are being sufficiently encouraged by universities, by the AACSB and its key committees, and indeed, by the business community itself. For the system as a whole, we believe that *more diversity of mission (but not of quality) is vital* if university-based management education and development is to make major strides toward improvement in the future. Such diversity of educational goals and approaches must take into account the reality that across the range of schools there are different modal populations of entering students, different career paths of graduating students, different needs of the nation/region/state/local area, and different missions of universities and schools themselves. Despite all these factors that would seem to lead schools in the direction of diversity one from another, what we found, in all candor, was a distressing tendency for schools to avoid the risk of being different. Many of them seemed to be attempting to emulate what they think are appropriate role models, but models which may, in fact, be *in*appropriate to their mission, rather than considering how they might be constructively distinct. A "cookie cutter mentality" does not seem to be too strong a term to describe the situation we encountered in a number of schools.

There are probably a number of reasons for what we believe to be a relative lack of creative and energizing diversity. One may be the unintended impact of the AACSB Standards. Although the statement of accreditation philosophy and preconditions at the beginning of the Standards is explicit about the fact that "departures from Standards will be accepted if the school can demonstrate that overall high quality is achieved" and Standard VII currently states that "schools are encouraged to develop and test new learning approaches and technologies," the vast majority of schools appear to be trying to avoid any deviation lest they run the risk of failure to obtain accreditation or reaccreditation. So, intended or not, the Standards, in general, seem to generate a tendency toward uniformity.

Another equally or (probably) more important influence on inhibiting diversity is the belief on many schools' part that doing something that would differentiate themselves from the majority of business schools would make them and their graduates less acceptable, or even unacceptable, to the business world. In our corporate interviews we did not encounter this kind of thinking in any explicit fashion, but neither, on the other hand, did we find any specific corporate support for diversity. Thus, if unique competency is to be developed, it is unlikely to be as the result of any direct encouragement from the corporate community. Rather, it must come from the active and strategically motivated efforts of the business schools themselves.

It appears to us that individual schools have more opportunity and more leeway to maximize their particular comparative advantages than they are currently exploiting. An obvious first step in this direction seemed to have been neglected by some of the schools that we visited. That is, they do not (as far as we could tell from our interviews) put into practice the age-old maxim of "know thyself" and thus do not made a careful and comprehensive review of exactly who they are. Although it is surely taught in one form or another in their own classes in the area of management, they do not put into practice SWOT—a systematic examination of their particular *s*trengths and *w*eaknesses and the *o*pportunities and *t*hreats in their specific environment. Some other schools (in our interview sample) had at least gone this far and appeared to have a good grasp of their distinctive advantages and disadvantages; however, they are, for some of the reasons noted earlier, unwilling to move ahead to implement changes that would accentuate the former and minimize the latter and, in effect, differentiate their school and "products" from others.

The desire to be like others, or at least not very different, is not an exciting way to advance the cause of management education. To "dare to be distinctive" in at least some respects, *and simultaneously, to be willing to be assessed rigorously on quality,* should be a major objective of more than just a few business/management schools in this country.

3 CURRICULUM: UNDERNOURISHED EMPHASES

There are a number of areas or issues that seem to us not to be receiving enough relative attention in contemporary business school curricula. While there potentially is almost an infinite set of possibilities for inclusion on such a list, in this section we discuss six of those we consider to be the most important.

Breadth

The focus of attention of the business/management school, as far as the curriculum is concerned, has been for some years, quite understandably, on the core—the definition of the "common body of knowledge"—along with limited specialization in a fairly wide variety of functional areas. The incorporation of concepts from mathematics and the social/behavioral sciences along with an emphasis on the analytical and rigorous, as opposed to the descriptive and superficial, has demonstrably improved the quality of business school curricula significantly over the span of the last two and a half decades.

However, in the course of our investigations we encountered some well-reasoned concern, particularly among senior executives in the business world, that business school students tend to be rather more narrowly educated than they ought to be if they are to cope effectively in a rapidly changing and increasingly complex world. From this perspective, business schools seem to be turning out focused analysts, albeit highly sophisticated ones, adept at measuring and calculating the probabilities of certain outcomes, but, at the same time, graduates who often are unwittingly insensitive to the impacts of these outcomes on factors other than the "bottom line." This is a view with which we ourselves strongly concur.

If these observations are close to the truth, it logically follows that not enough attention has been paid to the need for business students to broaden the scope of their interests. Business/management school faculties, in their responsibilities for undergraduate education, quite understandably concern themselves predominantly with the 40 to 60% of the student's total curriculum which is their direct responsibility; however, if they are to be true to their total charge—maximizing the value of the student's entire experience—they ought also to concern themselves with the education of the whole student. They should proactively engage their colleagues across the campus to help ensure that business students come away from 4 years of acculturation in the university with exposure to a wider range of issues and ideas than is true of the typical business school graduate today.

In our view, business/management schools need to recognize and support the importance of breadth for breadth's sake; they should avoid the temptation to specify business school electives and requirements at the expense of opportunities for enrichment elsewhere in the university—the course in Greek mythology should not always be sacrificed on the altar of advanced electives in business.

Most universities have extraordinary faculty resources across a broad spectrum of colleges and departments—that is why they are universities, after all, and not mere vocational institutes. It is our conviction that these resources ought to be tapped far more by business/management schools than is now the case; business school students need not only to be assured of having access to, but also to be induced to partake of, their fair share of these resources. In order to maximize the student's exposure to elements outside the business school, it will be necessary to streamline the undergraduate curriculum by reducing the business proportion of the total (4-year) program to as close to 40% as possible— that is, to the lower limit of the amount required for AACSB accreditation. At the same time, to ensure that quality control is exercised so that students do not simply avoid challenge and rigor, we suggest a *prescribed* set of courses from which the business students would choose electives that address their needs for breadth within the context of their overall program goals.

While the preceding discussion pertains to the design and implementation of undergraduate curricula, we believe the MBA program also should be enriched in a similar fashion for those students not having had this kind of exposure to breadth in their baccalaureate degree programs. Business schools certainly can— and should—co-opt other areas of the university to provide some breadth-enhancing courses for the elective part of the MBA curriculum. In addition, some of the leading graduate schools of business could include in their admission policies, if they were so inclined, a requirement of a certain amount of breadth in the undergraduate curriculum as a prerequisite for matriculation. Such a stipulation, well-advertised among undergraduate schools, could have a salutary effect on the motivation of students to broaden the scope of their interests.

On the basis of our interviews with senior managers in a variety of corporations and professional organizations, we believe any move by business schools toward broadening the academic experience of their students beyond the technical and functional will find enthusiastic endorsement by many employers. We are less sanguine about our colleagues in academia—there are many hurdles: inertia, suspicion of motives, departmental prerogatives (''turf''), and the opposition of some faculty members who themselves may have been somewhat narrowly educated and hence unappreciative of the value of a broad education, among others. Despite these obstacles, we believe that, with artful management, much could be done and would be well worth doing.

Whereas our counterpart researchers (Gordon and Howell, and Pierson) in the late fifties showed how the incorporation of concepts from mathematics and the social and behavioral sciences into the business school curriculum could improve these schools, we submit that it is now time for business schools to turn for enrichment to virtually all sectors of the university. We feel that this is one of the most important challenges for business schools as they prepare for the 21st century: to transcend the analytical and the methodological and to incorporate an understanding of the importance of a broad, well-rounded education in the preparation of business students.

The External Organizational Environment

It has been traditional for business/management schools to place much of their curriculum emphasis on what can be called the "internal" organizational environment, that is, on how to improve the operating and financial effectiveness of the firm. For the most part, this heavy internal orientation seems to have drifted along without major change in the past 20 years or so. Furthermore, as we reported in Chapter 3, there did not seem to be extensive expressions of opinion in either the corporate or the academic world in favor of concentrating more attention on the external environment. We were surprised by this apparent lack of concern because we believe that there needs to be a much more concerted effort to achieve a stronger external focus than before in the business school milieu in general and in the curriculum in particular.

There needs to be a proportionate increase in attention to the external environment—governmental relations, societal trends, legal climate, international developments, among other areas—for the obvious reason that these events "outside" the organization are increasingly penetrating into the internal operations of the firm and affecting its core efficiency and effectiveness. Moreover, for the next couple of decades, at least, it hardly seems likely that such outside influences will be decreasing. If anything, they are likely to increase.

It will not be an easy task for business/management schools to increase their external focus relative to an internal one. For one thing, there is the ever-present but very real issue of what gets less attention if other areas such as these get more attention. Second, external areas are generally more "messy" and do not clearly belong to any single discipline. As anyone who has spent any time in business schools can attest, given competition for scarce resources (faculty positions, curriculum space, funding, etc.), specific discipline areas tend to win out over multidiscipline or interdiscipline areas. In the past, this has led to such external-environment–focused areas being accorded "second-class citizen" status in many schools, as illustrated, for example, by the frequent use of part-time faculty to teach courses in these subject matter areas and the generally greater difficulty of full-time faculty members in these areas obtaining tenure. A third and related problem, not easily solved, is how to bring to bear high-level, scholarly research on issues not rooted in traditional disciplinary fields and hence not particularly amenable to rigorous and well-accepted methodological approaches. As with the problem of developing a stronger cross-functional focus within business/management schools, the first step toward adjusting the internal/external balance is to make it a much more salient topic for discussion and concern among both academic and corporate leaders. Without more "push," this issue will simply get shunted aside vis-à-vis more familiar, more concrete, and more easily addressed topics.

The International Dimension

In Chapter 2 we noted in some detail what "futurists" have been predicting about the developing globalization of the world's economy, including such concepts as "gross world product" (GWP). A critical issue, at least as far as the United States is concerned, is what part this country will in fact play in this expanding level of international trade. And one important aspect of this issue is how the education provided by business/management schools will facilitate and support that role. As we pointed out in Chapter 2, futurists are not at all certain about whether the United States will be the dominant player in the future in a worldwide economy, and likewise, there is no guarantee that business school education will contribute significantly to ensuring that America will in fact have a major position. What is already certain, however, is that a very large opportunity has been presented to business/management schools *if* they can, and will, take advantage of it.

It is our impression from our extensive interviewing that business schools, collectively, have not yet become really serious about the international dimension of management. (There is a great irony in this state of affairs, inasmuch as some U.S. business schools "export" parts of their programs to foreign countries and thus have become multinational in this sense and, furthermore, almost all schools "import" foreign nationals into their BBA and MBA programs. It is in educating their own U.S. domestic students to become more internationally knowledgeable that American business schools appear to have made relatively little headway.) As we observed in Chapter 9, the worldwide dimension of business is mentioned in the preamble to the AACSB's Curriculum Standard (and in an accompanying Interpretation that states that "every student should be exposed to the international dimension through one or more elements of the curriculum"), but it is not, in fact, an explicitly identified element of that Standard. Thus the AACSB, as the accrediting organization for business education, has given recognition to this area but has not yet made it a central feature that is backed up by the enforcement power of a specific Standard component. Even more important, however, than what the AACSB and its accreditation process has done to date in the international area is what initiatives individual schools have, or have not, instituted on their own. Our interviews leave us with this strong impression: not much. There are definite exceptions in the case of certain schools, of course, but the general response across a large sample of schools leads us to the conclusion stated earlier, namely, that business schools have a long way to go before it can be said that the international dimension of business and management has become an *integral* part of their educational programs. A beginning has been made, but much more remains to be done.

Both our interview and survey data gave us cause for some degree of optimism that more attention will be given to this area in the near future, because both deans and faculty members rated it as one of the higher priorities for curriculum areas needing increased emphasis. Thus in the *academic* community we encountered widespread sentiment for strengthening business schools' approaches to the international dimension. As always, the sticky issue is how to do this. We mentioned in Chapter 3 that a debate has gone on for some time within business/management schools about whether the worldwide dimension should be dealt with in separate courses or as part of existing courses in various functional areas (marketing, finance, etc.). For the foreseeable future, it is likely that some schools will do the former and some (probably the majority) will do the latter. Regardless of how this is dealt with by individual schools, they will need to proceed in a more purposeful manner than most have demonstrated to date.

Also, there is an additional issue relating to this area that we believe needs to be addressed by business schools: how much they should expect their domestic U.S. students—especially at the MBA level—to know about the culture, history, geography, economy, and politics of at least one major foreign country or region in addition to their own. America's future managers need to understand the degree to which U.S. methods are unique rather than universal and the related ethnocentric character of their own attitudes. They need also to appreciate the pluralist nature of the culture in their own society—black America, for example, may be as divergent from mainstream American business culture as that of many countries geographically far-removed from the U.S. The question, then, is whether American business school graduates can afford to continue to be as parochial—as culturally and internationally naive—as they have been in the past. We doubt it.

The responsibility for greater emphasis on the global aspects of business in business school education resides primarily with academic institutions. However, the business community itself surely has some role to play, even if indirect. In this specific area it has a great potential for influencing business schools and their curricula, but insofar as we could determine it has not exercised this influence to any great degree—at least to date. The lack of attention to the international dimension was seldom, if ever, voluntarily raised by the corporate respondents as an important issue. To put this another way, one could ask, if the American corporate community does not seem more concerned about education for the international aspects of business, why should business schools themselves? Our response is that regardless of the low degree of current pressure from the business world for more attention to the international arena, business/management schools ought to be doing more. Here is an area where the educational community can *lead* the business community, at least many parts of it. Perhaps back in the 1970s and early 1980s American managers would have been more attuned to global realities sooner than they were if business/management schools and their graduates had pushed harder on the corporate sector to face these issues. In any event, for there to be a vastly strengthened global perspective in U.S. business schools, synergistic efforts will be required on the part of both leading educators and their schools, on the one hand, and influential corporations and their executives, on the other.

The Information/Service Society

In Chapter 2 we stressed two trends that already were occurring and which seem likely to accelerate in the years immediately ahead: the move from a primarily industrial to an increasingly service-oriented economy and the related development of a strong focus on the generation, distribution, and management of information. These trends are intertwined and tend to reinforce each other. Service organizations, by their nature, depend on information as an integral part of most of their operations, and the rapid availability of particular kinds of information allows for the expansion of existing organizations of this type as well as the creation of new ones. However, it would be a mistake to overlook the fact that the modern industrial (manufacturing) organization is also becoming much more information-intensive. That sector will still be significant in the future, and information likely will be as important to it as to the service sector. This means that virtually all organizations, whether industrial or service, will have rapidly expanding needs for managers who can understand, comprehend, and utilize information for increased performance and productivity.

For these reasons, we believe that these two trends will have serious implications for management education and development, implications that so far seem (based on impressions from our university-based interviews regarding curriculum matters) not to have been incorporated into the educational programs of business schools as thoroughly and deeply as they could and should be. This is particularly true with respect to the movement toward more information-intensive organizations. As our interviews strongly confirmed, in the past decade the typical response of business/management schools has been to hire management information systems (MIS) faculty and build MIS departments or units. (In fact, in some schools to date there has been precious little activity even of this type.) While this is certainly a necessary and appropriate step, it would be our contention that the trend toward an information-rich external and internal organizational environment requires a broader response than merely the insertion of one or two MIS courses into the curriculum.

This trend will affect almost *all* areas traditionally covered in business schools because it is increasingly affecting all aspects of the way in which business organizations operate. For example, the availability of data bases clearly affects financial and accounting operations as well as those of marketing; information-processing capabilities coupled with other advances in technology such as the development of robotics are revolutionizing production systems; also, the fact that more people throughout the organization will have potential access, via personal computers and other advanced technological devices, to an increasing array of types of information hitherto unavailable to them (in any feasible and rapid manner) will have crucial implications for how people interact in organizations and how human resources can be successfully mobilized for effective performance. Since these kinds of effects are pervasive across different functional areas, business/management schools in the next decade will need to take a hard look at *how an information orientation can be incorporated into the entire curriculum and into fundamental research activities*. This can be accomplished through a variety of approaches, including changes in the specific content of courses, decisions regarding faculty selection and development, and generally through an attitude and intent of permeating the curriculum with this orientation. Business schools will need to do this individually, as suits each school's particular set of circumstances and capabilities, and collectively as the nation's primary agent for educating individuals for future leadership roles in business organizations that will be functioning in a rapidly changing and information-saturated society.

Cross-Functional Integration

A major issue that was discussed at some length in the Commentary section of Chapter 3 will be reemphasized here: the need for business/management education to provide sufficient attention—in the curriculum and in other activities—to an *integrated* approach to problems that cut across specific functional areas. As we stated in Chapter 3, it was our strong impression from our visits to a sample of more than sixty schools representing a wide range of types of institutions that (as in the past) there continues to be an overfocus on traditional functional areas as separate entities and a corresponding underfocus on how knowledge based on these specific functional areas can be put together to solve the complex, multifaceted problems in today's business world.

Business schools' primary response to the need for cross-functional integration has been to require a single and (by now universal) "capstone" business policy/strategy course that students take in their final term in the program (whether at the BBA or MBA level). Is this enough? We think not. For one thing, the increasing attention being given to entrepreneurial activities—at the national level and at the level of individual student interests—demands a more integrated, cross-functional approach. Anyone involved in developing a small, dynamic, and growing business cannot expect to work solely on marketing matters, for example, nor expect to have a lengthy career totally within the finance or production areas. The entrepreneurial problems to be faced will not come neatly wrapped in distinct functional packages, nor will the knowledge to solve them come from only a single functional area of expertise. A trend toward entrepreneurism, however, is only one of the forces pushing in the direction of a more integrated focus. The changing world described in Chapter 2 and especially the increasingly information/service-oriented economy and society discussed earlier constitute powerful pressures for developing a wholly revamped approach to this issue.

Obviously, modifying the curriculum is one direct way to meet this challenge. However, given the finite length of any program, whether at the undergraduate or master's level, the number of feasible curriculum options is clearly limited. One alternative would be simply to require students to take other integrative courses in addition to the capstone course. This would have the associated effect of reducing the number of available elective courses, which may or may not be desirable. The more important pedagogical issue, however, is the question of what the substance or content of those courses would be. It is beyond the scope of this project to define that content, but certainly there are a variety of possibilities that need to be actively pursued, but which would not have to be identical from school to school.

Another option might be to revise some of the existing functional courses to include more integrative material. However, this would create serious problems in how to build in enough of the necessary functional material and still have time left for including meaningful coverage of integrative issues. The same would be true for an alternative that proposed substituting some integrative courses for functional courses. In essence, these and other possible approaches to incorporating more cross-functional integration into the curriculum require careful consideration of (1) what the value of such an increased amount of attention to integration would be, (2) what would be traded off (i.e., reduced or eliminated) against it, and (3) how the change in relative focus would be accomplished. What is clear, however, is that the curriculum needs to reflect, in some way or another, a greater level of cross-functional integration than is currently the case in order to match the multifunctional nature of business problems.

We should note that while the curriculum may be the main vehicle for bringing a stronger integrative focus to management education, it is not the only approach. The attitudes, scope of knowledge, and interests of the faculty, also are important variables. The research activities of a school—in terms of the types of problems the faculty choose to tackle—represent one means for a school to highlight for its students and for the business community how functional areas of expertise and knowledge can be combined to increase individual and organizational performance and effectiveness. Likewise, faculty members can broaden the focus of their own field of teaching. Many might profitably spend some time attending classes of their colleagues to find out what is going on in other subject areas in their school. As one highly respected faculty member with whom we talked commented: "If I were the Ford Foundation today, I would seriously consider offering schools grants so that faculty could apply to buy out half of their teaching time; this time to be used not for research, but for attending classes of their colleagues in order to see for themselves where material overlaps and connects." We think this is an excellent idea. In any event, however, the important point, in our view, is that first, the issue of cross-functional integration be recognized as one for substantial attention and that second, it be addressed from multiple angles.

"Soft" (People) Skills

Developments occurring over at least the past decade or so indicate strongly that the very nature of organizations, particularly business organizations, is changing and the way they are carrying out their work is changing. They are becoming less hierarchical, which among other things means that lateral relationships are becoming at least as important as the traditionally emphasized superior/subordinate vertical relationships. Likewise, organizations are becoming, on average, more participative with diminished reliance on the exercise of "top down" autocratic authority. Such tendencies, which probably become accentuated in service organizations, have the effect of increasing the need for effective "soft" (i.e., people) skills even more than has been the case in the past.

As has been stressed at several points in this report (particularly in Chapters 3 and 4), this need—as it relates to management education—has been documented repeatedly throughout our data. Corporate respondents showed an overwhelming preponderance of opinion that behaviorally oriented subject matter should receive more attention in the curriculum. Deans and faculty members themselves perceive a gap between how much "soft" skills and personal characteristics are currently emphasized in the curriculum versus how much they "should be." Also, and perhaps most important, the corporate sector gives business school graduates relatively low ratings in terms of the strength (or lack thereof) of their leadership and interpersonal skills. Having said all this, however, it must be reiterated that while the corporate community wants more emphasis on the development of these skills, they do *not* want less emphasis on the development of analytical and quantitative skills.

Although there may be a fair degree of unanimity that business/management schools ought to endeavor to increase their students' behavioral skills, the task is daunting. Among a number of important problems in doing so are the following: First, students arrive at business schools (whether as juniors in the undergraduate BBA program or as entering MBA graduate students) with a considerable amount of prior conditioning—some 19 to 20 years, at a minimum. Thus the amount and nature of their skills in these areas have been affected by a lifetime (though usually of less than three decades' duration) of experiences. This can be contrasted with, for example, a student's (lack of) prior exposure to the principles of accounting, which are more easily imparted in a 2-year time span. This means, basically, that it is not an easy matter for the educational program of a business school to have an impact on the area of "soft" skills. Second, a business/management school has only 2 years (technically, about 21 months on a full-time basis) to make such an impact. This is not a long period in which to achieve a lasting change. Third, the educational program in a business school has to accomplish a number of other important instructional objectives and cannot devote an overly large amount of time to work on this type of skill development, even if it wanted to. Finally, and perhaps most critical, is the question of whether there are sufficiently well-validated and feasible methods available to the faculty to bring about a demonstrable increase in such skills as leadership and effective interpersonal influence. On this last point, however, it appears that some corporations, the military, and other organizations have achieved at least some success in improving these skills, so it would appear that the task is not an impossible one.

Faced with these obstacles that hinder any easy and quick solutions to strengthening these skills, business schools will need to be both aggressive and inventive in attacking the overall problem. One straightforward approach would be to examine course offerings to determine if there are opportunities in the classroom situation to focus on such skills to a greater extent than is now the case, through various assignments such as term projects and in-class presentations and other interpersonal activities. A second potential major avenue of attack could be through out-of-class activities related to the educational program, especially if they can be connected to classroom situations where these real-world experiences can be examined with the assistance of an instructor (and other students) such that guided and focused learning takes place. We found considerable sentiment, for example, in the business world for business/management schools to devote more attention to arranging for internships (paid or unpaid) for those students lacking substantial work experience. There are a number of feasibility problems—not the least of which is expense in time and effort in locating such positions and in matching students and firms—connected with this approach, but it probably has not been exploited to as full an extent as possible in many schools. Related to this is the possibility of greater use of co-op arrangements, where students go to school and then work during alternating terms. Such arrangements, again, take considerable effort by schools and a high level of cooperation by companies—the positions have to be made available—and therefore, they may not be appropriate in many circumstances. Nevertheless, some schools—especially those in urban areas—have used this method with considerable reported success, and it may offer wider possibilities than many schools realize.

Finally, an approach basically open to all schools is to provide increased incentives for students to participate in various student-run organizations and other extracurricular activities that furnish a variety of types of opportunities to build leadership and interpersonal skills. Our interview observations would lead us to believe that this is an underutilized option that schools could promote much more vigorously. Indeed, to focus more on developing student leadership skills will itself require the exercise of some degree of leadership on the part of the schools themselves.

There is one other important point that needs to be emphasized regarding the development of "soft" skills: The business world cannot expect all such development to have been accomplished in the 2 years that students have in their BBA or MBA programs. Such development is a classic example of a *lifelong learning need,* and firms will have to look to various types of postdegree executive education activities in combination with planned work assignment experiences to provide this kind of additional skill enhancement. The education received at the undergraduate or master's level can initiate the process, but it will take a commitment on the part of both individuals and their companies to continue it. Here, again, we see a strong link between management education at the front end and at later career stages. "Soft" skills indeed tend to become soft unless continually honed by a variety of recurring developmental activities and programs.

4 FACULTY: PREPARATION AND DEVELOPMENT

In many respects, business school faculties are seen as doing a good job by those within and outside the university setting. As detailed in Chapter 5, faculty members in business schools receive relatively favorable ratings both from provosts, whose job it is to deal with faculty throughout all parts of the campus, and from those individuals in the business community most closely connected with business/management schools, namely, BAC members. This general assessment, as we noted, is in marked contrast to the situation 25 years ago, as described in the two Foundation reports. Business schools collectively, it would appear, have made definite and commendable progress in upgrading the quality of their faculties during these past several decades. Despite this seemingly rosy picture, however, we believe that there is definite room for making additional improvements. In fact, we believe that it is time—past time, probably—for doctorate-granting business/management schools to take a hard look at how they are preparing Ph.D. students for their future roles as faculty members, and furthermore, it is also time for *all* schools to examine carefully how they can contribute to the further subsequent development of new faculty members once they are hired. Both these issues were discussed at some length in the Commentary section of Chapter 5, but the basic points bear reemphasizing here because of their importance.

Preparation: Modifying Doctoral Education

Our observations and interviews during the course of this project convinced us of the absolutely critical necessity for the AACSB or some other appropriate organization to commission a thorough and comprehensive study of doctoral-level education taking place within business schools. (Of course, business/management schools do not employ only those Ph.D.s educated in these schools, but also those trained in adjacent relevant disciplines such as economics, psychology, mathematics, and the like; however, the one segment of doctoral education they have the power to influence directly is that provided by business schools themselves. Thus such a study can be influential in relation to a large portion of the source of supply of new faculty members, even if it is not the total source.)

This kind of new study—or, at least, a national conference on the subject—is needed, in our opinion, since it appears, based on the indirect evidence we obtained, that new doctorates are emerging who are in many cases unduly specialized and lacking a sufficient appreciation of the complexities of business problems that extend beyond the narrow confines of their own discipline or functional area. (This problem is exacerbated, of course, by the increasing number of faculty members trained in other disciplines who do not even have the benefit of a business school socialization process.) We think that this particular issue is especially important because it also relates directly to the issue mentioned previously in this chapter concerning whether business school faculty members—especially younger and newer ones—are as well prepared as they should be to support, through both their teaching and their research, increased attention to cross-functional integration. Progress on the latter will be slow unless faculty members have a strong sense of its importance and well-grounded ideas about how to bring it about.

Insofar as we could detect, there seem to be few bold new initiatives currently taking place in business school Ph.D. programs. At least, we can state that if these kinds of innovations were being undertaken, they were seldom mentioned spontaneously in our interviews with the "producing" schools, nor were they mentioned by "employing" schools when discussing the merits of their recently hired faculty. Thus, if truly new approaches are occurring, they are well disguised. Assuming this is the case, we believe that doctorate-producing business/management schools could usefully begin to look at ways to break out of the conventional Ph.D. program mold—without having to sacrifice the development of rigorous research capabilities. Examples of features of doctoral programs that could benefit from some experimentation would include the development of greater cross-functional capabilities, significantly increased awareness of the international dimensions of business, and, for those Ph.D. students lacking it, exposure to appropriate full-time work experience (e.g., ideally as a result of meeting some type of entrance requirement in this regard or, alternatively, through 1-year internships or a co-op type of work/study arrangement after being enrolled in a Ph.D. program). This latter type of requirement, if implemented, could help produce a new type of Ph.D. graduate, one with "hybrid vigor" that combined the analytical sophistication of the typical Ph.D. program with the sharpened and broadened perspective of real-world work experience. In any event, these are only some of the elements of business doctoral programs that need fresh thought and action.

Development: Different Tasks for Different Schools

As with managers, the needed development of faculty members does not stop with the completion of their preemployment education. However, as we observed in Chapter 5, it is an interesting—if unfortunate—paradox that many business/management schools are heavily involved in providing management development programs for executives but themselves have drifted along without systematic development programs for their own faculties. Our data indicated that faculty members, across all categories of schools, believe strongly that more development efforts by their schools are needed than are now being provided. This should become a major agenda item for schools in the future. Presumably, the *lifelong learning perspective* surely applies as much to business school faculty members as it does to corporate executives.

Clearly, specific faculty development needs will vary by type of school, and thus there will be different developmental tasks facing different schools. Judging by the survey results from deans of Category I schools, the typical school of this type expects to put *relatively* more emphasis on *teaching* in the future in order to bring about a more effective teaching/research balance. Since faculty members in such schools have been selected and subsequently rewarded for their research skills and accomplishments, the further development of capabilities in this latter realm is not the primary challenge. For schools in the upper part of Category II, many of whom have strong aspirations to match the scholarly reputations and visibility of Category I schools, the developmental tasks might be several. The major emphasis likely would be on further improvement of the research proficiencies of faculty, but a strong secondary emphasis could also be on additional enhancement of teaching process skills.

In contrast, for those schools nearer the accredited/nonaccredited margin (i.e., the lower part of Category II and the upper part of Category III), where direct involvement by faculty in research activities plays a smaller role, the urgent developmental tasks might be to help their faculty members to be able to keep abreast of the most recent research advancements in their field. This could be accomplished in a variety of ways, such as individualized study leaves or opportunities to work directly with faculty members at other schools on particular research projects. Not only would this serve the primary purpose of helping to keep classroom course contents *au courant*, but it also would fulfill a secondary purpose of maintaining some type of involvement with research activities. For those schools in Category III that are strictly teaching-oriented and have no immediate accreditation aspirations, developmental activities could focus almost exclusively on an array of efforts to facilitate improved and strengthened course content and delivery. Overall, it seems apparent that there is no lack of developmental needs for faculty regardless of the type of school in which they are located—whether at the most elite or the most humble—and that any efforts directed at responding to such needs must be appropriately adapted to the specifically identified mission and objectives of the particular school.

5   AACSB ACCREDITATION: IMPACT AND POTENTIAL

At the time of the Ford and Carnegie reports in 1959, AACSB accreditation was relatively impotent—standards were vague and enforcement mechanisms were for all practical purposes nonexistent. The primary impact was on schools newly admitted to AACSB membership. The reports, propitiously timed, found fertile ground. They served as catalysts to galvanize action toward reform along the lines then recommended by many individual deans and groups. Since that time, standards have been delineated more sharply and have been enforced to a much greater degree. In general, the quality of higher education for management and business has surely improved, and we believe that AACSB accreditation has contributed in a major way to this improvement.

However, we also believe that while AACSB accreditation has had a definite positive impact on the overall quality of its accredited members in toto, there are two important areas of further potential which need to be addressed. The first is the fact that the predominant influence of AACSB accreditation is largely limited to those schools still at the threshold level and to (relatively weaker) schools striving for accreditation. Once a school is well established as an accredited member, the systematic incentive provided by accreditation to expend the resources to reach still higher levels of quality declines in intensity.

The second area of accreditation needing to be addressed, in our opinion, is the ignorance of, or indifference to (which could be caused by ignorance), AACSB accreditation by the corporate world and the general public. There appears to be little or no impact on corporate recruiting patterns or choices of tuition-reimbursed programs for employees, nor has accreditation had much influence on the general public, most of whom are not likely to know the difference between general institutional and AACSB accreditation. This problem is a serious one, since one of the major purposes of AACSB accreditation is to inform the relevant publics of the distinction between accredited and nonaccredited business programs.

We suggest two complementary mechanisms as a means of improving accreditation in these two respects: First, the creation of an additional threshold, with standards significantly above the entry level, and second, a notational scheme for providing key information about a business school.

The Need for an Additional Accreditation Incentive to Induce Higher Quality

The impact of accreditation at the threshold level is clear and impressive. However, once explicit Standards have been met and accreditation has been attained, there may be little additional incentive for many schools to continue to improve. Ironically, the threshold may in fact become a ceiling—an ultimate target to be perpetually focused upon rather than a stepping stone to higher elevations of quality. Under these circumstances the accreditation Standards become a constraint rather than a stimulant; satisfying, rather than maximizing, behavior results.

To help overcome the potential *limiting* nature of threshold Standards, other incentives for achieving excellence have to be devised. The AACSB has not been unaware of the problem, and has moved in recent years toward a more consultative approach to accreditation—as opposed to a more narrowly conceived audit process—i.e., the review process not only determines whether a school has met the minimum set of requirements, but also provides advice as to areas of relative weakness and how these weaknesses might be overcome. However, the impact of advice, no matter how well conceived or how persuasively presented, is unlikely to match the motivational whip of explicit Standards. We believe, therefore, that the AACSB should explore the possibility of establishing Standards beyond the entry-level threshold—in effect a second (higher) threshold.

We recognize that the introduction of a second threshold will not be without problems of design, implementation and acceptance. The specification of new, higher-level Standards will doubtless pose serious challenges but at the same time can provide the opportunity to identify new indices of high quality—e.g., outcome measures of performance as opposed to input measures. Despite the obstacles, and fully cognizant of the misgivings (if not outright hostility) this notion will arouse in many deans, we believe that the second threshold idea holds promise as a powerful device to motivate a significant number of schools to aim for higher levels of achievement than they might otherwise attempt to attain.

We realize, of course, that accreditation is by no means the only factor influencing the quality levels of business schools. Competition—the marketplace—obviously plays a powerful overall role in determining quality. However, competition alone does not necessarily ensure the motivation to achieve continual improvement and in fact in some situations may have the reverse effect. A school, under certain circumstances, may maximize revenues and volume by reducing its own standards of quality; there is, unfortunately, a market for low-quality "easy to get in and easy to get through" programs. In short, competition by itself does not guarantee high quality; accreditation is needed along with it. As we have pointed out in Chapter 9, a few schools at the top of the system are indeed driven by competitive forces to strive for higher quality as a way of organizational life, but that condition does not hold for all—or even most—schools. It is this larger group of schools, below the top but well above the current accreditation threshold, that could be strongly influenced in a positive direction of increased excellence if a second threshold were to be adopted.

The Need for More Information

The current system of all-or-nothing accreditation reveals precious little beyond the fact that a school met bare minimum standards the last time it was reviewed. Much more information could readily be made available to the public than is currently provided in the AACSB membership directory: Examples (in addition to the notation as to whether the member school is accredited or non-accredited) might include factual data such as the size of the school and its admissions standards; whether part-time or off-campus degree programs are available; the dates of the last accreditation visitation and the next one scheduled; and demographic data about the faculty—how many full-time, part-time, etc.

Limited qualitative judgments (by outside reviewers) also might be noted, such as the adequacy (or lack thereof) of computer and library facilities. We appreciate the potential risks in publishing subjective judgments—even informed ones—but nonetheless believe that AACSB accreditation falls short of the mark if it does not provide enough information to allow a prospective student or employer to draw inferences about the nature and quality of a school's programs beyond the mere fact of threshold accreditation status.

If these two measures—a second threshold and more disclosure—were to be adopted, we believe that AACSB accreditation could improve its capacity to induce quality improvement by providing not only an incentive for already-strong schools to improve still further, but also an improved service to both member schools and the public through recognition of superior accomplishment and the dissemination of information.

6 MANAGERIAL LIFELONG LEARNING IN THE FUTURE: A CHALLENGE FOR BOTH BUSINESS SCHOOLS AND CORPORATIONS

A basic objective for this Project, as determined by its sponsors, was to explore how university business/management schools, corporations, and other potential providers could improve their contributions to meeting the lifelong learning needs of managers. The Project objective was based on the simple premise that the development of managers cannot stop with the completion of the traditional front-end degree (BBA or MBA) but, instead, must be continuous—must be, in effect, lifelong. As reported in Part 3, we found considerable evidence to support this contention, in terms of the perspectives of senior executives responsible for corporate policies and line managers' own views of their needs. The necessity is irrefutable and growing increasingly stronger, if our data are any indication. The issue, however, is how to meet this need effectively, and in our opinion, to do so will represent a major future challenge for both business schools and corporations, because at the present time this need is being met only partially and inconsistently at best.

For business/management schools, the first critical challenge is to decide how postdegree executive education/management development programs should relate to their regular undergraduate and master's degree programs, that is, what *role* EE/MD programs should play in their total educational operations. There seems little doubt that in the future executive education/management development will constitute a larger segment of the overall programs of many business schools. Unfortunately, however, we found little evidence of any systematic planning and attention on the part of business/management schools concerning how to prepare for this increased need of managers and corporations for lifelong learning. Indeed, this constituted one of the clearest examples of business school ''drift'' that we encountered in the entire project. Schools need to determine explicitly where they want to be positioned in this type of enterprise. The decision will be different for different schools—with some choosing not to take part at all—depending on their mission and their distinctive comparative advantages vis-à-vis other schools, but the decision should be faced directly and with a good deal of thought and planning.

A second challenge for business/management schools in the area of EE/MD is to take advantage of such programs as potential *instruments for change*. What is learned (institutionally speaking) by undertaking these types of educational endeavors can be used to provide fresh ideas for curriculum restructuring and, in particular, for modified or improved instructional methods. If there is one thing that some schools and individual faculty members have discovered, it is that teaching methods that may be suitable for undergraduates and relatively inexperienced MBAs may not be at all appropriate for adult students who have moderate or greater amounts of real world experience. While methods suitable for the former may not work with the latter, the reverse is not necessarily true. That is, some different and effective approaches to delivering material in executive education programs may well transfer to teaching traditional BBAs and MBAs. Therefore, EE/MD activities provide a potentially significant opportunity for improving instruction in both degree and postdegree programs. In fact, one could argue that teaching executives is one kind of faculty development experience that should be insisted upon for any teacher in a professional school.

A third challenge facing business schools in general in the EE/MD area is whether they have the appropriate mix of faculty skills to instruct in these programs. The asking of this question does not imply that there is a "right" and a "wrong" type of faculty for this type of instructional activity. Rather, it is concerned with the extent to which faculty are *well prepared* to be effective instructors in such programs. Our data indicated that only a relatively modest percentage of faculty members were currently capable of performing effectively in these programs. In order to increase these percentages, especially in those schools that decide they want to make major efforts in executive education, the issue will be primarily one of development rather than selection. To be able to provide the quality instruction that adult learners and their corporate sponsors will demand in EE/MD programs, many schools will need to increase substantially their investments in faculty development in this particular kind of teaching activity with its special set of requirements. This will be no small task, and some schools are not well prepared for its magnitude or scope.

A fourth challenge that faces business/management schools is the question of how responsive they want to be to specific corporate needs. These can include highly specialized programs for particular industries or categories of companies as well as some companies' preference for contract programs designed solely for their own managers. A few schools in our interview sample indicated that they already are quite willing to attempt to accommodate any reasonable requests of this nature. Some other schools took almost the complete opposite position: They will not tailor-make courses to suit only one company and instead will offer an array of predetermined programs and leave it up to individual firms to decide whether or not to send their managers to such programs. Regardless of which route a school chooses to take, it appears, based on our corporate interviews, highly likely that in the future, as companies generally become more management development–oriented, they will tend to want increasingly specialized and company-specific services. Schools will need to plan for how, or if, they want to participate in this market.

A final challenge for university business/management schools in the EE/MD area is a major one—namely, increased competition from both corporate in-house programs and, especially, other independent (i.e., noncorporate, nonuniversity) third-party providers. We have elaborated on this issue in Chapter 12 and will not repeat those details here, except to reiterate that business schools cannot take for granted that they will necessarily share the expected increase in demand for EE/MD programs in the same proportion as they share the current demand. As the advertising slogan (paraphrased) states, "They will have to *earn* it."

As we stressed above and in earlier chapters (particularly Chapters 10 and 11), the challenges connected with managers' needs for lifelong learning confront not only university-based business schools but also companies themselves. The basic challenge for corporations and firms emerges from the fact, as documented in our survey and interview data, that managers themselves believe that they should be participating in systematic development activities to a much greater extent than they are currently. They want "more," and companies will need to decide whether they in fact need more and, if so, how best to provide this additional, planned development. No matter what decisions individual companies make with regard to these questions, one thing seems certain, as we emphasized in Chapter 10: on-the-job experiences *alone* are highly *un*likely to provide sufficient development opportunities for most managers in most companies. The tasks faced by managers and the environments in which their organizations operate are changing too fast and to too great an extent to rely solely on a series of job assignments to provide the needed development. Some firms have already heard this message and are acting accordingly, but others seemed (to us, at least) to be glaringly insensitive to the developmental needs of their managers in ways that not only hinder their progress, but also greatly handicap the abilities of the organization to compete in the contemporary and future world of business.

Heading the list of specific challenges facing corporations in deciding how to meet managerial development needs is the absolute necessity of first determining what those needs are. Although many of the companies we visited and 70% of the companies responding to our survey question in this area reported that they do carry out systematic needs analyses, there were numerous exceptions (amounting to almost 30% of the companies in the survey sample). For these latter companies as well as for some of the former, the failure to carry out systematic and thorough management development needs analyses frequently has resulted in what some managers have characterized as "smorgasbord" approaches—various programs and courses sponsored by the company without any coherent plan as to how the total set was designed to meet the organization's needs. To change from a smorgasbord to a well-designed and integrated menu with clear objectives is a challenge that more companies, in our opinion, ought to take on.

Corporations, as we pointed out in Chapter 11, become involved with EE/MD activities both as providers and as consumers. Challenges in the former area revolve around the issue of the extent to which a company wants to meet its managerial and executive development needs through in-house programs. While such programs have certain clear-cut advantages, notably that they can be geared to the specific needs of the company, they also have disadvantages, such as the overhead expense of maintaining a sufficient set of in-house instructional resources and the danger of too much institutional inbreeding that could cause a lack of innovative ideas from the external environment (including those from other organizations). Thus, as discussed in Chapter 11, in-house programs are appealing, but they do represent something short of a panacea. As consumers, the primary challenge is for corporations to become more sophisticated and knowledgeable about the programs they are buying and how those programs will meet specified objectives. Our interview data indicated that there has been progress on this front over the past couple of decades, but it has been uneven: Some firms have become very smart consumers—probably more so than many business schools recognize—but many others have a long way to go toward becoming wise purchasers of this important, and costly, product.

One other conclusion concerning managerial lifelong learning that should be emphasized is the growing role of the so-called third-party providers—consulting firms, individual consultants, firms specializing in providing management development, and the like. Given our findings, we expect that their role will grow considerably in the future and that this will have serious implications for both corporations and university business/management schools. For the former it will provide increased options in choosing how to meet the developmental needs of their managers. For the latter it will generate healthy competition and force business schools to be more cognizant of market needs and their abilities to capitalize on the particular advantages that can be provided in university-based programs. The overriding challenge for the third-party providers themselves, as brought out in Chapter 13, can be summed up in a single term: *quality control.* They will need to bring to bear mutual influence within this set of providers to help reduce the incidence of occasionally shoddy and inferior programs put on by a few who tend to mar the image and reputation of the total group.

Viewed from an overall perspective, the picture for managerial lifelong learning in the future is composed of three elements: the increasing need that managers will have for such learning, the role of corporations in responding to these needs (i.e., their consumer role), and the tripartite role of corporations, university business/management schools, and other (third-party) individuals and organizations in providing the developmental programs. One legitimately might ask whether in the future it will be possible, on a national basis, to achieve greater coordination and greater synergy among all these elements. While this might be theoretically possible, we strongly doubt that it will be attainable in any practical sense. There is simply too much and too varied demand on the part of both individual managers and corporations and, likewise, too many suppliers, whether they are the companies themselves, universities, consultants, or other providers.

No group of providers, nor any particular individual provider, is likely to agree to restricting its domain. Nor, in our opinion, should they. Our view is that the nation's management development needs can best be met through vigorous competition among a very large potential set of providers coupled with rigorous (i.e., sophisticated) selection standards and program evaluations by those who pay the bills for this type of service. In any event, the free market may be the only feasible method of ensuring an adequate supply of the ''right''

MD product at the "right" price in the "right" supply. In short, let many flow-ers bloom! And, as to potential inefficiencies in the total "system" supply of provider resources, the most that can be hoped for in reducing them by means of cross/provider coordination will probably lie in making increased informa-tion available to all concerned regarding corporate and managerial needs, on the one hand, and the developmental resources that can be supplied by the various individual providers and categories of providers, on the other. Whether or not this will occur is difficult to predict, but a safe presumption is that the total picture relating to managerial lifelong learning is likely to get more com-plex, rather than less so, in the future.

7 TOWARD THE FUTURE: THE CORPORATE COMMUNITY, THE AACSB, AND THE BUSINESS SCHOOL

Management education in the United States is primarily the responsibility of university business/management schools, and management development is pri-marily the responsibility of corporations. However, each type of institution also has a role to play in the other arena as well. In this final section we focus on the tasks that each faces in the coming 10- to 15-year period in the quest to improve MED. In addition, we also include a discussion of the challenges that confront the AACSB—the national reviewer of, and spokesperson for, higher education for business and management.

The Corporate Community

The corporate community as a whole has at least four important roles to play in management education and development: As a consumer, as a provider, as a "voice," and as a supporter. Each of these roles is discussed below, with particular emphasis on opportunities for enhanced involvement and contribu-tions in the future.

Consumer Role   A key corporate connection to management education and development is obviously in its consumer role, which can be further subdivided into several types of consumer functions. The principal one, of course, involves the hiring of graduates of business schools, both BBAs and MBAs. In this par-ticular consumer role, a significant challenge for the future for corporations and other firms is to increase their ability to match their hiring needs with the differentiated student products being turned out by different business schools. It was our clear impression (from our corporate interviews) that many firms were not making effective strategic decisions about what types of student prod-ucts they really needed or could use effectively. Hence they often seemed nei-ther to have a clear rationale for choosing the particular set of schools at which to recruit or from which to hire nor reliable information about which schools were producing which types of graduates. Moreover, in the absence of sound information, many companies have resorted to using indices of questionable validity, such as national rankings based on subjective impressions unverified by objective data. Therefore, it would appear that corporations and firms need to become more sophisticated in their recruiting practices by informing themselves to a greater extent than is now the case about the student product they are buying from business schools. This would include aspects such as the curriculum students are exposed to, the school's AACSB accreditation status, and information about student aptitudes specifically relevant to the types of jobs (and actual—not idealized—job characteristics) a company is able to offer. With graduates across a range of business/management schools possibly becoming even more differentiated in the future, this will intensify the need for corporations to become particularly cost-effective in their whole approach to recruiting.

Another MED consumer function of corporations is the (partial or total) "purchase" of particular degree programs for individual employees through the mechanism of tuition reimbursement. As we have noted elsewhere at several places in this report, many firms are remarkably blasé and unconcerned about what kind of a business/management school degree program qualifies for reimbursement. There is little or no attention to a program's AACSB accreditation status or to any other indications of the type or quality of a program that an employee chooses to attend and for which reimbursement is virtually automatic. The challenge for the future in this area for the business community would seem to be to put more effort into obtaining appropriate information about particular programs so that some estimation can be made of the value received for the not inconsiderable money invested in tuition reimbursement.

A third corporate consumer role that relates to MED has already been discussed in Chapters 10 and 11 and earlier in this chapter: the role of purchaser of nondegree executive education/management development programs, whether provided in-house or externally. As we emphasized, the key task in future years in this area will be to learn how to respond in a cost-effective manner to the increasing needs—and demands—of managers for formal developmental programs. Some companies will acquire the expertise necessary to spend their dollars wisely in this area and others will end up wasting money and other resources needlessly and with little to show for their efforts and expenditures.

Provider Role   While companies primarily play a consumer role in connection with the array of MED activities, they also can—and many do—fulfill at least one important provider function—namely, conducting in-house management development programs. Again, we have discussed this corporate provider role previously in this chapter and in Chapter 11, so we need only to reiterate here that the challenge for a given firm is to decide whether it wants to be a direct provider and, if so, how to do this efficaciously. Here, as in the EE/MD consumer role, companies' opportunities to misallocate resources are numerous.

One other possible corporate provider role for the future ought to be mentioned: providing academic degree programs at the BBA or MBA levels. At the outset of this project, several knowledgeable individuals suggested that this might become a "wave of the future" and therefore urged us to investigate this nascent development in some detail because of its potential significant consequences. Our corporate interviews, however, strongly indicate to us that this is *not* likely to become a major phenomenon in the near future (at least the next decade). While there are a few firms that are already offering degree programs, these are on very limited bases and for particular categories of clientele. Most companies (including the largest ones in our sample) were fairly vehement in asserting that they wanted to leave *degree* programs to the academic institutions because undertaking such operations is simply not a good use of their own resources or capabilities. Therefore, although anything is possible, we would be highly surprised to find that this—the corporate offering of accredited degree programs in business—becomes anything like a major trend or development before the turn of the century.

Active (Potentially Major) Voice   Ever since the establishment of the first American business school more than 100 years ago, managers and executives of business firms have been speaking out about what business schools should be doing and how they could be doing those things better. At times, as in the 1950s, corporate concerns with the quality of business education have reinforced similar concerns inside universities and consequently have contributed to forces for productive and needed change. In other instances, the corporate voice, at least as exemplified in the statements of some individuals, has at times been rather strident and thus the opinions expressed have often been dismissed— rightly or wrongly—by the intended academic (business school faculty) audience as, at best, overstated and, at worst, uninformed. The net effect over the years has been to create a certain kind of tension between the corporate community and the academic business school community—a tension that often could be labeled creative but which sometimes could be termed unproductive.

Looking to the future, there seems little doubt that the practicing world of business and its leaders have the potential to affect business education in areas such as curriculum, instruction, and research. For this to happen, however, will require more coordinated corporate efforts than we have seen in the recent past and a willingness to engage in a reciprocal influence process with the academic world. To the extent that such a corporate voice is dispersed, discordant, and inconsistent, it is unlikely to be heard. To the extent that it is informed, reasonably coherent, and thoughtful, it not only will be heard, but indeed can be a powerful and constructive stimulus for major change.

Potential Supporter   A final avenue for corporations to influence business education, if they choose to do so, is through their support, both moral and financial. The former category would include service by individual executives on business school advisory committees, guest appearances in classes, and the like. These types of activities have become more common in recent years to the apparent benefit of both the schools and the corporate community. Among other things, where this mutual outreach by managers and executives, on the one hand, and by schools, on the other hand, has occurred, it has been well received by both sides. It appears to us likely that such activities will—and no doubt should—increase rather than decrease.

Another area of nonfinancial corporate support for business education that remains largely underdeveloped and undernourished is cooperation in supplying data for research projects. One excellent example of the type of cooperation by the business sector, and where the progress of academic research can be influenced positively on a substantive level, is represented by the Strategic Planning Institute. This institute was established through the efforts of major corporations to be the custodian of financial and operating information on individual business units. The resulting data base (the well-known PIMS data), which is continuing to be supplied on a regular and ongoing basis by these companies, has been a boon to academic scholars in finance and corporate strategy and has facilitated important research advances of great value to the business community. Unfortunately, this is not necessarily a typical example of the business sector's proaction in (or even positive reaction to requests for) making data available about their operations that would aid business school researchers in their efforts to develop new knowledge. If the quality of such research is to be improved and become increasingly addressed to important issues relevant to both the academic and the business communities, greater corporate cooperation (both at the institutional and individual executive level) will be required.

Financial support by the business community for the business school, at least as seen by the schools themselves, has been definitely increasing. In recent years, for example, there have been extremely generous gifts by corporate-connected individuals and foundations for certain business schools, especially with respect to funds for "brick and mortar" improvements. However, one area of business school operations that seems not to have received much (relative) attention from the corporate community in the way of concrete financial support is faculty research. There are probably a number of reasons for this state of affairs, but certainly one of the main ones is the outright skepticism—as documented and discussed in Chapter 7—that many top corporate executives have concerning the value (to the business community) of such research and its findings to date. As expounded by a number of our (most thoughtful) corporate respondents, it is not the idea per se of business schools doing research that is seen by them as the problem, but rather the types and importance of the issues being addressed in the research and their perceived (lack of) relevance for the fundamental challenges faced by the modern business organization. (See Chapter 7 for the details of this line of reasoning.)

In our view, however, major players in the business community, those in the position to commit financial resources in the support of business school research, need to give consideration to whether various kinds of consortium efforts across a set of companies could—and should—be put together for major projects that could have significant impact. If the business community does not provide such funds, who will? The federal government? Highly unlikely. Wealthy individual donors? Again, unlikely, since their efforts most often get channeled into such tangible items as endowed professorships and new buildings. Foundations (i.e., those not connected with corporations)? Possibly, for very specific (and often limited in scope) projects, but this is not likely to be a source of widespread, sustained support. That leaves the business community as the major potential source of financial support for important and critical business research projects. In summary, it would appear that the relevant professional community for business schools, the managerial and corporate world, needs to assess what role it *wants* to play, and is *willing* to play, in affecting— and perhaps stimulating and improving—the course of business school research.

The AACSB

As the single collective organization of collegiate-based business schools in the United States, the AACSB has—without overstating the case—tremendous potential leverage to influence the future of American business education. Its most powerful carrot—or, in the view of some, stick—is accreditation, which has already been discussed in Chapter 9 and a previous section of this final chapter. Hence little further on this point needs to be said here except that we cannot repeat too often the conclusion that the AACSB's accreditation process (through the Standards and their enforcement) has been a force for quality improvement in the system in the past and that it has the possibility to become even more potent in the future *if the AACSB's members choose to make certain changes*.

The other major AACSB function that has had considerable positive influence to date on the quality of higher education for business has been the training and development programs sponsored by the organization (utilizing the expertise of its member schools and their personnel) for business school administrators and faculty in various topic areas. This is an activity that has increased in size and scope in recent years, and although we did not explore the reactions to this part of the AACSB's operations in detail, it has (as verified in our interviews) been quite well received by member institutions. The future challenge in this area, as we see it, is to utilize such educational programs and activities to their maximum to encourage and stimulate *innovation*. Such programs also offer a good opportunity to reinforce constructive diversity across different types of schools with different missions—opportunities to encourage breaking out of molds rather than folding into molds.

Another area in which the AACSB has begun to get more involved in recent years is in influencing national policies at the federal level that have important consequences for collegiate business education. While such efforts are necessarily rather costly in terms of staff time and financial resources to support them, they would seem to be of increasing necessity in future years if business schools collectively expect to increase their "clout" on a national basis in higher education and in society at large. The dollars and time expended may not always be successful, but failure to make the efforts will leave the university business education establishment a follower rather than a leader.

One other area that seems to us to be extremely important for the AACSB—in effect, for business schools jointly—to become more concerned about, and more actively involved in, is doctoral education. The rationale for doing so was discussed in Chapter 5 and basically involves the issue of whether doctoral education for business can and should be improved. Obviously, the nature and characteristics of particular doctoral programs are strongly influenced by the respective universities (and their graduate schools) in which they occur, but in principle the same reasoning also would apply to master's degree programs. Thus, although doctoral education differs in degree (no pun intended) from master's level education, we see no inherent reason why the national association of business schools should be so heavily involved in one but have absolutely no involvement in the other. We believe that the AACSB and its members could have a positive impact on this segment of business education—which, in turn would influence the quality of BBA and MBA programs—just as they (collectively) have had on the baccalaureate and master's segments. The time to start doing so—and the need to do so—in our judgment, and based on our observations from our interviews, is now.

To recapitulate, the AACSB, as an association of its member schools, has many tasks to do already and only limited resources to do them. It has been (especially in recent years) a significant force for improvement in business education. It should not, and indeed cannot, rest comfortably on its laurels, but instead needs to set its sights on how it can increase its positive influence in the future. To take on new tasks and undertake old tasks in new ways will require considerable perspicacity in setting priorities and making judgments among a set of alternatives, all of which are desirable but some of which probably will not be possible to pursue. The supreme challenge is to bring fresh perspective to these difficult choices.

The Business School

Whatever else can be said about the American collegiate business school, one thing is certain: It is *the mechanism* for bringing about any change in business education. If innovations are to be made, it will be *through* the business schools—albeit with the needed help and support of their own universities and the business community. So, in this final section of the final chapter of this report, we discuss what we see as the single, overriding challenge for business schools and the corresponding set of responses required of them.

The Business School Challenge: Doing "Everything" Expected of It   The all-encompassing challenge facing the business school of the future is how to se-

lect among all the demands that will be made on it. One dimension of this near-impossible task is the difficulty of integrating instruction in conventional degree programs and a set of other potential activities including instruction in postdegree executive education and management development programs, the conduct of meaningful and nontrivial research, and the maintenance of strong and positive relationships with the campus at large and the local/regional/national/international business community. The second and parallel dimension of the challenge is the difficulty in serving diverse constituencies, including, among others, degree students (typically) in their early twenties, adult postdegree managers and executives who (typically) range in age from their early thirties to their late fifties, the immediate campus community, the larger academic community, individual companies and firms, the corporate community at large, and the general society.

What makes all this an especially formidable challenge is that the typical school has a highly constrained set of resources with which to carry out its heterogeneous activities and meet the needs of its various publics. It has a finite time (usually 2 academic years or the equivalent) to educate its degree students; a set of faculty talents that may be especially suited for one or two activities (e.g., conventional classroom teaching and academic research) but not necessarily for other activities (such as executive education or highly applied research); only so many available person-hours to interact with other units on campus and/or with relevant members of the corporate and government communities; and so forth. Each activity and each constituency is worthy in its own right and justly expects to receive its requisite degree of attention from the business school. The fundamental question is: can all masters be served? If not, what are the priorities and what is sacrificed? This is what each school must decide, and the answer need not—and, in our view, *should not*—be the same for all schools, if the total system of American collegiate business education is to function at its maximum effectiveness for the greatest societal benefit.

Business School Response   In conclusion, we believe that if American business schools are to meet successfully this fundamental challenge—and to exert thrust and avoid drift—in the next 10 to 15 years, they must plan strategically, set priorities, and make tough but explicit choices. In this process, four main themes will need to be kept to the forefront:

• *Continuous quality assessment*   Each school needs to develop an insistent and persistent attitude of "how can we do it better tomorrow than we are doing it today" and then proceed to subject itself to continuous, tough, and independent external assessment, as well as self-assessment. It is incumbent on business schools *not* to wait for the AACSB accreditation process to get around to them every 9 years (if they are already accredited and in the indefinite future if they are not yet accredited) for a rigorous assessment of quality.

• *Continuous Attention to Theory/Practice Linkages*   Business/management schools represent both an area of knowledge *and* a professional area of practice. In the early history of American business schools it sometimes seemed the latter was emphasized to the detriment of the former, and in later years it has seemed to some that the former became overemphasized to the near-exclusion of the latter. In the future, a business school—in our opinion—cannot afford to focus only on one or the other, but instead must concentrate on both, and especially on the *connection* between the two. In effect, in both their MBA programs and their Ph.D. programs, business schools should consider—more so than they have up to now—how they can bring a strengthened *clinical* approach to the education of their students, an approach that simultaneously combines knowledge dissemination, research investigation, and on-site implementation of advanced methods of management analysis and practice. The U.S. medical school, which reputedly has successfully achieved this kind of synchronization in the education of physicians, provides a model that might well be emulated by U.S. business schools. No model, of course, is ever ideally appropriate, and other professional schools such as law and architecture also represent models of varying degrees of usefulness to business schools, but we believe that the medical school approach comes closest to what we regard as the target toward which business school education should aim in the future. For this to happen, not only will business schools themselves need to be willing to make some significant changes in this direction, but also the environment will need to be supportive: The university, and its campus officials, will need to recognize the professional obligations and responsibilities of the business school; and likewise the business community will need to recognize the anchorages of the business school in the academic setting and the importance of the independent search for new knowledge that often will challenge conventional wisdom and practices.

• *Continuous adaptability to change*   Specific future changes are nearly impossible to foretell with precision, but the fact that business schools in the future will have to become more adaptable to change than they have in the past is one of the safest predictions. Unsettling flux is more likely to be the constant than comfortable stability, and thus the business school of the future should put nimbleness at the top of its own list of desired attributes and stodginess at the bottom. To be forewarned in this sense is, indeed, to be forearmed.

• *Continuous innovation*   In our opinion, if any single element of organization culture ideally should characterize the U.S. business school in the next decade, it should be an ingrained, embedded, and pervasive spirit of innovation. If this occurs, society will be the winner.

BIBLIOGRAPHY

Adams, S., & Matrone, M. (Fall, 1985). Survey course: Pete Pond on what's new in university executive education programs. *UNC/Business*, 7–8.

American Assembly of Collegiate Schools of Business. (April 30, 1982). Accreditation Council Meeting Minutes. St. Louis: Author.

American Assembly of Collegiate Schools of Business. (1986–1987). *Accreditation Council, Policies, Procedures, and Standards*. St. Louis: Author.

American Assembly of Collegiate Schools of Business. (June/August, 1987). *Newsline*, pp. 1–5.

American Assembly of Collegiate Schools of Business, & European Foundation for Management Development. (1982). *Management for the XXI century*. Boston: Kluwer-Nijhoff Publishing.

American Association of Collegiate Schools of Business. (1946). *Standards for Admissions*. St. Louis: Author.

American Association of Collegiate Schools of Business. (August, 1949). Executive Committee Interpretations. St. Louis: Author.

American Association of Collegiate Schools of Business. (1958). *The Constitution and Standards for Membership*. St. Louis: Author.

Andrews, K. R. (1959). University programs for practicing executives. In F. C. Pierson, *The education of American businessmen* (pp. 577–608). New York: McGraw-Hill Book Co.

Arden House Colloquium. (1979). *Management and management education in a world of changing expectations*. American Assembly of Collegiate Schools of Business, & European Foundation for Management Development. St. Louis & Brussels, Belgium.

Behrman, J. N., & Levin, R. I. (January–February, 1984). Are business schools doing their job? *Harvard Business Review*, 140–147.

Bell, D. (1973). Notes on the post-industrial society. In F. Tugwell (Ed.), *Search for alternatives: Public policy and the study of the future*. Cambridge, MA: Winthrop Publishers.

Bickerstaffe, G. (August, 1981). Crisis of confidence in the business schools. *International Management*, 87–89.

Bluestone, I. (1979). Emerging trends in collective bargaining. In C. Kerr & J. Rosow (Eds.), *Work in America*. New York: Van Nostrand Reinhold.

Bolt, J. E. (November–December, 1985). Tailor executive development to strategy. *Harvard Business Review*, 168–175.

Bossard, J. H. S., & Dewhurst, J. F. (1931). *University education for business*. Philadelphia: University of Pennsylvania Press.

Bricker Bulletin. (1984). Vol. 3, no. 3.

Bridgman, D. S. (1959). Company management development programs. In F. C. Pierson, *The education of American businessmen* (pp. 536–576). New York: McGraw-Hill Book Co.

Butler, R. (1981). Overview on aging: Some biomedical, social, and behavioral perspectives. In S. B. Kiesler, J. N. Morgan, & V. K. Oppenheimer (Eds.), *Aging: Social change*. New York: Academic Press.

Cetron, M. (1985). *The future of American business: The U.S. in world competition*. New York: McGraw-Hill Book Co.

Copperman, L., & Keast, F. (1983). *Adjusting to an older work force*. New York: Van Nostrand Reinhold.

Dymsza, W. A. (Winter, 1982). The education and development of managers for future decades. *Journal of International Business Studies*, 9–18.

Fields, O. (1979). Simulation in business classes at the four-year college level. In B. B. Wakin & C. F. Petitjean (Eds.), *Alternative learning styles in business education* (pp. 99–107). Reston, VA: National Business Education Association.

Garvin, C. C., Jr. (1985). The future has a mind of its own. In R. Lamb, & P. Shrivastava (Eds.), *Advances in Strategic Management, 3*, 299–304.

Giauque, W. C., & Woolsey, R. E. D. (1981). A totally new direction for management education: A modest proposal. *Interfaces, 11*(4), 30–34.

Glickman, A. (Ed.). (1982). *The changing composition of the workforce: Implications for future research*. New York: Plenum Press.

Gordon, R. A., & Howell, J. E. (1959). *Higher education for business*. New York: Columbia University Press.

Gordon, T. (1969). The feedback between technology and values. In K. Baier & N. Reschew (Eds.), *Values and the future: The impact of technological change on American values*. New York: Free Press.

Hofstadter, R., & Hardy, C. D. (1952). *The development and scope of higher education in the United States*. New York: Columbia University Press.

Honig, M., & Hanoch, G. (1981). The labor market behavior of older people: A framework for analysis. In S. B. Kiesler, J. N. Morgan, & V. K. Oppenheimer (Eds.), *Aging: Social change*. New York: Academic Press.

Hunt, H., & Hunt, T. (1983). *Human resource implications of robotics*. Kalamazoo, MI: Upjohn Institute for Employment Research.

Jones, B. (1982). *Sleepers, wake!* Melbourne, Australia: Oxford University Press.

Kahn, H. (1979). *World economic development: 1979 and beyond*. Boulder, CO: Westview Press.

Katz, R. L. (January–February, 1955). Skills of an effective administrator. *Harvard Business Review*, 33–42.

Kerr, C. (1979). Industrialism with a human face. In C. Kerr & J. Rosow (Eds.), *Work in America*. New York: Van Nostrand Reinhold.

Kerr, C., & Rosow, J. (1979). *Work in America*. New York: Van Nostrand Reinhold.

Lindblom, C. (1977). *Politics and markets: The world's political economic systems*. New York: Basic Books.

Maret, E. (1983). *Women's career patterns: Influences on work stability*. Lanham, MD: University Press of America.

McNulty, N. C. (Ed.). (1985). *International directory of executive education*. New York: Pergamon Press.

Middlebrook, B. J., & Rachel, F. M. (November, 1983). A survey of middle management training and development programs. *Personnel Administrator, 27–31*.

Miles, R. E., & Snow, C. (1986). Network organization: New concepts for new forms. *California Management Review, 28,* 62–73.

Millard, R. M. (1983). Accreditation. In J. R. Warren (Ed.), *Meeting the new demand for standards. New directions for higher education: no. 43.* (pp. 9–28). San Francisco: Jossey-Bass.

Muller, H. (1970). *The children of Frankenstein: A primer on modern technology and human values*. Bloomington, IN: Indiana University Press.

Naisbitt, J. (1982). *Megatrends*. New York: Warner Books.

Nohl, R. L. (Winter, 1986). Executive development: An overview. *Selections,* 18–23.

Paris Conference. (1980). *Report of the international conference: Managers for the XXI century*. American Assembly of Collegiate Schools of Business, & European Foundation for Management Development. St. Louis & Brussels, Belgium.

Pierson, F. C. (1959). *The education of American businessmen*. New York: McGraw-Hill Book Co.

Schmotter, J. W. (Spring, 1984). An interview with Professor James E. Howell. *Selections,* 9–18.

Sheppard, H. (1982). When is old? In A. Glickman (Ed.), *The changing composition of the workforce: Implications for future research*. New York: Plenum Press.

Skinner, W. (1979). The impact of changing technology on the working environment. In C. Kerr & J. Rosow (Eds.), *Work in America,* New York: Van Nostrand Reinhold.

Smith, R. (1979). *Women in the labor force*. Washington, D.C.: Urban Institute.

Walton, C. C. (1982). *Lifelong learning for managers: Report of the Wingspread Conference*. St. Louis: American Assembly of Collegiate Schools of Business.

Williamson, O. (1975). *Markets and hierarchies: Analysis and antitrust implications*. New York: Free Press.

Windsor Castle Colloquium. (1979). *The changing expectations of society in the next thirty years*. American Assembly of Collegiate Schools of Business, & European Foundation for Management Development. St. Louis & Brussels, Belgium.

Yankelovich, D. (1979). Work, values, and the New Breed. In C. Kerr & J. Rosow (Eds.), *Work in America*. New York: Van Nostrand Reinhold.

RESEARCH DESIGN AND DATA COLLECTION PROCEDURES

A brief summary was provided in Chapter 1 concerning the methods used for collecting the three types of data utilized in this study: "factual" statistical data, interview data, and questionnaire data. This appendix provides additional details concerning the research design and data collection procedures pertaining to the latter two types of data: the information obtained from interviews and questionnaires.

INTERVIEWS

As was noted in Chapter 1, interviews (over 500) were conducted in both universities and business organizations. The design considerations and procedures for the interviews conducted in each setting are discussed separately below.

Universities

A target number of 60 schools—amounting to approximately 10% of schools holding membership in AACSB at the time the study was initiated in the latter part of 1984— was set for interview visits. In order to exercise reasonable control on travel time and costs, a decision was made to limit sampling to schools in six different defined geographical areas. These areas were selected to provide, collectively, a wide variety of types of schools (accredited and non-accredited, urban and rural, large and small, etc.) that would be reasonably—though not perfectly—representative of the total AACSB membership. The six areas (and the number of schools actually visited in each of them) were the following:

- Boston metropolitan area: eleven schools
- Chicago metropolitan area: ten schools
- San Francisco Bay Area: eight schools

- Part of the state of Texas (Dallas to Austin to San Antonio): thirteen schools
- State of Kansas: seven schools
- State of Georgia: twelve schools

As can be seen, this cluster sampling resulted in a total of sixty-one schools that were visited, with 61% (thirty-seven) of them being accredited (compared to approximately 40% of the total AACSB membership). Thus, in terms of schools visited, there was some overweighting toward accredited schools; however, since accredited schools (being larger, on average) produce a disproportionate share of graduates, the proportion of visits to accredited schools was considered justified. (A complete list of all schools visited for interviews is provided in Appendix B.)

A target set of categories of respondents to be interviewed at each school was identified before the first interviews were conducted. The intent was to interview administrators in four key positions: dean of the school, director of the school's placement office (or that person in the campus placement office who was responsible for business school graduates), the director of executive education programs (if a school had such programs), and in order to obtain a campus perspective, the provost (academic vice president). In addition, the dean was asked to select three faculty members to be interviewed, faculty members who would be from different functional areas (marketing, accounting, etc.) and, if possible, not all of the same academic rank. While the selection of these three faculty members was obviously not random, we asked for faculty members whom the dean considered to have a broad overview of the school's programs and issues (i.e., not faculty members who might be new to the school). The final category of university-affiliated respondents was composed of, in effect, "boundary-spanners": managers and executives from the business community who were members of schools' business advisory councils (BACs). For each school visited, the dean was asked to select (for an interview) someone who had been a BAC member long enough to be familiar with the school.

The content of the interviews was geared to the particular position (dean, faculty member, placement director, etc.) of each interviewee. An interview schedule of areas to be covered, and key questions in each area, was developed in advance for each category of interviewee. Because of time and scheduling pressures, not all relevant areas could be covered in each interview. (A list of the target content areas for each respondent category is provided in Appendix C.)

Most interviews were conducted individually, by either one or both of the Project directors. (Approximately 10% of the university interviews were conducted by the Project's two graduate research assistants.) Occasionally, faculty interviews were conducted with groups of two or three individuals at a time, but this was the exception rather than the rule. Most interviews lasted approximately one hour and, with the permission of the interviewee, were tape recorded. Notes were also taken during the interviews.

The total number of interviews conducted in each respondent category are listed below.

Deans:	61
Placement directors:	28
Executive education directors:	25
Provosts (Academic VPs):	44
Faculty members:	146
BAC members:	20
Total:	324

Corporations and Firms

An arbitrary target number of approximately 50 business organizations was set for obtaining corporate interview data. The selection of firms involved either or both of two principal criteria: being a recognized leader in corporate management development activities and/or being a significant regional or national employer of business school graduates (especially if located in one of the six geographical regions in which the business school interviews were conducted). About fifteen firms were included in the sample based primarily on the first criterion; that is, they were among the leading twenty-five firms nationwide in the quality of their overall management development programs as determined by a survey we conducted of human resources executives. Most of the remaining thirty-five firms were selected based on the second criterion, although there were a few organizations that were included based on special considerations (e.g., precisely because they had so far done almost nothing in the way of management development activities, or because they had a distinctly local as opposed to a regional or national orientation in hiring business school graduates). The resulting sample of firms was obviously biased toward medium and larger organizations because these were the ones that met either or both of the two major criteria for selection. Our view on this size bias is similar to that of Gordon & Howell nearly 30 years ago: "Since (the study) was primarily designed to secure information regarding company practices, experiences, and policies in reference to the employment of college and university graduates, we felt that the smaller companies, which individually employ few graduates, would not have enough experience in this area to provide meaningful responses" (1959, p. 467). [A somewhat broader range of size of firms, especially service organizations, was obtained as part of the questionnaire sample for the present study (see a later section in this Appendix).] The final total sample consisted of fifty-two firms, which are listed in Appendix B.

The target categories of respondents for the companies selected for interviews consisted of five sets: chief executive officers or senior corporate-level executives; vice presidents (or directors) of human resources, directors of management development, directors of college recruiting/relations, and operating (mid/lower level) line managers who had had some degree of contact with recent business school graduates.

The content areas targeted for coverage in each set of corporate interviews are shown in Appendix C. As with the university interviews, circumstances did not always permit each intended area to be covered in each interview.

Initial contact with a firm that was to be included in the interview sample was made by a variety of means, though typically it was through the office of the senior human resources executive. At the time of this first contact (ordinarily by phone), the purpose of the study was explained and a request was made to interview up to seven executives or managers in the firm (the relevant official in each of the first four categories listed above and one to three appropriate operating line managers). Similar to the way in which university interviews were carried out, almost all the corporate interviews were conducted individually by one or both of the two project directors, and most lasted about an hour (although some went as long as 2 hours).

The total number of interviews conducted in each respondent category are listed below:

CEOs and senior corporate executives:	21
VPs (directors) of human resources:	46
Directors of management development:	44
Directors of college recruiting/relations:	46
Operating line managers:	44
Total:	201

QUESTIONNAIRES

In addition to factual data and interview reports, responses to questionnaire surveys constituted the other primary set of data obtained for this study. Questionnaires, of course, have both advantages and disadvantages compared to interviews as a vehicle for data collection. They permit the researcher to reach a much broader sample, but there are severe constraints on the types of questions that can be asked and also an absence of flexibility to probe with follow-up questions. Recognizing these limitations, we attempted to construct forms of the questionnaire that provided the maximum amount of information for a given amount of respondent time in completing them. All told, sixteen different versions of the questionnaires were developed, each version being specially designed for a particular category of respondents. In each instance, we attempted to balance the (directly conflicting) twin goals of keeping the questionnaire relatively short in order to generate as large a response rate as possible, while at the same time including as many relevant questions as possible to obtain the maximum amount of useful information. The final versions of the questionnaires, of necessity, always represented compromises between these two objectives. Nevertheless, we view the extensive data thus obtained from these questionnaires as complementing the intensive interview data, in some cases reinforcing the bases for conclusions and in other cases providing findings that could not otherwise be obtained from the smaller number of interviews with a more limited sample.

As was done earlier with the description of interview procedures, we separately discuss questionnaire procedures for the university and corporate samples.

Universities

One of our objectives for the university surveys was to involve all (as of 1984) the U.S. member educational institutions (both accredited and nonaccredited) of AACSB in this Project, if at all possible. Therefore, the target sample of schools for those individuals holding relevant administrative positions (see below) was in fact the entire population of 620 such institutions. For other respondent categories associated with universities, different samples were utilized as will be described subsequently.

The target categories of university-based respondents for questionnaire surveys included the six categories designated for interviews (i.e., deans, directors of placement, directors of executive education, provosts/academic vice presidents, faculty members, and members of BACs). In addition, four other categories of respondents were surveyed: graduating BBA seniors and graduating MBA students, and BBA and MBA alumni (with each alumni group subdivided between those 5 years and those 10 years beyond graduation).

The samples within each of the ten university-affiliated response groups were drawn as follows:

- Deans: All U.S. member schools (of AACSB): total = 620.
- Placement directors: (Same as deans).
- Executive education directors: All AACSB member institutions involved in such activity to the extent (very small, in many cases) of having someone specifically designated as responsible for it for the school. (Exact number not known, but could be as high as 400, based on deans' replies to a relevant question.)
- Provosts (Academic vice presidents): (Same as deans).
- Faculty members: 10% of all faculty in AACSB member schools (in the United States). Total possible sample = approximately 2800.

- BAC members: Three per schools having a BAC. (Exact number of schools having a BAC not known, so total possible sample of BAC members not known.)
- BBA students: 2% of all graduating BBA students in Spring (only), 1985. Total possible sample = about 4000.
- MBA students: 5% of all graduating MBA students in Spring (only), 1985. Total possible sample = about 2500.
- BBA alumni: Five alumni (randomly selected) each, from the classes of 1975 and 1980, from a random sample of 100 AACSB member schools: Total possible sample = 1000.
- MBA alumni: (Same as BBA alumni, but a different random sample of 100 schools).

All the questionnaires were distributed through the office of the dean of each school. For the first four categories (deans, placement directors, executive education directors, and provosts), we asked the dean to send the relevant questionnaire form to the specific individual holding that position. For faculty members, we asked the dean to distribute the relevant questionnaire form to every tenth name on an alphabetical list of *full-time* faculty members. For BAC members, the dean was requested to send the appropriate form to three members having knowledge of the school. All questionnaires for all these groups were returned to the dean's office in *sealed* envelopes supplied by the researchers, and the total packet of all such individual envelopes were sent as a group to the Project office. The questionnaires for BBA and MBA students were distributed and completed in class in a last-semester (-quarter) course in business policy (or the nearest equivalent course required of all graduating students in their final term). Distribution of the alumni questionnaires was accomplished by asking the deans' offices of the randomly selected schools for a list of five randomly-selected names (in the 1975 and 1980 BBA and MBA classes) on the alphabetical roster of alumni for whom addresses were available; these lists were then forwarded to the Project office and the questionnaires sent by mail from there and returned by mail to the same office.

The content of the various versions of the questionnaires generally followed the topic areas covered in the interviews (and listed in Appendix C) for those categories of respondents that were involved in both the interviews and the administration of questionnaires. For BBA and MBA student questionnaires, the topics covered included reasons for choosing a business major (for BBAs) or the reasons for deciding to obtain an MBA degree (for MBAs), the degree to which their respective programs developed various managerial skills, their self-ratings of the extent to which they possess these various relevant skills and personal characteristics, and their evaluation of the quality of instruction they received in their respective programs. For BBA and MBA alumni, questions focused on (among a number of appropriate topics) self-ratings of various relevant skills and personal characteristics, opinions regarding the extent to which their respective programs prepared them for assuming eventual positions of managerial leadership, and ratings of which particular curriculum subject-matter areas had been most valuable to them in their careers to date.

The format of most questions on most versions of the questionnaires (for both the university and corporate samples) involved several different types of closed-end questions with fixed alternative responses. However, a small number of open-ended questions were also included on all questionnaire versions.

The number of questionnaires returned, and the corresponding response rate (where feasible to calculate), for each respondent category are listed in the table at the top of the next page. (It should be noted that all response rates, except those for deans, are rough estimates. The bases for these estimates are indicated following the report of the information.)

Deans:
    Number returned: 457
    Response rate: 74%
Placement directors:
    Number returned: 332
    Response rate: 73%(estimated)*
Executive education directors:
    Number returned: 245
    Response rate: 61%(estimated)†
Provosts (academic VPs):
    Number returned: 290
    Response rate: 63%(estimated)*
Faculty members:
    Number returned: 2,055
    Response rate: 73%(estimated)
BAC members:
    Number returned: 445
    Response rate: (not possible to ascertain)
BBA students:
    Number returned: 2,558
    Response rate: 64%(estimated)‡
MBA students:
    Number returned: 1,835
    Response rate: 73%(estimated)‡
BBA alumni:
    Number returned: 218
    Response rate: 44%
MBA alumni:
    Number returned: 282
    Response rate: 56%
Total number of all university-
    based questionnaires returned: 8,717

*Estimate based on the assumption that 74% of the deans distributed the relevant questionnaires.

†Estimate based on the assumption that only about 400 schools offer any type of executive education/management development programs.

‡Estimates based on assumptions of approximately 200,000 BBA graduates and 50,000 MBA graduates in the *Spring term* (*not* for the entire year), 1985. It is not known how many of the questionnaires were actually distributed in class but not completed, so response rates are probably underestimated.

Corporations/Firms

For purposes of questionnaire surveying in the corporate sector, we selected a target sample of companies and firms that would be most likely to hire business school graduates and most likely to have some degree of involvement in organized executive education and management development activities. To accomplish this objective, we surveyed executives and managers in the (1985 lists of) Fortune 500 industrial firms, the Fortune 500 service organizations, the 100 members of the American Business Conference, the 100 leading entrepreneurial firms as identified by *Inc. Magazine,* and the 100 leading small companies in America as selected by *Business Week.* The total set of companies obviously is again biased toward medium and large firms, for the reasons previously indicated, but the latter three groups (totaling 300 firms) were included in an attempt to sample a set of the most prominent smaller-size firms. The sample of corporate organizations also included the fifteen largest national public accounting firms.

Within each target company, the target categories of respondents were the same as for the corporate interviews—CEOs, Senior Corporate Executives (SCEs), Vice Presidents (Directors) of Human Resources (VPHRs), Directors of Management Development (DMDs), Directors of College Recruiting/Relations (DCRs), and Operating (mid/lower level) Line Managers (OLMs). One other target group of respondents, not connected with the target companies, was a separate special (limited) sample of 130 managers of extremely small firms employing less than 100 people.

Distribution of the questionnaires to each target category of respondents was accomplished as follows: a packet of questionnaires was sent to each of the Vice Presidents of Human Resources (or the persons holding the equivalent position in smaller companies) in all the target companies (totaling 1239 companies = all companies for whom we could obtain the specific name of the VPHR) requesting their cooperation with the Project by distributing the appropriate questionnaire forms to the specifically designated targeted individuals within their company. This mailing (to each VPHR by name) was preceded by an advance letter explaining the objectives of the Project, its sponsorship, and the subsequent procedures to be used for distribution of the individual questionnaire forms. The mailed packet of questionnaires included individual prepaid envelopes for return of the completed forms by each respondent directly to the Project office. The VPHR was asked to distribute the appropriately designated form to the CEO, to himself or herself as VPHR, to the DMD, and to the DCR. For the SCE form, the VPHR was asked to select a senior corporate executive *not* in the human resources area. For the OLM forms, the VPHR was asked to distribute the appropriate forms to three mid/lower-level line managers (preferably, according to the instructions, managers who had had some prior contact with recent business school graduates). Forms for the separate limited sample of managers of very small business firms were distributed through bureaus of business research at thirteen business/management schools (ten forms per school) located in different states around the country.

The contents of the questionnaires distributed to the six categories of respondents in the two sets of Fortune 500 firms and the 300 other smaller and medium sized firms paralleled the topics covered in the corresponding interviews (as listed in Appendix C). The contents of the questionnaires for managers of the very small firms included such topics as relations with business/management schools, recruitment of BBAs and MBAs, appraisal of new-hire business school graduates, and the relevance of current management education to the needs of small business enterprises.

The number of questionnaires returned from corporate-based respondents, and the corresponding response rate for each respondent category, are listed below. Most of the various corporate response rates cannot be calculated with precision for one major reason: the method of distribution of the questionnaire forms. Although it is known exactly how many questionnaires were sent to the offices of the VPHRs of each company, and exactly how many questionnaires were mailed back directly to the Project office, it is *not* known how many of the specific questionnaires actually reached the hands of the targeted individual respondents (other than the VPHRs). If a given VPHR did not distribute the forms to the designated set of respondents in his/her company, then these other individuals obviously did not have an opportunity to complete their forms. Given this situation, we have chosen to present three types of response rates:

1 *Raw response rate* Number of questionnaires returned/number of questionnaires (for each category of respondent) sent to the offices of the VPHRs.

2 *Adjusted raw response rate* Number of questionnaires returned/number of questionnaires that *could have been distributed* by the VPHRs (i.e., the total number of questionnaires sent minus those known *not* to have been distributed because of specific information received from particular companies that they would *not* be participating in this part of the study).

3 *Estimated net response rate* Number of questionnaires returned/number estimated to have been distributed by VPHRs. (This latter—denominator—number is an estimate based on the assumption that if a VPHR returned his/her own questionnaire, then it is likely that he/she distributed the other questionnaires; of course, almost certainly some VPHRs who did not complete their own questionnaires did nevertheless distribute all or part of the remaining set of questionnaires to the other target respondents. Thus, for estimation purposes for the net response rate, we took a figure of the actual VPHR response rate plus 30% as the number to be used in calculating the denominator.)

Since the raw response rates differed considerably between the Fortune companies, on the one hand, and the smaller non-Fortune companies, the rates are reported separately for the two aggregate groups.

FORTUNE COMPANIES
(958 companies)

CEOs:	
Number returned:	130
Raw response rate:	14%
Adjusted raw response rate:	16%
Estimated net response rate:	47%
SCEs:	
Number returned:	172
Raw response rate:	18%
Adjusted raw response rate:	21%
Estimated net response rate:	62%
VPHRs:	
Number returned:	213
Raw response rate:	22%
Adjusted raw response rate:	25%
Estimated net response rate:	n/a
DMDs:	
Number returned:	218
Raw response rate:	23%

Adjusted raw response rate:	26%
Estimated net response rate:	79%

DCRs:

Number returned:	222
Raw response rate:	23%
Adjusted raw response rate:	26%
Estimated net response rate:	80%

OLMs:

Number returned:	533
Raw response rate:	19%
Adjusted raw response rate:	21%
Estimated net response rate:	64%

NON-FORTUNE COMPANIES
(281 companies)

CEOs:

Number returned:	15
Raw response rate:	5%
Adjusted raw response rate:	6%
Estimated net response rate:	42%

SCEs:

Number returned:	32
Raw response rate:	11%
Adjusted raw response rate:	13%
Estimated net response rate:	89%

VPHRs:

Number returned:	28
Raw response rate:	10%
Adjusted raw response rate:	12%
Estimated net response rate:	n/a

DMDs:

Number returned:	32
Raw response rate:	11%
Adjusted raw response rate:	13%
Estimated net response rate:	89%

DCRs:

Number returned:	29
Raw response rate:	10%
Adjusted raw response rate:	12%
Estimated net response rate:	81%

OLMs:

Number returned:	68
Raw response rate:	7%
Adjusted raw response rate:	9%
Estimated net response rate:	63%

Total number of all corporate-based questionnaires returned:	1,692

The additional number of forms returned from the special sample of managers of very small companies was seventeen, with a resulting raw response rate of 13%. Since it is impossible to know how many of the 130 forms sent to thirteen schools for distribution actually reached the intended respondents, it is not possible to calculate an adjusted raw response rate nor an estimated net response rate for this group.

ORGANIZATIONS IN WHICH INTERVIEWS WERE CONDUCTED

UNIVERSITIES AND EDUCATIONAL INSTITUTIONS

Arthur D. Little Management Education Institute
Atlanta University
Augusta College
Babson College
Baylor University
Bentley College
Boston College
Boston University
University of California, Berkeley
California State University, Hayward
University of Chicago
Chicago State University
Columbus College
University of Dallas
DePaul University
Emory University
Emporia State University
Fort Hays State University
University of Georgia
Georgia College
Georgia Institute of Technology
Georgia Southern College
Georgia State University
Golden Gate University
Harvard University
University of Illinois at Chicago
University of Illinois at Urbana-Champaign
Indiana University
University of Kansas
Kansas State University

Loyola University (Chicago)
University of Massachusetts-Boston
Massachusetts Institute of Technology
Mercer University-Macon Campus
North Texas State University
Northeastern University
Northeastern Illinois University
Northwestern University
Pittsburg State University
Roosevelt University
St. Edward's University
St. Mary's University
University of San Francisco
San Francisco State University
San Jose State University
University of Santa Clara
Simmons College
Southern Methodist University
Southwest Texas State University
Stanford University
Suffolk University
The University of Texas at Arlington
The University of Texas at Austin
The University of Texas at Dallas
The University of Texas at San Antonio
Texas Christian University
Texas Wesleyan College
Valdosta State College
Washburn University of Topeka
West Georgia College
Wichita State University

CORPORATIONS, BUSINESS FIRMS AND OTHER ORGANIZATIONS

American Telephone & Telegraph Co.
American Express Company
American Management Association
American Society of Training Directors
American Standard Inc.
Amoco Corporation
Arthur Andersen & Co.
Bank of America NT & SA
Bank of Boston Corp.
Baxter Travenol Laboratories Inc.
Booz, Allen & Hamilton Inc.
Burlington Industries, Inc.
Forum Corporation
Center for Creative Leadership
The Chase Manhattan Bank, N.A.
Chemical Bank
Citicorp
The Coca-Cola Company
Digital Equipment Corporation
Dresser Industries Inc.
Eastman Kodak Company
Equitable Life Assurance Society of the
    United States
Exxon Corporation
Fidelity Investments
First Boston Corp.
GTE Corporation
General Electric Company
General Foods Corporation

General Motors Corporation
Goldman, Sachs & Co.
Hewlett-Packard Co.
Honeywell Inc.
International Business Machines Corp.
Koch Industries, Inc.
Marriott Corporation
MCI Communications Corp.
McKinsey & Company
Minnesota Mining & Mfg. Co.
Morgan Stanley Group Inc.
Motorola, Inc.
Pacific Bell
Pacific Gas & Electric Co.
Peat, Marwick, Mitchell & Co.
J. C. Penney Company, Inc.
Pepsico, Inc.
The Pillsbury Company
Polaroid Corporation
Price Waterhouse & Co.
Procter & Gamble Co.
Republicbank Corporation
Salomon Brothers Inc.
Sears, Roebuck and Co.
J. & W. Seligman & Co. Inc.
Shearson Lehman Brothers Inc.
Small Business Association of New England
Towers, Perrin, Forster & Crosby
Xerox Corporation

TOPIC AREAS
OF INTERVIEWS
FOR DIFFERENT CATEGORIES
OF RESPONDENTS

Note 1: Not every topic was covered in every interview.
Note 2: Order of topics across interviews within a given category of respondent was generally similar.

UNIVERSITIES AND EDUCATIONAL INSTITUTIONS

Deans of Business/Management Schools

1 The school's future
2 Faculty
3 Research
4 Executive education/management development
5 School's relationships with the business/management community
6 Accreditation
7 Curriculum
8 Students/graduates
9 Education delivery
10 Placement
11 School's relationships with the university
12 Criticisms/strengths of the school

Faculty Members of Business/Management Schools

1 The school's future
2 Faculty

  3 Research
  4 Executive education/management development
  5 School's relationships with the business/management community
  6 Curriculum
  7 Students/graduates
  8 Education delivery
  9 Criticisms/strengths of the school

Placement Directors for Business/Management Schools

  1 School's placement activities
  2 School's relationships with the business/management community

Executive Education Directors for Business/Management Schools

  1 Overview of school's executive education/management development programs
  2 Program content
  3 School's relationships with the business/management community
  4 Students (in executive education programs)
  5 Instructors (in executive education programs)
  6 Delivery of executive education programs

Provosts/Academic Vice Presidents

  1 Business/management school's relationships with the university
  2 The school's future
  3 Accreditation
  4 Executive education/management development
  5 Relationships (of the school) with the business/management community
  6 School's faculty
  7 School's students
  8 School's education delivery
  9 School's curriculum
  10 Criticisms/strengths of the school

Business Advisory Council Members

  1 Role of the business advisory council (BAC)
  2 School's relationships with the business/management community
  3 School's students/graduates
  4 School's faculty
  5 School's research
  6 School's executive education/management development programs
  7 The school's future
  8 Criticisms/strengths of the school

CORPORATIONS AND BUSINESS FIRMS

Chief Executive Officers/Senior Corporate Executives

1 Strengths/weaknesses of collegiate business education
2 Management development
3 Future roles for business/management schools

Vice Presidents (Directors) of Human Resources

1 Demographics of management component of own organization
2 Organization's recruitment and selection of college graduates (including business/management school graduates)
3 Organization's use of college graduates (including business/management school graduates) in management
4 Appraisal of new-hire MBAs and BBAs
5 Management education and development post-hire
6 Organization's policies re degree program participation
7 Relevance of current management education to corporate needs

Directors of Management Development

1 Organization's management development needs analysis
2 Organization's internal management development activities
3 Programs provided by external providers
4 Approach to make/buy decision in management development
5 Evaluation of effectiveness of management development programs
6 Future changes in the organization's management development activities

Directors of College Recruiting/Relations

1 Organization's approach to the recruitment and selection of college graduates
2 Organization's approach to the recruitment and selection of business/management school graduates
3 Organization's approach to the recruitment and selection of liberal arts graduates
4 Relevance of business education to corporate needs
5 Involvement of the organization with business schools

Operating (Mid/Lower Level) Line Managers

1 Exposure to business/management school graduates
2 Evaluations of the job performance of business/management school graduates
3 Opinions regarding business/management school education
4 Opinions regarding organization's management development programs
5 Opinions regarding approach to make/buy decision for management development programs
6 Personal background

INDEXES

NAME INDEX

SUBJECT INDEX